SADLIER
FAITH AND
WITNESS

LITURGY AND WORSHIP

A Course on Prayer and Sacraments

Annotated Edition

Guide Writer
Isabel F. Blevins

Text Author
Rev. Thomas Richstatter, O.F.M., S.T.D.

William H. Sadlier, Inc.
9 Pine Street
New York, New York 10005-1002
http://www.sadlier.com

Acknowledgments

General Consultant for Texts
Rev. Joseph A. Komonchak, Ph.D.

**Official Theological Consultant
for Texts**
Most Rev. Edward K. Braxton, Ph.D., S.T.D.
Auxiliary Bishop of St. Louis

Publisher
Gerard F. Baumbach, Ed.D.

Editor in Chief
Moya Gullage

Pastoral Consultant
Rev. Msgr. John F. Barry

Scriptural Consultant
Rev. Donald Senior, C.P., Ph.D., S.T.D.

General Editors
Norman F. Josaitis, S.T.D.
Rev. Michael J. Lanning, O.F.M.

Catechetical and Liturgical Consultants
William Sadlier Dinger
Eleanor Ann Brownell, D. Min.
Joseph F. Sweeney
Helen Hemmer, I.H.M.
Mary Frances Hession
Maureen Sullivan, O.P., Ph.D.
Don Boyd

"The Ad Hoc Committee to Oversee the Use of the Catechism,
National Conference of Catholic Bishops,
has found the doctrinal content of this teacher's manual to
be in conformity with the *Catechism of the Catholic Church*."

Nihil Obstat
✠ Most Reverend George O. Wirz
Censor Librorum

Imprimatur
✠ Most Reverend William H. Bullock
Bishop of Madison
November 3, 1997

The *Nihil Obstat* and *Imprimatur* are official
declarations that a book or pamphlet is free of
doctrinal or moral error. No implication is contained
therein that those who have granted the *Nihil Obstat*
and *Imprimatur* agree with the contents, opinions,
or statements expressed.

Printed in the United States of America.

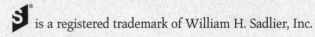 is a registered trademark of William H. Sadlier, Inc.

Home Office:
9 Pine Street
New York, NY 10005–1002

ISBN: 0–8215–5614–2
123456789/987

CONTENTS

Note: *Chapter 15 can be used at any time during the course, e.g., during retreat day, as a "break" week, or in a holiday shortened week. It needs to be scheduled and prepared well in advance.*

Sadlier's new FAITH AND WITNESS PROGRAM is a creative response to the needs of adolescents in the Catholic Church. It is rooted in a desire to serve effectively these young people, as well as those adults who teach, guide, and parent them on their faith journey.

It is shaped by an awareness of the multiple challenges and rewards of working with this vulnerable age group, which has been described as having one foot in childhood and the other groping toward adulthood.

At the heart of **Faith and Witness** is "a Person, the Person of Jesus of Nazareth, the only Son from the Father." And its aim is to draw adolescents into "communion with Jesus Christ." (*Catechism of the Catholic Church*, 426)

Just as Jesus himself related to and communicated with people "on their own level," so this program respects and responds to the adolescent's urgent questions: Who am I? Where am I going? What is my purpose in life?

Research done by the Carnegie Council on Adolescent Behavior verifies that many adolescents in our society have not been receiving the kind of guidance and support they need to thrive during this difficult period of metamorphosis. The Council's October 1995 report warns that youth between ten and fourteen have become "a neglected generation." It notes alarming increases in adolescent suicide, firearm use, smoking, drug and alcohol addiction, pregnancy, and poor grades. Its recommendations stress that schools should create programs better suited to adolescents' developmental needs, and parents should be encouraged

INTRODUCING
FAITH AND WITNESS

A Five-Course Program for Junior High Students

to become more involved in their young people's lives.

Sadlier's new **Faith and Witness Program** endeavors to meet these goals through an integration of the specific social, intellectual, religious, and spiritual needs of youth. It addresses "the desire for God [that] is written in the human heart" (*Catechism*, 27) as well as the Church's pastoral mission. Particular attention is paid to the following aspects of that mission: examining the reasons for belief, celebrating the sacraments, being integrated into the faith community, providing and calling forth gospel witness (*Catechism*, 6).

The semester courses that together comprise the program draw junior high youth into relationship with Jesus and the New Testament, Liturgy and Worship, Church History, Morality, and the Creed. Each course invites young people to venture further into the mystery of faith and the challenge of discipleship. Through shared study, reflection, prayer, and action in response to God's word, students experience themselves as a small faith community within the larger community of the parish and the Church itself.

We asked the writers of the five courses to share with you, in a few sentences, their response to the following question:

What hopes do you have for the young people who will use your book?

Creed

"We know what a privilege and a challenge it is to share with young people the dynamic teachings of our Catholic faith. Moreover it is important to share that faith in a clear and meaningful way with the next generation of believers. We hope that through the use of this book they will come to love Jesus and his Church even more and take their place as committed evangelizers in society."

**Dr. Norman F. Josaitis, S.T.D., and
Rev. Michael J. Lanning, O.F.M., authors**

New Testament

"The purpose of this book is to provide an introduction to the New Testament that will offer young people a mature appreciation of their faith. Knowing all about the good news of Jesus Christ is more than the work of one lifetime. But it is our hope that this book will help young people to become more committed disciples of Jesus and stronger members of his Church."

**Dr. Norman F. Josaitis, S.T.D., and
Rev. Michael J. Lanning, O.F.M., authors**

"This introduction, I hope, will make accessible to young people twenty centuries of Christian reflection on the New Testament."

**Dr. Mary Ann Getty, S.T.D.,
special consultant**

Liturgy and Worship

"We all know that it takes a lot more knowledge and skill to do something than to watch something. I hope that this book will provide the students—the next generation of young Catholics—with the help they need to celebrate the sacraments intelligently, joyfully, and fruitfully."

**Rev. Thomas Richstatter, O.F.M., S.T.D.,
author**

Morality

"Too many people think of morality as something negative and limiting. But the truth is that Christian morality is an invitation to become part of the most graced and promising life possible. Morality is all about authentic happiness and rich, lasting loves. My hope with this book is that students will discover that God loves them and wants the best for them, and that people who care for them will always challenge them to be good."

Rev. Paul J. Wadell, Ph.D., C.P., author

Church History

"I love Church history and agree with Cicero who said: 'To know nothing of what happened before you were born is to remain ever a child.' The same is true of Catholics who are unaware of our own religious heritage. The history of the Catholic Church is a marvelous story of saints and sinners, successes and failures, hopes and disappointments. For a person of faith, it is not only a human story but also a divine drama of God's grace at work in our world."

Rev. Thomas J. Shelley, Ph.D., author

It is our hope that FAITH AND WITNESS will strengthen the social, moral, and spiritual character of junior high youth. It is our prayer that they will experience more deeply and pass on more boldly the joy of living the Catholic faith.

You Are a Catechist

Grace and peace to you! You have been called to be a catechist, a faith-filled minister of the word to junior high youth. The aim of your ministry is to bring young people into intimate communion with Jesus Christ, and to draw them more deeply into the faith life of the Church. Think for a moment:

◆ Why do you think you were invited to do this work with young people?
◆ What gifts, talents or experiences do you bring to this ministry?

Ministry to the Needs of Youth

Ministry to young people has two main goals:

• to contribute to the personal and spiritual growth of each young person in your care;

• to invite young people into responsible participation in the life, mission, and work of the faith community. The components of your ministry include:

Evangelization—reaching out to young people who are uninvolved in the life of the Church and inviting them into a relationship with Jesus and the Catholic community.

Catechesis—promoting a young person's growth in the Catholic faith through a teaching process that emphasizes understanding, reflection, and conversation.

Prayer and Worship—guiding young people in developing their relationship with Jesus through personal prayer; drawing them more deeply into the sacramental life of the Church; involving them in a variety of prayer and worship experiences to celebrate their friendship with Jesus in a faith community of their peers.

Community Life—forming young people into the Christian community through programs and relationships that promote openness, trust, respect, cooperation, honesty, responsibility, and willingness to serve; creating a climate where young people can grow and share their struggles, questions, and joys with other young people and feel they are valued members of the Church.

Justice, Peace, and Service—giving direction to young people as they develop a Christian social consciousness and a commitment to a life of justice and peace by providing opportunities for service.

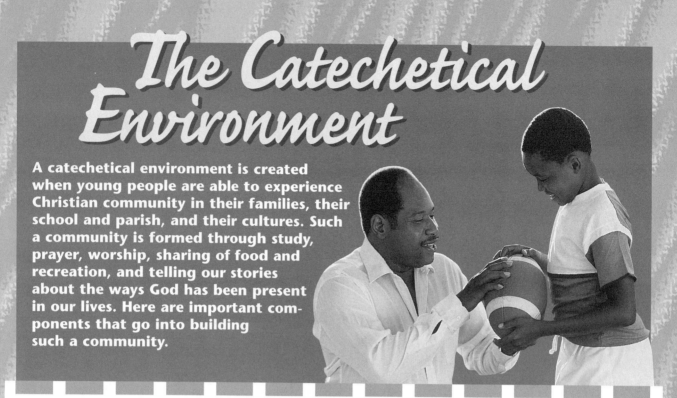

The Catechetical Environment

A catechetical environment is created when young people are able to experience Christian community in their families, their school and parish, and their cultures. Such a community is formed through study, prayer, worship, sharing of food and recreation, and telling our stories about the ways God has been present in our lives. Here are important components that go into building such a community.

Knowing the Students

The environment and practices in the home and neighborhood have had, and continue to have, a powerful influence on the faith development of the young people in your group. It is important to be aware of the world the young people inhabit. Here are ways to develop that awareness.

◆ Be sure that your consistency, dependability, and fairness are such to win students' confidence.

◆ Review the information you have been given regarding each student.

◆ Become familiar with where and with whom each student lives and who has legal custody.

◆ Make sure you are aware of young people who may be neglected or who come from homes that appear to be unhappy.

◆ Be available for private conferences with parents or family members, even if it means rearranging your schedule to meet their employment or family obligations.

◆ Be alert to signs of distress or abuse in the students.

◆ Be mindful of and sensitive to the language spoken in the home and the religious affiliation of parent(s) or guardians.

◆ Be alert to the general health and well-being of the student.

Getting Families Involved

The mission of Catholic education is to support, develop, enhance, and encourage the positive learning that takes place within the home. It is essential, therefore, to involve the family in the catechetical process. Encourage them to participate fully in ongoing religious development of the young person. Regular family conversations about God and religion have a tremendous positive effect on a young person's faith attitudes and practices.

◆ Welcome the families at the beginning of the year. Explain the catechetical program and invite their participation.

◆ Introduce them to the semester courses. The table of contents for each course provides an excellent overview of what the students will be expected to learn about our Catholic faith during the program.

◆ Encourage a conversation about ways they can share with their son or daughter the *Putting It Together* page and the weekly review *(Testing 1, 2, 3...)* that follows it. Duplicate and send home *Highlights for Home* from each chapter of the guide.

◆ Make positive telephone calls to parents. Conversations can be barrier-breakers, and from them catechists can gain great parental support and insight.

◆ Make a "Parents' Day" part of your yearly tradition so that the parents are given the opportunity to share their hopes and dreams for their daughters and sons.

Knowing the Neighborhood

◆ Become aware of the out-of-school activities both of the students and of those with whom they frequently associate. If possible, attend some of their athletic or musical events.

◆ Be available and willing to listen to your students without suggesting cures. When necessary, suggest that they seek professional advice as to how to deal with any unhealthy behaviors. Discuss these with the parents as well as any neighborhood influences and/or friends who are adversely affecting the young people's social, emotional, and spiritual development.

◆ Invite professionals to help the young people learn ways to cope with social pressures and problems such as alcohol, drugs, and peer pressure.

Sadlier's **Faith and Witness Program** is designed to nurture in young people a wholesome sense of self and a secure relationship with God in the context of the faith community. By integrating the teaching of Jesus and of the Church with the realities of their lives, they will be better prepared to minister to a world in which secular values often oppose the good news.

Making Discipline Positive

Positive discipline entails creating a climate in which young people feel secure, accepted, and supported. Here are suggestions for establishing and maintaining positive discipline in the classroom.

◆ Establish a sense of order immediately. Clearly and briefly explain to the students what is expected of them. Rules should be few and easy to remember.

◆ Use affirmation; acknowledge the students and remember to praise and affirm good behavior.

◆ Provide activities that build healthy self-esteem.

◆ Respect their thoughts and ideas, and expect them to do the same with you and their peers.

◆ Provide activities that challenge them to cooperate with one another.

◆ Deal with those who act inappropriately in a way that will calm them; set aside a space where they can think quietly about their actions and the consequences of them. If correcting is necessary, do it one-to-one, never publicly.

Developing Multicultural Awareness

True Christian community takes place within the context of the cultural heritage and the identity of the students we teach.

◆ Be aware of and sensitive to ethnic and cultural diversity.

◆ Encourage the young people to express their cultural uniqueness through art, music, dance, food, and dress.

◆ Send communications home in the languages of the families, if possible.

◆ Invite families to share their cultural symbols and food at celebrations.

◆ Be aware of possible conflicts because of ethnic or cultural diversity among students.

Youth With Special Needs

In recent years, the bishops of the United States have encouraged religious educators to pay particular attention to those students who have special needs and to integrate these students, when possible, into regular programs of religious education.

There are many different kinds of special needs. Some students have *physical* needs that must be taken into consideration. Physical needs may involve any of the five senses, as well as special motor needs. Some students have *emotional* needs that require our recognition, attention, and consideration. Still others have *special learning* needs. Learn about the special needs of these young people from the trained professionals who have dealt with them and their families.

Try to ascertain what adjustments or adaptations need to be made in your classroom. Be aware also of any adaptations necessary to enable the students to profit from their religion materials. Plan the seating arrangement so that each student feels part of the group. Be sure that the group is aware of and sensitive to the special needs of these students.

Recognize how all of us need to receive from as well as give to those who are disabled or challenged in any way. Jean Vanier, founder of the L'Arche communities in which people with disabilities and their caregivers live together, observes that those who are "broken" can reveal to us our own spiritual or psychological "brokenness." By this mutuality, we are strengthened, reconciled, and healed.

Understanding the Adolescent

Adolescence—the period that normally covers the years between eleven and fifteen—is a time of major change, development, and sometimes upheaval in the young person's life. To the young person everything seems to be in flux, in motion—physical development, emotions, ideas, relationships. It is a time of challenge and enormous potential for growth; it can also be a time of frustration and confusion both for the adolescents and for the adults—parents and teachers—who care for them.

Social Development

As young people move into adolescence, their interests begin to extend beyond family and school to wider horizons. As these new interests develop, relationships that had been of primary importance, especially those with family, sometimes seem to recede. Although there is still an essential need for the security and support of family and other adults, it is a time when old ties and the excitement of an enlarging world can conflict. The growing desire of the young people for greater freedom and their continuing need for support and security offer a real challenge to parents and catechists, who must find ways to facilitate this process of progressive emancipation. The sociability of the teenagers should be utilized and their energies channeled into common pursuits. It is the right age for such educational techniques as small-group projects or discussions, debates, panel presentations, retreat days, youth days, and service projects.

Intellectual Development

Young adolescents are increasingly capable of all the intellectual operations. There is specific growth in the ability to deal with abstract ideas and judgments in those young people who have matured beyond the egocentrism of an earlier stage. As they come more and more into contact with the judgments and opinions of others, they will need to be helped and challenged to think more accurately, perceptively, and critically. The broadening intellectual and social world of the young people stimulates a questioning and critical spirit. We can foster a *positive* questioning and critical attitude in the young people by challenging them to explore, probe, and reflect.

Also on a positive level, God's relationship with the young people is often expressed in a more "spiritual" way than before. Prayers become more other-oriented and less egocentric. The Church can be more readily understood as a community of believers, and worship is seen as a natural expression of belief and a way to become a better person.

The catechist should be aware that as real religious insights such as these occur, there can also be a tendency for negative attitudes to develop. This is often especially true for less mature students, who, when faced with the struggle to move from an egocentric to a more mature religious belief, find it difficult to wrestle with the problems this involves and retreat into indifference or hostility. The challenge to the catechist is great. The first challenge is to recognize some very basic needs of adolescents.

Some Basic Needs

1. *Affirmation and Approval.* Young people must consistently be affirmed by their parents, teachers, and peers. Most have a precarious sense of self-esteem. They suffer anxiety about their physical appearance, their popularity, their skills and talents. They need to be told and shown that they are accepted, appreciated, and approved for who they are right now.

2. *Security and Success.* Because intellectual and other abilities vary so broadly among adolescents, they need multiple opportunities to succeed. An effective teacher discerns and draws out the particular skills of each young person. When a relationship of trust is nurtured between teacher and student, the young person feels secure enough to do his or her best.

3. *Freedom and Structure.* Like fledgling pilots, adolescents love to fly but they depend heavily on the voice from the control tower. They want freedom to experiment and explore yet they require a reliable

home base to return to as needed. Catechists who come to the group well-prepared, who require students to abide by simple rules, and who consistently offer opportunities for choice and self-expression will do well with this age group. Giving clear directions and guiding young people step-by-step through a new process or ritual reinforces awareness of structure.

4. *Idealism and Self-Definition.* Youth have a great capacity for energetic idealism which can be effectively harnessed in the causes of justice, equality, and peacemaking. When motivated and well directed, they will unselfishly participate in the works of mercy—particularly in one-on-one situations. However, if their idealism and altruism are

not channeled by teachers and adult mentors, youth readily take refuge in cynicism and hostility. Their need for self-definition must be met through individual attention from adults and by enlisting their particular abilities in ways that serve others.

5. *Physical Activity and Social Interaction.* Driven by hormonal changes and uncontrollable growth spurts, adolescents literally "cannot sit still" for extended lectures. They need to move from place to place, activity to activity, individual to partnered or group pursuits. Their hunger for interaction with peers can be met in diverse ways (discussions, debates, art or craft projects, sharing food and music, games, dancing, human sculptures).

Thinking Skills for Discipleship

More and more often, a complex and technological society demands critical thinkers. Critical thinkers see beneath surface impressions to the root of an issue or event. They are able to discern causes rather than symptoms, and they are able to project consequences rather than to be satisfied with quick solutions. Above all, critical thinkers are capable of reflection—not only on issues outside themselves, but capable of their own responses and reactions as well. How can we help our students develop critical thinking skills? And how can we encourage them to use these skills as disciples of Christ?

The ability to think critically can be developed in young adolescents through questions and activities that involve the following:

• solving problems
• making decisions
• imagining outcomes

• setting up criteria
• finding reasons
• reflecting/meditating
• choosing applications to life

"Who do you say I am?" Jesus asked his disciples. It was a question that demanded the disciples to go beneath surface impressions to the heart of the matter. Instead, the disciples responded by repeating what *others* had said— "Some say John the Baptist; others Elijah; still others responded Jeremiah or one of the prophets." Jesus refused to accept the superficial, unreflective answer. He probed further. "But who do you say that I am?"

This is the basic question of our faith. This is the question that we want our young disciples to answer with personal conviction, commitment, and hope.

"You are the Messiah, the Son of the living God" (Matthew 16:13–16).

Prayer and the Young Person

A well-known youth minister was asked what advice he would give to religion teachers. "Be bold about the spiritual," he said. "These kids want and need religious experience. They need help with prayer."

Forms of Prayer

Many young people have experienced prayer as "talking to God" and reciting prayers. They are ready to explore new ways of expressing their relationship with God. Variety is the spice of their lives, and they will generally be open to prayer forms like the following:

- **The Breath Prayer**
  Seated with back straight and eyes closed, the person focuses on the flow of breath in and out of the body. As breath is exhaled, one can "breathe" a simple word or phrase like "Jesus" or "Here I am, Lord." This practice in being present is a prayer itself as well as being an excellent prelude to other forms of prayer.

- **Prayer with Scripture**
  Herein lie unlimited riches. Try gospel meditations using imagination, i.e., "place yourself in the scene . . ."; read the psalms in choral fashion; learn personally chosen passages by heart; and practice proclaiming the word of God.

- **The Symbol Prayer**
  Potent symbols from the Bible and the liturgy (water, wind, oil, fire, light, incense) may speak more powerfully to meditating youth than would many words or explanations.

- **The Prayer of Music**
  This native tongue of youth speaks to them of God as they reflect on, participate in and respond to music (religious, classical, contemporary).

- **The Prayer of Journaling**
  Prayers, Scripture responses, poems, dreams, doubts, questions, dialogues with Jesus and the saints are recorded in words and/or art in the young person's book of life. He or she comes to know God and self more intimately.

- **Traditional Vocal Prayer**
  Traditional prayers—prayers of the Catholic community—are the most used and taken-for-granted form of prayer. When they are prayed slowly and thoughtfully, instead of rattled off, they can be a source of comfort, rootedness, and connectedness for young people. One way to make traditional prayers take on new meaning is to pray them against a background of beautiful music or visual images.

Young people should be invited to help choose and prepare for these and other prayer experiences. Many junior high teachers find that the most fruitful time for exploring prayer forms is about midway in the session. However, brief opening and closing prayers (a minute or two) may be used to frame the session itself as an extended prayer. Sources for these include: a line or two from traditional prayers, the Mass, the psalms, inspired songs, prayers of the saints, collections of prayers by teenagers, and the words of Jesus.

Do not assume that young people reject prayer. They are hungry for the spiritual, for relationship with God. Prayer is a way for them to touch the living God who is with them and in them.

Some resources that might be helpful:

Caprio, Betsy. *Experiments in Prayer.* Notre Dame, IN: Ave Maria Press, 1973.

Hokowski, Maryann. *Pathways to Praying with Jesus.* Winona, MN: Saint Mary's Press, 1993.

Koch, Carl, FSC. *Dreams Alive: Prayers by Teenagers.* Winona, MN: Saint Mary's Press, 1991.

Bolton, Martha. *If the Pasta Wiggles, Don't Eat It. . . .* Ann Arbor, MI: Servant Publications, 1995.

Catucci, Thomas F. *Time With Jesus.* Notre Dame, IN: Ave Maria Press, 1993.

Questions That Matter

Questions have to be carefully prepared if they are to be truly effective. Part of preparation for teaching each lesson should be the formulation of questions that stimulate, challenge, and engender deeper thought. Besides simple recall, questions should motivate and stimulate emotion, evaluative thinking, imagination, and creative problem solving. Vary your techniques; allow time for responses (research shows that most teachers wait less than 4 seconds); above all, *listen* to the answers! Here are some sample questioning techniques.

Recall

- List the types of evidence for believing in God. Other "recall" words: name; define; outline; describe.

React

- Imagine a friend tells you that he no longer believes in God. List four questions you would ask your friend about his reasons for not believing.

Compare

- In what ways are the early Church (A.D. 33–300) and today's Church alike?

Contrast

- In what ways are they different?

Preference

- Which would you rather be—a stained glass window or a church bell?
- Which helps you to pray—silence or music?

Personification

- What questions would you like to ask Francis of Assisi (or Mary, or...)?
- What would Jesus think or say about this issue? How might he say it?

Creative Thinking

- What if there had been television in Jesus' time?
- What if you could trade places with Saint Paul (or Catherine of Siena...)?
- Suppose that Jesus had not come. What would the consequences be?

Application

- Give Luther a list of alternatives to leaving the Church.
- Ask several "when" questions about the Church.
- Ask five "why" questions about faith.

Research Skills

- Would it have been possible for Pope John Paul II to meet Hitler?
- Would it have been possible for Catherine of Siena to have dinner with Ignatius Loyola?

Synthesis

- What might be some of the moral consequences of violent or sexual content in some contemporary music?
- The answer is "life." What is the question?

Ways of Learning

In his 1983 book *Frames of Mind,* Dr. Howard Gardner identified seven types of intelligence of which educators need to be aware among their students.

Because young people vary so widely in their intellectual abilities, it is especially important that teachers recognize these multiple intelligences.

The following list describes seven intelligence types and suggests appropriate teaching strategies within the context of the FAITH AND WITNESS PROGRAM.

1. Linguistic Intelligence

Exhibits sensitivity to the meaning and order of words

- *Storytelling:* scriptural, traditional, contemporary and imaginary stories to be told, re-told, or written
- *Brainstorming:* unleashing a torrent of ideas on a specific issue or question, i.e., How would we describe Jesus to teen aliens who had never heard of him?
- *Speaking a New Language:* learning a prayer in Aramaic, Spanish, Latin, or American Sign Language
- *Publishing:* collecting and publishing a semester's worth of student reflections, prayers, responses to be placed in the school library

2. Logical-Mathematical Intelligence

Shows ability to discern patterns of reasoning and order; dexterity with numbers

- *Classification:* organizing information (on Church history, Creed, or New Testament) on attribute webs (listing attributes of a person, place or thing as spokes around the subject)
- *Devising Strategies:* for computer or board games on history or Scripture
- *Socratic Questioning:* teacher or leader questions student views to sharpen critical thinking skills (e.g., "Do you think human beings will eventually have the power to understand the mysteries of life?")

3. Spatial Intelligence

Demonstrates ability to grasp how things orient to each other in space

- *Making Maps and Architectural Models:* recreating scenes or places from Scripture and Church history
- *Making Timelines and Murals:* visualizing historical, liturgical and creedal developments

4. Bodily-Kinesthetic Intelligence

Using the body skillfully and handling objects with unusual aptitude

- *Drama and Dance:* roleplaying moral decision-making; acting out stories from Scripture and history; ritual prayer in which dance or choreographed movement is integrated
- *Human Sculptures and Relays:* small groups form "sculptures" of faith concepts or objects (community, steeple, fishermen's boat) using only their bodies; teams perform physical "feats" and respond to faith questions on relay "batons."
- *Crafts:* using clay, pipe cleaners, papier-maché, looms, wood, beads to make faith-related objects (from Scripture, Church history, prayer traditions)

5. Musical Intelligence

Using sensitivity to sound, melody, instrumentation and musical mood

- *Rhythms, Songs, Chants, Raps:* employing these as aids to internalization and memorization (composing songs on moral issues or chants of favorite prayer lines)

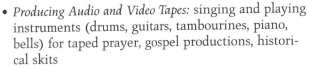

- *Producing Audio and Video Tapes:* singing and playing instruments (drums, guitars, tambourines, piano, bells) for taped prayer, gospel productions, historical skits
- *Collecting Disks:* classroom resource of religious, classical and contemporary music to illustrate, amplify or embody content themes ("Godspell," "Messiah," "Tears In Heaven," plus nature recordings)

6. Interpersonal Intelligence

Showing relationship skills, understanding and empathy

- *Peer Sharing:* interacting with partners or small groups to explore content questions and personal responses; peer tutoring and mentoring by older youth or adults
- *Doing Simulations:* groups participate in "as-if" environments (e.g., "You have just attended Jesus' Sermon on the Mount and are now on the road home. What are you feeling, thinking, planning to do?")
- *Making Murals, Puzzles, Banners:* working cooperatively to produce an art project illustrating a faith theme
- *Peacemaking Strategies:* roleplaying ways of reconciliation practiced by Jesus, saints, Gandhi, Martin Luther King, Jr., youth
- *Culture Sharing:* putting together prayer and worship experiences enriched by African-American, Hispanic, Asian, Native American and other cultural expressions within the Church

7. Intrapersonal Intelligence

Showing self-knowledge and self-discipline; awareness of one's inner life

- *Doing One-Minute Reflections:* taking "time out" in the midst of interactive learning for reflection or deep thinking (no talking; occasional background music)
- *Praying, Journaling, Retreats:* responding to youth's hunger for God and need for self-awareness
- *Offering Choices:* enhancing self-discipline and self-expression by offering choices on projects, methods, ways of responding to content
- *Expressing Feelings:* calling forth expressions of wonder, surprise, anger, joy, caring, humor, sadness in response to faith experiences (through stories, poems, videos, photos, music, personal witness, prayer)

The Learning/ Teaching Process

Junior high students need to feel some ownership of the learning situation. They do not respond positively to being "talked at" or "talked down to." They need to participate as much as possible in the planning, presentation, and carrying out of the program. Above all, they need to be challenged to take responsibility for their learning.

The semester courses in SADLIER'S FAITH AND WITNESS PROGRAM are designed with these realities in mind. The process suggested is simple yet comprehensive. Each lesson consists of three steps:

1. Introduction

The lesson begins with an *opening prayer*—preferably led by one or more of the students.

* The opening prayer is followed by the *forum* (see page 20) in which the young people present their responses, reflections, or reactions to the assigned reading and activity.

2. Presentation

* The catechist clarifies the material the students have read. This can be done through a variety of techniques including questions, activities, dialogue, highlighting, guest speakers, and so on.

3. Conclusion

* Students and/or catechist give a brief summary of the work of the lesson.

* Catechist gives forum assignment for the next lesson.

* Session closes with a brief prayer or song.

This guide will suggest a variety of techniques, activities, questions to facilitate this process. The key with young people is to have a balance of consistency and variety so that every lesson is solid but not predictable.

Preparing a Lesson

Here are a few suggestions for preparing to teach this course. The suggestions are especially intended for those who may be new—either to teaching religion or to teaching junior high students.

Note:

Chapter 15 is a unique chapter. It can be used at any time during the course. For example, it can be compressed to use during a shortened week, before a holiday, or inserted in the course to provide a change of pace from the intensity of the other chapters.

It is important that you examine Chapter 15 at the beginning of the course in order to plan its use and to gather the materials needed for its presentation.

Remote Preparation

- Read the whole text carefully. This will give you an understanding of the scope of the whole course and the sequence of ideas throughout.

- As you read make marginal notes about any ideas you have regarding the material and how to present it.

- Look at the list of resources and try to familiarize yourself with at least one of them.

- Check the references given throughout to the *Catechism of the Catholic Church*. Read over the cited paragraphs and make them your own.

Immediate Preparation

- Read the chapter that makes up the week's work.

- As you read highlight what you consider to be the main points of each lesson.

- List these main points for yourself. It will help to clarify and to focus your objectives.

- Read again the two pages that comprise the next day's lesson. Focus on the objective(s) for that lesson.

- Write out the questions you feel will help direct the students' understanding of the material. (See the suggestions for questioning on page 15.)

- Plan the activities you wish to use during the lesson. Make sure you know exactly what you wish the group to do. Assemble any materials you will need.

- Plan the *forum* assignment you will give the students for the following day's lesson. Make the assignment clear and simple, but be creative.

- Immediately before the lesson begins, talk to the students who are responsible for leading the opening prayer to make sure they have what they need.

- Take a minute for quiet reflection. Ask the Holy Spirit to be in your mind, heart, and mouth as you share the faith with your group.

Student Interaction

Student interaction is essential to the success of this program. Their participation in and ownership of the learning process provides stimulus, enthusiasm, and energy to the whole program.

The **Faith and Witness Program** is organized on the principle of student involvement and responsibility. The two most important elements in the program are, therefore, the student-directed prayer, and the student-led *Forum*.

Forum

The purpose of the student *forum* is to involve the students immediately and interactively in each day's work. We want them to become not simply passive receivers of information, but active partners and participants in the learning process.

It is essential, therefore, that the students assume responsibility for the *forum* and for the preparation necessary to take part in it. If this is not done, the religion lesson will become a reading exercise or a lecture. These are not acceptable alternatives.

How Does the Forum Work?

◆ At the end of each lesson ask the students to prepare for the next *forum* by doing two things:

• Read carefully the two text pages assigned, and underline key ideas.

• Prepare a written or oral response to the question, reflection, or activity assigned.

◆ Following the opening prayer, each lesson begins with the *forum* in which the young people share both the results of their reading and their responses to the *forum* assignment.

The *forum* should take approximately 15 to 20% of the total class time.

Ideas for Forum Assignments

Each *forum* assignment should act as an interesting and creative "doorway" for the students into the work of the lesson. Their responses and reactions at the outset of the lesson should provide an initial dialogue that helps them enter enthusiastically into the ideas and content of the lesson. Some ideas:

◆ Always the first part of the assignment is to read the next two pages of the lesson. Encourage the students to underline in pencil sentences that they feel are key ideas on these pages.

◆ Some of the suggestions on *Questions That Matter* are excellent ideas for *forum* assignments—especially those under *Recall, React, Personification, Creative Thinking, Application,* and *Synthesis.* (See page G15.)

◆ *Journaling* could occasionally be the *forum* assignment. Be careful not to require a response that would be too personal or too revealing for a young person to share with the group.

◆ *Simple Research* to discover more information about an idea is helpful if students have access to computer on-line services.

Journaling

The students keep a journal throughout the course. Journal suggestions appear in each chapter.

Purpose:
It provides an outlet for private, ungraded, uncensored expressions of students' thoughts, reflections, imaginations, feelings.

Outcomes:
• students become more in touch with themselves, their feelings, their personal questions;

• students become better writers;

• students have something to look back on that will give them insights into their own change and growth.

A special journal is available as a component to this program for each course.

Student-Led Prayer

Purpose:
- provides immediate responsibility for and involvement by the young people in the spiritual dimensions of their learning;
- gives them the opportunity to express their own spiritual concerns and to lead others in prayer.

Outcomes:
- young people are enabled to be less self-conscious about their faith;
- they are given the freedom to express their relationship with God and their concerns in personal and creative ways;
- the experience can draw them deeper into their personal life of prayer with God.

Needs:
- especially in the beginning: the catechist's help, support, and suggestions;
- scriptural and other resources (see *Teaching Resources* chart for each chapter);
- partners! Sometimes it is easier with a friend.

How to:
- at the beginning of the week meet with the students who will be leading prayer;
- if they request help, make resources available;
- encourage them—prayer does not have to be perfect; it only has to be sincere.

Faith in Action

*I*nvolvement in active service for others is an integral part of the FAITH AND WITNESS PROGRAM.

Purpose:
Young people have so much to give—energy, generosity, enthusiasm, idealism, compassion. It is essential that we help them find practical and immediate ways to share these gifts.

Outcomes:
They will find that they receive far more than they give—a humbling and joyful discovery. They will begin to develop and to live the values of God's kingdom in very real, practical, and sometimes demanding ways.

Needs:
Ideas and suggestions from the parish and communities concerning needs and opportunities the young people can address.

How to:
From the beginning, make it clear to the young people that an essential component of the program is their willingness to serve. A list of suggestions for projects is supplied on page G25, but you might find other ideas more appropriate for your particular situation. Set aside time during and at the end of a service project to help the young people evaluate their service, their attitudes, and their reflections.

FAITH AND WITNESS Program

Morality A Course on Catholic Living

We were made for happiness, a happiness that God alone can provide. Modeling our lives on Christ, we know that the only way to achieve happiness is by rejecting sin and freely choosing to do what is right. Through God's law and God's grace, we are called upon to form our consciences and make moral decisions as followers of Christ and members of the Church. The Church itself is the authentic teacher of the ways of Christ and the manner in which we are to live a moral life in the world.

Within this deeper framework of moral decision making, we explore the Ten Commandments in greater detail. Likewise, we concentrate on gospel formation (the Beatitudes) and what it means to live a life of virtue. This course will enable young people to navigate through challenging times with a clear and positive moral attitude that is essential for Catholics in the new millennium.

Church History A Course on the People of God

How important it is for young Catholics to be in touch with their roots, roots that took hold about two thousand years ago!

Beginning with the apostolic age and the age of persecution, students will be introduced to the accomplishments of men and women of faith throughout the centuries. The successes and difficulties that the Church has faced, both within and without, will be studied, but always with a view to help young Catholics of today face the challenges of their own time. As Catholics, we stand on the shoulders of giants. In helping others to know the story of this great Church community, we are preparing leaders for the new millennium.

The New Testament A Course on Jesus and His Disciples

Young Catholics need to rub shoulders with the culture of Jesus and his times. Likewise, they need to know that in Scripture things are not always what they appear to be. Scripture presents so much more, and young people should never be afraid of the truth as presented in Scripture. This text will introduce them to questions people have asked over the ages: Were the Magi historical figures? Did Jesus really raise people from the dead, or were they just asleep? Did Jesus really die, and did his body really come out of the tomb? By tackling such questions, this course will help young people to appreciate the contemporary Catholic understanding of Scripture and give them tools to avoid fundamentalistic leanings that distort real Catholic doctrine and Scripture itself.

Creed A Course on Catholic Belief

It is through divine revelation that we come to know God through the knowledge God has of himself. The gift of faith enables us to respond to this divine revelation.

Because our first parents rejected God's plan of original holiness and justice, the whole human race is born in the state of original sin. God promised us a savior and that promise was fulfilled through his only Son, who became flesh and took on our human nature. Jesus, the Son of God and the son of Mary, is true God and true Man. He offered himself as the perfect sacrifice for us and for our salvation.

We are the Church, the people of God. Jesus promised that he would be with the Church until the end of time. He sent the Holy Spirit to guide the Church in all things. The course concludes with Mary and the saints and our belief in the communion of saints and life everlasting.

Liturgy and Worship A Course on Prayer and Sacraments

It is in the Church's liturgy, especially the seven sacraments, that Catholics celebrate all that God has done for us in Christ Jesus through the working of the Holy Spirit. Our salvation was made possible through the paschal mystery of Christ's passion, death, resurrection, and ascension. This mystery is made present to us in the sacred actions of the Church's liturgy.

As members of the Church, we are called upon to enter into this mystery of faith and truly be people of both word and sacrament. This is where our lives of faith are proclaimed, formed, and nourished. If young people are to be strong and faithful followers of Christ, they must make the liturgical life of the Church their own.

Liturgy & Worship
Scope and Sequence

Chapter 1

MORE THAN MEETS THE EYE: the use of symbols to express one's deepest beliefs; the awareness of the divine, the sacred in human cultures; the meaning and characteristics of ritual

Chapter 2

THE PRAYER OF THE CHURCH: Catholic symbols and rituals; liturgy—the public prayer of the Church; characteristics of liturgy; the paschal mystery

Chapter 3

GOD'S MASTERPIECES: God's plan of salvation; Jesus, the Word made flesh; definition of sacrament

Chapter 4

THE SACRAMENT OF SACRAMENTS: Eucharist: source and summit of the Christian life; the Mass: sacrifice and meal; liturgical time; the eucharistic prayer

Chapter 5

CELEBRATING EUCHARIST: the Liturgy of the Word, the Liturgy of the Eucharist; the berakah form of the eucharistic prayer; the meaning of the Eucharist for our lives

Chapter 6

THE SACRAMENTS OF INITIATION: the process of becoming a Catholic; the need for conversion; initiation: Baptism, Confirmation, Eucharist; celebrating these sacraments

Chapter 7

OUR HOUSE OF PRAYER: need for sacred space; the parish—visible sign of faith; design that serves four liturgical functions; a place of worship

Chapter 8

SEASONS OF PRAISE: the liturgical year, an unfolding of the whole mystery of Christ; Sunday, the day of resurrection; the Lenten retreat; the solemn liturgies of the Triduum

Chapter 9

A YEAR OF GLORY: seasons of change, preparation and new beginnings; Easter, a season of fifty days; reflecting on the gospels; Pentecost, the Holy Spirit in the Church; the gift of mission; Advent and Christmas: the Kingdom of God among us

Chapter 10

THE SACRAMENT OF RECONCILIATION: Jesus and forgiveness; a sacrament develops; a reconciling Church; Reconciliation today; celebrating the sacrament: communal and individual rites; sign of the sacrament

Chapter 11

THE ANOINTING OF THE SICK: Jesus and healing; healing in the early Church; essential sign: anointing with oil; a public prayer directed toward healing; celebrating the sacrament

Chapter 12

THE SACRAMENT OF HOLY ORDERS: call to Holy Orders; the three ranks; a share in Christ's priesthood through ministry, divine worship, authority; an indelible mark; ordination of bishops, priests, deacons; essential signs of the sacrament

Chapter 13

THE SACRAMENT OF MATRIMONY: the meaning of marriage; preparation for marriage; life-giving sign of grace; ministers and sign of the sacrament; the marriage commitment; celebrating the sacrament

Chapter 14

MARY AND THE SAINTS: the communion of saints; the meaning of holiness; celebrating the saints; Mary, the mother of God; and first disciple

Chapter 15

PATHS OF PRAYER: the meaning of and need for prayer in the Christian life: kinds of prayer: scriptural, meditative, contemplative, Liturgy of the Hours

Why a Course on Liturgy and Worship?

By the time young people are in junior high they might have the feeling that they have "had" sacraments and liturgy ever since second grade. It is important to involve them in looking at the liturgical life of the Church in a new and more mature and profound way. In the liturgy, which is the public prayer of the Church, we share in the "work of God." What is the work of God? It is the work of our redemption; it is what Christ did for us. In the liturgy the work of Christ—his passion, death, resurrection, and ascension—continues today in the Church—in us.

The liturgical prayer of the Church makes present in our lives today redeeming actions of Christ in his paschal mystery. When Jesus passed from death to life, all creation was made new—including ourselves. His new life is now our new life. Why a course on liturgy and worship? Because it is the central vocation of every Christian to discover, to celebrate, and to live the meaning of Christ's passion, death, and resurrection in today's world.

Objectives

◆ to deepen the young people's understanding of the Church's liturgy as prayerful celebration of all that God has done for us in Christ through the working of the Holy Spirit.

◆ To develop a richer awareness that our salvation was made present to us in the sacred actions of the liturgy.

◆ To encourage them to enter more full into this mystery of faith and to become truly people of both word and sacrament.

Faith in Action

Active, attentive, responsible service of others should be the hallmark of the Christian moral life. Involve your group in individual or communal service projects to be carried out throughout this course. The young people should reflect on their commitment in their journals and give a report at the end of the course. (Note: All projects will need your support and coordinating efforts.) Some suggestions follow.

◆ Invite a friend who is not a Catholic to come with you to a sacramental celebration in your parish. Explain the significance of the sacrament and what it means to you. Help your friend follow the liturgy and to feel part of the celebration. Take time afterwards to discuss the liturgy you have shared.

◆ If possible, arrange to accompany a eucharistic minister in your parish when he or she brings the Eucharist to the sick in their homes. Join in any prayers that are offered and take a minute afterwards to talk to the sick person. Find out what it means to be a eucharistic minister.

◆ During this course, ask Jesus to help you become a healing presence in someone's life. "Adopt" a sick, handicapped, or elderly person. Each day pray that your friend may be healed spiritually and physically. Once a week visit or call or send a card to that person.

Cross Curriculum Projects

◆ Young people with an interest in music could research the vast treasury of Church music: chant, polyphony, congregational, oratorio, and modern, for example. They might prepare a program for the group with explanations and musical selections.

◆ Young people with an interest in the visual arts might research the area of modern liturgical art and architecture. They should prepare a report explaining the developments in the field in the last twenty years.

◆ Young scientists might compare and contrast Einstein's thoughts on time with the concept of liturgical time–God's time.

MORE THAN MEETS THE EYE

Adult Focus

As you gather together with the young people at the beginning of this course on Liturgy and Worship, help your group experience Christ's presence and the Holy Spirit's guidance. If the young people are to be strong and faithful followers of Christ, they must make the liturgical life of the Church their own. It is in the Church's liturgy, especially the seven sacraments, that we celebrate all that God has done for us in Jesus Christ through the working of the Holy Spirit. Our salvation was made possible through the paschal mystery of Christ's passion, death, resurrection, and ascension. This mystery is made present to us in the sacred actions of the Church's liturgy. As members of the Church, we are called upon to enter into this mystery of faith and truly be people of both word and sacrament. This is where our lives of faith are proclaimed, formed, and nourished.

In this chapter the young people explore the Church's teaching that an understanding of symbol and ritual is essential to a mature understanding of our worship as Catholics. And if we are aware and willing to participate, each ritual draws us more deeply into the life of faith that it expresses.

Catechism Focus

The theme of Chapter 1 corresponds to paragraphs 1145–1148 of the *Catechism of the Catholic Church*.

Enrichment Activities

More Than Meets the Eye

Have the young people make a cloth or paper banner with four sections. Provide fabric swatches or construction paper for the young people to use to make symbols. Suggest that they place a symbol of their favorite gift of God in nature in the first section of the banner. In the second section they may place a symbol of their favorite interest or hobby. In the third section they may place a symbol of peace and in the fourth section a symbol of happiness.

Computer Connection

Have the students use an electronic-mail feature of an on-line information service, such as *Prodigy*™, to exchange letters explaining their understanding of Matthew 18:20: "Where two or three are gathered together in my name, there am I in the midst of them." Also have them invite the young people with whom they are communicating to be part of a prayer "web."

Locate and verify other groups of Catholic young people that are willing to exchange letters. Have the young people in your group compose their letters off-line using an appropriate writing software program, such as *Student Writing Center*™. Then have them upload their letter files to the on-line information service in order to send the letters. Have the young people print and present to the class the letters and any responses they may receive.

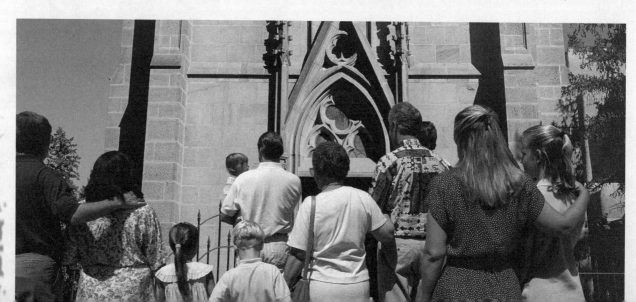

Teaching Resources

Overview	Opening Prayer Ideas	Materials
SESSION 1 **Discovery:** To discover that humans have the power and the imagination to think symbolically.	Look at the photo on pages 6 and 7. Reflect on 1 Corinthians 13:12.	These will be needed for every session: texts, Bibles, highlighters or colored pencils, journals. • large tub of water, small stones or pebbles and sponges • copies of handout *Thinking Symbolically*, page 6C
SESSION 2 **Exploring 1:** To explore the ways that we humans use symbols to communicate our belief in the sacred.	Pray the following Native American prayer: O Great Spirit, who dwells in the sky, lead us on the path of peace and understanding.	• photos of sacred places throughout the world • materials to set up a prayer corner
SESSION 3 **Exploring 2:** To explore three of the most important characteristics of ritual.	Offer to each other a gesture and greeting of peace.	• construction paper (optional) • string or yarn (optional)
SESSION 4 **Exploring 3:** To explore ways our cultural experiences and our maturity help us to be aware of symbolic meanings.	Offer spontaneous prayers of thanksgiving for God's gifts to us.	• bell • words to "America the Beautiful"
SESSION 5 **Putting It Together:** To deepen understanding of the importance of symbolism and ritual in our lives.	Look at the photo on pages 6 and 7. Ask God to help you to strengthen your roots of faith.	• *Chapter 1 Assessment*, page 17A, for each student • *Highlights for Home*, page 17B, for each student

If your religion class is on a four-day cycle, you may want to incorporate the questions and activities for Session 5 into your schedule where appropriate.

Supplemental Resources

Videos
The Wonders of God's Creation
Vision Video Inc.
2030 Wentz Church Road
P.O. Box 540
Worcester, PA 19490–0540

William
Franciscan Communications/
St. Anthony Messenger
1615 Republic Street
Cincinnati, OH 45210

Faith and Witness Journal:
Liturgy and Worship

For Chapter 1 see pages
4–7.

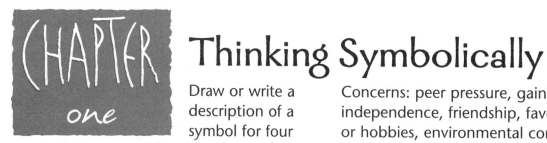

CHAPTER one

Thinking Symbolically

Draw or write a description of a symbol for four concerns that many young people have. Choose from those listed here.

Concerns: peer pressure, gaining more independence, friendship, favorite activities or hobbies, environmental concerns, peace in the world, God's love for you, your faith in God.

SESSION 1

More Than
Meets the Eye

At present we see indistinctly,
as in a mirror,
but then face to face.
1 Corinthians 13:12

Objective: To discover that humans have the power and the imagination to think symbolically.

Introduction ____ min.

Opening Prayer: Before the session begins, gather the following materials: a large tub of water, small stones or pebbles (the type used in aquariums), and sponges (as many as needed to provide each student with a small square piece).

Give to each young person some pebbles and the sponge piece. Then ask them to gather around the large tub of water. Sing together a hymn of gathering, such as "We Gather Together" (words and music appear in parish hymnals or missalettes) or "Gather Us In" (words and music by Marty Haugen, 1982).

Then use the following script to guide the first part of the prayer activity:

> Sometimes when we gather with our peers, self-doubt, fear, or other problems weigh on our hearts. Drop the pebbles you are holding into the container of water. Let this action symbolize your willingness to cast these negative feelings aside to help yourself and each other on your journey of faith.

Then read Psalm 34:12–15.

Use the following script for the second part of the prayer activity:

> Jesus told us, "Where two or three are gathered together in my name, there am I in the midst of them" (Matthew 18:20).
> Jesus is with us now. We have gathered in his name. Place the sponge piece you are holding in the container of water. Let this action symbolize your willingness to absorb a deep knowledge about the prayer and sacraments of the Church. Turn to each other and extend the invitation to celebrate your faith from the fourth verse of Psalm 34:
> Magnify the LORD with me;
> let us exalt his name together.

Chapter Warm-Up: Invite the young people to look at the photo on pages 6 and 7. Read together 1 Corinthians 13:12. Then explain that in this chapter you will be looking at ways humans engage in symbolic thinking. Discuss the symbolism of examining the roots and veins of the lily pads rather than just looking at them as they float on the surface of the water.

*A rock, a flower, a fire, a stream,
A touch, a smile, a goodbye, a dream—
Oh, how these are so much more than they seem!*

*In what ways can things like these be
"much more than they seem"?*

Presentation ___ min.

◆ Have a volunteer read the poem at the top of page 9. Ask the students, "What do you think about when you see or hold a rock?" "Do you think about strength or durability?" Then ask how all the things mentioned in the poem are much more than they seem.

◆ Ask a different volunteer to read each paragraph of "The Real World." Have the students highlight or underline in color the definition of *symbol*.

◆ List the following words and phrases on the board, and ask the young people to draw or write a description of a symbol for each in their journals: favorite activity or hobby, a close friendship, your mood at this time, growing pains, strength, faith in God, freedom.

Note: Throughout these lessons, journaling suggestions will be made, but the young people should be encouraged to express themselves in their journals whenever, and in response to whatever, they wish. Take a few minutes to explain the concept of journaling. You may want to share the ideas presented on page G19. Sadlier publishes a journal that reflects the journaling activities suggested in this text and guide.

◆ Have a volunteer read "The Power of Symbol" on page 9. Ask the students to highlight the statements shown highlighted in this section on the reduced student page. Have them form buzz groups. Invite each group to decide on a person or group whom they would like to honor for an outstanding achievement or positive contribution to society. Have each buzz group decide the following:

• What symbol would you draw or sculpt on the award you would present to this person?
• What words would you include?

Let a young person from each buzz group share the group's award symbol and words with all the students.

Note: The term *buzz group* in this guide refers to a small discussion group. Emphasize the importance of listening to what each person has to share.

The Real World

You are about to enter into a whole new way of looking at life and faith. Now that you are more mature, it is time to go deeper in understanding exactly what Christ meant when he said, "Where two or three are gathered together in my name, there am I in the midst of them" (Matthew 18:20).

Jesus is with us, especially when we gather to celebrate the liturgy. But how does this happen? To begin our challenging exploration, we must get back to basics and start with our human experience of signs and symbols.

Have you ever heard the expression, "There's more here than meets the eye"? It means that often things can suggest images, emotions, or meanings beyond what we can see with our eyes. When this happens, the things become symbols. A *symbol* is something that stands for or suggests something else. *Symbol* comes from a Greek word that means "to throw together." When something we observe with our senses is "thrown together" with the unseen—a memory, a feeling, or an idea—it can become a symbol.

How does this happen? To answer this question let's take a look at fire. The discovery of fire was an earthshaking moment in human history.

8

Conclusion ___ min.

◆ Take a few minutes to explain the *Forum*—its purpose and the students' participation in and responsibility for it. Here are some points to cover:

• *Forum* is a Latin word for the place where the ideas and work of the community were explored and discussed. It was the center of public life in a Roman city. So important was this concept that in English the word *forum* refers to an intense exchange of ideas, thoughts, and opinions.
• Each day's work will begin with this kind of exchange and dialogue. The *Forum Assignment* is prepared outside of class. It has two steps.

The Power of Symbol

Have you ever watched an award ceremony at the Olympics? What happens? The gold medal is given to the champion because gold is the most precious of all metals. If you have watched, however, you will observe that for most winners having the medal placed around their necks is not the most moving or symbolic moment. It's what comes next that stirs deep feelings. All stand as the flag of the champion's country is raised and its national anthem is played. This moment is so rich in symbolism that no matter who the gold medal winner is, all who watch understand the symbolic meanings behind the sound of the music and the sight of a flag.

Over time and cultures certain things or acts have come to have deeper meanings that are recognized by the people of that culture. There is a kind of "sign language" that uncovers a deeper world of meanings, ideas, and emotions. That sign language is made up of symbols. A multicolored piece of cloth, as we have seen, arouses feelings of patriotism. A dove suggests the human desire for peace.

Among all the creatures of earth, we humans are the only ones who have the power and the imagination to think symbolically, to interpret and make sense of our lives, and to express in symbols our deepest beliefs and concerns. What does all that have to do with our Catholic faith and with this course on liturgy and worship?

You're about to find out. This book will invite you to celebrate your faith in a way you have never done before. It will challenge you to look at things you thought were familiar in a whole new way. Why now? Because you are ready to experience your faith on a deeper and more mature level. Don't be afraid of the challenge. Let's begin!

And down through the centuries the image of fire has become a symbol of great power. Human beings see in fire so much more than simple scientific combustion. Fire has many symbolic meanings: light, energy, safety, warmth, even godlikeness.

We are so accustomed to the reality of fire that perhaps we are not always aware of its symbolism. But have you ever sat beside a campfire or before a fireplace and been fascinated by the flames—their movements, their sound, their warmth, their colors? If you have, you have engaged in symbolic thinking, just as so many others have done down through the ages.

9

FORUM Assignment

✔ Read pages 10 and 11. Underline in pencil the statements that express four main ideas.

✔ Work on the handout *Thinking Symbolically.*

Closing Prayer: Invite the students to look again at the photo on pages 6 and 7. Pray together:

> Jesus, be with us as we look at the symbols of our faith in a deeper, more mature way.

Note: Suggestions for the *Opening Prayer* are given in the *Teaching Resources* chart in the introductory pages for each chapter.

---

1. The two pages of the next lesson are read thoroughly. Key ideas are underlined in pencil.
2. The assigned activity or question is prepared for discussion. Stress the importance of both preparation for and participation in the forum.

◆ Explain that the *Forum Assignment* for Session Two is to work on the handout sheet. Distribute the handout *Thinking Symbolically*, and have a volunteer read the directions aloud.

Note: The *Forum Assignment*, which appears throughout the guide, is written in the voice of the teacher addressing the students.

FOR SESSION 2

- Prepare volunteers for the opening prayer.
- photographs of sacred places

SESSION 2

Objective: To explore the ways that we humans use symbols to communicate our belief in the sacred.

Introduction ___ min.

Opening Prayer

Forum: Have the students form small buzz groups to share the symbols they have written about or drawn. Ask each group to choose the members' favorite symbol for each of the concerns listed. Then have a representative from each group explain the reasons for the group's choices.

Discuss with the young people the statements they underlined.

Presentation ___ min.

◆ Have a volunteer explain the Native Americans' beliefs about sacred space. Ask another volunteer to explain some of the symbols of their beliefs and concerns.

Note: Throughout the text you will see the sunburst icon. It indicates directives or questions that are meant to be thought provoking. Responding to these will help the young people internalize the key ideas presented. In the guide these directives or questions will be referred to as *thought provokers.*

◆ Direct attention to the thought provoker on page 10. Have the young people share their experiences.

Discuss with the students the symbolism of sacred places as described in the first three paragraphs of "Symbols of Belief" on page 11. Have the students highlight the last paragraph in the left-hand column on this page. If you have brought in photographs of sacred places, show them to the students now.

◆ Ask, "If you could choose a place in which to build a church, where would it be? For what reasons?" Have the young people write their responses in their journals. Invite those who wish to share their thoughts with the group.

Sacred Space

We can see from the signs that have been left us that ancient peoples used symbols to express their deep beliefs and concerns about the great mysteries of life, concerns that we share today: Who are we? Who made us? Why are we here? Who directs our lives? Does anyone care for us?

This awareness of the divine, the holy, the sacred appears in every human culture. It is expressed differently in different cultures; but in all of them, symbols are part of the way we humans communicate our belief in the sacred. And just as we do today, the ancient peoples set aside symbolic *places* in which to celebrate the sacred mysteries of life.

Consider, for example, Native Americans. They saw no need to build sacred spaces because they believed deeply that the land—all of it—is sacred: every rock, every tree, every river, every canyon. Everything from the smallest insect to the highest mountain is sacred to them because it was placed here by the creator. And because all things are sacred, all places are sacred, too.

Still, Native Americans chose certain special places on the sacred land in which to celebrate their deepest beliefs. In these chosen places they have left us many symbols of their beliefs and concerns: serpent mounds, rock paintings, medicine wheels, rock carvings, and totem poles, among others. At the heart of these symbols is their belief in the relationship human beings have with one another, with the land, and with the Great Spirit, the creator.

At the summit of a mountain in northern Wyoming, there is a great stone wheel or circle impressed on the earth. Spokes radiate from the center of the wheel to its edge. Native Americans believe that the circle symbolizes infinity because it has no beginning and no end. Native peoples of the area have oral histories about the sacred ceremonies held at this symbolic place. Even today prayer offerings are left on the mountain.

Have you ever been to a place sacred to a culture other than your own? If so, share your experience.

10

Medicine Mountain, Wyoming

FYI Visitors to Palestine, the land of Jesus' birth, may stand in a spot near a ford in the Jordan River that is, according to tradition, the place where Jesus was baptized by John (Mark 1:9). In early Christian times thousands of people visited here on the eve of the feast of the Epiphany. They prayed and sang hymns as they processed to the Jordan, in which they bathed.

Today many visitors fill small bottles with water from the Jordan to take home as a memento of their visit to this holy place.

Machu Picchu, Acropolis, Saint Peter's Basilica

Symbols of Belief

Native Americans are not the only ones with sacred places, of course. In every age and culture, the holy place—a shrine, forest grove, temple, church—has been symbolically set apart as a sacred area. The placement of objects in the sacred place symbolizes the belief of the people. Sacred places are often considered to be reflections of the universe. The domes of Christian churches, often painted with stars, are symbols of heaven; the altar, a symbol of Christ. The inner sanctuary in Shinto shrines in Japan is a symbol of God, and the prayer niches in mosques of Islam are symbols of the presence of Allah.

The ancient Greeks saw their highest mountain, Mount Olympus, as the dwelling place of the gods, where they lived shrouded from men's eyes by the mists. The Athenians chose the highest hill in their city as their sacred place. There on the Acropolis (meaning high city"), they constructed a sacred temple to their gods, especially Athena, the protective goddess of their people.

The remains of Machu Picchu, the sacred city of the Inca, lie at the top of the Andes mountains, symbolically close to the heavens and suggesting symbolically the efforts humans must make to approach the sacred.

As we have seen, expressing our beliefs in symbol is part of our humanity. And one of the most profound symbols of all is that of the space we set apart in which to worship.

What about us? What do our sacred places symbolize? Our sacred places and spaces express our deepest beliefs as Catholics. Our most profound belief is that Jesus Christ, the Son of God, became one of us. He suffered, died, and rose again so that we might have new life. All our sacred places, objects, and actions help us to enter more deeply into this mystery of our salvation through Jesus Christ.

During this course we have the opportunity to look at and to celebrate these beliefs in a new and more mature way, to decide what they mean to us, and to allow them to change our lives.

CATHOLIC ID

For us Catholics, all our churches are sacred spaces. Each is the "house of God" because Christ is present there in the Eucharist. Your own parish church is a sacred space. Some places, however, hold deeper significance for us because of their location or because of something that happened there. Saint Peter's Basilica in Vatican City is one such sacred space. From the earliest centuries of the Church, Christians believed that this was the place where Saint Peter was martyred and buried. Excavations beneath Saint Peter's have uncovered a *necropolis*, a "city of the dead." Inscriptions and bones found there seem to confirm that this is indeed the burial place of Saint Peter.

11

• *Photographs of the Vatican City, Italy* at http://www.crols.com/g brown/travels/vatican.htm

FORUM Assignment

✔ Read pages 12 and 13. Underline in pencil the statements that express six main ideas.

✔ A friend is moving far away. Your friend has been part of your lives for as long as you can remember. You have shared good times and bad. Plan a simple going away ritual that you and your other friends would have to mark this moment.

Closing Prayer: You may want to take this time to set up your group's prayer corner. The students may want to use this space as a gathering place for communal prayer or as sacred space for personal prayer.

Have the young people gather in this space now. Ask a volunteer to read Psalm 23:1– 4 or Psalm 139:1–12, 23–24.

Then sing a favorite hymn or sing or pray together the Our Father.

Note: *FYI (For Your Information)* is a feature that will appear frequently throughout the guide. Its purpose is to provide you with some additional information about one of the topics mentioned on the pages. If you wish, share the information with your group.

Conclusion ___ min.

◆ Have the students highlight the main ideas high-lighted here.

◆ Have a volunteer summarize *Catholic ID*. You may want to show photographs of St. Peter's Basilica. They may be found in encyclopedias or at the following web sites:

• *Feature Story: St. Peter's Basilica, Rome* at http://www.christmas 95.com/xmas/features/story010.htm

FOR SESSION 3

• construction paper (optional)
• string or yarn (optional)

SESSION 3

Objective: To explore three of the most important characteristics of ritual.

Introduction ___ min.

Opening Prayer

Forum: Have the young people present the farewell rituals that they have planned for their friends. Ask the students to choose one of these rituals or plan a different one to use to celebrate the birthdays of the group's members.

Discuss with the students the statements they underlined. Have them highlight the main ideas highlighted on these pages.

Presentation ___ min.

◆ Have volunteers write the symbols included in the description of the President's funeral. The following should be listed:

• a soldier leading a riderless horse (a symbol of a fallen leader)

• no music, only muffled drums (symbols of silence and grief caused by murder)

• folding of flag (symbolizes service of person to his or her country)

• playing of "Taps" (symbolizes eternal sleep)

• lighting of eternal flame (symbolizes the person's good deeds that live on)

◆ Direct attention to the thought provoker on page 12. Have the students form buzz groups to discuss the ways the wedding ritual expresses deeper meanings and beliefs.

◆ Have the young people form buzz groups to discuss specific rituals they may have celebrated. Ask the groups to note any ritual that was marked by the three important characteristics described on page 13: interpersonal, repetitive, and acted out.

◆ Have the young people remain in their groups. Explain to them that some sociologists and psychologists have claimed that the people of today's fast-paced world do not participate in ritual enough and that family life and the world in general would improve greatly if people did so. Ask each group to discuss its members' agreement or disagreement with this claim.

Symbols in Action

It is 1963. An assassinated president is being laid to rest. President Kennedy's flag-draped coffin is brought from the cathedral and placed on a horse-drawn gun carriage for the procession to Arlington National Cemetery. Behind the gun carriage a soldier leads a riderless horse. There is no music for this procession, only the sound of muffled drums and the creaking of the carriage wheels.

At the cemetery members of the military fold the flag, with solemn precision, into an intricate and prescribed triangle and present it to the widow. Three buglers play in echoing sequence the plaintive *Taps*, the sound that ends a soldier's day. Mrs. Kennedy then lights an "eternal flame," a light that will never go out, on the president's grave.

This event, indelibly imprinted on the memories of those who witnessed it, is rich in symbols. How many can you discover?

When symbols are connected like this in meaningful action, we have what is called a ritual. *Rituals*, then, are symbolic actions that often express our deepest beliefs or concerns. Some rituals, of course, are very simple, such as placing candles on a birthday cake, doing the wave at a baseball game, or giving a teammate a high five after a victory.

Other rituals, such as the funeral described above, the opening ceremonies of the Olympic Games, or a graduation ceremony, have deeper and more complicated symbolism.

Recall a wedding that you have attended or seen. Describe some of its symbolic ritual. In what way does the ritual express deeper meanings and beliefs?

These pictures show people of other faiths expressing their beliefs in rituals. How do we express our Catholic beliefs?

12

FYI Does your family or school have a special ritual to welcome visitors? Today citizens of the state of Hawaii continue the ancient native custom of welcoming visitors with garlands of leaves, or flowers (originally shells, fruits, beads, or feathers were also used). These garlands, called leis, are also given when saying farewell. Hawaiians celebrate Lei Day on May 1 to symbolize their tradition of friendliness and hospitality.

Think of a single welcoming ritual that you might initiate within your families or groups of friends.

What Makes a Ritual?

Anthropologists tell us that rituals, or symbolic actions, are at the heart of human experience. From earliest times human beings have developed rituals to celebrate, remember, and express in a public way their deepest concerns, their most profound beliefs. Rituals are found among human beings in every age and from every culture, from the cave paintings of prehistoric humans to the Eucharist celebrated today in our parish churches. Somehow rituals meet deep human needs of individuals and communities. They often mark transitions from one stage of life to another. They help us make sense of life's mysteries.

What are some characteristics of ritual? Here are three of the most important ones.

Ritual is *interpersonal*. It is something one does not alone but with others who share the same beliefs or concerns. When symbolic action is expressed by people as a community, its deepest meanings are revealed and experienced.

Ritual is *repetitive*. Humans repeat rituals because these actions express what is most constant, most meaningful in their lives. We celebrate ritually

what is unchanging to us in a changing world. If an action is true and meaningful to us, it must be repeated, celebrated, over and over again.

• Ritual is *acted out*. It uses symbolic movements and gestures to express deeper meaning. These actions are symbolic because they go beyond what is seen on the surface.

For example, do you know why the ritual of greeting someone by shaking hands arose? What to us is now an automatic action of greeting was once a very serious and very symbolic action. In the early Middle Ages, it was a sign to strangers or possible foes that one was not holding a weapon and therefore was not a threat to the other. Once men shook hands, both were committed by honor to obey its meaning and not to attack one another during their meeting. The symbol persisted into later ages, when a man's handshake was equivalent to his word. "Let's shake on it" came into the language of business and diplomacy as a symbol of one's word of honor.

An understanding of symbol and ritual is essential to a mature understanding of our worship as Catholics. All the sacraments of the Church involve ritual. And if we are aware and willing to participate, each ritual draws us more deeply into the life of faith it expresses.

Scripture UPDATE

One beautiful way to look at symbols in Scripture is found in the story of the prodigal son (Luke 15:11–32). Remember when the younger son came home? His father *ran* to meet him. He *hugged* and *kissed* his son even before saying a word. What clearer symbols could the son have had of his father's love?

13

FORUM Assignment

✔ Read pages 14 and 15. Underline in pencil the statements that express two main ideas.

✔ Complete the chart on page 14.

Closing Prayer: Invite the students to stand and form a circle. Stand in the middle of the circle, and offer the following blessing from Numbers 6:24–26:

> The LORD bless you and keep you!
> The LORD let his face shine upon
>   you, and be gracious to you!
> The LORD look upon you kindly
>   and give you peace!

Then have the young people exchange their leis.

Conclusion___ min.

Note: The following activity is optional.

◆ Provide construction paper and string or yarn for the young people to make leis to present to each other at the end of the *Closing Prayer*. They may choose to use one of the traditional Hawaiian symbols or other symbols of peace or friendship.

◆ Have a volunteer summarize the *Scripture Update* on page 13. You may wish to read together the story of the prodigal son (Luke 15: 11–32).

FOR SESSION 4

- a bell
- words for "America the Beautiful"
- words for "The New Colossus" by Emma Lazarus (inscription poem on the Statue of Liberty)

13

SESSION 4

Objective: To explore ways our cultural experiences and our maturity help us to be aware of symbolic meanings.

Introduction ___ min.

Opening Prayer

Forum: Have the young people present the meanings for the symbols listed in the chart on page 14.

Ask the students to discuss the key ideas they chose to underline on pages 14 and 15. Encourage all to participate in the discussion. Then have the group highlight the statements highlighted here.

Presentation ___ min.

◆ Have the young people discuss the symbolism of the Statue of Liberty. If possible, have a volunteer read aloud the poem at its base. Invite anyone who has visited the statue to share the experience. Ask, "What are other symbols of liberty or freedom?"

◆ Direct attention to the thought provoker on page 14. List the students' responses on the board.

◆ Have the students write their descriptions of the rituals they celebrate on Thanksgiving, Christmas, and Fourth of July. Then have the young people form buzz groups to discuss their responses.

◆ Ask, "How does the Church celebrate the civil holidays of Thanksgiving and Fourth of July?" Point out that on both holidays most parish communities participate in Mass. Before Thanksgiving the Church asks us to donate food and clothing to share with those less fortunate than ourselves.

◆ Have a volunteer summarize *Catholic Teachings* on page 15. Discuss with the students signs and symbols that are "bearers of the saving and sanctifying action of Christ" (*Catechism*, 1189).

What does this picture symbolize to you?

Thinking Symbolically

In this chapter we have explored symbols: objects, places, and actions that have meanings beyond what we can perceive with our physical senses alone. All people of a given culture recognize and identify with these meanings. Of course a person has to have had some cultural experiences and a certain maturity to be aware of symbolic meanings. You are certainly ready to begin to think symbolically.

See if you can recognize the meanings of these symbols. If you are not sure, use your imagination. See how close you can come to the universal understanding of each one.

Symbol	Meaning
At the coronation of Elizabeth II, the young queen was given symbolic objects: a scepter and a golden orb (a sphere). What do these stand for?	
A bishop carries a shepherd's staff. It is called a *crosier*. Why a shepherd's staff?	
A traditional symbol of justice is a statue of a woman. She wears a blindfold and holds balanced scales in her hands. What do these symbols say about justice?	
A Chinese proverb says, "It is better to light one candle than to curse the darkness." How are these words symbolic?	

Share your ideas. See how aware you already are of complex symbolism.

 Can you describe some other symbols that are universally recognized?

14

FYI Saint John Damascene (about A.D. 675–749) was a monk and priest who was also a gifted writer and speaker. In 726, when the Byzantine ruler, Leo the Isaurian, condemned the use of religious images by Christians, John wrote the following defense:

What a book is for those who can read, such is an image for those who cannot. What a word is for hearing, such is an image for sight. The holy images are a memorial of God's work.

Ritual Celebrations

Like symbols, rituals, such as a salute or a handshake, can be very simple. They can also be much more complex, much richer, especially those dealing with people's cultural memories and deepest beliefs.

In the spaces here describe the rituals that are celebrated on each occasion. To the general rituals that most people celebrate, add any further details that are a part of your family's rituals.

We have spent a great deal of time on symbol and ritual in this opening chapter. Why? Because symbolic thinking is one of the most essential and profound things humans can do. Symbolic thinking is certainly the most essential and profound thing we do as Catholics. And when we grow in appreciating and understanding the symbols and rituals of our faith, they will speak to us as nothing else in the world does.

This will take hard work and effort. But by the time we finish this course, we will see with new eyes the power and effect of what we do together as Catholics. As we will see, the Church takes elements from creation and from our human activity and sanctifies them—makes them holy— and enables them to be signs of grace.

CATHOLIC TEACHINGS

About Symbol and Ritual

The Church's sacramental celebrations involve not only signs and symbols relating to creation and human life but also to God's mighty deeds for his people, above all the Passover. Through the power of the Holy Spirit, these signs and symbols become "bearers of the saving and sanctifying action of Christ" (*Catechism*, 1189).

Thanksgiving

_____

Christmas

_____

Fourth of July

_____

15

Turn our hearts toward the family of nations:
to understand the ways of others,
to offer friendship,
and to find safety only in the common good of all.

FORUM Assignment

✔ Read pages 16 and 17. Prepare your responses for *Things to Think About* and *Things to Share*.

✔ Read *On Line with the Parish* on page 16. List your favorite hymns, and explain the reasons the words have special meaning for you.

Closing Prayer: Ring a bell to symbolize the ringing of the Liberty Bell, and sing together one verse of "America the Beautiful." Then invite the shared-prayer groups to stand and act out their prayerful gestures as you read aloud the Prayer for Independence Day. Conclude the prayer by inviting the young people to offer spontaneous prayers of petition and/or thanksgiving.

Conclusion ___ min.

◆ Have the young people form shared-prayer groups. Write A Prayer for Independence Day on the board. Have the groups reflect on the words and then plan prayerful gestures for some of the phrases or verses. Explain that they will use these gestures during the *Closing Prayer*.

God, source of all freedom,
this day is bright with the memory
of those who declared that life and liberty
are your gift to every human being.

Help us to continue a good work begun long ago.
Make our vision clear and our will strong:
that only in human solidarity will we find liberty,
and justice only in the honor that belongs
to every life on earth.

FOR SESSION 5

• If you wish to give a standardized-format test for this chapter, duplicate *Chapter 1 Assessment* on page 17A and plan time for its use.

• *Highlights for Home*, page 17B, can be duplicated and sent home to families.

SESSION 5

Objective: To deepen understanding of the importance of symbolism and ritual in our lives.

Introduction ___ min.

Opening Prayer

Forum: Invite the young people to form buzz groups to share their favorite hymns and the special meaning the lyrics have for them in their prayer life.

Note: The fifth lesson of each chapter, as the title *Putting It Together* suggests, provides the students with the opportunity to review, summarize, and internalize the work of the week. Each part of the page is like a piece of a jigsaw puzzle. The aim is to get all the pieces to fit so that the chapter becomes a whole.

Presentation ___ min.

◆ Invite the young people to share their reactions and responses to *Things to Think About* and *Things to Share*. Encourage everyone to participate actively with questions, comments, and suggestions.

◆ Direct attention to *Words to Remember*. Ask the young people to find and define the words. The definition for *symbol* is on page 8; the definition for *ritual* is on page 12.

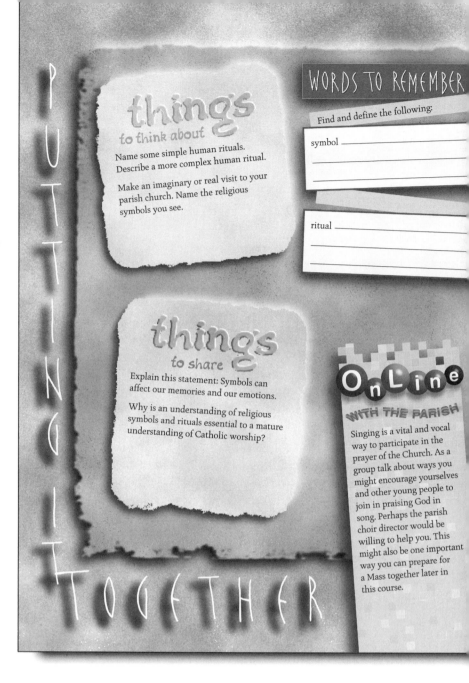

things to think about

Name some simple human rituals. Describe a more complex human ritual.

Make an imaginary or real visit to your parish church. Name the religious symbols you see.

things to share

Explain this statement: Symbols can affect our memories and our emotions.

Why is an understanding of religious symbols and rituals essential to a mature understanding of Catholic worship?

WORDS TO REMEMBER

Find and define the following:

symbol _____

ritual _____

OnLine WITH THE PARISH

Singing is a vital and vocal way to participate in the prayer of the Church. As a group talk about ways you might encourage yourselves and other young people to join in praising God in song. Perhaps the parish choir director would be willing to help you. This might also be one important way you can prepare for a Mass together later in this course.

Note: Definitions will be easy for the students to find because in every chapter key words are printed in italics.

◆ *On Line with the Parish*, which appears in each chapter, will suggest ways the young people can connect with, participate in, and serve their parish. Take time to talk about these suggestions with the students and find ways to facilitate their parish endeavors. In this particular chapter the group may want to write their suggestions for ways they can show enthusiasm for singing.

Assessment: *Testing 1, 2, 3* can be used in a variety of ways. One way is to have the students write their responses and share them with the group. If they can articulate their thoughts clearly in this section, they have truly understood the ideas of this chapter.

If you wish to give a standardized-format test for this chapter, administer *Chapter 1 Assessment* on page 17A.

Conclusion ___ min.

◆ End the lesson and the chapter by setting aside time for *Life in the Spirit*. It is essential that this component not be omitted because its aim is to draw the young people into a spiritual awareness and appreciation of the intellectual ideas they have been exploring. Everything that is explored, discovered, and learned in a chapter should lead to prayer.

Closing Prayer: Invite the young people to look again at the photograph of the pond on pages 6 and 7. Encourage them to reflect silently and peacefully on what they have discovered and explored "beneath the surface" this week.

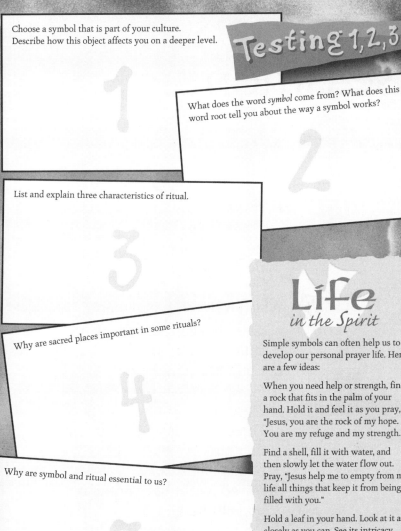

Choose a symbol that is part of your culture. Describe how this object affects you on a deeper level.

Testing 1,2,3

What does the word *symbol* come from? What does this word root tell you about the way a symbol works?

List and explain three characteristics of ritual.

Why are sacred places important in some rituals?

Why are symbol and ritual essential to us?

Life in the Spirit

Simple symbols can often help us to develop our personal prayer life. Here are a few ideas:

When you need help or strength, find a rock that fits in the palm of your hand. Hold it and feel it as you pray, "Jesus, you are the rock of my hope. You are my refuge and my strength."

Find a shell, fill it with water, and then slowly let the water flow out. Pray, "Jesus help me to empty from my life all things that keep it from being filled with you."

Hold a leaf in your hand. Look at it as closely as you can. See its intricacy and beauty. Thank God for the wonders of his creation.

17

Evaluation: Have the young people discovered that symbols can affect our memories and emotions? Do they recognize that an understanding of religious symbols and rituals is essential to a mature understanding of Catholic worship?

Note: There is no *Forum Assignment* at the end of a chapter.

Testing 1,2,3

1. See pages 8 and 9. Accept any reasonable response.

2. See page 8. *Symbol* comes from a Greek word that means "to throw together." When something we observe with our senses is "thrown together" with the unseen—a memory, a feeling, or an idea—it can become a symbol.

3. See page 13. Ritual is *interpersonal*, something one does with others who share the same beliefs or concerns. Ritual is *repetitive*. Humans repeat rituals to express what is most constant, most meaningful in their lives. Ritual is *acted out*, using symbolic movements and gestures to express deeper meaning.

4. See pages 10 and 11. One of the most profound symbols is that of the space we set apart in which to worship. For Catholics all our sacred places help us to enter more deeply into the mystery of our salvation through Jesus Christ.

5. See page 13. An understanding of symbol and ritual is essential to a mature understanding of our worship as Catholics. All the sacraments of the Church involve ritual. And if we are aware and willing to participate, each ritual draws us more deeply into the life of faith it expresses.

Answers for Chapter 1 Assessment
1. c 2. b 3. c 4. a 5. b
6. a 7. a 8. c 9. d 10. See page 13.

Assessment

 1 *Symbol* comes from a Greek word that means
- **a.** "a sacred place."
- **b.** "a repeated action."
- **c.** "to throw together."
- **d.** "an important discovery."

 2 For Native Americans a circle symbolizes
- **a.** deep beliefs.
- **b.** infinity.
- **c.** God's dwelling.
- **d.** humanity.

 3 We say that ritual is _____ because it is expressed by people as a community.
- **a.** repetitive
- **b.** acted out
- **c.** interpersonal
- **d.** none of the above

 4 We say that ritual is _____ because rituals express what is most constant, most meaningful in our lives.
- **a.** repetitive
- **b.** acted out
- **c.** interpersonal
- **d.** frequent

 5 We say that ritual is _____ because we use symbolic movement to express deeper meaning.
- **a.** repetitive
- **b.** acted out
- **c.** interpersonal
- **d.** frequent

 6 An example of symbolic thinking is
- **a.** seeing fire as warmth and safety.
- **b.** seeing fire as scientific combustion.
- **c.** both a and b
- **d.** neither a or b

 7 Which is the true statement?
- **a.** Catholics consider all our churches to be "houses of God."
- **b.** Catholics consider only St. Peter's Basilica to be a sacred place.
- **c.** The Church teaches that symbols are non-essential to human life.
- **d.** sacred places have nothing to do with belief.

 8 Rituals are _____ that often express our deepest beliefs or concerns.
- **a.** symbolic objects
- **b.** sacred places
- **c.** symbolic actions
- **d.** symbolic words

 9 Which of the following would be considered a complex ritual?
- **a.** a handshake
- **b.** a victory sign
- **c.** wishing someone "Happy Anniversary"
- **d.** a wedding

 10 Explain briefly the symbolism found in the story of the prodigal son. Write your response on the reverse side of this page.

Highlights for Home

Focus on Faith

During this course, *Liturgy and Worship*, the young people will examine closely the uniqueness of Catholic worship: its roots, its transforming power, and its deep spirituality. It is in the Church's liturgy, especially the seven sacraments, that we Catholics celebrate all that God has done for us in Jesus Christ through the working of the Holy Spirit. Our salvation was made possible through the paschal mystery of Christ's passion, death, resurrection, and ascension. As members of the Church, we are called upon to enter into this mystery of faith and truly be people of word and sacrament. This is where our lives of faith are proclaimed, formed, and nourished. If our sons and daughters are to be strong and faithful followers of Christ, they must make the liturgical life of the Church their own. In this chapter the young people will begin to see that if they are to be men and women of prayer and mature people who know how to celebrate God's presence in their lives, they must be at home with the rituals, signs, and symbols that are part of our Catholic identity.

Conversation Starters

. . . . a few ideas to talk about together . . . .

◆ What places do I consider sacred?

◆ What symbols or rituals help me make sense of life's mysteries?

◆ What religious symbol causes pleasant memories or emotions?

Feature Focus

Scripture Update on page 13 describes the symbolic actions of the loving father in the story of the prodigal son (Luke 15:11–32). Instead of waiting to be approached, the father *ran* to meet his son, who was returning after a long period of time. He *hugged* and *kissed* his son before the young man said a word. Reflect on the ways the relationship between the father and son symbolizes the relationship between God, our loving Father, and each of us.

Reflection

What images come to mind as you reflect on Psalm 91:1–4?

*You who dwell in the shelter of the Most
    High,
    who abide in the shadow of the Almighty,
Say to the LORD, "My refuge and fortress,
    my God in whom I trust."
God will rescue you from the fowler's snare,
    from the destroying plague,
Will shelter you with pinions,
    spread wings that you may take refuge;
    God's faithfulness is a protecting shield.*

THE PRAYER OF THE CHURCH

Adult Focus

It is essential that our young people develop a deep understanding and appreciation for the public prayer of the Church, which is called *liturgy.* In this chapter they will learn that the liturgy is public because each liturgical celebration includes, concerns, and affects the whole Church. It is the official prayer of the Church.

Liturgical prayer is different from private prayer in an important way. Liturgical prayer is the prayer of Christ himself and as such has unique value far beyond what we ourselves can do. Liturgical prayer is always a prayer to the Blessed Trinity offered to God the *Father* in, through, and with his *Son, Jesus Christ,* in the unity of the *Holy Spirit.* In liturgical prayer we use the words and actions given to us by the Church. These words and actions have been treasured and handed down to us across the centuries in the rites and rituals of the liturgy.

Above all, our liturgy celebrates our relationship with the Father in and through the paschal mystery of Jesus Christ. Liturgy is a communal, public experience and, at the same time, a personal experience because of that relationship. That is why we say that good liturgy is never private, but good liturgy is always personal.

Catechism Focus:

The themes of this chapter correspond to paragraphs 1146–1152 of the *Catechism.*

Enrichment Activities

Video View

You may want to show the video *Journey to the Mountain Top,* the story of World Youth Day 1993. Viewing this dialogue of the Church with the young people from around the world and watching Pope John Paul II celebrating Mass with the youth may help the young people respond to the questions on page 22 about the concerns of Christ that we pray for in liturgical prayer. Watching various youth groups in their ministry to the needy will demonstrate the statement in *Catholic Teachings:* "Liturgy sends us out to serve others, and that experience sends us back to celebrate liturgy."

The video is made available by Liguori Publications. The address is:

Redemptorist Pastoral Communications
Liguori, MO 63057
(314) 464-2500

CHAPTER 2

Teaching Resources

Overview	Opening Prayer Ideas	Materials
SESSION 1 **Discovery:** To discover that when we Catholics pray together, we celebrate in and through symbolic activity.	Look at the photo on pages 18 and 19. Lift up your minds and hearts to God by praying together Psalm 63:5.	These will be needed for every session: texts, Bibles, highlighters or colored pencils, journals. • tree branch and potting soil, sand, or aquarium pebbles in large pot (optional)
SESSION 2 **Exploring 1:** To explore the characteristics of liturgy in which we proclaim and celebrate the mystery of Christ.	Pray together Psalm 105:1–6.	• sacramentary and/or lectionary • lyrics for songs "All That We Have" or "All Our Joy" (optional)
SESSION 3 **Exploring 2:** To discover what we mean by the paschal mystery; to explore ways we live the paschal mystery.	Sing or pray together: Dying you destroyed our death, rising you restored our life. Lord Jesus, come in glory.	• yarn, string, or ribbon (optional)
SESSION 4 **Exploring 3:** To discover the ways in which our liturgical history has helped to shape our liturgical life.	Pray together Psalm 150.	• copies of handout *To Proclaim God's Love*, page 18C • recordings of Gregorian chant and processional and recessional hymns we sing at Mass
SESSION 5 **Putting It Together:** To explore the words, feelings, or images the word *Catholic* brings to mind; to review the ideas presented in the chapter.	Pray together Glory to the Father on page 186.	• copies of *Chapter 2 Assessment*, page 29A • copies of *Highlights for Home*, page 29B

Supplemental Resources

Video
Gregorian Chant: The Monks and Their Music
Ignatius Press
P.O. Box 1339
Ft. Collins, CO 80522

Faith and Witness Journal:
Liturgy and Worship
For Chapter 2 see pages
8–11.

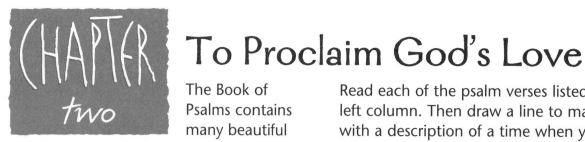

CHAPTER two

To Proclaim God's Love

The Book of Psalms contains many beautiful words our ancestors of faith used to address God. Jesus prayed the psalms, and today when we celebrate and live out the paschal mystery, we pray these verses.

Read each of the psalm verses listed in the left column. Then draw a line to match it with a description of a time when you would find it helpful to pray these words.

1. Psalm 148:1–14

2. Psalm 34:2–4

3. Psalm 130:1–8

4. Psalm 59:17–18

5. Psalm 96:7–13

6. Psalm 121:1–8

7. Psalm 103:1–18

8. Psalm 143:4–11

a. after the sacrament of Reconciliation

b. when you are upset and want God's guidance

c. when you want to praise God for his gifts of creation

d. a national holiday

e. when you want to ask God's forgiveness

f. when you want to invite others to pray

g. when you want God's help to overcome temptation

h. when you want to ask God to help you be strong and courageous

Write your favorite psalm verse. Think of the ways the words help you to lift your mind and heart to God.

_____

_____

_____

_____

_____

_____

_____

_____

_____

_____

SESSION 1

The Prayer of the Church

Lord, teach us to pray.
Luke 11:1

Objective: To discover that when we Catholics pray together, we celebrate in and through symbolic activity.

Introduction ___ min.

Opening Prayer: Invite the young people to look at the photo on pages 18 and 19 as you read aloud Ephesians 3:14–21. Ask the young people to write in their journals a prayer thanking Jesus for his great love.

Explain to the young people that when we pray, we lift up our minds and hearts to God. Invite them to stand and extend their arms as if each of them was one of the tree branches shown in the photo. Direct them to pray the response from Psalm 63:5 to each of the following situations you will describe and any others that volunteers may choose to add:

Response: I will lift up my hands, calling on your name.

Situations: When I am happy and my life is running smoothly. . .

When I am upset and everything seems topsy-turvy. . .

When I have achieved a goal I have set for myself. . .

When I cannot seem to overcome a stumbling block. . .

Conclude the prayer by praying together the Our Father, the prayer that Jesus taught us.

Note: The following activity is optional.

Chapter Warm-Up: Place a tree branch in a container and support it with potting soil, sand, or aquarium pebbles. Distribute drawing paper, and have the students cut out a speech-balloon shape. Ask each student to write on the balloon a one-sentence prayer of praise or thanks. Then use paper clips or string to attach the prayers to the tree branch.

From posterboard cut out a large heart shape. Write on the shape, "We lift up our minds and hearts to the Lord." Glue the heart onto a stick and plant it at the base of the tree branch.

Invite the volunteers responsible for the opening prayers to choose a few of the prayers from the tree to read at the beginning of each of the sessions of this chapter.

Presentation ___ min.

◆ Brainstorm with the young people about ways we as Catholics express our hopes and beliefs. List the responses on the board.

◆ Have the students read pages 20 and 21 independently. When most are finished, direct attention to the photographs on these pages. Explain the following symbolism:

• The fragrant smoke that rises when incense is burned is a symbol of the people's prayers rising to God.

• By the lighting of the paschal candle, the priest expresses our hope in Christ our Light, who has risen from the dead.

During solemn celebrations of the Mass, the altar, the gifts of bread and wine, the celebrant and the participants, and the paschal candle are incensed as a sign of reverence.

◆ Discuss with the students some of their ordinary daily rituals. Ask, "Does performing these rituals make you feel secure?" "bored?"

◆ Then ask:

• What do our Catholic rituals help us to do? (celebrate Christ's saving action in our lives)

• What should we never forget about the signs and symbols of our faith? (They put us in touch with the divine. Through them we share in God's own divine life.)

◆ Have the students highlight the statements that are highlighted on these pages.

◆ Ask volunteers to explain why it is important for us to look more closely at the liturgy and the sacraments, the Church year, and Catholic devotions. What value do they have for us? How can they help us?

In every culture human beings express their beliefs and hopes in symbolic ways. Think of the ways that we as Catholics express our hopes and beliefs.

Catholic Symbols and Rituals

Words alone can never fully express the deep meanings of our Catholic faith. Because we are human beings, because we have bodies and live in the world of created things, we often use symbols to express our thoughts and feelings, our understandings and insights. As we have seen, a symbol is an object or action that stands for something else. For example, people in love not only talk about loving each other; they also exchange gifts. That is, they give symbols of their love. In the same way, when we celebrate our love relationship with God, we do so not only with words but also with objects and gestures. These are symbols, too.

When we Catholics pray together, we celebrate in and through *symbolic* activity. We must use the language of symbol in our prayer because we are

20

FYI Share the following reflection of James Turro, an author of contemporary spiritual books:

Man is God's most precious thought. This is one of the truths the sacraments disclose to us. Just as in the human community signs are used by men to manifest their thoughts and intentions toward one another, so God uses these signs to put beyond doubt his affection for us. No need to wonder or fear what God thinks of us; he declares himself through the sacraments.

discovering and celebrating what is invisible to our eyes. Remember that signs and symbols put us in touch with what we cannot see. Catholic worship is filled with symbols: eating and drinking, being plunged into water and anointed with oil, standing and sitting, processing from place to place, raising our hands, speaking out and singing together. As Catholics we must never forget that these signs and symbols of our faith put us in touch with the divine. Through them we share in God's own divine life.

The church, the sacred place where we meet for worship, is full of symbols: light, fire, water, word, incense. Often the very architecture of a church is symbolic. Many of our churches are cross-shaped in design, a symbol of our redemption. Others are circular, symbolic of the public nature of our worship.

We use the things of this earth in our prayer because we believe that creation is good. By using created things, we worship the God of creation, the God who "looked at everything he had made, and he found it very good" (Genesis 1:31).

The prayer of the Church is not only *symbolic* activity; it is also *ritual* activity. Rituals are actions we do over and over in prescribed, formal, and set ways. In our daily lives we carry out many ritual actions. Can you think of some ordinary things we do ritually each day?

The prayer of the Church, too, is expressed in rituals. We do things over and over in prescribed, formal, and set ways. Rituals are characteristic of Catholic worship. It would be obvious to a visitor attending Mass for the first time that Catholics know the rituals and are comfortable with them. Catholics know "what happens next," what to expect. When the priest greets us with, "The Lord be with you," we respond, without any thought or hesitation, "And also with you." When the priest invites us, "Let us pray," we stand up. Our rituals help us to do together what we came to do: celebrate Christ's saving actions in our lives.

We Catholics perform many ritual actions during our liturgical celebrations. Perhaps you have never thought about the meaning of these rituals. But understanding what is being said and done through ritual helps us to participate in the prayer of the Church. This is true of anything we do. Isn't it true that the activities which we find boring are often the ones which we do not understand?

The same is true of the prayer of the Church. We can't participate well if we don't understand its symbols and rituals. In order to pray well and to come to know what that prayer means in daily life, it is important for us to acquire the skills and understanding that are necessary to celebrate the prayer of the Church with enthusiasm and joy.

In this course we will discover how Catholics have traditionally prayed and worshiped God. We will explore the liturgy and the sacraments, the Church year, and Catholic devotions. We will learn about the rituals and ceremonies that Catholics have used through the centuries to become God's friends. In this way we, too, can come to know how much we are loved by God. Through that knowledge we will come to appreciate even more what it means to be a Catholic.

21

✔ Read pages 22 and 23. Underline in pencil the statements that express six main ideas.

✔ Prepare what you would say to a friend who told you, "I don't think liturgical prayer is for me. I'll stay at home and pray privately."

Closing Prayer: Invite the young people to look again at the photo on pages 18 and 19. Then ask the group to stand and sing or pray the first stanza of "Now Thank We All Our God."

> Now thank we all our God
> With heart and hands and voices,
> Who wondrous things hath done,
> In whom his world rejoices;
> Who, from our mother's arms,
> Hath blessed us on our way
> With countless gifts of love
> And still is our today.

Conclusion ___ min.

◆ Have the young people describe in their journals their current attitudes about celebrating the prayer of the Church. Encourage them to be honest. Emphasize that they should respect one another's privacy as they write in their journals.

FOR SESSION 2

- sacramentary and/or lectionary
- lyrics for songs "All That We Have" or "All Our Joy" (optional)

SESSION 2

Objective: To explore the characteristics of liturgy in which we proclaim and celebrate the mystery of Christ.

Introduction ___ min.

Opening Prayer

Forum: Have the young people work in pairs to reenact the conversation between friends about private and liturgical prayer.

Discuss with the students the statements they underlined. Then have them highlight the definition for *liturgy* on page 22.

Presentation ___ min.

◆ Ask the young people, "Would you consider the prayer service we celebrated in Session 1 to be liturgical prayer?" Then write the following statement beginnings on the board and have the students complete them:

• The prayer service was public prayer because . . .

• We included personal prayer when . . .

• It was not liturgical prayer because . . .

◆ Ask volunteers to explain the characteristics of liturgical prayer that are described on pages 22 and 23. Then have the young people highlight the statements that are highlighted here.

◆ Ask your pastor's permission to borrow the parish's sacramentary and lectionary. Have the students form small groups to take turns examining the contents of both books.

◆ Have the young people form small groups to discuss the questions in the thought provoker on page 23. Ask a representative from each group to report its findings.

◆ Have a volunteer summarize *Catholic Teachings*. On the board draw a large circle, and divide it into four equal segments. As you point to each segment, use the following script to demonstrate that "liturgy and loving service form one unbroken circle."

• Segment 1: You have a concern about peace in the world.

A deacon accepting the offerings of bread and wine at the preparation of the gifts

The Prayer of the Church

Liturgy is the public prayer of the Church in which we proclaim and celebrate the mystery of Christ. Originally the word *liturgy* meant "a public work"—literally, a work for the people, for everyone.

Because the public prayer of the Church is for everyone, it came to be called *liturgy*, which now means "the participation of the people in the work of God." What is the work of God? It is the work of our redemption; it is what Christ did for us. Liturgy is a work by and for the people, but above all it is God's work. In liturgy the mission of Christ—the work of his passion, death, resurrection, and ascension—continues today.

Liturgical prayer, as God's work and the work of the people, the Church, is a very particular kind of prayer. What are some of its characteristics?

Public First, as we have already seen, liturgical prayer is *public* prayer. Yet it is public in a very special way. Not all prayers said in public are liturgical. For example, a group of people may gather in church to say the rosary. Or perhaps you have seen pictures of the Holy Father on Good Friday leading the stations of the cross in the Coliseum in Rome. Hundreds of people participate. These are certainly public acts, but liturgical prayer is public in a deeper sense.

Liturgical prayer is public because each liturgical celebration, such as the Mass or the sacraments, includes, concerns, and affects the whole Church community. It is the official prayer of the Church. And because liturgical prayer is always for the entire Church, it is public even when only a small number of people are present.

22

• Segment 2: During the general intercessions at Sunday's Mass, the assembly prays for peace.

• Segment 3: At the dismissal the celebrant prays "Go in peace to love and serve the Lord."

• Segment 4: During the week you help to defuse rather than escalate an argument among your friends.

Then point to the second segment, and explain that during next Sunday's liturgy you will give thanks for the peace Christ brings and that sometimes you can be an instrument of his peace.

Ask the young people to think of other examples of liturgy that send us out to serve others and of experiences that send us back to celebrate liturgy.

Prayer of Christ Liturgical prayer is the prayer of Christ himself. Because it is the prayer of Christ, liturgical prayer has unique and special value above and beyond anything else we, as Church, could possibly do.

Worship of the Trinity Liturgical prayer is always prayer to the Blessed Trinity. Every liturgical celebration is offered in, with, and through *Jesus Christ*, in the unity of the *Holy Spirit*, to the honor and glory of the *Father*. Liturgical prayer is always worship of the Trinity.

Addressed to God Liturgical prayer is always addressed to God. Even when we honor Mary and the other saints in the liturgy, we praise and thank God for them. In our private prayer we are always free to call on Mary and the saints directly. In the liturgy, however, our focus is God. In our private prayer we can ask God for all sorts of things. In liturgical prayer, because it is the voice of Christ, we pray for those things that Christ wants. What things do you think Christ wants?

In the Words of the Church In our private prayer we are free to use whatever words we choose. We are encouraged to pray freely and spontaneously, both alone and sometimes with others. In liturgical prayer, however, we pray in the words and with the actions given to us by the Church. Words and actions, carefully preserved and treasured for centuries, are handed down to us in the rites and rituals given in liturgical books.

You may already be familiar with a few of these liturgical books. One, the large book that you see the priest use at the altar during Mass, is the sacramentary. It contains the prayers for the Eucharist. Another book you might know is the lectionary. The name comes from *lectio*, the Latin word for "reading." This is the book that the reader, or lector, carries in procession at the beginning of the Eucharist and from which the Scriptures are proclaimed.

Communal and Personal

Liturgy is the public prayer of the Church in worship of the Trinity. In the liturgy we pray with Christ, the head of the Church, and with his whole body, the Church on earth and in heaven. Now that's public!

Do you think it is possible to be both *public* and *personal* at the same time? Have you ever been with a group of people celebrating a victory, a memorial, or another special moment in life? You are all experiencing something together, but at the same time you are feeling it personally, individually.

That is what liturgy is like. It is a communal experience and a personal experience at the same time. Good liturgy is never private, but good liturgy is always personal.

Liturgical prayer is the prayer of Christ. What do you think might be some of the concerns of Christ that are expressed in the liturgy? Which of those concerns are yours as well?

CATHOLIC TEACHINGS

About Liturgy

The liturgy is the most important activity of the Church because it is the work of Christ himself. However, liturgy can never be the *only* activity of the Church. We must believe the good news and live as Jesus' disciples. This means we "love and serve the Lord" by loving and serving others. Liturgy sends us out to serve others, and that experience sends us back to celebrate liturgy. Liturgy and loving service form one unbroken circle.

23

◆ Prepare the young people for the *Forum Assignment* by explaining that when Peter was waiting in the courtyard after Jesus was arrested, someone accused him of being a friend and follower of Jesus (Matthew 26:69–75). Ask, "If someone made the same accusation of you today, what evidence would be found to convict you?" Have the young people write their responses in their journals.

FORUM Assignment

✔ Read pages 24 and 25. Underline in pencil the statements that express five main ideas.

✔ Design a "wanted" poster that lists reasons young people might be considered suspects for committing acts to show that they are friends and followers of Jesus.

Closing Prayer: Invite the young people to offer spontaneous prayers of petition for the Church leaders and the entire Church, world leaders, the local community, family and friends, those who are sick, and those who have died. The response for each petition is: "Lord, hear our prayer."

Conclusion ___ min.

◆ Discuss with the group the ways that liturgy is a communal experience and a personal experience at the same time.

Sharing the lyrics for the following songs may help with this discussion:

- "All That We Have," *Glory & Praise Comprehensive Edition* (North American Liturgy Resources, 1987)
- "All Our Joy" from *Songs of the New Creation* by the Dameans (**GIA** Publications)

FOR SESSION 3

- yarn, string, or ribbon (optional)

SESSION 3

Objective: To discover what we mean by the paschal mystery; to explore ways we live the paschal mystery.

Introduction ___ min.

Opening Prayer

Forum: Invite the young people to act like detectives as they present their "wanted" posters. Encourage them to "ham it up" when they describe the suspects' "crimes," such as acts of friendship and kindness.

After all the presentations, have the young people provide reasons the "suspects" should be considered upstanding and desirable neighbors and friends.

Have the young people share the statements they underlined on pages 24 and 25. Ask them to highlight the main ideas that are highlighted here.

Presentation ___ min.

◆ Write the words *paschal* and *mystery* on the board. Have volunteers explain the meaning of both. Then ask what we mean by the term *paschal mystery.* (all that God has done to redeem us in Christ Jesus, especially in his suffering, death, resurrection, and ascension)

Emphasize that when we proclaim the paschal mystery at Mass, we remember what Jesus has done for us, we thank him for his great love, and we proclaim our belief that he will return in glory.

◆ Have the young people form small groups to prepare dramatic readings of the following Scripture accounts:

• Jesus' crucifixion (John 19:16–30)
• Jesus' resurrection (John 20:1–10)
• Jesus' ascension (Luke 24:36–53)

Allow the groups about ten minutes preparation time. Then ask them to present their readings to the entire group.

Note: The following activity is optional.

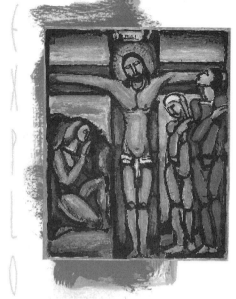

The Crucifixion, Georges Rouault, 1939

From Death to Life

There is an ancient saying in the Church: "The way we pray shows what we believe." The liturgy, the public prayer of the Church, is the official way we pray as Catholics. In what way does the prayer of the Church show what we believe?

What makes us who we are as Catholics is our relationship to the Father in and through Jesus Christ. We believe in Jesus Christ—in who he is and in what God has accomplished in him. What makes us Catholic is our belief in the paschal mystery of Jesus.

What is the paschal mystery of Jesus Christ? By the *paschal mystery* we mean all that God has done to redeem us in Christ Jesus, especially in his suffering, death, resurrection, and ascension. We proclaim this paschal mystery at every Eucharist when we say:

24

Dying you destroyed our death, rising you restored our life. Lord Jesus, come in glory.

Christ has died, Christ is risen, Christ will come again.

The word *paschal* refers to Passover, the feast of freedom for the people of Israel. During this great feast, the Jewish people celebrate their deliverance, their passing over, from slavery to freedom. During Holy Week and Easter, we Christians celebrate the "passing over" of Jesus from death to new life. As the liturgy tells us, Jesus Christ is now and always "our Passover and our lasting peace."

Mystery means more than just something that cannot be fully understood. It also means *a truth that continually calls us to deeper understanding,* a truth so wonderful that we are continually drawn to investigate the depths of its meaning.

To discover what the paschal mystery really means is the work of a lifetime. Catholics believe that the birth, life, suffering, death, resurrection, and ascension of Jesus Christ is the very center of all that exists. When Jesus, in his paschal mystery, passed from death to life, all of creation was made new—including ourselves. His new life is now our new life. It is the central vocation of every Christian to discover and live the meaning of Christ's passion, death, and resurrection in today's world. How do we do this?

Scripture UPDATE

The liturgy of the Church has adopted many Jewish liturgical symbols and rituals. Many of these are mentioned in Scripture: praying the psalms as responses; using musical instruments and incense in worship; setting aside one day a week, the Sabbath, as a day of rest and prayer. Among the most important of these practices that we still observe is the reading of the Old Testament in our liturgy. This practice is "irreplaceable" (*Catechism,* 1093).

◆ Have each student follow each step of the directions given here to make friendship wristbands.

• Cut three long pieces of colorful yarn, string, or ribbon.
• Tie the pieces together at one end.
• Make a braid as you proclaim the following words slowly by yourself or with a prayer companion:

> Dying you destroyed our death,
> rising you restored our life.
> Lord Jesus, come in glory.

• When you have finished, make a knot at the end of the braid.
• Tie both ends together, and place the braid around one of your wrists.

Living the Paschal Mystery

The first step is to begin to develop a personal relationship with God, for it is our *person* that we bring to the public prayer of the Church. We do not come to the celebration of Christ's paschal mystery as strangers in God's presence or even as mere acquaintances. We come as Jesus' own friends and disciples, just as his first followers did.

Usually friendship does not just happen. We have to work at a relationship. We have to spend time with the other person. We have to develop common interests. We have to want what is good for the other, and we need to be willing to sacrifice for the other.

We become friends with God in much the same way, spending time with him, developing common interests, learning about God, sharing our concerns, our dreams, our hopes. That is what praying really is.

And even though we may not realize it, God is waiting for us to come to him. God, after all,

tops the list of those who love us. He sees, knows, and loves us as we really are. God shows his love for us through Jesus Christ and through the Church. And it is in praying with the Church "through Jesus Christ, our Lord" that we come to recognize and respond to him in a personal way.

If some people find the liturgy long or dull or boring, it may be because they have not yet grown up enough to establish a real relationship, a friendship with God.

As Saint Gregory of Nyssa, a fourth-century bishop, said, "The one thing worthwhile is becoming God's friend."

What is your relationship with God like? Do you work at it? How? Do you come to celebrate liturgy as a stranger, as an acquaintance, or as a friend?

Conclusion ___ min.

◆ Direct attention to *Scripture Update* on page 24. Have volunteers name the Jewish liturgical symbols and rituals that the liturgy of the Church has adopted.

FORUM Assignment

✔ Read pages 26 and 27. Underline in pencil the statements that express six main ideas.

✔ Ask yourself and five other people of different ages to name a favorite hymn that is sung during liturgical prayer. Ask each person to explain why it is a favorite and to share the words that she or he finds most meaningful.

Closing Prayer: Explain to the young people that after you read each verse of Psalm 136, you would like them to respond, "God's love endures forever."

Invite the young people to look again at the photo on pages 18 and 19 as you pray the psalm together.

Now explain the symbolism of the band, using the following script:

> You may want to wear the wristband often to remember Jesus' words at the Last Supper, "No one has greater love than this, to lay down one's life for one's friends" (John 15:13). When you look at the band, remember that the central vocation of every Christian is to live the meaning of Christ's passion, death, and resurrection in today's world.

◆ Have volunteers name ways in which we live the paschal mystery. List the responses on the board. Then invite the young people to respond in their journals to the questions in the thought provoker on page 25.

FOR SESSION 4

- copies of handout *To Proclaim God's Love*, page 18C
- recordings of Gregorian chant and processional and recessional hymns we sing at Mass

SESSION 4

Objective: To discover the ways in which our liturgical history has helped to shape our liturgical life.

Introduction ___ min.

Opening Prayer

Forum: Have the young people form small groups to discuss the results of their interviews about favorite hymns. Then have the members choose their group's top three favorites. Ask the members to label the hymns as traditional or recent. Have a representative from each group report its findings to the general group.

Discuss with the young people the statements they underlined. Have them highlight the main ideas that are highlighted on pages 26 and 27.

Presentation ___ min.

◆ Ask the following questions to help the young people reflect on the roots of Catholic liturgy:

• Before Jesus died, how did he and his first followers pray? (They prayed as Jews.)

• What did Jesus' followers continue to do after his death? (They continued to pray in the Temple in Jerusalem and at the synagogue on the Sabbath.)

• What did Jesus' followers do differently after he died? (See the first paragraph in the right column on page 26.)

• Why were the gospels and the letters of Saint Paul translated into Greek? (When the good news of Jesus was first spread, Greek was the common language spoken at that time.)

• Why did Latin become the principal language of the liturgy? (It was the official language of the Roman Empire.)

◆ Have volunteers explain the ways in which the liturgy is still celebrated as it was by the early Christians. Have the group chart the similarities and differences explained in the second paragraph of "The Liturgy Today" on page 27.

A Little History

A great part of understanding something is knowing where it comes from, its history. Most of us probably enjoy looking through family albums or other family mementos. These things tell us something about the lives of our parents and grandparents. They are part of our family history, a history that shapes our lives.

How did liturgy come to be the way it is today? Our liturgical family has a history, too, a history that has helped to shape our Catholic life. It is a rich and interesting history formed by many languages, many cultures, and many historical events.

What are the roots of our liturgical life? Where do these symbols and rituals come from? We begin with Jesus himself. As we shall see, it is really Jesus who gives us the sacraments and entrusts them to the Church.

When the Son of God became one of us, he did so in a particular culture: Jesus was a Jew who lived in first-century Palestine. His first followers were also Jews. They prayed as Jews. After the resurrection and ascension of Jesus, they continued to pray in the Temple in Jerusalem on the Sabbath. But now they did something new as well.

We read that "every day they devoted themselves to meeting together in the temple area and to breaking bread in their homes" (Acts 2:46). In the Temple they listened to readings from the Old Testament and responded with psalms and prayers. In their homes they shared the Eucharist, as Jesus had instructed them. Even at this early date, we can trace the origin of the two parts of the Mass as we know them today: the Liturgy of the Word and the Liturgy of the Eucharist.

As the good news of Jesus spread from Palestine to Syria, Greece, Africa, and the ends of the Roman Empire, the message was translated into new languages and planted in new cultures. Greek was the common language spoken at that time, so the gospels and the letters of Saint Paul were written in Greek. Later, when Latin became the official language of the Roman Empire, both the Bible and the liturgy were translated into Latin. For many centuries the Latin language served as the principal means for understanding and explaining our faith. It is still used as the official language of the Church in important documents, such as papal encyclicals.

◆ Play a recording of Gregorian chant sung in Latin. Help the young people to appreciate the atmosphere of quiet and peace made possible by the use of the human voice unaccompanied by musical instruments. Play the recording again, inviting the young people to sing along or hum the chant.

Then play a recording of a hymn or psalm that we sing as a processional or recessional hymn at Mass. Ask the young people to explain how the musical accompaniment helps us to express ourselves prayerfully and joyfully.

The Liturgy Today

In what ways do we still celebrate the liturgy as the early Christians did? How are we different?

We no longer go to the temple for prayer; instead we go to our parish churches. But we still read the same readings and pray the same psalms as the first Christians did. We no longer read the Scriptures in Latin, as the Romans did; now we read them in our own language. We celebrate the same breaking of the bread, the same Eucharist. The most important parts of the liturgy have not changed. They have been given to us just as they were given to the first followers of Jesus.

Yet our culture today does influence some aspects of liturgy because our culture expresses who we are and what we believe. For example, the kind of music we play and sing at the liturgy is a reflection of our culture. Various instruments are used in church music: pipe organ, guitars, drums, violins, and flutes. The music can range from the quiet reflection of chant to the exuberance of a mariachi band.

The liturgy is a major part of the tradition of the Church. The word *tradition* means "what is handed down." Because the liturgy is handed down to us from the earliest days of the Church, we look to the teaching authority of the Church to guide our liturgical celebration.

But the liturgy is also flexible and open to various cultures. Can you discover unique cultural expressions in African liturgical worship? Latin American? Asian? Magazines from missionary societies may help you with your search.

The question of change—of what should or should not be changed based on changing culture—is always a very important and serious question for the Church. It is the Church that teaches and guides us in what can be changed and what can never be changed. For example, for two thousand years we have celebrated the Eucharist as the memorial of Christ's death and resurrection. Through sacramental signs we share in this mystery of faith. Bread and wine are transformed into the Body and Blood of Christ. This will never change. The words of institution will never change. How wonderful it is that the Church guides us to this truth and will do so for all time.

"The way we pray shows what we believe." Give one example from the liturgy that shows what we believe as Catholics.

Assignment

✔ Read pages 28 and 29. Complete *Words to Remember.*

✔ Complete the handout *To Proclaim God's Love.*

Closing Prayer: Have the young people sing their favorite psalm of praise.

27

Conclusion ___ min.

◆ Discuss with the young people what will never change about our liturgical celebrations. Emphasize the first part of *Catholic ID:* We look to the teaching authority of the Church to guide our liturgical celebration.

◆ Invite volunteers to describe various unique cultural expressions in liturgical celebrations.

◆ Distribute the handout To *Proclaim God's Love.* Have a volunteer read the directions, and ask if there are any questions. Explain that work on the handout is part of the *Forum Assignment.*

FOR SESSION 5

• copies of *Chapter 2 Assessment,* page 29A
• copies of *Highlights for Home,* page 29B

SESSION 5

Objective: To explore the words, feelings, or images the word Catholic brings to mind; to review the ideas presented in this chapter.

Introduction ___ min.

Opening Prayer

Forum: Have the young people check their handout sheets as you share with them the following matches. (Answers: 1. c, 2. f, 3. e, 4. h, 5. d, 6. g, 7. a, 8. b) Then ask the students to keep the handout for *Closing Prayer.*

Ask volunteers to define the *Words to Remember.* The definition for *liturgy* may be found on page 22; the explanation for *paschal mystery* may be found on page 24.

Presentation ___ min.

◆ Discuss *Things to Think About* with the entire group. Include in your discussion the roots of Catholic liturgical life as described on pages 26 and 27.

◆ When discussing the questions in *Things to Share,* have the young people imagine what their lives would be like if they were not able to participate in the liturgical prayer of the Church.

Assessment: Have the students work in pairs to complete *Testing 1, 2, 3.* If time permits, have the partners share their responses with the group.

If you are administering *Chapter 2 Assessment,* page 29A, allow about ten minutes for the students to complete the test.

◆ Have a volunteer summarize *On Line with the Parish.* Explain that a representative from the group may want to call your diocesan offices to find out where the liturgies are celebrated.

◆ Direct attention to *Life in the Spirit* on page 29. Ask the young people to discuss the symbols that help them to focus when they pray privately.

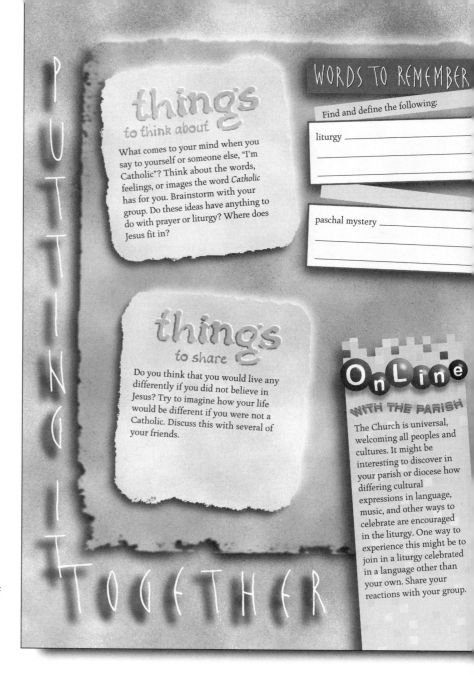

PUTTING IT TOGETHER

things to think about

What comes to your mind when you say to yourself or someone else, "I'm Catholic"? Think about the words, feelings, or images the word *Catholic* has for you. Brainstorm with your group. Do these ideas have anything to do with prayer or liturgy? Where does Jesus fit in?

things to share

Do you think that you would live any differently if you did not believe in Jesus? Try to imagine how your life would be different if you were not a Catholic. Discuss this with several of your friends.

WORDS TO REMEMBER

Find and define the following:

liturgy _____

_____

_____

paschal mystery _____

_____

OnLine WITH THE PARISH

The Church is universal, welcoming all peoples and cultures. It might be interesting to discover in your parish or diocese how differing cultural expressions in language, music, and other ways to celebrate are encouraged in the liturgy. One way to experience this might be to join in a liturgy celebrated in a language other than your own. Share your reactions with your group.

Conclusion ___ min.

◆ Encourage the young people to share *Highlights for Home,* page 29B with their families.

Closing Prayer: Have each student share with a prayer companion the psalm verse he or she has written on the handout.

Proclaim together or sing a joyful psalm. After each verse, you may want to suggest that the young people use the Latin words of praise *Gloria in excelsis Deo* (**Glow**-ree-a in ex-**chel**-sees **day**-oh), meaning "Glory to God in the highest."

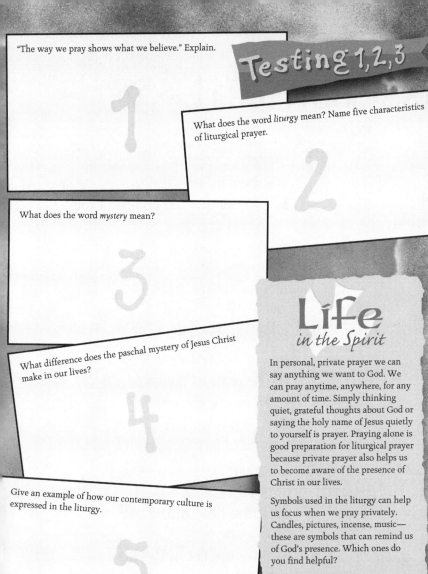

"The way we pray shows what we believe." Explain.

Testing 1,2,3

1

What does the word *liturgy* mean? Name five characteristics of liturgical prayer.

2

What does the word *mystery* mean?

3

What difference does the paschal mystery of Jesus Christ make in our lives?

4

Give an example of how our contemporary culture is expressed in the liturgy.

5

Life
in the Spirit

In personal, private prayer we can say anything we want to God. We can pray anytime, anywhere, for any amount of time. Simply thinking quiet, grateful thoughts about God or saying the holy name of Jesus quietly to yourself is prayer. Praying alone is good preparation for liturgical prayer because private prayer also helps us to become aware of the presence of Christ in our lives.

Symbols used in the liturgy can help us focus when we pray privately. Candles, pictures, incense, music—these are symbols that can remind us of God's presence. Which ones do you find helpful?

29

Testing 1,2,3

1. See page 24. The liturgy is the way we pray together as Catholics. In the liturgy we show that we believe in Jesus Christ—in who he is and in what God has accomplished in him. What makes us Catholic is our belief in the paschal mystery of Jesus.

2. See pages 22 and 23. It means "the participation of the people in the work of God." The characteristics are that it is: public, the prayer of Christ, worship of the Trinity, addressed to God, and expressed in the words of the Church.

3. See page 24. *Mystery* means a truth that continually calls us to deeper understanding, a truth so wonderful that we are continually drawn to investigate the depths of its meaning.

4. See page 24. When Jesus passed from death to life, all of creation was made new—including ourselves. His new life is now our new life.

5. See page 27. Accept any reasonable responses.

Evaluation: Have the young people explored the differences between private prayer and liturgical prayer? Have they discovered the meaning of the paschal mystery in our lives?

Answers for Chapter 2 Assessment

1. d	2. b	3. d	4. a	5. c
6. c	7. b	8. a	9. b	10. See page 27.

Assessment

1 Which of the following is not characteristic of liturgical prayer?
a. prayer of Christ himself
b. prayer to the Blessed Trinity
c. always addressed to God
d. includes our own words

2 _____ are characteristic of Catholic worship.
a. Personal words
b. Rituals
c. Foreign languages
d. Prayers to the saints

3 Today Catholics define *liturgy* as
a. a work for the people.
b. personal and public prayer.
c. reading.
d. the participation of the people in the work of God.

4 The sacramentary contains
a. the prayers for the Eucharist.
b. the Scripture readings for Mass.
c. the Book of Psalms.
d. suggestions for developing our friendship with God.

5 Circle the true statement.
a. Good liturgy can be private.
b. Liturgy may sometimes be the only activity of the Church.
c. Liturgy sends us out to serve others.
d. Liturgy is never personal.

6 Current culture
a. never influences liturgy.
b. has completely changed the liturgy.
c. does influence some aspects of liturgy.
d. none of the above

7 *Paschal* refers to
a. the birth of Jesus.
b. the feast of Passover.
c. Jesus' ascension.
d. a psalm response.

8 The two parts of the Mass originated
a. at the time of the early Christians.
b. after the fall of the Roman Empire.
c. during the Middle Ages.
d. in recent times.

9 The most important parts of the liturgy
a. have always been changed.
b. will never change.
c. may change in the future.
d. can be changed at any time.

10 Name two ways we celebrate the liturgy as the early Christians did. Write your responses on the reverse side of this page.

CHAPTER 2: The Prayer of the Church

Highlights for Home

Focus on Faith

In this chapter the young people have learned that when we Catholics pray together, we do so through symbol and ritual. It is essential that your son or daughter develop a deep understanding of and appreciation for the liturgy, the public prayer of the Church. You can help him or her to do this through your example.

In liturgical prayer we use the words and actions given to us by the Church. These words and actions have been treasured and handed down to us across the centuries in the rituals of the liturgy.

Help your son or daughter understand that the Church's liturgy celebrates our relationship with God the Father in and through the paschal mystery of Jesus Christ.

Conversation Starters

. . . . a few ideas to talk about together . . . .

◆ What words and symbolic gestures help me to lift up my mind and heart to God?

◆ What symbols or rituals help me make sense of life's mysteries?

◆ How do I discover and live the meaning of Christ's paschal mystery in today's world?

◆ Do I come to celebrate liturgy as a stranger, as an acquaintance, or as a friend?

Feature Focus

Catholic Teachings on page 23 explains that liturgy sends us out to serve others and that those experiences of love and service in turn send us back to celebrate liturgy. We hear the good news at Mass and we show our belief by living as Jesus' disciples.

Reflection

Think about and pray these words (Psalm 36:6–10) that have been repeated since the time of David.

LORD, your love reaches to heaven;
your fidelity, to the clouds.
Your justice is like the highest mountains;
your judgments, like the mighty deep;
all living creatures you sustain, LORD.
How precious is your love, O God!
We take refuge in the shadow of your
wings.
We feast on the rich food of your house;
from your delightful stream you give us
drink.
For with you is the fountain of life,
and in your light we see light.

GOD'S MASTERPIECES

Adult Focus

On December 17 the Church begins praying the "O antiphons" as we wait for the celebration of Jesus' coming into the world to save us from sin and death. On this day we pray:

O Wisdom, O holy Word of God,
you govern all creation with
your strong yet tender care.
Come and show your people the way to
salvation.

Jesus came to show us what God is like by what he did, what he said, and what he was. The invisible life of God, first made visible in Jesus Christ, is now made visible in the Church. Jesus has given the Church seven sacraments, visible and effective signs, through which we share in God's grace. Through the sacraments our faith is nourished and made strong.

When we celebrate the liturgy and the sacraments, we celebrate God's plan and our Christian story, which is part of that plan. That is why we can say that Catholics are truly people of word and sacrament.

Catechism Focus

The themes of this chapter correspond to paragraphs 1077–1109, 1114–1118, and 1122–1130 of the *Catechism*.

Enrichment Activities

Sacraments Are . . .

Explain to the young people that the sacraments have been referred to as "doors to the sacred" because through the sacraments we enter into communion with our God. Have the young people choose a word or a picture that says best what sacraments mean to them. On construction paper have them draw a personal symbol or logo that best illustrates the word or visualization they have chosen. Then have them mount the illustrations on black construction paper. Make stained-glass doors by hanging the young people's work on the doors of your room.

Computer Connection

Have the students use a multimedia software program, such as *Hyperstudio®,* to make a multimedia Sunday Readings Journal. Using the *Hyperstudio®* program, the students can set up the Journals as a stack of cards by making "buttons" that allow them to manipulate the stack and progress from card to card. Have students add a button for each date. Inform them that any word or icon can be used as a button.

Journal entries may take the form of questions to God, prayers, and reflections about Sunday readings. Students may also wish to include scanned-in pictures, digitized photographs, imported sounds, and clip art. Encourage them to use different borders, backdrops, and features such as fading to black or white from card to card. Students should update these entries each week.

Teaching Resources

	Overview	Opening Prayer Ideas	Materials
SESSION 1	**Discovery:** To discover that in Jesus we see and come to know the invisible God.	Look at the photos on pages 30 and 31. Meditate on Scripture passages listed on guide page 30–31.	These will be needed for every session: texts, Bibles, highlighters or colored pencils, journals. • recording or lyrics for a song of thanksgiving (optional)
SESSION 2	**Exploring 1:** To explore the four essential qualities that are always present in the celebration of each sacrament.	Look at the stained-glass collage on page 34. Reflect on the ways we encounter Christ in the sacraments.	• posterboard • copies of handout *Poetic Expression*, page 30C • recordings of nature sounds (optional)
SESSION 3	**Exploring 2:** To understand the prominent role that the proclamation of Scripture has in every liturgical celebration.	Pray together the prayer Upon Waking on page 186.	• lectionary (optional) • parish missalettes (optional)
SESSION 4	**Exploring 3:** To discover that remembering, knowing Christ is present with us, giving glory to God, calling upon the Holy Spirit, and saying a prayer of blessing are part of celebration of the sacraments.	Pray together Glory to the Father on page 186.	• posterboard cut in squares (optional) • masking tape (optional) • poster paint (optional)
SESSION 5	**Putting It Together:** To affirm the belief that in Jesus we see and come to know the invisible God; to recall that Jesus has given the Church seven sacraments through which we share in his saving work.	Pray together Prayer After Communion on page 189.	• parish missalettes (optional) • copies of *Chapter 3 Assessment*, page 41A • copies of *Highlights for Home*, page 41B

Supplemental Resources

Pamphlets
• *Youth Update:* "Why We Have Sacraments"

Catholic Update
• "Sacraments: It All Starts with Jesus"

• "The Seven Sacraments — Symbols of God's Care"
• "What Are Sacraments?"

St. Anthony Messenger
1615 Republic Street
Cincinnati, OH 45210

Faith and Witness Journal: Liturgy and Worship

For Chapter 3 see pages 12–15.

Poetic Expression

Use poetic form to express your thoughts about the sacraments or your thanks to Jesus for them. You may wish to follow one of the patterns given below:

Haiku

Example
You gave us signs of
your great love for us, Jesus.
For these, I thank you.

Cinquain

Example
Sacraments,
Jesus' signs,
Showing the way,
Filling, energizing, making holy,
Celebrations!

Pattern

Line 1 has five syllables.
Line 2 has seven syllables.
Line 3 has five syllables.

Pattern

In Line 1, one word names the subject.
In Line 2, two words describe the subject. In Line 3, three words describe an action about the subject. In Line 4, express your feelings using four words. In Line 5, one word renames the subject.

Your poetic verse

_____
_____
_____
_____
_____
_____
_____
_____
_____
_____

THROUGH HIM
WITH
HIM
IN
HIM

SESSION 1

God's Masterpieces

How great are your works, Lord!
Psalm 92:6

Objective: To discover that in Jesus we see and come to know the invisible God.

Introduction ___ min.

Opening Prayer: Invite the young people to look at the panoramic view on pages 30 and 31. Proclaim together Psalm 92:6.

Have a volunteer read Luke 24:44–53. Then use the following script to guide the young people's meditation as they focus on the photos on pages 30 and 31.

Imagine that you are with the disciples in Jerusalem after Jesus' ascension. You are sharing your memories of all Jesus has told you.

- One in your midst remembers Jesus telling the Samaritan woman, "Whoever drinks the water I shall give will never thirst; the water I shall give will become in him a spring of water welling up to eternal life" (John 4:13–14).

- Another person remembers Jesus telling his disciples, "I am the bread of life; whoever comes to me will never hunger, and whoever believes in me will never thirst" (John 6:35).

- John reminds everyone of Jesus' words after the Passover meal: "I am the true vine, and my Father is the vine grower. He takes away every branch in me that does not bear fruit, and everyone that does he prunes so that it bears more fruit" (John 15:1–2).

- Mary, the mother of Jesus, asks the group to recall her son's words: "I am the good shepherd. A good shepherd lays down his life for the sheep" (John 10:11).

- You remind everyone about Jesus telling people that he . . . . (Have the young people take turns sharing their memories.)

As a response to Jesus' words, look again at the photos on pages 30 and 31. Pray Psalm 23 together with confidence and trust in God's great love.

You may want to conclude prayer by singing or playing a recording of a song of thanksgiving. "All Good Gifts" from the musical *Godspell* is appropriate.

Presentation ___ min.

◆ Have a volunteer read the questions in the first paragraph on page 32. Ask the young people to explain their understanding of what a sacrament is.

◆ Ask the young people to look at the reproduction of *Jesus as the Comforter* on page 32. Invite them to share their thoughts about what Jesus might be saying.

Have the young people look through their *Liturgy and Worship* books to find their favorite images of Jesus. Ask them to explain their reasons for their choices.

◆ Direct the students to read pages 32 and 33 independently. Then discuss the ways original sin shattered the harmony of God's plan for the world.

Ask what made the Father's plan of peace and harmony possible for us and for the world. (Jesus' sacrifice on the cross and his victory over sin and death)

◆ Have the students highlight the main ideas that are highlighted on these pages.

◆ You may wish to share with the young people the following meditative dialogue of Saint Catherine of Siena. Explain that Catherine wrote as if God were speaking to her.

But first I want you to look at the bridge of my only-begotten Son, and notice its greatness. Look! It stretches from heaven to earth, joining the earth of your humanity with the greatness of the Godhead. This is what I mean when I say it stretches from heaven to earth—through my union with humanity.

This was necessary if I wanted to make the road that had been broken up so that you might pass over the bitterness of the world and reach life. From earth alone I could not have made it great enough to cross the river and bring you to eternal life. . . .

And why should he have made himself a roadway? So that you might in truth come to the same joy as the angels. But my Son's having made of himself a bridge for you could not bring you to life unless you make your way along that bridge.

Ask the young people to reflect for a moment on where they are on the "bridge" of Jesus.

Jesus as the Comforter, August Jerndorff, 1846–1906

Is a sacrament something we pray? something we do? something we receive or something we watch? or something else? What do you think a sacrament is?

God's Master Plan

What is a sacrament? To answer this question, we should start at the very beginning. At the very beginning, when God created the world and everything in it, he had a plan. He didn't start one day and make sky, then make earth, then make light, and then make darkness. He did not continue to create one thing after another without knowing from the very beginning what it would be when it was all finished. The Father had a plan in mind.

32

Throughout the Old Testament we read about God's plan. Little by little the plan is revealed in the history of his chosen people and through his prophets and messengers. And when the right moment came, this plan was revealed in all its wonderful mystery in the birth, life, passion, death, and resurrection of Jesus Christ. The plan God had in mind was Jesus Christ! In Jesus, God would reveal himself to us most fully. In Jesus, we see God made visible, at once truly human and truly divine.

Jesus, the Word Made Flesh

On page after page of Sacred Scripture, we read of God's mysterious plan. At the very beginning of the Bible, we see God creating this magnificent universe and all that is in it. He creates the world. Then, from the earth, he creates an "earthling," a human person, breathing into it his own image. And all is at peace.

In these first chapters of the Book of Genesis, we glimpse the harmony God plans for the world:

• Men and women are at peace *with each other*: They are partners and helpers to each other.

• The human creatures are at peace *with the earth*: Adam names the animals. He tills the earth, and it brings forth fruit.

• These human creatures are at peace *with God*: Adam walks and talks with him in the garden.

And it is good. This is God's plan: He wants all creation to be reconciled and at peace.

Then sin shatters every layer of the dream. Peace between human beings dissolves; peace with the earth becomes toil and struggle. And peace with God? When God calls to Adam, Adam hides. He no longer walks and talks freely with God. This is the first sin—the *original* sin. And all of us share in its effects: weakness of will, tendency to sin, suffering, and death.

But God did not give up on the plan. When the time was ripe, God sent his only Son to bring it to

fulfillment. This is Jesus, the Word made flesh. Jesus spent his life showing us how to be at peace with one another, with creation, and with his Father and ours. He spent his life teaching love and forgiveness, healing sickness and division. His resurrection and ascension was his victory over death and sin. Jesus is our redeemer. Through him we are saved from sin. His sacrifice on the cross and his victory over sin and death made the Father's plan of peace and harmony possible for us and for our world. The paschal mystery is the promise that God's plan will be fulfilled.

 *Think for a moment. How are you at peace with others, with creation, and with God? How can you deepen and strengthen this peace?*

The Son of God, the second Person of the Blessed Trinity, became one of us in Jesus. In Jesus the invisible God becomes visible! In Jesus we see and come to know the invisible God, whom no eye has ever seen.

This understanding of Jesus is expressed clearly and beautifully in a prayer from the Mass at Christmas. It proclaims that in Jesus,

> we see our God made visible
> and so are caught up in love of the God we
>   cannot see.

33

✔ Read page 35. Underline in pencil the statements that express five main ideas. Consider the sacraments' four essential qualities as one main idea.

✔ Find two or more photographs to show the ways people live in peace with others, with creation, and with God.

Closing Prayer: Pray spontaneously, thanking Jesus for spending his life showing us how to be at peace with one another, with creation, and with his Father and ours.

Conclusion ___ min.

◆ Have the young people read the thought provoker on page 33. Allow a few minutes of quiet time for their reflection or journaling.

◆ On the board or on a sheet of posterboard, draw a large cross like the symbol shown at the bottom of page 33 or a bridge. Ask each person to name a sign of God's care that he or she has seen in the past few days. On or near the illustration, have a volunteer write the young people's responses.

FOR SESSION 2

• posterboard

• copies of handout *Poetic Expression*, page 30C

• recordings of nature sounds (optional)

SESSION 2

Objective: To explore the four essential qualities that are always present in the celebration of each sacrament.

Introduction ___ min.

Opening Prayer

Forum: Have the young people work in small groups to make collages that show the ways people live in peace with others, with creation, and with God. Provide each group with a sheet of posterboard. Suggest that group members write captions for the photos they choose for the collage. Have a representative from each group present its collage to the group as a whole.

Presentation ___ min.

◆ Direct the students' attention to the collage of stained-glass windows on page 34. Have volunteers identify the sacrament symbolized in each window. (Starting with Baptism, shown in upper left, and moving in clockwise direction: Confirmation, Reconciliation, Anointing of the Sick, Holy Orders, Matrimony, and Eucharist) Ask, "Why do you think the window for Eucharist is in the center?"

◆ Allow a few minutes of quiet time for young people to reflect on the following question: "We've already learned about the sacraments; why are we going to study about them again?"

After the quiet time have students discuss their responses with a partner.

◆ Invite volunteers to use their own words to define *sacrament*. Then have them highlight the definition in the last paragraph in the left-hand column on page 35.

◆ Ask the young people, "What is the purpose of the sacraments?" Direct the young people to highlight the statements in the first paragraph of "Celebrating the Sacraments" that explain the purpose.

34

◆ Discuss the four essential qualities that are always present in the celebration of each sacrament. Have the young people highlight the statements that are highlighted here.

◆ Distribute the handout sheet *Poetic Expression*. Have a volunteer read the directions. While the young people are reflecting and writing, play recordings of nature sounds or quiet instrumental music. Circulate among them, and help those who may be having difficulty. When most have finished writing their verse, invite those who wish to share their poetry to read their verse to the group.

...the Sacraments

...we ever wonder what God is like, all we have to ...o is look at Jesus of Nazareth—at what he did, ...hat he said, what he was.

...he plan of God did not end with the birth of ...sus. It did not even end with the death of Jesus. ...or even after death, Jesus carried out God's plan. ...ow? After his resurrection, the risen Christ ...ppeared to his apostles and said, "Receive the ...oly Spirit" (John 20:22). In handing over the ...pirit, Jesus handed over to his descendants— ...s followers, the Church—his very own life.

...his life of Jesus, this Spirit, dwells now in the ...hurch, in us. The invisible life of God, first made ...isible in Jesus Christ, is now made visible in the ...hurch. And Jesus has given the Church seven ...pecial signs to draw us into union with him and ...he Father through the power of the Spirit. Through ...e sacraments we encounter Christ. Through the ...craments we share in the saving work of Jesus ...hrist our redeemer.

...sign is something that points the way. ...acraments are signs but they are unique signs. ...hey are signs unlike any other signs in the world. ...his is because they do more than point the way. ...hey are the way. For example, the water of ...aptism is not only a sign of life. Through these ...aters of Baptism, we receive life. In the Eucharist ...e bread and wine are not only signs of the Body ...nd Blood of Christ. They become the Body and ...lood of Christ.

...sacrament actually brings about—that is, makes ...al and present—what it signifies. When we ...elebrate the sacraments, we do not simply ...elebrate salvation, forgiveness, and ...nion with God. We are in fact saved, ...rgiven, and made one with Jesus ...hrist. A sacrament is a visible and ...ffective sign, given to us by Christ, ...rough which we share in God's grace. ...o wonder that the Church calls the ...craments "God's masterpieces" ...atechism, 1091).

Celebrating the Sacraments

The Church celebrates the seven sacraments. Rejoicing in that faith we received from the apostles, we understand the purpose of the sacraments: to sanctify us, to build up the Church, and to give praise and worship to God. Through the sacraments, our faith is nourished and made strong.

In the celebration of each sacrament, four essential qualities are always present.

Ritual Action A sacrament is God's life in us—grace—expressed in ritual action. Each sacrament has its own symbols and gestures, its own ritual way of expressing the gift of grace being shared. For example, in the sacrament of the Anointing of the Sick, the sick person is anointed with oil in the sign of the cross. The oil and the cross are signs of the healing given by Christ.

Worship of God The sacraments are liturgical prayer, public prayer, and their focus is God. In every sacrament we praise and worship the Holy Trinity in public liturgical prayer.

Paschal Mystery In every sacrament we remember and enter into the paschal mystery. In every sacrament we ourselves are made part of the paschal mystery in a deeper way.

The Power of the Holy Spirit The sacraments are not magic or wishful thinking. They make the paschal mystery present and effective by the power of the Holy Spirit—by what God does.

 Are sacraments something we only receive? How would you answer this, knowing what you know?

CATHOLIC ID Because the sacraments are so important, the Church reminds us that the sacramental rites cannot be changed by anyone. Even the supreme authority in the Church can only change the liturgy after faithful reflection and "with religious respect for the mystery of the liturgy" (*Catechism*, 1125).

35

FORUM Assignment

✔ Read pages 36 and 37. Underline in pencil the statements that express five main ideas.

✔ Read the following passages from the Gospel of Matthew: 6:19–21, 6:25–34, and 7:24–29. Then choose your favorite passage. Practice proclaiming the words with expression. Prepare an explanation of the symbolism Jesus used to teach an important lesson.

Closing Prayer: Read together the second paragraph in the left column on page 35. Invite the young people to reflect quietly on the last sentence.

Pass Gina to Rel. LTingle 9/24 2:31

FOR SESSION

- lectionary (optional)
- parish missalettes (optional)

Conclusion ___ min.

◆ Discuss the thought provoker on page 35. Write the following statements on the board. Have a volunteer underline the verbs in each statement.

- We <u>celebrate</u> salvation, forgiveness, and union with God.
- We <u>share</u> in God's grace.
- We <u>praise</u> and <u>worship</u> God.
- We <u>remember</u> and <u>enter</u> into the paschal mystery.

◆ Have a volunteer summarize *Catholic ID* on page 35.

SESSION 3

Objective: To understand the prominent role that the proclamation of Scripture has in every liturgical celebration.

Introduction ___ min.

Opening Prayer

Forum: Have the young people form buzz groups to discuss the symbolism used in the readings from Matthew. Invite the members of each group to prepare a dramatic presentation of one of the readings. If time permits, have the groups make props and/or scenery.

Presentation ___ min.

◆ Have the young people work with a partner to role-play a conversation between two friends, one of whom is a poor listener. (Explain that they should each take a turn being the poor listener.) Then discuss the following questions with the group:

• How might having good listening skills affect our friendships?

• How might having poor listening skills affect our friendships?

• Do your friends, coaches, parents, and teachers expect you to listen to them more closely now than when you were younger?

Emphasize the importance of listening to the Scripture readings during our liturgical celebrations. Give some suggestions for learning how to listen to the Scriptures. For example:

• listen for key words

• listen for key questions

• listen for the ending sentence

• ask yourself, "What is God asking me to hear?"

Then have the young people highlight the main ideas presented in the first paragraph in the right-hand column on page 36.

Invite the young people to reflect on these words. Ask them to write in their journals what they remember about the readings of last week's liturgy. Have them use that as a way to evaluate their listening skills during liturgical celebrations.

God's Plan in Writing

God wanted the story of his plan to last through the centuries and to have meaning for all peoples. Eventually, from the Book of Genesis in the Old Testament to the Book of Revelation in the New Testament, God's plan was put into writing under the inspiration of the Holy Spirit. This written story of God's plan is what we now call Sacred Scripture.

Each of the seven sacraments celebrates some aspect of the plan of God that has come to fulfillment in Christ and in the Church. Sacred Scripture is the written record of this divine plan as it unfolds in history. But it is more than a history. Sacred Scripture, we know, is the inspired word of God. When it is proclaimed, God is speaking to us. When Catholics celebrate the liturgy, they hear the word of God.

The proclamation of Sacred Scripture plays a prominent role in every liturgical celebration. In every liturgy we read aloud some part of the story of God's plan. Through the Scriptures we are continually reminded of what God has done for us and what God still plans to do—with our cooperation. We listen to the Scripture story to keep alive our faith in God's plan, God's dream for unity and reconciliation: "Thus faith comes from what is heard, and what is heard comes through the word of Christ" (Romans 10:17).

When we celebrate the liturgy and the sacraments we celebrate God's plan and our Christian story, which is part of that plan. We need the word of God in the Scriptures to help us to hear our story with faith and understanding and to urge us on to complete the work of Christ in the world. That is why we can say that Catholics are truly people of word and sacrament.

36

◆ As a quick review, play "What's the Question?" One student is the host who gives the answers to which the rest of the group must supply the questions. For example:

• This is taken from the Old Testament except during the Easter season, when it is taken from the Acts of the Apostles. (What is the first reading?)

• This is from the Book of Psalms. (What is the response to the reading?)

• This is taken from the epistles or the Book of Revelation in the New Testament. (What is the second reading?)

• This is from one of the accounts of Matthew, Mark, Luke, or John in the New Testament. (What is the gospel?)

Scripture in Liturgy

Let us look more closely at the ways the Scriptures are used in our liturgical celebrations.

The readings given are from Scripture and are explained in the homily. The psalms, too, are from Scripture.

The prayers and liturgical songs are drawn from Scripture.

The symbols and rituals in the liturgy take their meaning from Scripture.

In recent times the Church expanded the amount and the variety of the Scripture readings to be proclaimed. These readings are found in an official liturgical book called the *lectionary*. The *lectionary* contains the Scripture readings assigned to the various days of the Church year. It provides us with a great variety of Scripture readings all through the year. Because it contains the word of God, we treat the lectionary with great respect.

If possible, borrow a lectionary or a missalette from your parish church. Find and read the Scripture readings for Christmas, Easter, or perhaps the feast days of your favorite saints.

As Catholics living in this sin-torn world divided by war and greed, we must continually retell the story of God's plan for unity and reconciliation. We must keep God's dream alive among us. We do this most significantly in the celebration of the liturgy and the sacraments. The sacraments are the celebration of our Catholic story. Sacraments are worded signs. Scripture is the word, the word that gives the sacramental sign its meaning.

Scripture UPDATE

The reading of the Scriptures is an essential part of the celebration of every sacrament. The Church has provided a variety of readings to help us understand the meaning of each sacramental event. Of the readings listed below, which would you choose for these sacraments?

Baptism	Reconciliation
John 3:1–6	Micah 6:1–4, 6–8
Matthew 28:18–20	1 John 4:16–21
Mark 1:9–11	Luke 15:1–10

37

◆ Have the young people highlight all the statements highlighted on pages 36 and 37.

FORUM Assignment

✔ Read pages 38 and 39. Underline in pencil the statements that express six main ideas.

✔ Read *Scripture Update* on page 37. Choose a reading for the sacraments of Baptism and Reconciliation.

Closing Prayer: Invite the young people to look at the picture of Jesus on page 32 as you read the following passage (John 1:14).

> And the Word became flesh
> and made his dwelling among us,
> and we saw his glory,
> the glory as of the Father's
>   only Son,
> full of grace and truth.

Conclusion ___ min.

◆ Have a different volunteer read each of the following readings for the feast of the Holy Family, which the Church usually celebrates on the Sunday after Christmas:

- Reading 1—Sirach 3:2– 6, 12–14
- Reading 2—Colossians 3:12–21
- Gospel—Luke 2:22, 39– 40 (Cycle B in the lectionary)

Then ask, "How do these readings keep God's dream alive among us?" "What does the gospel reading tell us about Jesus?"

FOR SESSION 4

- posterboard cut in squares (optional)
- masking tape (optional)
- poster paint (optional)
- Have four volunteers prepare for a Reader's Theater presentation of the story of Emmaus (Luke 24:13–35).

SESSION 4

Objective: To discover that remembering, knowing Christ is present with us, giving glory to God, calling upon the Holy Spirit, and saying a prayer of blessing are part of the celebration of the sacraments.

Introduction ___ min.

Opening Prayer

Forum: Have the young people share the readings they chose for Baptism and Reconciliation.

Discuss the statements the students underlined on pages 38 and 39.

Presentation ___ min.

◆ Have the four volunteer Readers' Theater actors present their enactment of the story of Jesus' appearance on the road to Emmaus (Luke 24:13–35). Then ask the young people to form shared-prayer groups to reflect on the story. Ask the following questions to spark their reflections:

• What were the two disciples thinking and feeling as they walked along the road?

• Did talking with the stranger about the death and resurrection of Jesus help them?

• How did the disciples realize that Jesus was the stranger?

• Did realizing that Jesus had been with them help change their feelings?

• How did they share the good news with others?

Note: The following activity is optional.

◆ Distribute squares of light-colored posterboard. Have the young people draw a cross. Ask them to write on one side of the cross words or phrases to describe what they are happy about and what is causing them trouble.

Then give each young person a few long strips of masking tape. Have them cut small squares of tape and layer the squares on the shape of the cross to cover the words they have written, to give the effect of the cross shown on page 38. Then have them paint over the tape with their favorite color of poster paint. Lay out

In Every Liturgy

The liturgy of the Church has been influenced by many cultures and many languages. We use important words rooted in Hebrew, Greek, and Latin to explain the meaning behind the rituals and symbols of our liturgy. Some of these important words common to every sacrament are *anamnesis, presence, doxology, epiclesis,* and *berakah.* At first these terms may seem strange. But after we are introduced to them and we see how they function in each of the sacraments, they will begin to seem like old friends.

Remembering As we have already seen, recalling and celebrating the paschal mystery is at the heart of liturgical prayer. The term for this "remembering" is *anamnesis.* This word from the Greek means "memory," as in, "Do this in memory [*anamnesis*] of me." *Anamnesis* is the liturgical act of remembering. This special kind of remembering not only calls to mind a saving act of God that happened in the past but also makes that event present to us now.

When we celebrate the sacraments, we are not merely recalling events that happened long ago and far away. We are celebrating events that are present to us now. What began in the past, in the death and resurrection of Jesus, is continued into the present. *Now* Jesus Christ is risen. *Now* the Holy Spirit comes upon us. And *now* we are sent forth by Christ to love and serve.

Presence Christ is always present. The word *presence* comes almost directly from Latin, and means "to be before one"—that is, to be here. The real presence of Christ in the Eucharist has always been at the heart of our Catholic belief. Yet the risen Christ is present and active with us here in each and every sacrament and in every liturgy.

38

THROUGH HIM WITH HIM IN HIM

How is Jesus present in Liturgy

•He is present in the Mass under the signs of bread and wine and in the person of the priest.

•He is present in his power in the sacraments. When a person baptizes, it is really Christ who baptizes.

•He is present in his word when the Scripture is read.

•He is present in the assembly, the community. Jesus himself said, "Where two or three are gathered together in my name, there am I in the midst of them" (Matthew 18:20).

Glory Whenever we recall and make present God's plan for us, we experience feelings of thanksgiving and praise, and we give God glory. Each sacrament and liturgical action is a *doxology,* a prayer that gives God glory. In a more narrow sense, two prayers in particular have been given the title *doxology.* One of these is the Glory to God, the prayer of praise that we sing or recite at the beginning of the Eucharist. Another doxology is "Glory to the Father, and to the Son, and to the Holy Spirit," said at the end of each psalm.

Calling Upon the Holy Spirit In each sacrament we call upon the Spirit to make us holy and to build up the body of Christ. The technical term for this petition is *epiclesis.* Although the words may vary, at each Eucharist we ask God:

Let your Spirit come upon these gifts to make them holy,
so that they may become for us
the body † and blood of our Lord, Jesus Christ.

As we study each of the seven sacraments, look for this prayer of petition, the epiclesis, and see what the prayer asks for. The epiclesis is often the key to understanding the meaning of a sacrament.

the crosses to dry. Tell the young people that they will use their crosses during the *Closing Prayer.*

◆ Ask the young people, "Do you think that participating in the liturgy helps us to celebrate our lives?" "In what ways?" Write the word *anamnesis* on the board. Ask a volunteer to explain the meaning. Have the young people highlight the definition of this liturgical act on page 38. Point out to the young people that this special kind of remembering helps us to keep in mind that Jesus loved us so much that he suffered, died, and rose again to save us.

◆ Write the word *presence* on the board. Ask a volunteer to explain the ways the risen Christ is present and active with us in each and in every liturgy. Have the young people highlight these ways listed at the top of the right-hand column on page 38. Ask, "Should our hearts be burning within us at Mass when we listen to the Scriptures and when we receive the Eucharist?"

 Blessing One of the prayer forms familiar to Jesus and available to the early Church was the berakah. The *berakah* is not a specific prayer; rather, it is a prayer *form*. The berakah, or prayer of blessing, usually involves three elements: We call on the name of God (invocation). We gratefully remember (anamnesis) all that God has done for us. We make our petition (epiclesis).

Here is an example:

Blessed are you, Lord, God of all creation.
Through your goodness we have this bread
  to offer,
which earth has given and human hands
  have made.
It will become for us the bread of life.

This last sentence is really a prayer of petition meaning, "God, make it become for us the bread of life."

In the prayer above indicate the invocation, anamnesis, and epiclesis.

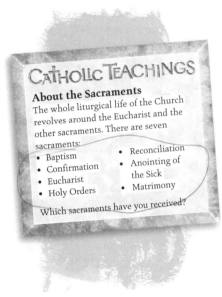

CATHOLIC TEACHINGS

About the Sacraments

The whole liturgical life of the Church revolves around the Eucharist and the other sacraments. There are seven sacraments:

- Baptism
- Confirmation
- Eucharist
- Holy Orders
- Reconciliation
- Anointing of the Sick
- Matrimony

Which sacraments have you received?

39

◆ Direct attention to the thought provoker. Have different volunteers indicate the invocation, anamnesis, and epiclesis of the prayer.

Conclusion ___ min.

◆ Have the young people summarize *Catholic Teachings* on page 39. Ask each person to reflect on the celebrations of the sacraments that they have received or in which they have participated.

FORUM Assignment

✔ Read pages 40 and 41. Prepare your responses for *Things to Share*.

✔ Read *Life in the Spirit*. List ways Jesus is the Good Shepherd in your life.

Closing Prayer: Ask the young people to write on their crosses the inscription on the cross pictured on page 38. Have them hold their crosses as a volunteer reads Philippians 4:4–7. Suggest that the young people use the crosses as bookmarks for their Bibles.

◆ Write the word *doxology* on the board. Have the young people highlight the definition highlighted in the second paragraph in the right-hand column on page 38. Ask, "How does concentrating on all that we have to be thankful for and giving thanks and praise to God help us to love and serve God?"

◆ On the board write the word *epiclesis*. Have a volunteer explain the meaning of this technical term. Ask, "Is it comforting to know that during the celebration of the Eucharist, we call upon the Holy Spirit to make us holy?" Have the students highlight the meaning of *epiclesis* in the section "Calling Upon the Holy Spirit" on page 38.

◆ Then write on the board *berakah*. Discuss this prayer form, and have the young people highlight the meaning and the three elements of the prayer on page 39.

Just in case... some pronunciation helps

anamnesis . . . . *an-am-**nee**-sis*
epiclesis . . . . *eh-peh-**klee**-sis*
berakah . . . . *beh-**rah**-kah*

FOR SESSION 5

- parish missalettes (optional)
- copies of *Chapter 3 Assessment*, page 41A
- copies of *Highlights for Home*, page 41B

SESSION 5

Objective: To affirm the belief that in Jesus we see and come to know the invisible God; to recall that Jesus has given the Church seven sacraments through which we share in his saving work.

Introduction ___ min.

Opening Prayer

Forum: Have the young people discuss the questions in *Things to Share*. Also ask them to list the reasons they depend on Jesus, the Good Shepherd. Read together John 10:11–18.

Presentation ___ min.

◆ If possible, borrow parish missalettes. Have the young people find and read quietly the readings for this coming Sunday. Ask, "What key words did you hear?" "What does God want me to hear?" "What part of God's plan is emphasized in the readings?" Have the young people write their responses in their journals.

◆ Have a volunteer summarize *On Line with the Parish*. You may want to suggest that volunteers plan a discussion for the group each week to help prepare themselves for Sunday readings.

◆ Direct attention to *Words to Remember*. The definition for *sacrament* may be found on page 35; the definition for *lectionary* may be found on page 37.

Assessment: Suggest that the young people work with partners in writing the answers for *Testing 1, 2, 3*. If time permits, have the partners share their answers with the entire group.

If you are administering *Chapter 3 Assessment*, page 41A, allow about ten minutes for the students to complete the test.

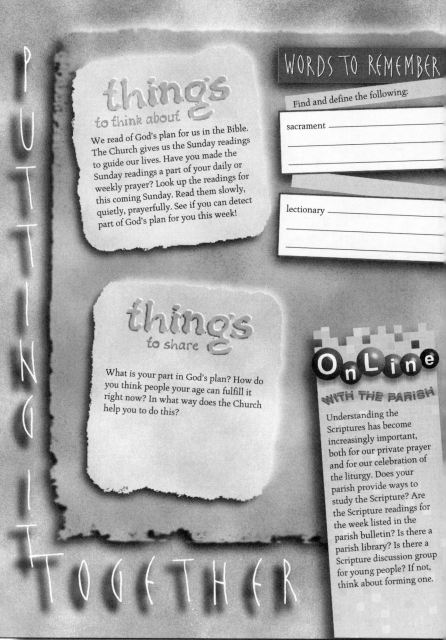

things to think about

We read of God's plan for us in the Bible. The Church gives us the Sunday readings to guide our lives. Have you made the Sunday readings a part of your daily or weekly prayer? Look up the readings for this coming Sunday. Read them slowly, quietly, prayerfully. See if you can detect part of God's plan for you this week!

things to share

What is your part in God's plan? How do you think people your age can fulfill it right now? In what way does the Church help you to do this?

WORDS TO REMEMBER

Find and define the following:

sacrament _____

lectionary _____

OnLine WITH THE PARISH

Understanding the Scriptures has become increasingly important, both for our private prayer and for our celebration of the liturgy. Does your parish provide ways to study the Scripture? Are the Scripture readings for the week listed in the parish bulletin? Is there a parish library? Is there a Scripture discussion group for young people? If not, think about forming one.

Conclusion ___ min.

◆ Encourage the young people to share *Highlights for Home*, page 41B, with their families.

◆ Have a volunteer read *Life in the Spirit*. Remind the young people of the three elements of the berakah: calling on the name of God, remembering all that God has done for us, and making our petition.

Closing Prayer: Invite the young people to look at the panoramic view on pages 30 and 31. Then read together Psalm 23.

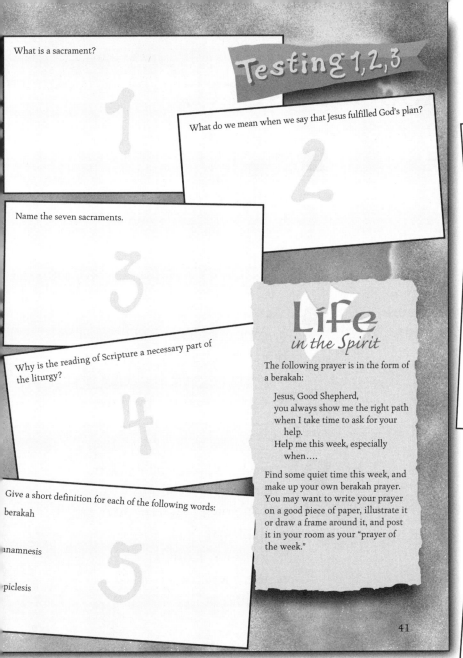

What is a sacrament?

What do we mean when we say that Jesus fulfilled God's plan?

Name the seven sacraments.

Why is the reading of Scripture a necessary part of the liturgy?

Give a short definition for each of the following words:

berakah

anamnesis

piclesis

Life in the Spirit

The following prayer is in the form of a berakah:

Jesus, Good Shepherd,
you always show me the right path when I take time to ask for your help.
Help me this week, especially when….

Find some quiet time this week, and make up your own berakah prayer. You may want to write your prayer on a good piece of paper, illustrate it or draw a frame around it, and post it in your room as your "prayer of the week."

41

Testing 1,2,3

1. See page 35. A *sacrament* is a visible and effective sign, given to us by Christ, through which we share in God's grace.

2. See page 33. Through Jesus we are saved from sin. His sacrifice on the cross and his victory over sin and death made the Father's plan of peace and harmony possible for us and for our world.

3. See page 39. The seven sacraments are Baptism, Confirmation, Eucharist, Reconciliation, Anointing of the Sick, Holy Orders, and Matrimony.

4. See pages 36 and 37. When we celebrate the liturgy and the sacraments, we celebrate God's plan and our Christian story. Sacraments are worded signs. Scripture is the word, the word that gives the sacramental sign its meaning.

5. See page 39. berakah: a prayer form, a prayer of blessing

   See page 38. anamnesis: the liturgical act of remembering

   See page 38. epiclesis: a petition to the Holy Spirit

Evaluation: Have the young people discovered that through the sacraments we encounter Jesus Christ? Have they explored the prominent role the proclamation of Sacred Scripture plays in every liturgical celebration?

Answers for Chapter 3 Assessment

1. c   2. b   3. d   4. d   5. c
6. b   7. a   8. c   9. a   10. See page 35.

Assessment

1 _____ is the liturgical act of remembering.
   a. Epiclesis
   b. Presence
   c. Anamnesis
   d. Berakah

2 The word _____ comes almost directly from Latin and means "to be before one."
   a. epiclesis
   b. presence
   c. anamnesis
   d. berakah

3 _____ is a prayer that gives God glory.
   a. Berakah
   b. Anamnesis
   c. Epiclesis
   d. Doxology

4 _____ is the technical term for calling upon the Holy Spirit to make us holy.
   a. Berakah
   b. Doxology
   c. Anamnesis
   d. Epiclesis

5 The proclamation of Sacred Scripture _____ every liturgical celebration.
   a. is not part of
   b. is not important in
   c. plays a prominent role in
   d. is the most important part of

6 In _____, God reveals himself to us most fully.
   a. the Book of Genesis
   b. Jesus
   c. Baptism
   d. the gifts of nature

7 Sacramental rites
   a. cannot be changed by anyone.
   b. can be changed at any time.
   c. are changed every ten years.
   d. can be changed by those participating in them.

8 The whole liturgical life of the Church revolves around _____ and the other sacraments.
   a. Baptism
   b. Reconciliation
   c. the Eucharist
   d. Confirmation

9 A sacrament is a _____ and _____ sign, given to us by Christ.
   a. visible, effective
   b. invisible, effective
   c. visible, ineffective
   d. invisible, ineffective

10 Explain briefly why the Church calls the sacraments "God's masterpieces."

_____
_____
_____
_____

Highlights for Home

Focus on Faith

Jesus came to show us what God is like by what he did, what he said, and what he was. The invisible life of God, first made visible in Jesus Christ, is now made visible in the Church. Jesus has given the Church seven sacraments, visible and effective signs, through which we share in God's grace. Through the sacraments our faith is nourished and made strong.

In previous years, the young people have studied the sacraments. Help your son or daughter to avoid the "Been there; done that" syndrome. Help them to deepen their understanding and heighten their participation as people of word and sacrament. When we celebrate the liturgy and the sacraments, we celebrate God's plan and our Christian story, which is part of that plan.

Conversation Starters

. . . . a few ideas to talk about together . . . .

◆ How is Jesus a sign of God's love?

◆ In what ways are the sacraments "doors to the sacred" for me?

◆ How can I, as a member of the Church, be a visible and effective sign of God's love?

Feature Focus

In reading *Scripture Update* on page 37, the young people learn that the reading of the Scriptures is an essential part of the celebration of every sacrament. The Church provides a variety of readings to help us understand the meaning of each sacramental event.

Reflection

In this chapter your sons and daughters learned about the berakah, a prayer of blessing. In some parishes it is a custom that homes be blessed during the Easter season by a parish minister or a member of the household. Reflect on and pray the following blessing:

Lord,
we rejoice in the victory of your Son over death:
by rising from the tomb to new life
he gives us new hope and promise.
Bless all the members of this household
and surround them with your protection,
that they may find comfort and peace
in Jesus Christ, the paschal lamb,
who lives and reigns with you and the
 Holy Spirit
one God, for ever and ever.

THE SACRAMENT OF SACRAMENTS

Adult Focus

In the Eucharist Jesus gave his Church a memorial of his saving passion, death, and resurrection. Now and for all time, we, the followers of Jesus, can gather in the presence of the risen Savior at the Eucharist and enter into his paschal mystery. We can be united with the sacrifice of Jesus Christ and give praise to the Father through him.

The Eucharist is a sacrifice. Sacrifice is a ritual action that brings about our joyful reunion with God. Through the sacrifice of Jesus on the cross our sins were forgiven and we were reunited with God. Every celebration of the Eucharist makes present the sacrifice of Jesus. The Eucharist is also a sacred meal. The *meal* is the external sign of the sacrifice. In the eucharistic celebration what we *see* is a meal; what the meal *makes present* is the sacrifice.

In this chapter we want the young people to come to a deeper and richer understanding of this great sacrament of love in which our redemption is carried on, we are filled with grace, and a pledge of future glory is given to us (*Catechism*, 1402, 1405).

Catechism Focus

The themes of this chapter correspond to paragraphs 1324–1332 of the *Catechism*.

Enrichment Activities

Video View

Note: It is essential that all videos be previewed before showing them to the group. This is part of teacher preparation. Choose the particular part of the video you wish to share with the students. Develop the questions or ideas you wish to use as follow-up.

The film *Jesus of Nazareth* (Zeffirelli) is one that can be used over and over again, each time showing and discussing a different segment. You might wish to add it to your library.

From *Jesus of Nazareth* show the segment on the Last Supper. Invite reactions, comments, and responses to your questions. Then, as time allows, show the segment again as part of a *Closing Prayer*. Allow time for silence and reflection. (See *Supplemental Resources*.)

Guided Meditation

Invite the group to pray using a guided meditation on the Eucharist. An excellent source is *Guided Meditations for Youth on Sacramental Life*, Arsenault and Cedor, St. Mary's Press, 702 Terrace Heights, Winona, MN 55987–1320, 1–800–533–8095. The meditations are on audio cassette. There is also a leader's guide available.

Teaching Resources

	Overview	Opening Prayer Ideas	Materials
SESSION 1	**Discovery:** To discover in a deeper way that the Eucharist is "the source and summit of the Christian life."	Pray or sing one verse of a eucharistic hymn.	These will be needed for every session: texts, Bibles, highlighters, journals. • construction paper, markers, scissors • paper (2' x 8") with outline of words "I am the Bread of Life."
SESSION 2	**Exploring 1:** To explore the meaning of liturgical time; to develop an understanding of sacrifice.	Read and reflect on Luke 22:14–20.	• mobile (optional) • copies of handout *Jesus Broke Bread with Them*
SESSION 3	**Exploring 2:** To study the eucharistic prayer of the Mass; to understand the Eucharist as both meal and sacrifice.	Gather in silence. Volunteer reads the words at the top of page 48. All reflect in silence.	• missalettes, hymnbooks • copies of Eucharistic Prayer III from missalette • cards with words MEAL, SACRIFICE, THE EUCHARIST IS BOTH, AND
SESSION 4	**Exploring 3:** To understand more fully that in the Eucharist we become one body in Christ; Christ is totally identified with us, his Church.	Invite each young person to offer a prayer for the needs of the world. After each intercession all pray: "Jesus, living Bread, feed us."	• strips of paper, basket
SESSION 5	**Putting It Together:** To deepen understanding of and appreciation for the gifts and graces of the Eucharist.	Offer together the Prayer After Communion, page 189.	• journals • copies of *Chapter 4 Assessment*, page 53A • copies of *Highlights for Home*, page 53B

Supplemental Resources

Videos
Jesus of Nazareth
Vision Video, Inc.
2030 Wentz Church Road
P.O. Box 540
Worcester, PA 19490–0540

"Eucharist" from *Sacraments— Loving Actions of the Church*
Ikonographics
P.O. Box 600
Croton-on-Hudson, NY 10520

Faith and Witness Journal: Liturgy and Worship

For Chapter 4 see pages 16–19.

Jesus Broke Bread with Them

There are many stories in the gospels about the times when Jesus shared a meal with others. From the list below choose two accounts. Find them in the New Testament. For each account tell with whom Jesus eats and what happens. Select a line from the account that you wish to remember and write it.

Matthew	Mark	Luke	John
9:9–13	6:34–44	7:36–50	13:1–15
14:13–21	14:3–9	14:1–6	21:9–17

Gospel Account: _____

_____

Description: _____

_____

_____

_____

Quote:_____

_____

_____

_____

Gospel Account: _____

_____

Description: _____

_____

_____

_____

Quote:_____

_____

_____

_____

The Sacrament of Sacraments

The cup of blessing that we bless, is it not a participation in the blood of Christ?

The bread that we break, is it not a participation in the body of Christ?
1 Corinthians 10:16

43

Objective: To discover in a deeper way that the Eucharist is "the source and summit of the Christian life."

Introduction ___ min.

Opening Prayer: Give each student a piece of construction paper. Make sure markers are available. Ask the young people to draw or outline on the paper a symbol that stands for the truest thing they know about themselves right now. For example, some might feel the truest thing is that they are honest or creative or confused or energetic or lonely. They must find a way to illustrate that thing with a symbol. Allow about five minutes. Then gather the group in a circle around a prayer table on which is placed wheat or bread and grapes or grape juice.

The Leader prays: Lord, be present with us. We bring you ourselves.

(In turn, each student quietly places his or her symbol on the table, saying, "Here I am, Lord.")

(When all have done this, the bread and grape juice, or wheat and grapes, are passed slowly and quietly

around the circle. Have music playing softly in the background. The last student returns the symbols to the table.)*

Leader: Lord Jesus, you give yourself to us as life-giving food. In the Eucharist you say to us, "Here I am."
All: "I am the living bread that came down from heaven; whoever eats this bread will live forever" (John 6:51).
(All return quietly to their places.)

Chapter Warm-up: Form two teams. Give the teams names and write each team name on an opposite side of the board. Each team has one minute to huddle and brainstorm (quietly!) as many names for the Eucharist as they can. Then each team forms a line. When the start signal is given, team members run to the board and write a name for the Eucharist under their team's name. This is a relay race, so team members must wait until they are tagged by the person ahead of them before going to the board. Allow about two minutes; then judge which team has the most names. If a name makes no sense, it is discounted.

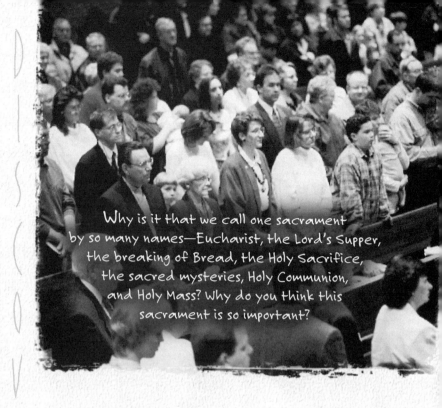

Why is it that we call one sacrament by so many names—Eucharist, the Lord's Supper, the breaking of Bread, the Holy Sacrifice, the sacred mysteries, Holy Communion, and Holy Mass? Why do you think this sacrament is so important?

Chapter 4
SESSION 1

Presentation ___ min.

◆ Have a volunteer read the opener on page 44. Ask the young people to check the lists to see whether the teams have used all these names. Then ask, "Why is this sacrament so important?"

◆ Have volunteers read page 44. Share with the group examples of the power of the Eucharist in the lives of people:

- Missionaries in Africa tell of people who walk twenty miles or more just to take part in the Eucharist.
- When the communists banned religious services in countries of Eastern Europe, people risked their lives to meet together secretly to celebrate Mass.
- When Catholics were imprisoned in China, a priest would save a piece of bread from the small amount of food the prisoners were given. He would consecrate the bread so that the prisoners could receive Jesus in Holy Communion.

Then ask, "What is your attitude toward the Eucharist?" Ask the young people to write a response to that question in their journals.

◆ Select five students to read the five paragraphs on page 45. Then have the group highlight or underline in color the ideas highlighted here on pages 44 and 45.

◆ Write the word *symbol* on the board. Talk about the symbols the young people drew to represent their truest selves. Invite volunteers to share their illustrations. Point out that their symbols are certainly signs that tell something about them. The eucharistic symbols, however, are very different. In the Eucharist the bread and wine do not simply stand for Christ; they *become* Christ.

Source and Summit

From the very first moments of the Church's life, it has been true. The Eucharist is the center of our lives. The early Christians knew this. That is why even under threat of persecution and death, they would risk their lives to come together and celebrate this sacrament. Hidden away in the catacombs or meeting secretly in people's homes, the early Christians knew why the celebration of the Eucharist was so important to them.

Contemporary Catholics know the same truth. All over the world, whenever and wherever the Mass is celebrated, Catholics will travel for miles just to receive Communion. We know that despite any suffering the Church may endure, men and women will still come together as a eucharistic assembly of faith.

Why is this so? What draws people to this sacrament? After all, it has not really changed that much in two thousand years. We still offer the simple gifts of bread and wine. We still gather around the priest who presides at each Mass. Let's take a moment to look more deeply at this sacrament of sacraments that the Church says is the source and summit of our life.

44

◆ Now write the word *memorial* on the board. Ask for one-or two-word definitions or descriptions of what this word means. Then have a volunteer read the third paragraph on page 45. Ask, "What is different about the memorial Christ gave us in the Eucharist?" Help the students to see that the Eucharist as a memorial of Christ's passion, death, and resurrection is not just a memory of something that happened long ago; it is a living memorial. Each time we celebrate the Eucharist, we enter into and become part of the one sacrifice of Jesus Christ. This is a great mystery, and we grow in understanding the mystery of the Eucharist only by coming to it as often as we can.

The Body and Blood of Christ

The first thing that Catholics must understand is that the sacrament of the *Eucharist* is really and truly the Body and Blood of Christ. The bread and wine are not just symbols to remind us of Christ. In the Eucharist they have become Christ—body and blood, soul and divinity. Jesus himself told us this. Even before the Last Supper, he said, "I am the living bread that came down from heaven; whoever eats this bread will live forever; and the bread that I will give is my flesh for the life of the world" (John 6:51).

He went on to say, "Unless you eat the flesh of the Son of Man and drink his blood, you do not have life within you. Whoever eats my flesh and drinks my blood has eternal life, and I will raise him on the last day. For my flesh is true food, and my blood is true drink" (John 6:53–55).

On the night before he died for us, Jesus instituted this sacrament of his Body and Blood. At the Passover feast commemorating God's saving action of bringing the Jewish people from death to life, Jesus took the gifts of unleavened bread and wine and said, "This is my body which will be given up for you. This is the cup of my blood, the blood of the new and everlasting covenant. Do this in memory of me." What had Jesus done? He had given to his Church a memorial of his saving passion, death, and resurrection. Now, for all time, his disciples could gather together in the presence of their risen Savior and once again enter into the paschal mystery. They could make themselves part of the one sacrifice of Jesus Christ and give praise to God the Father through him.

How wonderful! How simple and yet full of mystery. The Savior of the world would now be with his Church for all time in a most

marvelous way. In this sacred meal the Church would be nourished as the body of Christ by Christ himself. In the liturgy the Church would give thanks—the meaning of Eucharist—for all that God had done through his Son. By the power of the Holy Spirit, the Church would unite itself to Christ by sharing in his Body and Blood.

So vital is this sacrament that we will spend two chapters exploring its meaning and celebration for our lives—even before looking at the other sacraments. We will be celebrating the Eucharist throughout our lives. How important it is, then, that we as mature Catholics realize how critical we are at the celebration of the Eucharist. When we assemble, we are Christ's body, the Church, and we make this reality visible. We are never more the Church than when we are celebrating the Eucharist around the table of the Lord. In this sacrament of love, our redemption is carried on, we are filled with grace, and a pledge of future glory is given to us (*Catechism*, 1402, 1405).

45

Chapter 4 • Session 1

Conclusion ___ min.

◆ Write the word *mystery* on the board. Ask for a definition. (a truth that we cannot fully understand) Ask the young people to reflect for a moment about the Eucharist. Then encourage them to write in their journals one question they would like to ask Jesus about the mystery of the Eucharist or one thought they would like to share with him. If volunteers wish to share their reflections, allow time for them to do so.

FORUM Assignment

✔ Read pages 46 and 47. Underline in pencil six main ideas.

✔ Devise a symbol or make a collage that expresses the following truth: "For God all time is *now*." Be sure you read page 46 carefully.

Closing Prayer: Tell the young people that this prayer activity will help them to remember that we are totally united with Christ in the Eucharist. On a paper about two feet long and eight inches deep, print a *faint* outline in block letters of the words I AM THE BREAD OF LIFE. Invite the students to write their names inside of one of the letters. The signatures can be as elaborate or as simple as the signer wishes. Display the banner in the room during the sessions on the Eucharist.

FOR SESSION 2

- journals
- mobile (optional)
- copies of handout *Jesus Broke Bread with Them*

FYI During World War II, in the little village of La Chandon in Nazi-occupied France, a community of Christians risked their lives to shelter Jews. By the end of the war, the little village had protected five thousand Jews—one person for every man, woman, and child in the village. When asked why they had risked their lives, one villager replied, "I receive Jesus in Holy Communion each week. It is Jesus in me who risked his life."

What do you think this person had learned about the Eucharist?

Objective: To explore the meaning of liturgical time; to develop an understanding of sacrifice.

Introduction ____ min.

Opening Prayer

Forum: Invite the students to share and discuss their symbols or collages interpreting "God's time is *now*." Allow time for questions and comments, and display their efforts.

Presentation ____ min.

◆ Expand and explore the concept of liturgical time. Point out the diagram on page 46. Ask, "Do we tend to think of the past as going on now? What about the future? Is it happening now?"

Draw a very large circle on the board. Ask, "Where is the past in the circle?" "Where is the present?" "Where is the future?" Explain that a circle is a whole with no beginning and no end. It is all one. It is all now. This is true of our past, present, and future with God. It is all one; it is all *now*.

◆ Divide the circle into three equal sections. In each part write one of the following days: Holy Thursday, Good Friday, Easter Sunday. Invite volunteers to tell the events that happened to Jesus and the disciples on each of these days. List the information in the appropriate section of the circle. Direct attention to the language that has been used in describing the events. Point out that all the verbs are in the past tense!

Now on the entire circle, write "God's time is *now*." Underline the word *now*. Remind the students that in the liturgy, especially the celebration of the Eucharist, we enter into God's time. Ask, "How can the Last Supper be now?" "Does Christ die and rise again for us every time we celebrate the Mass?" Encourage a discussion of these ideas; then have the students highlight the last six lines in the top paragraph of the second column on page 46, beginning with "When we celebrate the liturgy." Have them read aloud together the same paragraph beginning with "These events are made present."

◆ If possible, hang a mobile in the room. Ask the young people to describe what a mobile is. If some have made mobiles in the past, ask them to explain the

Our Time, God's Time

Remembering (anamnesis) is at the heart of each of the sacraments. This is especially true of the Eucharist. Every time we celebrate the Eucharist, we hear the words "Do this in memory of me." We remember what Jesus did on Holy Thursday at the Last Supper. We remember what he did for us on Calvary on the first Good Friday. We remember how he rose from the dead on Easter Sunday. Indeed we remember the entire life of Jesus, all that he said and did for us as our redeemer.

When we remember these events at the Eucharist, we do not merely think about events that happened long ago in Jerusalem. The liturgy makes them *present* to us here and now.

This kind of presence may be difficult to understand at first. We are used to thinking of time in a "straight line":

past time > present time > future time

It seems only common sense to chop time up this way. The past is what used to be; the future is what has not yet happened. Only *now* is truly real to us.

But imagine that you are looking at a house you have never seen before. If you are standing in front of the house, for example, you see only the front; you can only imagine what the back is like. If you are directly above the house, you have a completely different view, but you still do not see *all* of it. Time is something like that for us. We see only what is before us: the present. We can only read about the past; we can only imagine the future.

For God, however, our past, present, and future are all one. For God all time is *now*. This is a hint of what "God's time of salvation" means. In the liturgy the events we might think of as "past" are actually present. In the liturgy we do not just recall the events of Holy Thursday, Good Friday, and

46

Easter Sunday. These events are made present. This does not mean that these events are repeated. No. Only the celebrations are repeated. But "in each celebration there is an outpouring of the Holy Spirit that makes the unique mystery present" (*Catechism*, 1104). When we celebrate the liturgy, the mysteries of our faith are made present so that we may enter into the event. When we enter the story, we encounter the presence of Christ, and we are filled with God's grace. When we celebrate the liturgy, we stand in God's time and God's presence.

A Beautiful Balance

We must keep in balance the three mysteries—Holy Thursday, Good Friday, and Easter Sunday—and not let any one outweigh the others. A true Catholic understanding of the Eucharist is achieved only when we balance all three. If we think of the Mass as a meal but do not see the relation of the meal to Christ's sacrifice on Good Friday, we do not have a balanced understanding. If we reverence Christ present in the Eucharist but fail to reverence Christ present in the Church (in one another and in the poor), we do not have a balanced understanding of the Eucharist.

necessity of *balance* among all the parts. Point out that a true understanding of Eucharist demands that we keep in balance the three mysteries of Holy Thursday, Good Friday, and Easter Sunday.

◆ In large letters print the word *sacrifice* on the board. If available, use colored chalk. First ask, "What do you think of when you hear this word?" Have one or two student "scribes" list these word associations on the board, but *not* under the word *sacrifice* itself.

Now invite someone to describe animal sacrifice in the Old Testament (see page 47). Ask, "What did the sprinkling of blood symbolize?" (God's life being shared with the people) "What is the major emphasis of the ritual?" (the people's joyful reunion with God) Write this response on the board under *sacrifice*. Have the students highlight the last sentence in the third paragraph of the first column on page 47.

We begin with Good Friday in order to understand what we mean when we say the Mass is a *sacrifice*. Today when we think of sacrifice, we usually think of giving up something—giving up candy for Lent or giving up softball in order to play in the band. When we think of sacrifices in the Old Testament, we might picture the sacrifice of an animal.

In this kind of sacrifice, the blood of the animal was a symbol of life. On the Day of Atonement, the holiest of all Jewish feast days, the high priest sprinkled this blood on the assembled community. This ritual action was a sign that it was God's own life which gave life to the people. In the life the people now shared with God, their sins were forgiven; they were at one (at-one-ment) with God and with one another.

The emphasis in this ritual is, not on the killing of the animal, but on the celebration of *the people's joyful union with God*. The central meaning of sacrifice, then, is union with God, not death or giving something up. For the Hebrews, for Jesus, for the early Church, and for us today, *sacrifice* is a ritual action that brings about and celebrates our joyful union with God.

Crucifixion, Sadao Watanabe, 1970

Eucharist and Sacrifice

As the early followers of Jesus began to reflect on his death and resurrection, they began to understand the Good Friday event as a sacrifice. Jesus began to be seen as the Lamb of God and the paschal victim—slain, yes, but victorious in the end. Jesus broke the chains of death. Through his sacrifice our sins were forgiven and we were reunited with God. Only Jesus, the spotless victim, could have done this.

We believe that the celebration of the Eucharist makes present to us the sacrifice Jesus offered once and for all on the cross. At the Eucharist we remember Good Friday not merely as a story or an event from the past. The sacrifice of Jesus is a *mystery*; it is more than words can say. It is a mystery we remember and make present each time we celebrate the Eucharist.

CATHOLIC ID
The words that Catholics use reflect what they believe about the Eucharist. Out of deep respect for Christ's real presence in the Eucharist, we call the consecrated Bread the *Host*, and the consecrated Wine the *Precious Blood*.

 Have you ever made a sacrifice that gave life, even in a small way?

47

FORUM Assignment

✔ Read pages 48 and 49. Underline in pencil the statements that express four main ideas.

✔ At every Mass we hear the story of the Last Supper. Sometimes because we are so used to the words, we do not stop to think about their meaning. Using one of following gospel accounts as a basis, rewrite the story as if you were there: Matthew 26:26–30, Mark 14:17–26, or Luke 22:14–20. What do you see, hear, touch, smell? What do you feel?

Closing Prayer: Read the following script as a reflective prayer. Invite the young people to look at the photo of the wheat field on page 54 and 55.

The bread of the Eucharist has deep meaning for us. Think of the way it is produced. Wheat is grown in the fields. After it is cut, the grains are separated from the seed coverings. The grains of wheat are ground into flour from which the bread is made. The bread of the Eucharist does not come from a single grain of wheat; many grains go into its making. So in the Eucharist we, though many, are made one in Christ.

Conclusion ___ min.

◆ Have a volunteer read *Catholic ID* on page 47. Ask the students if they have ever received Holy Communion under both species, the Host and the Precious Blood.

◆ Point out the thought provoker on page 47. Allow time for reflection, and then ask the young people to write their thoughts in their journals.

◆ Have the students underline in color all statements highlighted here.

◆ Distribute the handout *Jesus Broke Bread with Them*. Have the young people work with partners to complete it. Allow time for sharing the results.

FOR SESSION 3

- missalettes and hymnbooks
- copies of Eucharistic Prayer III from missalette
- cards with the words MEAL, SACRIFICE, THE EUCHARIST IS BOTH, AND

Objective: To study the eucharistic prayer of the Mass; to understand the Eucharist as both meal and sacrifice.

Introduction ___ min.

Opening Prayer

Forum: Select a student to lead the *Forum* by inviting individuals to share their "eye witness" accounts of the Last Supper. The leader should encourage reactions and responses to the accounts.

Presentation ___ min.

◆ Have the students tell what key ideas they have underlined on pages 48 and 49. Ask them to give reasons for their choices. Then have the group highlight the main ideas that are highlighted here.

◆ Do a quick review of the following terms by writing each word on the board and asking a volunteer to define it: *berakah* (a prayer of blessing), *anamnesis* (the liturgical act of remembering), *epiclesis* (the prayer of petition), *invocation* (calling on God's name), *doxology* (praise to God), and *sacrifice* (a ritual action that brings about and celebrates joyful reunion with God).

Repeat the definition of *sacrifice*. Then ask the young people whether they have ever thought of a meal as a sacrifice. Ask why the Eucharist is a sacrifice. (The sacred meal of the Eucharist is a sacrifice because it symbolizes and brings about our joyful reunion with God.)

◆ Call for three volunteers. Give one a card with the word MEAL. Ask that person to explain the Eucharist as a meal. Give the second volunteer a card with the word SACRIFICE. That person must explain that the Eucharist is a sacrifice. The third volunteer holds a card that says THE EUCHARIST IS BOTH. He or she explains in what way the Eucharist is both meal and sacrifice. Then have the volunteers stand facing the group so that their cards can be read as a sentence. (You hold a card saying AND.)

"This is my body"

The Eucharistic Prayer

At each Eucharist we hear these or similar words:

> While they were at supper,
> he took bread, said the blessing, broke
> the bread,
> and gave it to his disciples, saying:
> Take this, all of you, and eat it:
> this is my body which will be given up for you.

What a wonderful phrase to reflect on: "my body which will be given up for you." In joining with Christ to celebrate this Holy Thursday meal, we celebrate and make present the sacrifice of Good Friday. Sacrifices are celebrated in many different ways. One form of sacrifice known to Jesus and the early Church was the sacred meal: Eating and drinking together symbolized and brought about joyful union with God.

Today, at the Holy Sacrifice of the Mass, the meal is the external sign of the sacrifice. We do not ask whether the Mass is a sacrifice *or* a meal; it is *both*. The sharing of food and drink, the meal itself, is the sacrament. It is the external sign of the sacrifice. What we *see* is a meal; what the meal *makes present* is the sacrifice.

48

Before meals most Catholics "say grace." They say a prayer thanking God for the food they are about to eat and asking God to bless them as they share their meal. At the Eucharist, the greatest of all meals, we say, through the priest, the eucharistic prayer, the greatest of all meal prayers.

The basic shape of this meal prayer is that of the prayer of blessing (berakah) known to Jesus and the apostles. This prayer, spoken in our name by the priest, involves three elements:

• We call upon the name of God (invocation).
• We gratefully remember all that God has done for us (anamnesis).
• We make our petition (epiclesis).

The eucharistic prayer begins with a dialogue between the priest and the people, "The Lord be with you. . . . Lift up your hearts. . . ." Then we call on God, our loving Father, and give thanks for all the wonderful things he has done for us. We thank God most especially for Jesus. We remember what Jesus did for us at the Last Supper; we remember his passion, death, and resurrection. And we make

◆ Distribute copies of Eucharistic Prayer III. Have a volunteer read it aloud slowly and clearly. Then ask the young people to write above the title the word *berakah*. Point out that the eucharistic prayer is the greatest of meal blessings.

Challenge the group to identify the *invocation*, in which we call upon God's name (from the beginning to "at whose command"); the *epiclesis* ("And so Father . . . by the power of the Holy Spirit"); *anamnesis* ("Father, calling to mind the death . . . holy and living sacrifice); *doxology* ("Through him, with him, in him . . . forever and ever. Amen").

When the students have named these sections, point out that between the anamnesis and the epiclesis, there is the *offering* of the sacrifice and intercessions.

our petition. We ask God to send the Holy Spirit to change the bread and wine into the Body and Blood of Christ. We ask that we who eat the Bread and drink the Cup may become one body in that same Spirit.

When we listen closely to the words of the eucharistic prayer and understand the meaning of this greatest "grace before meals," we understand the relationship between Holy Thursday and the meaning of the Eucharist.

Meal and Sacrifice

To understand the Eucharist we must balance the Good Friday and Holy Thursday events. This is not always easy. *Sacrifice* suggests an altar; *meal* suggests a table. Can one object be both altar and table? Can we balance the reverence required by a sacrifice with the hospitality and warmth expected at a meal? Yes, we can. And we do, every time we celebrate the Eucharist.

At a sacrifice great care is taken that what is sacrificed is pure and spotless. At a meal we are concerned that the food is tasty and abundant. Can the bread we use for the Eucharist be both? At a meal we eat and drink; we take the food in our hands. How are these gestures balanced with the reverence required by a sacrifice?

Good Friday and Holy Thursday must be balanced in our reverence and devotion at the Eucharist. We are, as the hymn says, "kneeling at the foot of the cross." But we are also "sitting with Christ and the saints at the heavenly banquet, listening to Christ's words, sharing the bread and wine." The songs we sing at Mass speak not only of adoration but also of eating and drinking. We sing about meals, suppers, and banquets. Besides calling it "the Holy Sacrifice of the Mass," we also speak of "celebrating the Eucharist."

In order to understand the Eucharist well, we must hold the images of Good Friday and Holy Thursday in their proper balance. And to these two we add a third: the image of Easter Sunday.

 *Find a song about the Eucharist in a hymnal or a missalette. What does it say about a meal? a sacrifice?*

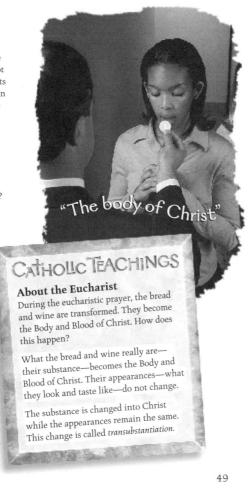

"The body of Christ"

Catholic Teachings

About the Eucharist
During the eucharistic prayer, the bread and wine are transformed. They become the Body and Blood of Christ. How does this happen?

What the bread and wine really are— their substance—becomes the Body and Blood of Christ. Their appearances—what they look and taste like—do not change.

The substance is changed into Christ while the appearances remain the same. This change is called *transubstantiation*.

49

FORUM Assignment

✔ Read pages 50 and 51. Underline in pencil four main ideas.

✔ Paul wrote to the Corinthians reminding them of something very important about the Eucharist. If Paul were alive today, what would he say to you about you and the Eucharist? Write your ideas in the form of a letter from Paul to you.

Closing Prayer: On the board write the following verse from the Sequence for the Mass of Corpus Christi. Gather in a prayer circle and invite the young people to stand and join hands to form a vine. Read the verse together and end with the response "Amen, Alleluia."

> Very bread, good shepherd, tend us,
> Jesu, of your love befriend us,
>   You refresh us, you defend us,
>   Your eternal goodness send us
> In the land of life to see.

Conclusion ___ min.

◆ Have a volunteer read *Catholic Teachings* on page 49. Write the word *transubstantiation* on the board. Under it write the word again, separating it in this way: *tran substantia tion*. Point out the source of each part: *tran* means "change"; *substantia* means "substance"; *tion* means "the act of." The word, then, means "the act of changing the substance." In the Eucharist the substance of the bread and wine is changed into the Body and Blood of Christ.

◆ Have the young people form five groups. Give each group a hymnal or a missalette. (Note: There are more choices in a hymnal.) Direct each group to find a song or hymn that speaks of the Eucharist as a meal and a sacrifice. Allow about five minutes for this search, then ask the groups to share their choices and answer the questions in the thought provoker on page 49.

FOR SESSION 4

• strips of paper, basket

Objective: To understand more fully that in the Eucharist we become one body in Christ and that Christ is totally identified with us, his Church.

Introduction ___ min.

Opening Prayer

Forum: Call on several "Pauls" to read the letters they have written to themselves about their celebration of the Eucharist. Do not critique the letters; simply let them be heard.

Presentation ___ min.

◆ Invite class actors to do a dramatic interpretation of Paul's conversion; the characters might include a narrator, Paul, Jesus, fellow travelers, and the high priest. Direct the actors to use Acts 9:1–8 as the basis for their dramatization. Encourage them to improvise the dialogue between Paul and the high priest, possible remarks by those traveling with him, and possibly Paul's thoughts in Damascus. Allow the actors a few minutes to prepare.

Note: If the young people in your group are not comfortable doing this kind of dramatic improvisation, read the account to them, supplying all the drama you can.

◆ Ask, "What was the important revelation Paul received when Jesus said, 'I am Jesus, whom you are persecuting'" (Acts 9:5)?

The young people should be able to see that Jesus is so united to us that what we do to one another we do to him. Have the students highlight this idea in the first paragraph in the right-hand column on page 50. Then have them highlight the three sentences in the first paragraph on this page that are highlighted here.

Supper at Emmaus, Ivo Dulčić, 1916

I Am with You

At the end of Matthew's Gospel, Jesus tells us, "I am with you always, until the end of the age" (Matthew 28:20). The Eucharist is the celebration of this abiding presence of Jesus in our midst. When Jesus returned to heaven, he did not leave us orphans. The risen Jesus makes us one with him in the Church. Through Baptism, Confirmation, and Eucharist, we have become the body of Christ. This is the heart of Easter Sunday: Christ is totally identified with us, his followers, his Church. Our work now is to be the presence of Christ in the world.

This is what Paul the Apostle, once called Saul, learned on the road to Damascus. In the Acts of the Apostles we see Saul on his way to persecute the followers of Jesus. Suddenly, "he fell to the ground and heard a voice saying to him, 'Saul, Saul, why are you persecuting me?' He said, 'Who are you, sir?' The reply came, 'I am Jesus, whom you are persecuting'" (Acts 9:4–5).

This experience taught Paul that Christ cannot be separated from his members. The risen Lord is so united to us, his followers, that what we do to one another we do to Christ. This fact is central to our understanding of the real presence of Christ at the Eucharist. Paul met Christ who was so identified with us that to persecute Christians was to persecute Christ himself.

We Are One Body

Around A.D. 50, Paul wrote to the Corinthians regarding some concerns he had about the way they were celebrating the Eucharist. At issue was their understanding of the presence of Christ in the Eucharist.

He had no praise for the Corinthians in the way they celebrated the Eucharist. In fact he told them that their meetings were doing more harm than good. He had heard of the divisions between the rich and the poor that separated the community.

50

◆ With the group recall why Paul was so angry with the Corinthians. Have a volunteer summarize his criticism. Stress that in the Eucharist we are united with Christ; Christ lives in us. Everything we do and say is now "in memory of" him.

Ask, "Has your understanding of the Eucharist been deepened by your study of the story of Paul's conversion and his letter to the Corinthians? In what ways?"

He told the Corinthians that when they gather for the Eucharist, "It is not to eat the Lord's supper, for in eating, each one goes ahead with his own supper, and one goes hungry while another gets drunk. Do you not have houses in which you can eat and drink? Or do you show contempt for the church of God and make those who have nothing feel ashamed?" (1 Corinthians 11:20–22).

Paul scolds the Corinthians for celebrating the Eucharist without recognizing the body of Christ—his Church. The poor are going hungry while the rich eat and drink all they want. His criticism of their eucharistic devotion goes to the heart of the matter, to the very meaning of the Eucharist. Nourished by Christ himself, we are to live as Jesus did and work for true justice and true peace. The Eucharist commits us to this.

Saint Paul tells the Corinthians that this is the "body of Christ" they must see at the Eucharist if they are to celebrate worthily. He reminded them that all who eat and drink without recognizing this body eat and drink judgment on themselves. Sharing the Eucharist is a promise that we will

Scripture UPDATE

In their gospels Matthew, Mark, and Luke describe the supper Jesus celebrated with his disciples on the night before he died. Each tells how Jesus took bread and wine, gave it to the disciples, and said, "This is my body; this is my blood."

These important words of Jesus do not appear in John's Gospel. Instead we read how Jesus "poured water into a basin and began to wash the disciples' feet" (John 13:5). What does Jesus say this action means? (See John 13:12–20.) What do you think Jesus' gesture tells us about the Eucharist?

treat all people as Christ would treat them—indeed, as we would treat Christ himself. This is also what it means to "do this in memory of me."

So the next time you hear the words "Body of Christ" at Communion remember and believe that:
• Christ is our Lord and reigns forever in heaven.
• Christ is really and truly present in the Eucharist.
• We the Church are the body of Christ.

If we believe these things about the Eucharist, then the words of Saint Augustine can both make sense to us and challenge us: "We become what we eat"—that is, in the Eucharist we can be transformed into Christ.

How wonderful then is this sacrament of sacraments. Through it we are united with Christ. We are strengthened in holiness to keep free from sin. And we are united as the Church, the body of Christ.

 Why do you think it is so important to prepare to receive Christ in the Eucharist and to receive him worthily?

◆ Have the young people reflect on the thought provoker on page 51. The intent here is truly thoughtful responses, not rote replies. What have the students understood in this chapter that will help them with their response? Allow time for responses and discussion.

FORUM Assignment

✔ Read pages 52 and 53. Prepare your responses to *Things to Think About*. Be ready to participate fully in the discussion.

✔ Do the interviews for *Things to Share*.

Closing Prayer: Hand out strips of paper. Ask each person to think of one way he or she wants to share Christ with others. Have the young people write their thoughts on the strips of paper, using this formula: "Jesus, help me to bring you to others by ____." Collect the strips of paper in a basket. Then gather in a prayer circle. Invite the young people to pass the basket around the circle. As each person receives the basket, have him or her draw a paper and read the prayer. After each prayer the whole group should respond: "Body of Christ. Amen."

Conclusion ___ min.

◆ Have the young people look at the painting on page 50. Discuss that the disciples at Emmaus, to whom Jesus revealed himself in the breaking of bread, understood the need for courage. They took the risk of returning to Jerusalem to spread the good news of the risen Jesus.

◆ Ask a volunteer to read *Scripture Update* on page 51. Remind the group that having the feet of guests washed was a ritual of hospitality in Jesus' time. The washing, however, was done by a servant. In John's Gospel it is Jesus who washes the feet of his disciples. What is he teaching them?

FOR SESSION 5

• copies of *Chapter 4 Assessment*, page 53A
• copies of *Highlights for Home*, page 53B
• Prepare hosts for newsmagazine program.

SESSION 5

Objective: To deepen understanding of and appreciation for the gift and graces of the Eucharist.

Introduction ___ min.

Opening Prayer

Forum: Introduce your version of a TV newsmagazine program. Choose two hosts to be the program's moderators. The hosts will invite several "reporters" to present the results of their interviews with longtime Catholics about the Eucharist. Allow time for questions and general discussion. For the second part of the program, the hosts ask others in the group to report on what they have learned about worship services in other Christian churches. What is similar? What is different?

Presentation ___ min.

◆ Have a volunteer read *Things to Think About*, and allow time for reactions and a brief discussion before having the students write in their journals.

◆ In the Eucharist Jesus calls us to be bread for the world. Ask the young people what that means to them. What kinds of "hunger" do they see in their world?

◆ Draw attention to *Words to Remember*. The definition for *sacrifice* can be found on page 47. The definition for *Eucharist* can be found on page 45. Have individuals read their definitions aloud.

◆ If time allows, go together to the parish church. Ask the young people to examine the images and furnishings that emphasize Holy Thursday, Good Friday, and Easter Sunday. They might wish to write down their observations. When you return from your visit, discuss *On Line with the Parish*.

Assessment: Suggest that the young people work with partners to discuss their responses to *Testing 1, 2, 3*.

If you are planning to administer *Chapter 4 Assessment*, page 53A, allow about ten minutes for the students to complete the test.

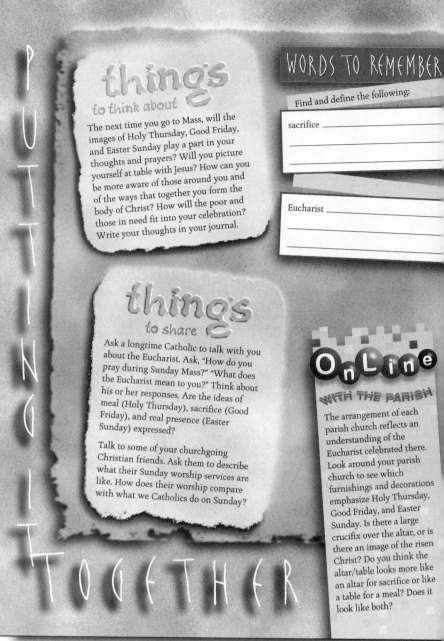

PUTTING IT TOGETHER

things to think about

The next time you go to Mass, will the images of Holy Thursday, Good Friday, and Easter Sunday play a part in your thoughts and prayers? Will you picture yourself at table with Jesus? How can you be more aware of those around you and of the ways that together you form the body of Christ? How will the poor and those in need fit into your celebration? Write your thoughts in your journal.

things to share

Ask a longtime Catholic to talk with you about the Eucharist. Ask, "How do you pray during Sunday Mass?" "What does the Eucharist mean to you?" Think about his or her responses. Are the ideas of meal (Holy Thursday), sacrifice (Good Friday), and real presence (Easter Sunday) expressed?

Talk to some of your churchgoing Christian friends. Ask them to describe what their Sunday worship services are like. How does their worship compare with what we Catholics do on Sunday?

WORDS TO REMEMBER

Find and define the following:

sacrifice _____

_____

_____

Eucharist _____

_____

OnLine WITH THE PARISH

The arrangement of each parish church reflects an understanding of the Eucharist celebrated there. Look around your parish church to see which furnishings and decorations emphasize Holy Thursday, Good Friday, and Easter Sunday. Is there a large crucifix over the altar, or is there an image of the risen Christ? Do you think the altar/table looks more like an altar for sacrifice or like a table for a meal? Does it look like both?

Conclusion ___ min.

◆ Go over *Life in the Spirit* together. Point out that you have already looked at some of these hymns. Discuss the ones that really seem to resonate with the group. Have the students respond to the questions in their journals.

Closing Prayer: Have the young people turn to the Prayer Before Communion on page 189. Gather in a prayer circle, and reverently and quietly read this prayer together.

◆ Encourage the young people to share *Highlights for Home*, page 53B, with their families.

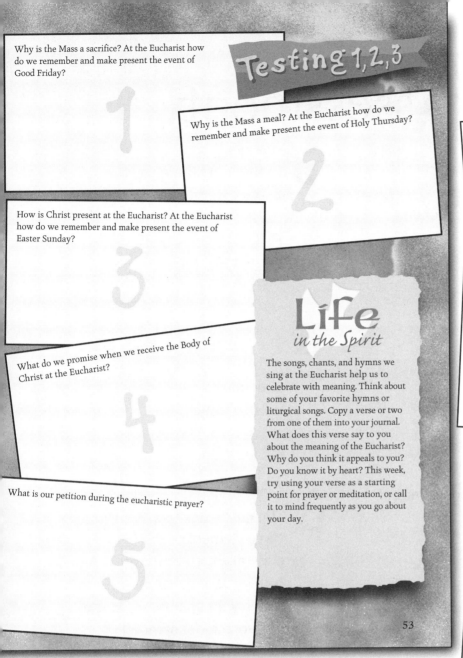

Why is the Mass a sacrifice? At the Eucharist how do we remember and make present the event of Good Friday?

1

Why is the Mass a meal? At the Eucharist how do we remember and make present the event of Holy Thursday?

2

How is Christ present at the Eucharist? At the Eucharist how do we remember and make present the event of Easter Sunday?

3

What do we promise when we receive the Body of Christ at the Eucharist?

4

What is our petition during the eucharistic prayer?

5

Testing 1,2,3

Life
in the Spirit

The songs, chants, and hymns we sing at the Eucharist help us to celebrate with meaning. Think about some of your favorite hymns or liturgical songs. Copy a verse or two from one of them into your journal. What does this verse say to you about the meaning of the Eucharist? Why do you think it appeals to you? Do you know it by heart? This week, try using your verse as a starting point for prayer or meditation, or call it to mind frequently as you go about your day.

53

Evaluation: Have the young people come to a deeper understanding of the Eucharist as the source and summit of their lives as Catholics? Do they recognize the Eucharist as both meal and sacrifice?

Testing 1,2,3

1. See page 47. The Mass is a sacrifice because we believe that the celebration of the Eucharist makes present to us the sacrifice Jesus offered once and for all on the cross. The sacrifice of Jesus is a mystery we remember and make present each time we celebrate the Eucharist.

2. See pages 48 and 49. The Eucharist is a meal because we eat and drink together. The meal is the external sign of the sacrifice. The sharing of the meal itself is the sacrament. On the first Holy Thursday, Jesus gave us his Body and Blood under the appearances of bread and wine.

3. See pages 49 and 50. Christ is present in the Eucharist in his Body and Blood. He is also present in the body of Christ, the Church. At the Eucharist, we remember and make present the event of Easter Sunday by the celebration of the abiding presence of Jesus in our midst.

4. See page 51. Sharing the Eucharist is a promise that we will treat all people as Christ would treat them— indeed, as we would treat Christ himself. This is also what it means to "do this in memory of me."

5. See page 49. We ask God to send the Holy Spirit to change the bread and wine into the Body and Blood of Christ. We ask that we who eat the Bread and drink the Cup may become one body in that same Spirit.

Answers for Chapter 4 Assessment
1. b 2. b 3. c 4. b 5. c
6. a 7. b 8. d 9. b 10. See pages 44 and 45.

Assessment

 1 Christ is in the Eucharist
   a. through anamnesis.
   b. body and blood, soul and divinity.
   c. in the Church.
   d. in the priest.

2 God's time is
   a. a memorial.
   b. always now.
   c. "straight line" time.
   d. past time.

3 In each liturgy the mysteries of the faith are
   a. repeated.
   b. simply symbols.
   c. made present to us.
   d. recalled.

 4 In the Old Testament the animal's blood
   a. was poured on the earth.
   b. was a symbol of life.
   c. was a sign of atonement.
   d. both b and c

 5 The emphasis of ritual sacrifice is on
   a. killing of animals.
   b. instilling fear.
   c. the people's union with God.
   d. the reminder of death.

6 In the Mass the meal is
   a. the external sign of the sacrifice.
   b. the most important part.
   c. the least important part.
   d. both a and c.

7 The greatest of all meal prayers is the
   a. berakah.
   b. eucharistic prayer.
   c. words of consecration.
   d. Our Father.

8 The eucharistic prayer includes three elements:
   a. berakah, epiclesis, great Amen.
   b. invocation, anamnesis, sanctus.
   c. berakah, anamnesis, epiclesis.
   d. invocation, anamnesis, epiclesis.

 9 The change of bread and wine into the Body and Blood of Christ is called
   a. consecration.
   b. transubstantiation.
   c. invocation.
   d. atonement.

 10 Explain this statement: The Eucharist is the center of our lives. Write your response on the reverse side of this page.

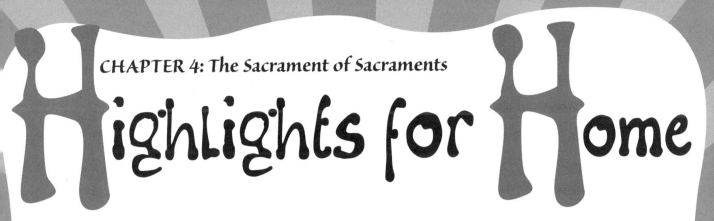

CHAPTER 4: The Sacrament of Sacraments

Highlights for Home

Focus on Faith

Often teenagers tend to feel that they have "had" lessons on the Eucharist since second grade. They can be unaware that the mystery of the Eucharist is so profound and so transforming that even a lifetime of prayer and study would never be sufficient. The Church teaches that "the Eucharist is 'the source and summit of the Christian life'" (*Catechism*, 1324). The Eucharist is Christ himself, the giver of life, the nourishment of our souls.

In this chapter on the Eucharist, the young people are asked to deepen their understanding of what it means to enter into the paschal mystery of Christ—his saving passion, death, and resurrection—made present in each celebration of the sacrament through which our redemption is carried on, we are filled with grace, and a pledge of future glory is given (*Catechism*, 1402, 1405).

Conversation Starters

. . . . a few ideas to talk about together. . . .

◆ What do I find most difficult to understand about the Eucharist?

◆ What efforts do I make to deepen my understanding?

◆ When was the last time I fully participated in the Eucharist, tuning out distractions?

Feature Focus

The *Scripture Update* on page 51 points out that John's Gospel does not relate the words Jesus said over the bread and wine. Instead John recounts the action of Jesus in washing the feet of his disciples. This was a task usually reserved for servants. This action of Jesus tells us something very important about the Eucharist. What do you think it is?

Reflection

Saint Paul reminds the Corinthians that simply to receive the Eucharist without recognizing the body of Christ—the Church—is to miss the whole point of the sacrament. We are fed by the Body and Blood of Christ so that we, in turn, may be "bread" for others. Saint Augustine reminds us that "we become what we eat." In the Eucharist we become Christ.

This week:
How can I be Christ for others?
How can I be bread for the poor?

CELEBRATING EUCHARIST

Adult Focus

This is the Lamb of God . . . .
Happy are those who are called to his
supper.

The celebration of the Eucharist is the focus of this chapter. We who are called to share the Bread of Life understand that we are called to celebrate both a meal and a sacrifice. We celebrate this sacrificial meal within a fourfold structure that can be found in any celebratory meal: 1) We gather (the Introductory Rites); 2) We tell our stories (the Liturgy of the Word); 3) We share our meal (the Liturgy of the Eucharist); 4) We return home (the commissioning).

As the young people follow this outline, they are gradually led to a deeper and more complete understanding of each part of the Mass. They are encouraged to examine in detail the celebration they have experienced countless times, in order that the meaning of these familiar rites might emerge in a new and more profound way.

A complete understanding of the celebration of the Eucharist requires a broad view—a view of the past (the Last Supper), the present (Christ's living presence today), and the future (a foretaste of the banquet of heaven). As this broad view comes into focus for the young people, they can be encouraged to put this new understanding into practice through a more informed participation in the holy sacrifice of the Mass.

Catechism Focus

The theme of this chapter corresponds to paragraphs 1346–1355, 1384–1387, and 1396–1405 of the *Catechism*.

Enrichment Activities

🖥 Computer Connection

Have the young people use a writing program to compose letters thanking Jesus for the wonderful gift of himself in Holy Communion.

If your class is using the *Student Writing Center™**, begin by selecting the letter icon and then "With Letterhead" from the Letter Layout window. Instruct the students to choose an appropriate letterhead from the "Choose a Letterhead" window. Make sure they clear the letterhead of any existing text by highlighting the text and then pressing the delete key. Encourage the students to add pictures to enhance their letters either before or after they finish writing. To access the picture library, students should click on the picture icon or select "Choose Picture," listed under "Graphics" in the main menu.

Have the students print their letters. Have each student roll up his or her letter and tie a decorative ribbon around it. Collect the scrolled letters into a box, and present them at a group prayer service or liturgy.

Sacred Vessels

Invite a priest to show and explain the use of the sacred vessels used during the celebration of the Eucharist.

Teaching Resources

	Overview	Opening Prayer Ideas	Materials
SESSION 1	**Discovery:** To discover that the celebration of the Eucharist has a fourfold structure: gathering, story-telling, meal sharing, and commissioning.	Write a note to Jesus to express your thoughts about celebrating the Eucharist.	These will be needed for every session: texts, Bibles, highlighters or colored pencils, journals, and parish missalettes. • basket
SESSION 2	**Exploring 1:** To explore the parts of the Liturgy of the Word.	Read together Matthew 7:24–27. Pray together: "Lord, give us the wisdom to listen to your word and act on it."	• three stalks of wheat cut from construction paper • sheet of posterboard
SESSION 3	**Exploring 2:** To explore the meaning of the words and actions of the eucharistic prayer.	Pray or sing together the preface acclamation: "Holy, holy, holy Lord. . . ."	• copies of the handout *For Granted*, page 54C
SESSION 4	**Exploring 3:** To understand the words and gestures of the communion rite and commissioning of the Mass.	Pray or sing together the Our Father. Invite the young people to exchange a sign of peace with those who are near them.	• recordings or copies of lyrics of eucharistic hymns
SESSION 5	**Putting It Together:** To discuss the importance of our full participation in the Mass.	Pray together the Prayer Before Communion on page 189.	• copies of *Chapter 5 Assessment*, page 65A • copies of *Highlights for Home*, page 65B • basket of notes to Jesus

Supplemental Resources

Videos
Living Eucharist
A Eucharist Parable
Saint Anthony Messenger
http://www.american
catholic.org

*A Teen's Guide to
Living the Mass*
Liguori Publications
1 Liguori Drive
Liguori, MO 63057

Faith and Witness Journal:
Liturgy and Worship

For Chapter 5 see pages 20–23.

For Granted

Imagine that thirty-five years have passed and that you have been stationed on Space Base 10 for a few years. Your chaplain has not been able to visit to celebrate Mass for almost a year. On the lines below finish the conversation with the chaplain to express your feelings about this matter.

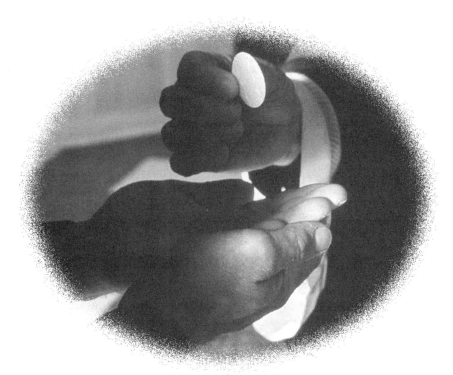

You: I think I took for granted the privilege of participating in Mass and receiving Jesus' Body and Blood every Sunday while I was based on earth!

Chaplain: _____

_____

You: I really miss _____

_____

_____

Chaplain: _____

_____

_____

You: When I return home, _____

_____

_____

_____

Chaplain: _____

_____

_____

Celebrating Eucharist

He was made known to them in the breaking of the bread.
Luke 24:35

Objective: To discover that the celebration of the Eucharist has a fourfold structure: gathering, storytelling, meal sharing, and commissioning.

Introduction ___ min.

Opening Prayer: Ask the young people to write a note to Jesus to express their thoughts about attending and participating in Mass each week. Encourage them to be honest, and assure them that no one will read their notes.

When you see that most students have finished writing, ask them to read over and then fold the notes. You may want to provide envelopes, tape, or staples for sealing the notes. Then ask the young people to print their initials on the outside of the notes. Have a volunteer take around a basket to collect the notes. Then place the basket on the group's prayer table. Explain that you are going to return the notes during the fifth session of this chapter.

Invite the young people to look at the photos on pages 54 and 55. Have them imagine that Jesus is walking with them on the road through the field. He is speaking to them personally, responding to their notes. Allow a few minutes of quiet time.

Direct the young people's attention to the painting of the supper at Emmaus on page 55. Have a volunteer read the account in Luke 24:28–35. Ask the young people to pray quietly, answering Jesus' request to celebrate the Eucharist.

Play a recording or share the lyrics of the song "Gather Us In" from *Gather Us In* by Marty Haugen (GIA). Have the young people pay particular attention to the third verse.

Chapter Warm-up: Explain that in the Middle Ages, in village churches and cathedrals alike, it was customary for someone to ring the church bells on Sunday morning to call people to Mass. Today some parish communities follow this custom. Discuss whether this practice would encourage individuals to gather with their parish communities for the weekly celebration of the Eucharist. Ask, "What other sensory aids might be used to invite us to gather?"

Presentation ___ min.

◆ Have the young people form small groups to discuss the following questions:

• Do you notice a pattern to the parts of the parties or celebrations you have been going to in the past year?

• What is the pattern you would describe to friends who have moved to another community?

• Do you enjoy the parties if you go with a poor social attitude or in a bad mood?

◆ Then read the following scenario:

You have invited all of your best friends to a party at your home. A few of the guests do not speak or participate in the party activities.

Ask, "How do these people affect the spirit of the entire group?"

While the young people are discussing, write on the board the four parts of any meal of celebration listed in the last paragraph on page 56. Have the groups compare and contrast their patterns with this list.

◆ Direct attention to the introductory question on page 56. Then have the students read this page quietly.

◆ Have a volunteer read "The Eucharistic Meal" on page 57. Explain that this structure does not include the official names for the parts of the Mass but that it shows us the overall pattern.

◆ Direct the young people's attention to the photo on page 57. Ask, "Has anyone participated in the entrance procession of the Mass?" Ask what the procession might symbolize. Also ask why parish liturgical committees usually choose upbeat songs or hymns for this procession.

◆ Have a different volunteer read each paragraph of "Gathering" on page 57. As each student finishes reading, write on the board the official title of the prayer.

• Paragraph 2: Greeting

• Paragraph 3: Penitential rite
　　　　　　Glory to God

• Paragraph 4: Opening prayer

What would you say if a friend who had never been to Mass asked you, "What do you Catholics do when you go to church on Sunday?"

Owning the Eucharist

Most of us have been celebrating the Eucharist almost all our lives, so we may think we know it well. This chapter, however, may open our eyes to the Eucharist in a new way. By learning more about the elements of the Eucharist, we can more clearly understand how best we can think, pray, and act during the celebration. We can better own the Eucharist, enter into it, as *our* celebration.

Of course none of this would matter so much if the Eucharist were an action we simply watched as spectators. But the Eucharist is a community action, a liturgical action. It requires the participation of each and every one of us, the entire body of Christ.

"Doing" is different from just "watching." Doing requires information and skills. Playing the trumpet in the band requires more information and skills than standing on the curb, watching the parade go

by. At the Eucharist we are the "players"; we *all* celebrate the Eucharist together. We each have an active part, whether that be reading, listening, bringing up the gifts, singing, or responding together with our "Amen!" In the last chapter we studied what the Eucharist means. Now we want to learn how to celebrate that meaning.

The external shape of the Mass is a meal. It will help us understand how to celebrate the Eucharist if we first think of what we do when we celebrate a special meal in our homes. For example, how might you celebrate Thanksgiving dinner at your grandmother's house?

Each person's Thanksgiving might be a little different, but we would probably find these same four parts in any meal of celebration: (1) We gather. (2) We tell our stories. (3) We share our meal by putting food on the table, saying the blessing, and eating and drinking. (4) We return home.

56

Distribute parish missalettes. If possible, have the young people find these prayers in the Introductory Rites. Explain that the celebrant has the option of using one of two greetings and one of three penitential rites. Also explain that there is a different set of two opening prayers that the priest may choose to use for each Sunday.

◆ Explain to the young people that the rite of blessing and sprinkling of holy water may be used in place of the penitential rite. The prayer of blessing reminds us that water brings new life to the earth and that in Baptism water is the sign of being cleansed from sin.

The Eucharistic Meal The Eucharistic meal has a similar four-fold structure:

gathering

storytelling

meal sharing: preparation of the gifts, the eucharistic prayer, the communion rite

commissioning

Each of these elements has its own special purpose. The better we understand each of these four parts of the Eucharist, the better will we be able to celebrate the Eucharist with meaning.

Gathering

We come together in one place for the eucharistic assembly. We gather together as the Church to make the body of Christ visible.

The priest invites us to make the sign of the cross. He greets us, saying "The Lord be with you." We respond, "And also with you." This greeting is used several times during the Mass. It is intended both as a wish, meaning "*May* the Lord be with you" and as a profound statement of faith, meaning "As you assemble for worship, the Lord *is* with you." This is an ancient greeting, found frequently in the Old Testament. It is a blessing that we exchange among ourselves in our everyday lives, although we may not realize it. This blessing, our familiar "good-bye," is a shortened form of "God be with you."

This greeting and all the other ritual acts of these Introductory Rites are intended *to gather us together into a worshiping assembly*. We are asked to pause and recall our common need for salvation (the penitential rite). On Sundays and feasts, we sing or recite the hymn "Glory to God in the highest." The "Gloria" has been part of the Mass since the sixth century.

At the close of these rites that gather us together, the priest asks us to join our hearts and minds in prayer. After a few moments of silence the priest "collects" our intentions into one prayer. We make it our own by responding "Amen."

When we gather to celebrate the Eucharist, we gather to experience the presence of Christ. This reality begins even during this first part of the Eucharist, the Introductory Rites. Here we experience together what Christ has promised: "Where two or three are gathered together in my name, there am I in the midst of them" (Matthew 18:20).

57

Conclusion ___ min.

◆ Have the young people highlight the statements that are highlighted here.

FORUM Assignment

✔ Read pages 58 and 59. Underline in pencil the statements that express six main ideas.

✔ Think about the reading from Scripture about the disciples at Emmaus. If you were helping the priest prepare the homily for this reading, what concerns or points would you recommend he address? Write three or more ideas to share.

Closing Prayer: Ask the young people to open their parish missalettes to the Glory to God prayer. Then invite them to form a circle and pray these words, remembering Jesus is in their midst.

FYI The prayer of blessing used during the Easter season reminds us that the Israelites were led through the waters of the Red Sea to freedom, and that we are led through the waters of Baptism to life in Christ and freedom from sin. In this prayer we ask to share the joy of all who were baptized at Easter.

After the people are sprinkled with the holy water, the priest faces the people and says:

May almighty God cleanse us of our sins, and through the eucharist we celebrate make us worthy to sit at his table in his heavenly kingdom.

The people answer: Amen.

FOR SESSION 2

• three stalks of wheat cut from construction paper
• sheet of posterboard

SESSION 2

Objective: To explore the parts of the Liturgy of the Word.

Introduction ___ min.

Opening Prayer

Forum: Have the young people form small groups to discuss *Scripture Update* on page 59 and to share the points that they would like to have addressed in a homily about the disciples at Emmaus. Then ask each group to compose a homily that would be given for this gospel reading. Emphasize that they should consider the various ages and concerns of the parish congregation. Then have a representative from each group deliver the homily to the others.

Presentation ___ min.

◆ At the top of a sheet of posterboard, write "The Word of God Gives Us Food for Thought." Choose a Sunday in the season that the Church is currently celebrating. Try to choose one that has readings the young people can easily understand. Ask the students to open their parish missalettes to that Sunday's readings. Have a volunteer read the first reading. Then discuss the ways in which the message of this reading helps us recall God the Father's original covenant with us.

Tape or paste one of the wheat stalks you have cut out or trace it on the poster. Write a statement near this stalk to summarize your discussion about the first reading.

Have a different volunteer read the second reading. Discuss the ways in which this reading relates to our lives today. Tape or paste another stalk of wheat on the poster. Write a summary statement near this stalk.

Have a third volunteer read the gospel. Tape or paste the third stalk of wheat on the poster. Write a statement to summarize the message in this reading near this stalk.

Discuss the theme of the three readings, and write a theme statement at the bottom of the poster.

Storytelling

When we gather for a meal, we usually begin with conversation: telling our stories. At the Eucharist, after the Introductory Rites, we sit down and enter into the ritual of conversation with Sacred Scripture, the inspired word of God. We do this in the Liturgy of the Word.

Through the reading of the Scriptures, we listen to the Father's story once again. As we hear God's story, we are reminded of our own stories, our own hopes and dreams. As we grow and change from day to day, we listen to the Scriptures from a slightly different perspective. At every liturgy, we are given the opportunity to hear God's story in a new way.

On Sundays we have three such opportunities, because there are three readings. The first reading is ordinarily taken from the Old Testament, and is related in theme to the gospel of the day. This Old Testament reading recalls, in some way, God the Father's original covenant with us. Following the first reading we sing or recite a psalm, a song from God's own inspired hymnal, the Book of Psalms. The second reading is usually from one of the letters of Paul or from another apostolic writing. The first two readings conclude with "The word of the Lord." To this we all respond with our liturgical "yes" as we say, "Thanks be to God."

The third reading is taken from one of the four gospels. Because of the unique respect given to the gospel words of Jesus, it has long been the custom in the Church to stand in attentive reverence during the proclamation of the gospel.

Before proclaiming the gospel, the priest greets us with "The Lord be with you." As he announces the particular gospel of the day, he traces with his right thumb a series of three small crosses on his forehead, on his lips, and on his heart. Silently he prays that God will cleanse his mind and his heart so that his lips may proclaim the gospel worthily. In many places the congregation makes these small signs of the cross along with the priest. The gospel reading concludes with, "The gospel of the Lord." We respond, "Praise to you, Lord Jesus Christ." We thus proclaim our faith in the presence of Christ in the word. Then we sit for the homily.

The *homily* takes the word of God and brings it to our life today. Just as a large piece of bread must be broken to be eaten, a good homily "breaks open" the word of God in order that we might hear, understand, and act upon it.

58

◆ Discuss with the young people the statements they underlined in "Storytelling" on pages 58 and 59. Then have them highlight the statements that are highlighted here.

◆ Remind the group that Scripture is the inspired word of God. As God's word, Scripture has a unique place and exercises a unique power in our lives. We can truly say that Scripture is God's word in power, which brings about what it proclaims.

◆ Invite volunteers to list on the board the different parts of the Liturgy of the Word in the correct sequence.

good homily helps us connect God's story with ~~r~~ own lives. The homily is often followed by a ~~w~~ moments of silence. We take this time ~~t~~o thank God for the word we have heard and ~~t~~o consider how we can apply the readings ~~an~~d the homily to our lives.

~~O~~n Sundays we then stand and together recite ~~th~~e Nicene Creed. The creed is a statement ~~of~~ our faith in the word we have heard ~~pr~~oclaimed in the Scripture and the homily.

~~O~~riginally the creed was the profession of faith ~~of~~ those to be baptized at this point in the ~~M~~ass. Today the creed reminds us of our own ~~Ba~~ptism. As we make our profession of faith, ~~w~~e are reminded that each time we come to ~~th~~e Eucharist, we come through Baptism.

General Intercessions The Liturgy of the Word comes to a close with what are called the general intercessions.

At Mass, the general intercessions help us recall that we are the body of Christ by Baptism. Now, as we prepare to approach the table for Eucharist, we look into the readings as we would look into a mirror. We examine the picture of Christ and the Church presented in the Scripture. Does our assembly, the body of Christ present here, resemble that picture? In the general intercessions, we pray that we will really come to look like the body of Christ proclaimed in the Scripture: a body at peace, providing shelter for the homeless, healing for the sick, and food for the hungry.

In the general intercessions, we pray that our Church and our world might come to look like the plan God has for us. Our petitions usually fall into four categories: the needs of the universal Church, all nations and their leaders, people in special need, and the needs of our local parish. As these petitions are announced, we all pray for these intentions in our hearts. Then we make our common response aloud: "Lord, hear our prayer."

What will you pray for so that your parish community will "reflect" the body of Christ proclaimed in the Scripture?

*Scripture*UPDATE

In Luke's Gospel we read the story of two disciples on the road to Emmaus. This story is the source of the fourfold structure we are using to understand the Mass. Read Luke 24:13–35 in your Bible. See if you can identify the four movements:

• Who gathers?

• What stories do they tell?

• Where do they recognize the presence of the risen Lord?

• What do they do at the end of the story, "after Mass"?

59

FORUMAssignment

✔ Read pages 60 and 61. Underline in pencil the statements that express the main ideas.

✔ Before you read pages 60 and 61, write what you recall about the prayers, priest's actions, and our responses during the eucharistic prayer. Compare what you have written with the explanation given on these pages of your text.

Closing Prayer: Have each pair of prayer partners offer one of the petitions they have written for each category of general intercessions. Then direct all the young people to respond to each petition with the words "Lord, hear our prayer."

Conclusion ___ min.

◆ Ask a volunteer to summarize "General Intercessions" on page 59. Have the young people work in pairs to write general intercessions that would be appropriate for next Sunday's Mass. Remind the pairs to include the four categories. Explain that the group will pray for these intentions during the *Closing Prayer*.

FOR SESSION 3

• copies of handout *For Granted*, page 54C

SESSION 3

Preparation of the Gifts

The Dialogue

Objective: To explore the meaning of the words and actions of the eucharistic prayer.

Introduction ___ min.

Opening Prayer

Forum: Have the young people give an honest appraisal of what they wrote about the eucharistic prayer before reading pages 60 and 61. Discuss the following questions:

- Is it important for us to develop a greater understanding and a deeper appreciation of the words we pray and the gestures we use during the preparation of the gifts, the eucharistic prayer, and the communion rite?

- Why is it important?

- How do we develop this understanding and appreciation?

Then discuss with the young people the statements they underlined. Have them highlight the statements that are highlighted here.

Presentation ___ min.

◆ Ask volunteers to explain the words and actions of the preparation of the gifts. You may want to discuss the following points with the young people:

- In the past, when society was agricultural, the gifts given at the Eucharist often included garden and farm produce. Some of this food helped to support the parish priest; some of it was given to the poor.

- This tradition continues today. In some parishes it is customary to bring food for the poor to the altar at the same time that the gifts of bread and wine are carried up. This becomes a symbol of our unity with one another in the body of Christ.

- During the preparation of the gifts, the weekly collection is also taken up. In modern times most people are given money in exchange for the work of their hands and minds. It is only right to give part of those earnings to help maintain the parish community and to support its efforts to spread the good news in the local community and even around the world.

Meal Sharing

Following the Liturgy of the Word, we move to the table of the Lord. In any meal celebration there are three movements: We bring the food to the table, say grace, and share the food. At Mass these actions are called the preparation of the gifts, the eucharistic prayer, and the communion rite.

Preparation of the Gifts Members of the community bring the bread and wine for the Eucharist to the priest at the altar. Then begins the preparation of the gifts. The priest places the bread and wine on the table. He mixes water with wine and washes his hands. These gestures remind us of the Last Supper: Mixing water with the wine and washing hands were rituals the Jews followed at all meals in Jesus' time. The priest then invites us to pray that our sacrifice be acceptable to God. We respond "Amen" to the prayer over the gifts and stand to participate in the central prayer of the Mass.

The Eucharistic Prayer

The eucharistic prayer brings us to the very center of the Mass and to the heart of our Catholic faith. The structure of this prayer is that of a berakah:

1. We call upon God the Father to remember all the wonderful saving deeds of our history.

2. We then recall Jesus Christ and, in particular, the memorial he left us on the night before he died. We narrate the institution of the Eucharist at the Last Supper, and we recall (anamnesis) his passion, death, and resurrection.

3. Then as we gratefully (eucharist) remember all the wonderful saving acts God has done for us in the past, we petition (epiclesis) the Father to send the Spirit to continue those deeds of Christ in the present and future. Now let us see how the berakah is expressed at Mass.

The Dialogue The eucharistic prayer begins with a dialogue between the priest and the assembly: "The Lord be with you. . . ." The priest then asks if we are ready and willing to approach the table, to renew our baptismal commitment, to offer ourselves to God: "Lift up your hearts." And we say that we are prepared to do so: "We lift them up to the Lord." The priest invites us to give thanks to the Lord our God. And we respond: "It is right to give him thanks and praise." (The word *eucharist* comes from the Greek, "to give thanks and praise.")

The Preface The priest begins the preface. In most cases *preface* means simply an introduction. Here *preface* retains its original meaning of speaking in the presence of God. We are brought into God's presence and speak directly to God, thanking him for his wonderful works. We ask to join the choirs of angels, who praise God unendingly in the heavenly liturgy. We cannot hold back our joy, and sing aloud with them:

> Holy, holy, holy Lord, God of power and might, heaven and earth are full of your glory.

Epiclesis The priest continues the eucharistic prayer, giving praise and thanks. He then invokes the Father (epiclesis) to send the Holy Spirit to change our gifts of bread and wine into the Body and Blood of Christ.

60

◆ Have the young people open their parish missalettes to the eucharistic prayer. Ask the students to focus on the appropriate photo at the top of pages 60 and 61 and then read quietly the prayers for the dialogue, preface, epiclesis, consecration, anamnesis, and doxology. Choose the first or second eucharistic prayer for this exercise.

◆ Discuss the thought provoker on page 61. Ask why we should pray "Amen" with our entire minds and hearts.

Epiclesis   *Consecration and Anamnesis*   *Doxology*

We also pray that we who take part in this Eucharist may become one body and one spirit. Only then can we experience the fullest presence of Christ.

Anamnesis The priest recalls the events of the Last Supper and the story of the institution of the Eucharist. (These words are called the "words of consecration.") He then speaks to us, inviting us to "proclaim the mystery of faith." Among the choices given for this acclamation, a short and familiar one is:

Christ has died,
Christ is risen,
Christ will come again.

The priest continues to recall with us (anamnesis) the wonderful deeds which saved us: the passion, death, and resurrection of Christ.

Epiclesis for Unity The grateful memory of God's salvation leads us to make the second half of our petition—our primary petition (epiclesis) at every Eucharist—the petition for unity. In the second eucharistic prayer we pray:

May all of us who share in the body and blood of Christ
be brought together in unity by the Holy Spirit.

We look forward to that glorious feast of never-ending joy in heaven and join our voices with those of all the saints who have gone before us as the priest raises the bread and wine and offers a doxology, a prayer of glory to God in the name of Christ:

Through him,
with him,
in him,
in the unity of the Holy Spirit,
all glory and honor is yours,
almighty Father,
for ever and ever.

Our "Amen" to this prayer acclaims our assent and participation in the entire eucharistic prayer.

Look back at the parts of the eucharistic prayers on these pages. What do you think we are saying "yes" to in each of the parts?

CATHOLIC TEACHINGS

About the Mass

It is Christ himself, acting through the ministry of priests, who offers the eucharistic sacrifice. Only validly ordained priests can preside at the Eucharist and consecrate the bread and wine. Through Baptism, however, all of us share in the priesthood of Christ. This is called "the common priesthood of the faithful." Laypeople may take on special roles in the liturgy, serving as readers, altar servers, and eucharistic ministers.

61

Conclusion ___ min.

◆ Have a volunteer summarize *Catholic Teachings* on page 61. Ask the young people whether they would like to be eucharistic ministers when they are older. Explain that the diocese or individual parishes usually ask those people who wish to serve in this role to attend preparation seminars.

FORUM Assignment

✔Read pages 62 and 63. Underline in pencil the statements that express five main ideas.

✔Complete the handout *For Granted*.

Closing Prayer: Invite a volunteer to read the doxology on page 61. Have everyone sing a familiar "Amen."

FYI The preface is one of the parts of the Mass that can change. There are special prefaces said during each liturgical season of the year, for special feasts, for Sundays and weekdays, and even for special civic holidays such as Independence Day and Thanksgiving Day. As we listen, we are reminded of the reasons we are gathered. For example, in the first Preface for Independence Day and Other Civic Observances, we hear:

We thank you, Father, for your blessings
in the past
and for all that, with your help, we
must yet achieve.

The prefaces may be found in the sacramentary.

FOR SESSION 4

• recordings or lyrics of eucharistic hymns

SESSION 4

Objective: To understand the words and gestures of the communion rite and commissioning of the Mass.

Introduction ___ min.

Opening Prayer

Forum: Have the young people work in pairs to share the conversations they wrote on the handout *For Granted*. Then have the pairs form small groups representing Catholics who live on Space Base 10. Have the groups plan a Mass that the chaplain will celebrate with them on his next visit to the base. Explain that they should choose the hymns and write general intercessions for this imaginary liturgical celebration. Then have a representative from each group share the members' plans with the group as a whole.

Discuss with the young people the statements they underlined in pencil. Have them highlight the key concepts that are highlighted here.

Presentation ___ min.

◆ Ask, "Why is it appropriate to pray the Our Father and extend the sign of peace before we receive the Body and Blood of Christ?" If students do not give the following responses, include them in your discussion:

• All during his public life, Jesus preached forgiveness and reconciliation. The Our Father summarizes Jesus' message.

• In order to be united with Jesus, we should be united with one another.

◆ Direct attention to the fourth paragraph in the first column on page 62. Then read together the words the priest uses to invite us to "come to the table." Ask what our response is. You may want the young people to find the response in their parish missalettes.

Explain that these words are taken from the Gospel of Luke in the story of Jesus' healing of the centurion's slave (Luke 7:1–10). Have a volunteer read the account. Ask, "Why do you think we pray these words at this particular time during the communion rite?"

The Communion Rite

The meal sharing or Liturgy of the Eucharist consists of three parts: the preparation of the gifts, the eucharistic prayer, both of which we have already studied, and the communion rite, to which we now turn.

We prepare to eat and drink at the Lord's table by praying together the Lord's Prayer: "Give us this day our daily bread; and forgive us our trespasses as we forgive those who trespass against us."

Communion is the sign and source of our reconciliation and union with God and with one another. Therefore, we make a gesture of union and forgiveness with those around us and offer them a sign of peace.

The priest then shows us the Bread and Cup and invites us to come to the table:

> This is the Lamb of God....
> Happy are those who are called to his supper.

Here we are once more reminded that the Mass is both a sacrifice and a meal. We come forward to eat and drink the Body and Blood of Christ.

As God fed our Hebrew ancestors in the desert on their pilgrimage to the promised land, so God gives us food for our journey today. We approach the minister, who gives us the eucharistic Bread with the words "The body of Christ." We respond "Amen." We then go to the minister with the Cup who offers it to us with the words "The blood of Christ," to which we again profess our "Amen."

During this procession we usually sing a hymn which unites our voices, thoughts, and spirits, even as the Body and Blood of Christ unites us as one body in Christ. Then we pray silently in our hearts, asking for all that this sacrament promises. The priest unites our prayers in the prayer after Communion, to which we respond "Amen."

Commissioning

Finally we prepare to go back to that world in which we work and play, study and live. The burdens we have laid down at the door of the church for this Eucharist we know we must take up again. But now we bear them with the strength received from this Eucharist and this community. The priest again says "The Lord be with you," this ritual phrase serving now as a farewell.

62

◆ Discuss some of the hymns or songs we sing at communion time. You may want to play a recording or read the lyrics of one that clearly explains that the Body and Blood of Christ unite us as one body in Christ. The following are suggestions: "At That First Eucharist" and "How Blest Are We" (found in many missalettes); "We Remember" by Marty Haugen, *With Open Hands*, GIA.

◆ Direct attention to the photos on page 62. Ask, "How are the young people showing that they believe they are receiving Christ in the Eucharist?" Emphasize that when we receive the Host, we must be careful to hold our hands in the position of the person shown in the photo on page 63. You may want the young people to practice the gestures involved in receiving communion in the hand. Have them use the photos on these pages as models.

As the bread and wine are brought to the altar, we picture ourselves sitting at table with Jesus at the Last Supper. We become present to that moment and give thanks. As we listen to the eucharistic prayer and ask the Holy Spirit to make us one, we remember Jesus' own prayer: "I pray. . . . Father. . . . that they may be one, as we are one" (John 17:20–22).

We place ourselves at the foot of the cross and offer our lives to God. We promise God that we will do his will, even as Jesus did on Calvary.

We say the Lord's Prayer and ask forgiveness for our sins. We step forward to share in the eucharistic meal, which is past (the Last Supper), present (Christ's living presence today), and future (a foretaste of the banquet of heaven).

Strengthened by this meal, we are commissioned to go forth and be bread for the world.

 Reflect for a moment. Decide on one way you will go forth from the Eucharist to be "bread" for someone.

We bow our heads to receive a blessing. As the priest blesses us in the name of the Trinity, we make the sign of the cross as we did at the beginning of the Mass. The priest or deacon then dismisses the assembly: "Go in peace to love and serve the Lord." And we give our liturgical "yes" as we say "Thanks be to God." ⑨

Personal Overview

How do we celebrate the Eucharist? We see that the answer to this question depends on what part of the Eucharist we are celebrating. During the time of gathering we become aware that together with all those around us we are the body of Christ. During the storytelling we listen attentively to the words of Sacred Scripture and enter into the story. During the homily we learn how the Scriptures apply to our lives today. During the general intercessions we pray that God's story might become real for us.

CATHOLIC ID ⑩

Do you know that we Catholics consider the Eucharist a sacrament of reconciliation? The Church tells us that when we receive the Eucharist worthily our venial sins are forgiven. The Eucharist strengthens our love for God, self, and others, and this love wipes out sin. The Eucharist also preserves us from future sin. "The more we share the life of Christ and progress in his friendship, the more difficult it is to break away from him. . . ." (*Catechism*, 1395). Forgiveness of sin springs from the principal effect of the Eucharist in our lives: union with Christ.

Conclusion ___ min.

◆ Have a volunteer summarize *Catholic ID* on page 63. Read together the words of the *Catechism*.

◆ Ask a volunteer to read the thought provoker on page 63. Have the young people write their decision in their journals.

FORUM Assignment

✔Read pages 64 and 65. Prepare your responses for *Things to Think About*.

✔Read *Things to Share*. Prepare your response. Write a pledge to include one thing you can do to make "liturgy a good experience."

Closing Prayer: Have a volunteer reread the first paragraph on page 63. Ask the young people to bow their heads as you share the following words taken from the solemn blessing for Passion (Palm) Sunday:

> The Father of mercies has given us
>   an example of unselfish love
> in the sufferings of his only Son.
> Through your service of God and
>   neighbor
> may you receive his countless
>   blessings.
> Response: Amen.

FYI Father Joseph Champlin, who has written extensively on the sacraments, reminds us of the following:

And when we come to the altar for Communion, our unity in the Lord becomes even more evident to all. The gesture of reaching outward and upward for the consecrated bread when receiving Communion in the hand is another. We are like a hungry child holding the bowl out and crying, "May I please have some more?" Hungry for the Lord's Body and Blood, we reach out in our need and humbly ask Christ, by that gesture, to give us our daily bread.

FOR SESSION 5

• copies of *Chapter 5 Assessment*, page 65A
• copies of *Highlights for Home*, page 65B

SESSION 5

Objective: To discuss the need for everyone's full participation in the Mass.

Introduction ___ min.

Opening Prayer

Forum: Have a volunteer hold the basket of notes to Jesus that the young people wrote at the beginning of Session 1. Ask the young people to take their notes from the basket, open them, and read them quietly. Ask them to reflect quietly on whether their opinions or concerns have changed after discussing the parts of the Mass explained in this chapter.

Have the young people form buzz groups to discuss *Things to Think About* and *Things to Share*. Then invite each group to compose a contract agreement in which the members pledge to enter as fully as possible into future celebrations of the Eucharist. Have them write the contract on construction paper and design it to look like a legal document.

With the young people's and pastor's permission, display the contracts in the church vestibule. The display might encourage the full participation of other parishioners.

Presentation ___ min.

◆ Have a volunteer summarize *On Line with Parish*. Have the young people highlight the last sentence.

◆ Direct attention to *Words to Remember*. The definition for *preface* may be found on page 60; the definition for *communion* may be found on page 62.

Assessment: Have the students work in pairs to answer the questions in *Testing 1, 2, 3*. Then discuss the responses with the general group.

If you are administering *Chapter 5 Assessment*, page 65A, allow the students about ten minutes to complete the test.

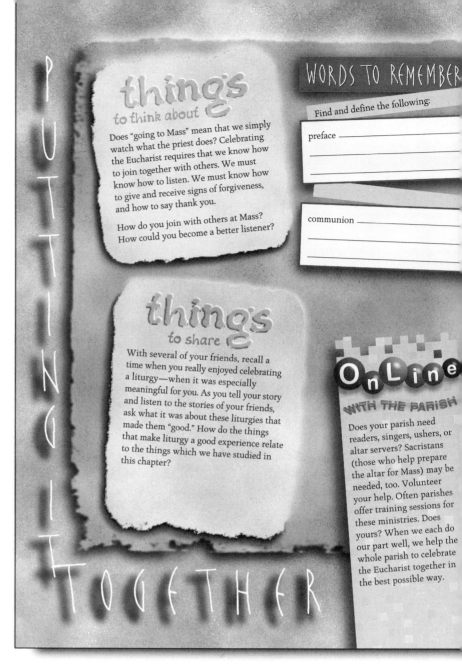

PUTTING IT TOGETHER

things to think about

Does "going to Mass" mean that we simply watch what the priest does? Celebrating the Eucharist requires that we know how to join together with others. We must know how to listen. We must know how to give and receive signs of forgiveness, and how to say thank you.

How do you join with others at Mass? How could you become a better listener?

things to share

With several of your friends, recall a time when you really enjoyed celebrating a liturgy—when it was especially meaningful for you. As you tell your story and listen to the stories of your friends, ask what it was about these liturgies that made them "good." How do the things that make liturgy a good experience relate to the things which we have studied in this chapter?

WORDS TO REMEMBER

Find and define the following:

preface _____

_____

communion _____

_____

On Line WITH THE PARISH

Does your parish need readers, singers, ushers, or altar servers? Sacristans (those who help prepare the altar for Mass) may be needed, too. Volunteer your help. Often parishes offer training sessions for these ministries. Does yours? When we each do our part well, we help the whole parish to celebrate the Eucharist together in the best possible way.

Conclusion ___ min.

◆ Encourage the young people to share *Highlights for Home*, page 65B, with their families.

Closing Prayer: Allow a few quiet moments for the young people to read *Life in the Spirit*. Then ask them to look at the photos on pages 62 and 63. Sing or pray the words of a hymn that is often used in your parish for the recessional. "God's Blessing Sends Us Forth" and "Now Thank We All Our God" are found in many parish missalettes.

How would you respond if a friend who had never been to Mass asked you, "What do you Catholics do when you go to church on Sunday?"

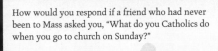

1

What do we remember in the eucharistic prayer? What do we ask for?

2

Name the elements of the Introductory Rites. What is their purpose?

3

What is the purpose of the general intercessions?

4

How is the eucharistic meal a celebration which is past, present, and future?

5

Life in the Spirit

Why do we pray the Our Father at the Eucharist? Because Jesus himself gave us these words to pray. As adopted children of God, we, like Jesus, can also call God "our Father." The Our Father is the best "prayer before Communion" that the Church could possibly pray, for when we pray the Our Father, we are in *communion* with the Father, with his Son, Jesus Christ, and with the entire body of Christ, the Church.

Pray the Our Father quietly. Choose one phrase, like "Our Father," "thy will be done," or "forgive us our trespasses." Try to recall it during the week and the next time you receive the Eucharist.

65

Testing 1,2,3

1. See page 57. Answer should be based on the fourfold structure of the Eucharist: gathering, storytelling, meal sharing, and commissioning.

2. See page 60. In the eucharistic prayer we recall Jesus Christ and the memorial he left us. We remember all the saving acts God has done for us in the past. We ask the Father to send the Spirit to continue those deeds of Christ in the present and in the future.

3. See page 67. The elements of the Introductory Rites are gathering together, the sign of the cross, the greeting, the penitential rite, the Glory to God on Sundays and feasts, and the prayer. The purpose of the Introductory Rites is to gather us together into a worshiping assembly.

4. See page 59. In the general intercessions we pray that we will come to look like the body of Christ proclaimed in the Scripture and that our Church and our world might come to look like the plan God has for us.

5. See page 63. The eucharistic meal is past (the Last Supper), present (Christ's living presence today), and future (a foretaste of the banquet of heaven).

Evaluation: Have the young people explored the fourfold structure of the Mass? Do the young people see the need for their full participation in the celebration?

Answers for Chapter 5 Assessment

1. b   2. f   3. h   4. i   5. c
6. a   7. d   8. e   9. g   10. See pages 62 and 63.

Assessment

Choose the correct letter for the term that completes each statement.

    a. general intercessions
    b. preface
    c. homily
    d. Liturgy of the Eucharist
    e. gospel
    f. words of consecration
    g. creed
    h. Introductory Rites
    i. first reading

1 We sing "Holy, holy, holy Lord," during the _____.

2 In the _____ the priest recalls the events of the Last Supper and the story of the institution of the Eucharist.

3 The _____ are intended to gather us together into a worshiping assembly.

4 The _____ is ordinarily taken from the Old Testament.

5 The _____ takes the word of God and brings it to our life today.

6 In the _____ we pray for the needs of the universal Church, all nations and their leaders, people in special need, and the needs of our local parish.

7 The _____ consists of three parts: the preparation of the gifts, the eucharistic prayer, and the communion rite.

8 During the proclamation of the _____, we stand in attentive reverence.

9 The _____ is a statement of our faith in the word we have heard proclaimed in the Scripture and homily.

10 Explain briefly what happens during the commissioning part of Mass.

_____
_____
_____
_____
_____
_____
_____
_____
_____

Highlights for Home

Focus on Faith

Today many families regret that a busy schedule sometimes prevents a family meal but are creative in scheduling a weekly "family night" instead. The sacrificial meal of the Eucharist is the family meal of the Church. We gather together as baptized brothers and sisters, as followers of Jesus Christ. We celebrate his death, his resurrection, and his presence with us in the sacrament. The outward structure of this eucharistic meal is the same as for any family meal: (1) We gather (the Introductory Rites). (2) We talk and tell stories (the Liturgy of the Word). (3) We bring food to the table, ask God's blessing, and share the food (the Liturgy of the Eucharist), (4) We end the meal (the commissioning).

This chapter reintroduces our young people to the celebration of the Eucharist in a deep and detailed way. Most have been celebrating and receiving the Body and Blood of Christ for many years. Now, from the perspective of belonging, they are able to reflect on their own experience of Eucharist as they explore the celebration of the holy sacrifice of the Mass.

Conversation Starters

. . . . a few ideas to talk about together . . . .

◆ When do you look forward to the celebration of the Eucharist and appreciate it most? Advent? Christmas? Easter? a special day when a family member is involved?

◆ Do you look forward to the Sunday celebration of the Eucharist? How do you prepare for it? How do you participate in it?

Feature Focus

The *Scripture Update* on page 59 explains how the four-fold structure of the Eucharist is related to the story of the two disciples on the way to Emmaus. Try reading the Scripture passage suggested (Luke 24:13–35). Answer the questions with the passage in mind. Then see whether you can apply the questions to a contemporary celebration of the Eucharist. The risen Lord is just as present in the Eucharist today as he was at Emmaus!

Reflection

The opening pages of this chapter present Caravaggio's *Supper at Emmaus.* The scene is early evening, in a wayside inn, as Jesus blesses, breaks, and then gives the bread to his disciples. Up to this point Jesus had been an anonymous wayfarer, someone who had been with them on the road and had been cordially invited to supper. But at the moment of recognition, at the breaking of the bread, Jesus was revealed to them as their friend and Savior.

Picture yourself in this scene. Jesus has been with you all along the road. He has taught you from the Scriptures and from your own experience of life. Now he is about to offer you the greatest gift of all: himself, his life. How will you respond?

THE SACRAMENTS OF INITIATION

Adult Focus

In recent years a new way of preparing adults and young people for the sacraments of initiation (Baptism, Confirmation, and Eucharist) has been adopted by the Church. You may have experienced this new way implemented in your own parish. It is called the *Rite of Christian Initiation of Adults (RCIA)*.

This chapter introduces our young people to the RCIA as a means of their learning more about the sacraments of initiation. The chapter explains that this new method of instruction and gradual incorporation into the Church is not really new; rather, it is very old. The liturgical rites we celebrate as part of the RCIA today have their origins in the practices of the early Christians.

The important process we share with the early Christians is the lifelong process of conversion. Begun at Baptism, our conversion continues in our Christian lives today. Confirmation strengthens and affirms this process as we are sealed in the Spirit. The Eucharist, as it unites us to Christ and to one another in his body, nourishes us in this lifelong journey to God.

Catechism Focus

The themes of this chapter correspond to paragraphs 1214–1215, 1226–1241, 1243–1274, 1285–1289, and 1293–1305 of the *Catechism*.

Enrichment Activities

In Support

Write a group note of encouragement to the catechumens of your parish who are preparing for the sacraments of initiation or to the candidates who are preparing for Confirmation. Offer prayers of support, and thank the groups for their example in turning toward a life that is filled with the Holy Spirit.

Sacraments of Initiation Triptych

Have the students work in small groups to make large triptychs (artwork presented in three panels or sections side by side).

Explain that on each panel the group should symbolize in words and/or illustration the meaning and significance of one of the sacraments of initiation. Display the triptychs in the church vestibule or parish hall to remind the parish community that conversion is "an uninterrupted task for the whole Church" (*Catechism*, 1428).

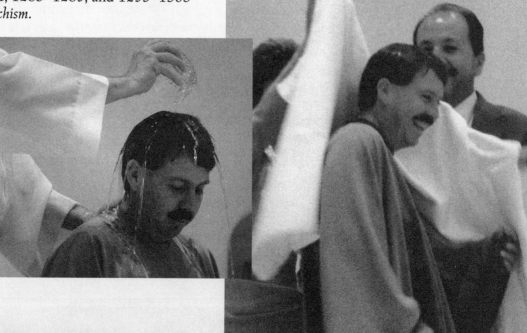

Teaching Resources

Overview	Opening Prayer Ideas	Materials
SESSION 1 **Discovery:** To discover that Baptism is our first act of conversion, the process of coming to believe that Jesus Christ is the Savior of the world.	Look at the photograph on pages 66 and 67. Pray together Psalm 42:2–6. As you pray, imagine yourself in this procession to the house of God.	These will be needed for every session: texts, highlighters, Bibles, journals. • sunrise drawing • posterboard
SESSION 2 **Exploring 1:** To explore how the Church prepares catechumens for the reception of the sacraments of initiation.	Read together Isaiah 42:6–9. Recall your own Baptism, and think about what these verses would mean to someone preparing for Baptism.	• material for *Closing Prayer:* construction paper, paper cups, potting soil, container of water
SESSION 3 **Exploring 2:** To explore the meaning of the symbols and images of Baptism.	Read together Isaiah 43:1–4a. Ask, "What does it mean to belong to the Lord, to be called by name?" Reflect on the feelings evoked by this reality.	• cassette recorder, cassette • birthday candles (optional)
SESSION 4 **Exploring 3:** To explore the ways the sacrament of Confirmation strengthens and continues Baptism.	Read together Joel 3:1–2. Spend some time "dreaming dreams" by praying for particular situations that need the touch of the Holy Spirit.	• poster "On Fire with God's Love" • construction paper for pennants • yarn or string for clothesline • copies of handout *Sealed in the Spirit*
SESSION 5 **Putting It Together:** To deepen understanding and appreciation of the sacraments of initiation.	Listen to a recording of a song based on baptismal or Confirmation themes: water, light, life, following Jesus, witness.	• posterboard or newsprint for statements of commitment • copies of *Chapter 6 Assessment*, page 77A • copies of *Highlights for Home*, page 77B

Supplemental Resources

Videos
- *Confirmation: Commitment to Life*
- *What Catholics Believe About*
  —*Baptism*
  —*Confirmation*
  —*RCIA*

Videos with Values
1944 Innerbelt Drive
St. Louis, MO 63114–5718

Faith and Witness Journal: Liturgy & Worship

For Chapter 6 see pages 24–27.

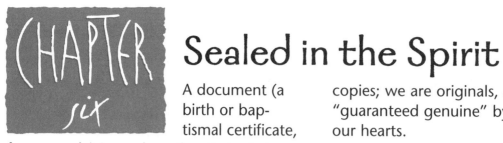

CHAPTER six

Sealed in the Spirit

A document (a birth or baptismal certificate, for example) is made authentic by being stamped with a seal. The seal is a small device that is used to press or emboss a design into a piece of paper. This embossed design cannot be copied or forged. It certifies that this particular document is an original.

Because we are sealed with the Spirit in the sacraments of Baptism and Confirmation, we are authenticated as Christians. For God "has also put his seal upon us and given the Spirit in our hearts" (2 Corinthians 1:22). We are not merely copies; we are originals, authentic, "guaranteed genuine" by the Spirit in our hearts.

In the space below design a "seal of authenticity" that expresses your life as a genuine Christian. Try to symbolize the work of the Holy Spirit in your life. Don't be afraid to be original!

The Sacraments of Initiation

I am the light of the world. Whoever follows me will not walk in darkness, but will have the light of life.

John 8:12

Objective: To discover that Baptism is our first act of conversion, the process of coming to believe that Jesus Christ is the Savior of the world.

Introduction ___ min.

Opening Prayer: Invite the young people to look at the photo of the roadway on pages 68 and 69. Have them respond in their journals to the questions in the opening paragraph on page 68.

While they are writing, draw on the board or on posterboard an illustration of a sunrise like the one shown on page 68. Explain to the young people that when we celebrate the sacraments of Baptism, Confirmation, and Eucharist, we signify our willingness to turn from selfishness and sin to walk in the light of Jesus and with the Holy Spirit's guidance.

Then invite the young people to stand and face in the opposite direction from the sunrise drawing. Ask them to turn slightly in a clockwise direction toward the "light" after each response to the questions you will read. (After responding to the third question, they should be facing the sunrise drawing.) Then say,

"Let us take the time to renew our determination to renounce sin and selfishness. These questions were first asked of our parents and godparents at Baptism. Respond to each question with the words 'I do.'"

• Do you reject sin to live in the freedom of God's children?

• Do you reject the glamour of evil and refuse to be mastered by sin?

• Do you reject Satan, father of sin and prince of darkness?

Invite the young people to gather near the sunrise drawing. Have a volunteer read Jesus' words from page 67 (John 8:12). Then ask all to reflect quietly as you read the exhortation that the celebrant proclaims to the newly baptized:

You have been enlightened by Christ. Walk always as children of the light, and keep the flame of faith alive in your hearts.

Note: If you wish, before beginning the session, make a holy card for each person showing a beam of light, a flame, or a sunrise on one side and this prayer on the reverse side. Distribute the cards after reading the prayer.

Presentation ___ min.

◆ Have the young people look again at the photo of the open road on pages 68 and 69. Point out that the road is a symbol of a Christian's faith journey and that the early Christian community called itself the "Way." Ask, "Why do you think the early Christians used this term?" (Jesus told his followers, "I am the way and the truth and the life." See John 14:6.)

Note: Be sure the young people appreciate the ancient and constant tradition of the Church of baptizing infants. The *Catechism* has a beautiful and concise section on the Baptism of infants in paragraphs 1250 to 1252.

◆ Have a different volunteer read each paragraph on page 68 and the left-hand column on page 69. Ask the young people, "What did Paul have to turn away from before becoming a great missionary?" (persecuting Christians) Then together do a dramatic reading of the account of Saul's conversion and Baptism (Acts 9:1–19).

◆ Have the young people form small groups. Give each group a sheet of posterboard on which to list and/or illustrate roadblocks or side roads that we should turn away from on our journey of faith. When the groups have completed their posters, ask a representative from each to present the group's work.

◆ Have a different volunteer read each paragraph in the right-hand column on page 69. Emphasize Paul's words to the Galatians quoted in the second paragraph. Explain that after Paul was baptized, he helped others to abandon selfish ways and turn toward the life of grace. Read together Acts 9:19–30.

◆ Have the young people highlight the main ideas highlighted on pages 68 and 69.

◆ Share with the young people the story of the life-long process of conversion of Saint Elizabeth Ann Seton.

Think about one new beginning you might already have made in your life. Was it hard? Did you have help? Has it made your life better? What beginnings are you looking forward to?

Beginnings

How do you begin to become a Catholic? This probably doesn't seem to be a very important question if you already are a Catholic! Many of us were baptized when we were infants and have been Catholics ever since. In fact, since the earliest times, Baptism has been administered to infants and children. This continues today. But even so, the question of becoming Catholic is very important. That is because the *process* by which an unbaptized person becomes a Catholic is like a map that helps us understand how to follow Jesus.

The Church realizes that people coming to the Catholic faith as adults need a different kind of preparation, the kind that the early Church gave to the first converts from paganism. This preparation is called the *Rite of Christian Initiation of Adults (RCIA)*. Through the liturgies and prayers it provides, the RCIA prepares adults and young people to become members of the Catholic Church. Sometimes this preparation can last one or two

68

years. These new Catholics are initiated into the Church by receiving the three *sacraments of initiation*—Baptism, Confirmation, and Eucharist—all at once, usually at the Easter Vigil. So understanding the RCIA is a good way to understand the three sacraments of initiation.

We have already studied the meaning of the Eucharist. Yet we will continue our study in this chapter because Eucharist is so closely connected to Baptism and Confirmation. Every time we come to the Eucharist, we come "through Baptism." (This is why we dip our fingers into the baptismal water and make the sign of the cross when we enter a church.) At each Eucharist we renew the promises of our Baptism: the promises to renounce evil and to follow Christ.

In order to understand our baptismal promises, we first need to learn about conversion. *Conversion* is a key word that is important for an understanding of the sacraments. *Conversion* is the process of

---

FYI Elizabeth Seton was an exemplary member of the Episcopalian Church in New York City. When her husband died of tuberculosis at the beginning of a trip to Italy, Elizabeth and her daughter were welcomed into the home of their Catholic friends, the Filicchi family.

This family's faith and Catholic devotion to the Blessed Sacrament awakened Elizabeth's interest in the Catholic Church. After she returned home to New York, she studied Catholic doctrine and prayed for almost a year about the decision to convert. Elizabeth was received into the Catholic Church in March, 1805.

FORUM Assignment

✔ Read pages 70 and 71. Underline in pencil the statements that express six main ideas.

✔ Draw a road to symbolize your journey of faith. On the road or on either side of it, note significant events such as sacrament celebrations, new family members, moving to a new neighborhood, and other memorable experiences. You may want to draw symbols next to the written description of the event. For example, draw waves to symbolize the waters of Baptism.

Closing Prayer: Sing or listen to a recording of "Day by Day" from *Godspell*.

...oming to believe that Jesus Christ is the Savior of the world. The word literally means "turning around, going in the other direction." This helps us understand the meaning of the following related words: "convert," "repent," "do penance."

Conversion may seem to be something that we do. But even more important, it is something that *God does.* Faith in Christ—coming to believe that Jesus is the Savior of the world—is a gift. It is God's free gift. It is Jesus who calls us to conversion: "This is the time of fulfillment. The kingdom of God is at hand. Repent, and believe in the gospel" (Mark 1:15).

If conversion is a turning around, what do we *turn from*? What do we *turn toward*? Saint Paul tells us we are to *turn from* the flesh, all that is selfish, all that seeks "me first" without considering what God wants, all that is sinful. We are to *turn toward* the spirit, all that is life-giving and selfless, all that is generous, all that is filled with the Holy Spirit.

Conversion is a lifelong task. Baptism is our first "turning," or act of conversion, but this process continues throughout our lives. Conversion "is an uninterrupted task for the whole Church" (*Catechism*, 1428). This task is made possible by the paschal mystery of Jesus Christ.

We have learned that the celebration of the paschal mystery lies at the heart of every sacrament. This is especially true of Christian initiation. The sacraments of Baptism, Confirmation, and Eucharist can be thought of as one "moment." When we celebrate this moment, we signify our turning from selfishness and sin to a life in the Spirit of Christ Jesus. We can then say with Saint Paul: "I live, no longer I, but Christ lives in me" (Galatians 2:20).

As we look at the steps a person would take to become a Catholic, the process described in the RCIA, ask yourself these questions: "Am I turning more and more toward Jesus and the Spirit?" "Where am I on my road?" "Am I following this road map?"

69

Conclusion ___ min.

◆ Explain to the young people that both Saint Paul's and Saint Elizabeth Seton's conversions brought about many important developments in the Church. Saint Paul became a great missionary, and Saint Elizabeth Seton founded a religious community of women, the Sisters of Charity. Today the sisters continue Elizabeth's ministry in schools, hospitals, and other charitable institutions.

Ask the following questions:

• How can we follow these saints' example?
• Who, by his or her example, helps us to realize that conversion is a lifelong task?

FOR SESSION 2

• Prepare volunteers for opening prayer.
• material for *Closing Prayer:* construction paper, paper cups, potting soil, container of water

SESSION 2

Objective: To explore how the Church prepares catechumens for the reception of the sacraments of initiation.

Introduction ___ min.

Opening Prayer

Forum: Use a TV talk show as the format. Invite a volunteer "cartographer" to host the segment in which the young people present the "journey of faith" maps they have prepared.

Then invite a volunteer "time traveler" to host the segment in which the young people discuss what they might add to their maps in the future.

Presentation ___ min.

◆ List the four steps of the catechumenate on the board: *instruction, moral conversion, worship, ministry.* Invite the young people to formulate a question for each step. For example: "What do I have to know to be a Catholic?" "How should I live as a Catholic?" "How do I worship as a Catholic?" "What is ministry for a Catholic?"

Ask two volunteers to role-play a conversation using the questions on the board. One volunteer asks about becoming a Catholic; the other responds with appropriate answers.

◆ Challenge the young people to find evidence of these four steps in their own lives. Stress that the steps are part of preparation for the sacraments of initiation but that they are also the work of a lifetime. List the responses on the board.

Give each person a quarter page of construction paper. Ask each to cut out four seedlike shapes from this paper. Direct the young people to think of these seeds as the four parts of the catechumenate and the four parts of their own Christian lives. On the "seed of instruction," have them write one way in which they hope to grow in this area. Then have the young people do the same for the other three seeds. Tell them to keep the seeds for the *Closing Prayer*.

◆ Ask a volunteer to summarize the first paragraph in the right-hand column on page 70. Explore the meaning of the words *elect* and *election*. Ask volunteers to define these words.

Becoming a Catholic

When an unbaptized person wants to become a Catholic or to see what the Catholic Church is all about, he or she usually seeks out a parish and participates in a series of inquiry evenings or information sessions. In some cases, moved by the grace of the Holy Spirit, the person might decide to take the first formal steps toward becoming a Catholic. This is called becoming a catechumen, or entering the catechumenate. The catechumenate has four parts: instruction, moral conversion, worship, and ministry.

The root meaning of *catechumenate* is instruction. *Instruction* is the first step, an important part of the catechumenate. A person who wants to become a Catholic will naturally want to know what Catholics know. Above all, a catechumen must know Jesus and his Church.

The second step along the journey is "changing one's way of life," or *moral conversion*. This part of the process concerns morality, right and wrong behavior. As we come to know Jesus, we will want to act like Jesus. We will want to convert, "to turn around" and follow Jesus.

Worship is the third step along the way. Part of becoming a Catholic is worshiping together with Catholics, praying in a Catholic way. Catechumens will usually participate in Sunday Mass. They will leave after the homily in order to continue their reflection on the word of God while the baptized community celebrates the Eucharist. Until they are baptized, catechumens are not able to participate fully in the Eucharist.

This worship step of the catechumenate normally leads to the fourth step: *ministry*. Those who know Jesus will want to tell others about Jesus. They will want to share their faith and serve others in his name.

 Have you ever felt called to conversion, to changing your way of life? What did you do about it?

70

Initiation

There comes a day when a catechumen decides to ask for the sacraments of initiation: Baptism, Confirmation, and Eucharist. Because the catechumen chooses or elects the Church and the Church chooses or elects the individual, the catechumens are now called the elect. The *Rite of Election* takes place on the first Sunday of Lent.

The season of Lent is a season of spiritual retreat during which the catechumens prepare for their reception of Baptism, Confirmation, and First Eucharist at the Easter Vigil. It is a time for those who are already baptized to encourage the catechumens, and to pray with them. At the Easter Vigil, the Saturday night before Easter, all that the catechumens have been preparing for comes together.

A *vigil* is a time to wait and watch. The liturgy begins after nightfall. We gather around the Easter fire and listen to Scriptures that call to mind the wonder of our salvation. We shout forth our alleluia, which is fresh and new because we have not used it during the forty days of Lent. And we hear in the gospel the proclamation that Jesus has risen from the dead.

Rite of Acceptance into the Order of Catechumens: presenting the gospels

◆ Ask, "Who has participated in the Easter Vigil?" Invite volunteers to relate their experiences. Help them to focus their response by asking questions such as these: "What do you remember most—the new fire, the paschal candle, the Baptisms?" "Did you have friends or relatives among the newly initiated members of the Church?"

Explain that participating in the Easter Vigil is not obligatory. Ask, "Why, then, do Catholics take the time to do so?" Discuss this question with the group as a whole. Then, have the students work in small groups to plan brief radio or TV spots inviting Catholics to participate in the Easter Vigil. The theme of "welcoming new Catholics" as a reason for coming should receive special emphasis.

Now the waiting and watching are over. The elect come forward, and we pray that what happened to Christ may now happen to them. They go down into the baptismal water, down into the tomb with Jesus: They are baptized. They emerge from the baptismal pool dripping wet with new life. The newly baptized are then clothed with a white garment, symbolizing that they have "clothed [themselves] with Christ" (Galatians 3:27). They are given candles lit from the Easter candle. Then they are anointed with oil: They are confirmed.

The vigil comes to its climax with the celebration of the Eucharist. The newly initiated join us for the first time at the table of the Lord.

CATHOLIC ID

The ordinary minister of Baptism is a bishop, priest, or deacon. But did you know that in case of necessity, anyone can baptize? In an emergency a person baptizes by pouring water over the head of the one to be baptized while saying, "I baptize you in the name of the Father, and of the Son, and of the Holy Spirit."

Rite of Election

Easter Vigil

71

Closing Prayer: Ask the young people to put the four paper seeds in front of them. Then give each student two cups: one half full of potting soil, the other half full of water. Take the leader's part in the prayer below.

Leader: On these seeds you have written your intentions to grow in the Christian way of life. Plant your seeds now in the good soil of the Catholic faith. Our life of faith began with the waters of Baptism. As we pour this water on our seeds of growth, we pray: (*Have the young people pour water on the soil after each prayer part below.*)

• Father, Son, and Holy Spirit, help us to learn more about your life in us and more about our Catholic faith.

• Help us to know and do what is right, and to follow the way of Jesus.

• Help us to worship with joy and thanksgiving and to receive the Body and Blood of Christ at the Sunday Eucharist.

• Help us to serve others whenever we can in the name of Jesus. Amen.

Leader: Let us conclude by praying together, "Our Father. . . ." Keep your cup of soil in a place where you will see it often. Remember that we grow in the light of God's love.

Conclusion ___ min.

◆ Have a volunteer summarize *Catholic ID* on page 71.

◆ Ask the students to highlight or underline in color the statements highlighted on these pages.

FORUM Assignment

✔ Read pages 72 and 73. Underline in pencil the statements that express four main ideas.

✔ Write at least five ways young people can show that they are trying to keep their baptismal promises.

FOR SESSION 3

• cassette recorder, cassette
• birthday candles (optional)

Objective: To explore the meaning of the symbols and images of Baptism.

Introduction ___ min.

Opening Prayer

Forum: Invite the students to form small groups to discuss the ways young people may show that they are trying to keep their baptismal promises. Have each group discuss all suggestions and then choose five actions or ways. Emphasize that "doability" with the least amount of help from adults should be a deciding factor in the choice of the final five actions.

Ask each group to select a volunteer to read its final five suggestions on tape. After each suggestion the volunteer will add this phrase: "Walk this way, the way of Jesus Christ." After all the suggestions have been taped, place the tape player near the door of your room for use during the *Closing Prayer*.

Presentation ___ min.

◆ Discuss the statements the young people have underlined on page 72. Have them highlight or underline the main ideas highlighted on this page. Then discuss the young people's responses to the thought provoker.

◆ Ask, "Why does the Church recommend that the celebration of the Baptism of adults take place during the Easter Vigil? Why does the Baptism of infants take place on Sunday?" (Both the Easter Vigil and Sunday celebrate the resurrection of Jesus Christ. Resurrection means new life and eternal life.) Ask, "Why does the Church suggest that the sacrament be celebrated at times during Sunday Mass?" (The parish community is present and can see the relationship between Baptism and Eucharist more clearly. The parish community can welcome the new members of the household of faith.)

Note: If you have invited a priest or deacon to demonstrate and explain the baptismal rite, ask that he demonstrate it as it would be celebrated during Sunday liturgy. If you have not invited a guest speaker, you may want to use the explanation as given in *The Rites of the Catholic Church, Volume One*. Ask to borrow it from your parish.

Baptism

Baptism is so important. It is the gateway to the Christian life. In the New Testament Christian initiation is described by means of many symbols and images. Baptism is "being born again." As Jesus said to Nicodemus, "No one can see the kingdom of God without being born from above" (John 3:3). The experience of those emerging from the waters of Baptism is an experience of birth. At our human birth we came forth from the waters of our mother's womb and were born into a human family. We were welcomed and loved and received our family name.

In this sacrament we come forth from the waters of Baptism and are born into God's family. We are filled with the Spirit of love, welcomed by the Christian community, and receive the family name "Christian." We start afresh. All our sins—original sin and all personal sins—are taken away.

Baptism is also a "dying." In Baptism we go down into the tomb. The baptismal font itself can be seen as a symbol of both the womb, which brings forth life, and the tomb, a place of death. In baptism we are buried with Christ. We die to selfishness and sin so that the Spirit of Christ might be born in us.

Baptism is "seeing things in a new light." We emerge from the waters of Baptism and see things with God's eyes. We see a world in which we are no longer alone, a world in which we are connected with every other creature. We see a world in which we are no longer left to ourselves, a world in which we are loved and given power by the Spirit of God.

Baptism is "being adopted into a new family," the family of God. As family members we are brothers and sisters of Jesus Christ. We inherit everything that God has given to his own Son, especially the great gift of eternal life.

Through these baptismal images the Church has come to believe that "Baptism is the basis of the whole Christian life, the gateway to life in the Spirit . . . and the door which gives access to the other sacraments" (*Catechism*, 1213). Through Baptism we are made members of Christ and members of his body, the Church. We are in Christ and Christ is in us. His work, his mission in the world, is now our own.

 Which image of Baptism has greatest meaning for you? Why?

72

◆ Remind the young people that water and the words "I baptize you in the name of the Father and of the Son and of the Holy Spirit" are the signs of the sacrament.

◆ Ask the students to recall, from their own experiences, the life-giving and death-dealing properties of water. (for example, a devastating flood, a cool shower on a hot day) You may want to chart their responses on the board under the headings "Life" and "Death."

Ask the group to look again at page 72 and add any words from the text that would fall under these two headings. (For example, *womb* means life; *tomb* means death.)

Celebrating Baptism

Another way we can learn the meaning of Baptism is by participating in the celebration of the sacraments of initiation, paying careful attention to both prayers and actions.

We have learned that the principal prayer of each sacrament is often expressed as a prayer of blessing (berakah): (1) We call God by name, "Father." (2) We gratefully remember what God has done for us. (3) We invoke the Holy Spirit.

At Baptism the blessing of the water takes this form. The priest moves to the water and calls upon God. He prays that the Father will give us grace through the sign of the gift of water. As the prayer continues, we remember (anamnesis) God's saving acts, especially those involving water. Then we make our petition:

> We ask you, Father, with your Son
> to send the Holy Spirit upon the waters
>   of this font.
> May all who are buried with Christ in the
>   death of baptism
> rise also with him to newness of life.

The candidates are plunged into this water three times (or water is poured over their heads three times), and the priest baptizes them in the name of the Father, and of the Son, and of the Holy Spirit.

This triple immersion gives the sacrament its name, for to baptize comes from a Greek word that means "to plunge" or "to immerse." Here the water is a symbol of Christ's death, and rising up from it is a symbol that the newly baptized person is risen with Christ and is now all new.

CATHOLIC TEACHINGS

About Baptism

Sometimes people may worry about those who die without being baptized. The Church teaches that those who have not been baptized but who die for the faith receive the grace of Baptism by their martyrdom. This is called the *Baptism of blood.* Unbaptized people who die, if they are catechumens or people who have sincerely tried to do the will of God, even without knowing the Church, are saved by what is called the *Baptism of desire.*

Baptism and clothing with white garment

73

As a group, compose a "sentence poem" using the words and phrases from the chart. The following is an example:

> Baptism leads from death to life.
> Baptism is a shower of refreshing water.
> Baptism is tomb and womb and eternal life.

Ask the students to copy the sentence poem in their journals. Encourage them to feel free to reorder the sentences or to add more if they like.

Conclusion ___ min.

◆ Direct attention to *Catholic Teachings* on page 73. Ask volunteers to summarize the meaning of *Baptism of blood* and *Baptism of desire.*

FORUM Assignment

✔ Read pages 74 and 75. Underline in pencil the statements that express six main ideas.

✔ When we are confirmed, we may choose another name in addition to the one we received at Baptism. As permitted by the Church, many have chosen the name of a saint whom they admire. Choose two or three saints' names that you would like to take for Confirmation. Be prepared to explain to others the reasons for your choices. If you have already been confirmed, choose two or three saints' names that you would recommend to a friend.

Closing Prayer: Remind the young people that light is another symbol of Baptism. Each newly baptized person is given a candle and a new white garment. After the Baptism of a child, the parents and godparents are told: "These children of yours have been enlightened by Christ. They are to walk always as children of the light."

Say, "We have learned that Baptism is the gateway to the Christian life and the door to the other sacraments." Ask the group to file out the door one by one. Before the first person leaves, start the tape of suggestions made earlier. As the reader on tape says, "Walk this way," you may want to hand each person a small birthday candle (unlit) as she or he walks through the door, carrying the light of Christ into the world.

FOR SESSION 4

- poster "On Fire with God's Love"
- copies of handout *Sealed in the Spirit*

SESSION 4

Objective: To explore the ways the sacrament of Confirmation strengthens and continues Baptism.

Introduction ___ min.

Opening Prayer

Forum: Before the session begins, have volunteers help you make a poster. On the poster print the phrase "On Fire with God's Love" in large letters. From colored construction paper cut out twelve flames. Tape or paste them around the phrase. On each flame write one of the fruits of the Holy Spirit: charity, joy, peace, patience, kindness, goodness, generosity, gentleness, faithfulness, modesty, self-control, and chastity.

Begin the *Forum* by explaining that the Holy Spirit develops in us certain qualities or virtues that are traditionally called the *fruits of the Holy Spirit*. Have the young people choose one saint from their list and then decide which two fruits of the Spirit can be most easily identified with that saint. As the young people take turns presenting their chosen saint and the reasons for their choices, ask them to announce the two prominent virtues of this ancestor in faith. Conclude the *Forum* by prayerfully thanking the saints for passing on the flame of God's love to us.

Confirmation

At the Easter Vigil the sacraments of initiation are celebrated together in one liturgy. The meaning of each of the three sacraments is found in the meaning of the other two and in the meaning of the whole ceremony. Catholics who were baptized as infants receive Confirmation later, usually at a time when they can understand what the sacrament means.

Before we study the meaning of Confirmation as a separate sacrament, we must know something of its history. The ceremonies for Baptism and Confirmation were influenced by Roman bathing practices. In second-century Rome, the body would be rubbed with oil after a bath to moisturize the skin. In a similar way the bath of Baptism is followed by an anointing with oil, the sacrament of Confirmation.

We do not find many writings about Confirmation dating from the early days of the Church because it was thought of as part of Baptism. When they spoke of Baptism, the early Christians meant Baptism-Confirmation. Baptism is the washing; Confirmation is the anointing.

Baptism washes away sin and frees us from original sin. *Original sin* was the rejection of God by our first parents, resulting in the loss of sanctifying grace. With their sin, Adam and Eve deprived themselves and all their descendants of the original state of grace given by God. Because of original sin, we need to be saved by Jesus and restored to God's grace.

Original sin and sanctifying grace exist in a relationship similar to that of a vacuum and air. A vacuum is not something; rather, it is the absence of something—air.

Original sin is like that. It is the absence of something—God's grace.

74

Presentation ___ min.

◆ Ask the students to recall the four parts of the catechumenate. (instruction, moral conversion, worship, ministry) Stress that the sacrament of Confirmation is a sacrament of initiation and that *initiation* means "beginning." What we began in Baptism, we continue in Confirmation. We continue to live the Christian life in these four ways.

◆ Ask the young people to look at the photographs on pages 74 and 75. The first shows a bishop. Ask a volunteer to describe what the bishop is doing. (See the third paragraph in the right-hand column on page 75 for a precise description.) Explain that the bishop is the ordinary minister of the sacrament of Confirmation. A priest may confirm only with the permission of the bishop and in special circumstances. For example, a priest confirms at the Easter Vigil. When priests confirm, they use the sacred chrism (oil), which has been consecrated by the bishop at the Chrism Mass on Holy Thursday.

◆ Direct attention to the second photo on page 74. Ask a volunteer to describe what is happening. (A precise explanation can be found in the third paragraph of the second column on page 75.) Explain that the anointing with oil and the words "Be sealed with the Gift of the Holy Spirit" are the essential signs of the sacrament.

Point out the presence of the sponsor in the photo. Note that the sponsor literally "stands behind" the one being confirmed and has a hand on the candidate's shoulder. Ask, "What do you think this body language means?" (possible responses: spiritual support, help, prayers, guidance in life) Explain that the Church encourages candidates for Confirmation to choose their godparents (sponsors at Baptism) as sponsors.

...ike a vacuum, original sin can best be understood ...y looking, not at what it is, but at what it is the ...bsence of, what it is in need of.

...he great vacuum of original sin is removed when ...he person begins to share in God's own life through ...he power of the Holy Spirit. This is what we call ...*anctifying grace.* In God, the source of all holiness, ...e share in holiness.

...Baptism and Confirmation exist in a similar ...elation: Baptism washes away original sin and fills ...s with grace; Confirmation seals us with the ...pirit, strengthening the grace of Baptism.

What is original sin the absence of? What is taken away by Baptism? What is given ...y Confirmation?

The Effects of Initiation

It is important to remember that Confirmation and Baptism go together. Confirmation is saying yes to our Baptism, and this is the same yes we say each day of our ongoing conversion and especially each time that we celebrate the Eucharist. Baptism changes us so radically that we can never be "unbaptized." Baptism makes us members of Christ's body, and this change is so radical that it can never be undone. It is an indelible spiritual mark, or character, that cannot be taken away.

Confirmation strengthens and continues our Baptism. We receive the Holy Spirit in a special way. We are incorporated more firmly into Christ. Like Baptism, Confirmation marks us with an indelible character. The sacrament never needs to be repeated—nor can it be.

A good way to understand Confirmation is to look at the way the Church celebrates it. First, the bishop or the delegated priest extends his hands over you (the typical gesture of invoking the Holy Spirit). Then, as he lays his hand on your head, he anoints your forehead with oil (remember that the name *Christ* means the "anointed one") and says, "Be sealed with the Gift of the Holy Spirit."

In Confirmation we are anointed with oil. It is a sign of consecration. We are anointed in order to share more fully in the mission of Jesus Christ. We are anointed as a sign that we have the seal of the Holy Spirit. Now we belong totally to Christ; we are enrolled in his service forever.

*Scripture*UPDATE

Very often during the rite of Confirmation, you may hear these words of Jesus about the Holy Spirit: "The Advocate, the holy Spirit that the Father will send in my name—he will teach you everything" (John 14:26). Here are a few more Scriptures from the rite of Confirmation. What do they say about the Holy Spirit in your life?

Luke 4:16–22   John 7:37–39

75

✔ Read pages 76 and 77. Prepare your responses for *Testing 1, 2, 3.*

✔ Complete the handout *Sealed in the Spirit.* Seals used for documents are usually plain embossings, but feel free to make yours as colorful as you like.

Closing Prayer: The following prayer is similar to the blessing the bishop says over the people at the end of the Mass at which Confirmation has been conferred. Tell the young people to respond "Amen" to each petition.

- God our Father made us his children by water and the Holy Spirit: may he bless us and watch over us with his fatherly love.

- Jesus Christ promised that the Spirit of truth would be with his Church for ever: may he bless us and give us courage in professing the true faith.

- The Holy Spirit came down upon the disciples and set their hearts on fire with love: may he bless us, keep us one in faith and love, and bring us to the joy of God's kingdom.

Conclude with a recorded song about the Holy Spirit.

Note: You may want to review the effects of original sin that are presented on page 33: weakness of will, tendency to sin, suffering, and death.

Conclusion___ min.

◆ Direct attention to *Scripture Update* on page 75. Ask volunteers to look up and read the two gospel passages. Take a few moments to discuss each separately.

◆ Discuss the thought provoker on page 75.

◆ Summarize the session by having the young people highlight or underline in color the key concepts highlighted on these pages.

FOR SESSION 5

- posterboard or newsprint
- copies of *Chapter 6 Assessment*, page 77A
- copies of *Highlights for Home*, page 77B

Objective: To deepen understanding and appreciation of the sacraments of initiation.

Introduction ___ min.

Opening Prayer

Forum: Ask the young people to gather in small groups. Explain that they will take turns presenting their seals to their own small group. Remind them to explain any symbols and meanings that might not be clear to others. Point out that the members of the group may have questions about the seal and its meaning. Remind the young people that these questions should be asked in a polite way because we should treat the work of others with respect.

Ask each group to compose a statement of commitment to the process of conversion. They may wish to begin the statement this way: "We, the undersigned, promise to turn toward Spirit-filled activities. These include. . . ." Direct the groups to write the statement on a piece of posterboard or newsprint and sign their names to the statement. Then ask them to cut their seals from the handout sheet and paste them at the bottom of the statement.

Presentation ___ min.

◆ Direct attention to *Things to Think About*. Make two lists on the board: one labeled "Turn From," the other labeled "Turn Toward." Brainstorm to answer the questions and write the responses in the appropriate list. Have the students form buzz groups to discuss the imaginary picture in *Things to Share*.

◆ Direct the students' attention to *Words to Remember*. The definition of *sacraments of initiation* can be found on page 68; the definition of *conversion* appears on pages 68 and 69.

Assessment: Suggest that the young people work with partners to complete *Testing 1, 2, 3*. If time permits, ask the partners to share their answers with the entire group.

If you are administering *Chapter 6 Assessment*, page 77A, allow about ten minutes for the students to complete the test.

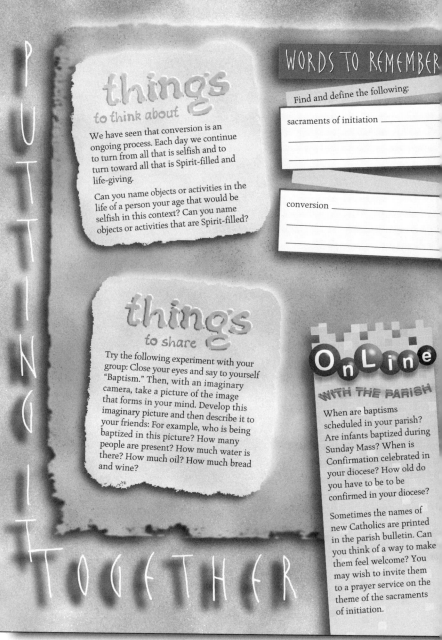

PUTTING IT TOGETHER

things
to think about

We have seen that conversion is an ongoing process. Each day we continue to turn from all that is selfish and to turn toward all that is Spirit-filled and life-giving.

Can you name objects or activities in the life of a person your age that would be selfish in this context? Can you name objects or activities that are Spirit-filled?

things
to share

Try the following experiment with your group: Close your eyes and say to yourself "Baptism." Then, with an imaginary camera, take a picture of the image that forms in your mind. Develop this imaginary picture and then describe it to your friends: For example, who is being baptized in this picture? How many people are present? How much water is there? How much oil? How much bread and wine?

WORDS TO REMEMBER

Find and define the following:

sacraments of initiation _____

_____

_____

conversion _____

_____

OnLine
WITH THE PARISH

When are baptisms scheduled in your parish? Are infants baptized during Sunday Mass? When is Confirmation celebrated in your diocese? How old do you have to be to be confirmed in your diocese?

Sometimes the names of new Catholics are printed in the parish bulletin. Can you think of a way to make them feel welcome? You may wish to invite them to a prayer service on the theme of the sacraments of initiation.

◆ Direct attention to *On Line with the Parish*. You may want to hand out copies of the weekly parish bulletin as a source for this information. To stay *On Line with the Parish*, see the *Enrichment Activities* suggested on page 66A.

Conclusion ___ min.

◆ Give the students a few moments to copy into their journals the prayer to the Holy Spirit given in *Life in the Spirit*.

◆ Encourage the young people to share *Highlights for Home*, page 77B, with their families.

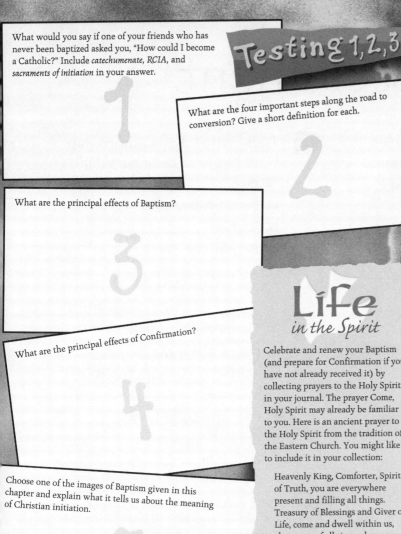

Testing 1,2,3

1. What would you say if one of your friends who has never been baptized asked you, "How could I become a Catholic?" Include *catechumenate, RCIA,* and *sacraments of initiation* in your answer.

2. What are the four important steps along the road to conversion? Give a short definition for each.

3. What are the principal effects of Baptism?

4. What are the principal effects of Confirmation?

5. Choose one of the images of Baptism given in this chapter and explain what it tells us about the meaning of Christian initiation.

Life in the Spirit

Celebrate and renew your Baptism (and prepare for Confirmation if you have not already received it) by collecting prayers to the Holy Spirit in your journal. The prayer Come, Holy Spirit may already be familiar to you. Here is an ancient prayer to the Holy Spirit from the tradition of the Eastern Church. You might like to include it in your collection:

Heavenly King, Comforter, Spirit of Truth, you are everywhere present and filling all things. Treasury of Blessings and Giver of Life, come and dwell within us, cleanse us of all sin, and save our souls, O Good One.

77

Closing Prayer: Play a tape of quiet instrumental music. While the music is playing, ask the small groups to hang their conversion statements around the room. Then pray together the prayer found in *Life in the Spirit.*

Evaluation: Have the young people discovered the importance and significance of the sacraments of initiation? Do they understand the relationship between Baptism and Confirmation?

Testing 1,2,3

1. See pages 68–70. To become a Catholic, you would need to prepare by participating in the RCIA. You would enter the catechumenate and prepare to receive the sacraments of initiation (Baptism, Confirmation, Eucharist).

2. See page 70. The four important steps along the road to conversion are: instruction, moral conversion, worship, and ministry. Accept specific explanations of each step.

3. See page 75. The principal effects of Baptism are taking away original sin and filling us with grace; making us members of Christ's body.

4. See page 75. The principal effects of Confirmation are sealing us with the Spirit and strengthening the grace of Baptism. We are incorporated more firmly into Christ and share more fully in the mission of Jesus Christ.

5. See page 72. Accept reasonable responses.

Answers for Chapter 6 Assessment

1. d	2. b	3. a	4. d	5. a
6. b	7. b	8. d	9. b	10. See page 75.

Assessment

 1 The sacraments of initiation are
   a. Baptism and Reconciliation.
   b. Baptism, Confirmation, and Reconciliation.
   c. Reconciliation and Eucharist.
   d. Baptism, Confirmation, and Eucharist.

 2 Conversion
   a. only happens before Baptism.
   b. is a lifelong task.
   c. means "to plunge."
   d. means "a time to watch and wait."

 3 The first step of the catechumenate is
   a. instruction.
   b. moral conversion.
   c. worship.
   d. ministry.

 4 At the Easter Vigil the newly baptized
   a. must leave church after the homily.
   b. begin religious instruction.
   c. do not receive the Eucharist.
   d. are also confirmed.

 5 _____ is the gateway to the Christian life.
   a. Baptism
   b. Eucharist
   c. Reconciliation
   d. Confirmation

 6 Those who have not been baptized but who die for the faith receive
   a. Baptism by water.
   b. Baptism of blood.
   c. Baptism of desire.
   d. all of the above

 7 At Confirmation the bishop
   a. pours water over a person.
   b. anoints a person's forehead with oil.
   c. only gives the homily.
   d. only asks questions of those to be confirmed.

 8 The second step of the catechumenate concerns
   a. religious instruction.
   b. ministry.
   c. worship.
   d. moral conversion.

 9 In _____ we are made members of Christ's body, the Church.
   a. the RCIA
   b. Baptism
   c. Confirmation
   d. the Rite of Election

 10 Explain the symbolism of anointing with oil at Confirmation. Write your response on the reverse side of this page.

Highlights for Home

Focus on Faith

In recent years the Rite of Christian Initiation of Adults (RCIA) has been adopted as a way of preparing adults and young people for Baptism and full communion with the Church. You may have noticed this rite in your own parish, especially during Lent and its culminating point, the Easter Vigil.

This chapter uses the RCIA as a jumping-off point to a deeper understanding of Baptism and Confirmation. Baptism is the beginning of our conversion, our turning toward the life of the Spirit. Confirmation strengthens, affirms, and deepens that conversion. The four points given to the RCIA candidates as points of preparation are areas of lifelong growth for all of us: instruction, moral conversion, worship, and ministry.

During Lent we have the opportunity to support our parish's catechumens and candidates in prayer as they prepare to receive Baptism, Confirmation, and Eucharist at the Easter Vigil. We welcome, promise our prayerful support, and realize how grateful we are for the gift of our Catholic faith.

Conversation Starters

. . . . a few ideas to talk about together . . . .

◆ Have I ever felt "called to conversion" in some way? What was it like? Did I feel good about making a new beginning? Did it have a long-term effect on my life?

◆ Has anyone asked me to change lately? How did I feel? How did I respond?

◆ How do I see Baptism, Confirmation, and Eucharist as a call to follow Christ?

Feature Focus

The *Scripture Update* on page 75 reminds us of the presence of the Holy Spirit in our lives. The first Scripture reference, Luke 4:16–22, recounts the incident in which Jesus read from the scroll in the synagogue and proclaimed, "The Spirit of the Lord is upon me." In the second, John 7:37–39, Jesus compares the Spirit to a river of living water within the believer. How is the Spirit upon you? In what direction is the river of living water, the Spirit, carrying you?

Reflection

The opening photograph on pages 66 and 67 shows a procession of young people, their hopeful faces illuminated by the candles they carry. Echoing Saint Ignatius of Antioch, they seem to be saying, "We are Easter people." What does it mean to be Easter people?

Easter is a time of new birth. The waters of Baptism are the womb of the Church. The Spanish phrase *dar a luz* ("to give birth") can be literally translated, "to give a light." New birth, new life, is new light. Baptism brings the new light of Christian life into the world.

My light is needed, too. Where? When?

OUR HOUSE OF PRAYER

Adult Focus

The ancient Hebrews were nomads. They had no fixed dwellings. They moved across the land, following their flocks and using tents for shelter. The ark of the covenant was sheltered in a tent. When Solomon built a Temple, another level of civilization was established. The Temple became the center of worship in Judaism.

Like the Temple, our churches are centers of worship. We gather in our churches in the name of Jesus to "continually offer God a sacrifice of praise" (Hebrews 13:15). Our church buildings symbolize what we live for in the present and long for in the future: the presence of God among us.

This chapter explores the significance of a parish church building as a gathering place for the celebration of the Eucharist and as a symbol of the body of Christ, which we, as the Church, are called to be. The artistic and architectural demands of such a building are explained, especially as Catholics seek a balance among the three elements of "seeing, hearing, and doing" in worship.

Catechism Focus

The themes of this chapter correspond to paragraphs 1179–1186 and 1197–1199 of the *Catechism*.

Enrichment Activities

Guest Speaker/Church Tour

You may want to arrange a church tour guided by a priest, deacon, or staff member of your parish. It might be helpful to make a copy of this chapter for the tour guide, highlighting the discussion of those parts of the church in which your group has expressed a special interest. Be sure to include the sacristy on your tour, with a look at vestments made and worn for special feasts and seasons.

Computer Connection

As a midsemester review, have the students use a crossword software program, such as *WordCross*®, to develop a crossword puzzle. Have the young people form small groups to develop lists of words or terms and corresponding clues used in Chapters 1 through 7. Then explain to the students that they can design their own puzzle step-by-step or let the computer automatically make a variety of puzzles from the same word list. Have the groups enter the word list and clues into the computer. Then have them print and exchange the puzzles.

Teaching Resources

	Overview	Opening Prayer Ideas	Materials
SESSION 1	**Discovery:** To understand the history of sacred space in the Christian tradition; to appreciate the parish church as a sign of Christ's presence among his people.	Look at the photographs on pages 78 and 79. Then pray together Ephesians 2:19–22. As you pray, think of your own parish church.	These will be needed for every session: texts, Bibles, highlighters or colored pencils, journals. • large cardboard boxes • half sheets of construction paper • recording of a song on the theme of God's house
SESSION 2	**Exploring 1:** To explore the ways in which the design of a church helps us participate in each of the four parts of the celebration of the Eucharist.	Ask volunteers to take turns reading the story of Jacob's dream in Genesis 28:10–22. Pray aloud together verse 17.	
SESSION 3	**Exploring 2:** To become more familiar with the parish church as a place of prayer and worship.	Express your thanksgiving for the house of God by prayerfully reading Psalm 27A.	
SESSION 4	**Exploring 3:** To understand the reasons for different styles, arrangements, and decoration of churches; to realize where the principal beauty of a church is found.	Picture yourself in your parish church. You may want to picture one part of it or something in it that helps you pray. As a prayer of thanksgiving, pray Psalm 26:6–8.	• recording of Gregorian chant with English translation
SESSION 5	**Putting It Together:** To deepen appreciation of the parish church building as a symbol of Catholic life and worship.	Read aloud Matthew 4:8–10. Ask Jesus for the courage and strength you need to worship and serve God.	• copies of handout *Standing Faithfully*, page 78C • copies of *Chapter 7 Assessment*, page 89A • copies of *Highlights for Home*, page 89B

Supplemental Resources

Videos
• *St. Etheldreda's: A Silent Witness* (Story of Britain's oldest Catholic Church)
• *Seven Cities of God* (Story of Father Junipero Serra's founding of missions)

Ignatius Press
P.O. Box 1339
Ft. Collins, CO 80522

Faith and Witness Journal: Liturgy & Worship

For Chapter 7 see pages 28–31.

CHAPTER
seven

Standing Faithfully

Read the prayer below. Then write your responses to each question.

The Brick

The bricklayer laid a brick on the bed of cement.
Then, with a precise stroke of his trowel, spread another layer
And, without a by-your-leave, laid another brick.
Then foundations grew visibly,
The building rose, tall and strong, to shelter men.

I thought, Lord, of that poor brick buried in the darkness at
    the base of the big building.
No one sees it, but it accomplishes its task, and the
other bricks
    need it.
Lord, what difference whether I am on the rooftop or in the
    foundations of your building, as long as I stand faithfully
    at the right place?

—Michel Quoist

Reflection

◆ I am a brick, a "living stone" in the Church. How do I feel about my position in the body of Christ? in my parish?

◆ Do I ever feel buried in darkness? When? Why?

◆ Do I ever feel recognized for what I am or do? When?

◆ When do I feel needed in my family, school, or parish? among my friends?

◆ Do I feel that I am in the right place for now? Why? Why not?

Our House of Prayer

LORD, I love the house where you dwell,
the tenting-place of your glory.
Psalm 26:8

Objective: To understand the history of sacred space in the Christian tradition; to appreciate the parish church as a sign of Christ's presence among his people.

Introduction ___ min.

Note: Before the session begins, have volunteers help you gather large cardboard boxes. Use the containers to construct a church wall. On a sheet of construction paper, print "Jesus Christ." Explain that this sheet represents the church cornerstone. Tape or paste this sheet onto one of the bottom church wall corners.

Opening Prayer: Have the young people imagine a world that has no churches, temples, synagogues, or mosques. Ask, "What do you think society would be like if there were no buildings in which to worship or if people were kept from gathering in churches to pray?"

Invite the young people to look at the photo collage on pages 78 and 79. Proclaim together Psalm 26:8

on page 79. Read each of the following prayer beginnings, and ask the young people to write their own conclusions in their journals.

- Jesus, when I see church steeples or domes, . . .
- Jesus, when I look at the crosses against the blue sky, . . .
- Jesus, when I hear the bells ringing, . . .
- Jesus, when I feel the glow and warmth of the lights and candles, . . .
- Jesus, when I see the pillars and arches, . . .
- Jesus, when I gather with the parish community, . . .

Ask a volunteer to read Ephesians 2:19–22. If possible, play a recording of the song "This Alone" by Tim Manion (*Lord of Light*, Oregon Catholic Press) or another song on the theme of God's house. As the young people listen, have them tape their stones to the church wall. Then pray together:

We are living stones, built upon Christ,
who is God's chosen cornerstone.

Presentation ___ min.

◆ Read aloud the question posed in the introductory paragraph on page 80. Invite a volunteer to list the young people's responses on the board.

◆ Emphasize that during Jesus' public ministry, he gave witness by praying with the Jewish community in the Temple in Jerusalem and by reading Scriptures and praying in village synagogues. Ask a volunteer to read page 80.

◆ Point out that the disciples of Jesus did not need symbols of him because he was with them physically. Ask a volunteer to read the first four paragraphs on page 81. Then have the young people highlight the statements that are highlighted here.

◆ Point out that churches are not immune from natural disasters or man-made tragedies. You may want to tell this story of one parish community. A parishioner wrote this to a friend:

Several years ago our little church was completely gutted by fire. The outside of the building and many of the stained-glass windows were saved, but everything else was destroyed. We celebrated Mass in the school auditorium and at the Methodist church nearby. Some of our parishioners refused to worship with our community until the original church building was restored. Those of us who stayed were strengthened by the Spirit in bonds of friendship, genuine concern for each other, and a deeper sense of fellowship. One Sunday the pastor asked, "What *is* a church, anyway?" A small child raised her hand and replied, "The church needs people. The Church is *us*!"

◆ Invite reactions to the story. Ask, "If you had been in that situation, what would you have done? Would you have stayed with the community even if you had to celebrate Mass in less-than-perfect conditions?" "What does this story tell us about the place of the church building in our lives?"

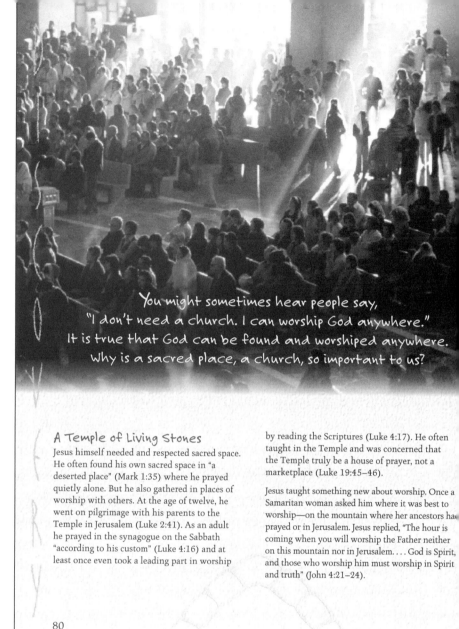

You might sometimes hear people say, "I don't need a church. I can worship God anywhere." It is true that God can be found and worshiped anywhere. Why is a sacred place, a church, so important to us?

A Temple of Living Stones

Jesus himself needed and respected sacred space. He often found his own sacred space in "a deserted place" (Mark 1:35) where he prayed quietly alone. But he also gathered in places of worship with others. At the age of twelve, he went on pilgrimage with his parents to the Temple in Jerusalem (Luke 2:41). As an adult he prayed in the synagogue on the Sabbath "according to his custom" (Luke 4:16) and at least once even took a leading part in worship by reading the Scriptures (Luke 4:17). He often taught in the Temple and was concerned that the Temple truly be a house of prayer, not a marketplace (Luke 19:45–46).

Jesus taught something new about worship. Once a Samaritan woman asked him where it was best to worship—on the mountain where her ancestors had prayed or in Jerusalem. Jesus replied, "The hour is coming when you will worship the Father neither on this mountain nor in Jerusalem. . . . God is Spirit, and those who worship him must worship in Spirit and truth" (John 4:21–24).

80

Conclusion ___ min.

◆ Have the young people form small buzz groups to discuss the following questions:

• How would you react if public worship was forbidden in this country?

• How can you show appreciation for having a church building within which to worship and having the freedom to worship there?

◆ Ask, "What happens when tyrants or dictators close churches and do not allow people to gather to celebrate the sacraments?" Direct attention to the photo on page 80. Explain that it shows the gathering of the worshiping community in the Basilica of Our Lady of Guadalupe in Mexico City. Then share the story of Father Miguel Pro.

hat does this mean? It means that we now
orship God in the Spirit and truth of Jesus, the
n of God. Although we do need places to worship,
sus tells us that he himself is the primary place,
e temple where God dwells. As he said on one
casion, "'Destroy this temple and in three days I
ll raise it up.' . . . He was speaking about the
mple of his body" (John 2:19–21). Through the
craments of initiation, we are incorporated into
is new temple, this body of Christ. We are now
e sign and sacrament of God's presence on earth.

ur worship of God in the body of Christ, in the
irit and truth of Jesus, "is not tied exclusively to
y one place. The whole earth is sacred" (Catechism,
79). In this sense it is true that we do not need
urch buildings. But this is not the whole story.

ter Jesus ascended into heaven, his disciples
ould gather on the first day of the week to keep
s message alive and to celebrate his risen presence
the Eucharist. They needed a *place* to do this: a
ace to come together, to tell their stories, and to
are their meal.

first the early Christians met in one another's
mes. Later, when assemblies grew larger
d worship in public became more
ceptable, they used Roman basilicas
r their gatherings. A *basilica* was
t a temple or a place of worship;
ther, it was a building designed
r public meetings and other
isiness. Even later, when
hristians began to design and
iild their own churches, they
sed the familiar basilica form as
model, often adapting it to the shape
a cross.

any churches all over the world were
iilt according to this model. The words
se, nave, and narthex are still used to describe
ese areas in a church building:

apse: a semicircular domed area

nave: a large open assembly area

narthex: a lobby, porch, vestibule.

The House of God

Our parish church, the place where we gather
to worship, is a visible sign of our faith. It is the
place where God dwells, the tenting place of
his eucharistic presence. It is not only a house
for us, for the Church, but also God's house.
Churches are not simply gathering places; they
symbolize and "make visible the Church living
in this place, the dwelling of God" with us in
Christ (*Catechism*, 1180).

The parish church is a visible witness to the
presence of Christ, who lives among his people:
"Behold, God's dwelling is with the human race.
He will dwell with them and they will be his
people and God himself will always be with them"
(Revelation 21:3).

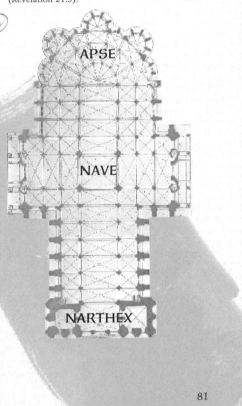

APSE

NAVE

NARTHEX

81

FORUM Assignment

✔ Read pages 82 and 83. Underline in
pencil the statements that express
five main ideas.

✔ Imagine that you are living in the
year A.D. 2100. Write a letter to the
editor to dispute someone's suggestion that the churches in your area
be closed and torn down because,
according to this person's opinion,
only outside space is sacred.

Closing Prayer: Explain to the young
people that as a firing squad raised its
guns to kill Father Pro, he stretched out
his arms to form a cross and cried,
"Viva Cristo Rey" ("Long live Christ the
King"). Invite the young people to
stand and to stretch their arms out to
form a cross. Ask them to listen carefully as you read Ephesians 3:14–21.
End the prayer with the acclamation,
"Viva Cristo Rey!" or "Long live Christ
the King!"

FYI Father Miguel Pro was a Mexican Jesuit
priest who was ordained in Belgium in
1925. Upon his return to Mexico City
in 1926, he found that religious persecution in
Mexico had increased and that public worship
was forbidden. But this did not stop Father Pro
from bringing the word of God and the sacraments to the people. He celebrated Mass in
their homes, traveling secretly and often in
disguise.

One day in November 1927, he was seized by
the police. He was executed ten days later.

FOR SESSION 2

• Prepare volunteers for opening prayer.

Objective: To explore the ways in which the design of a church helps us participate in each of the four parts of the celebration of the Eucharist.

Introduction ___ min.

Opening Prayer

Forum: Have the young people form small groups to share their letters to the editor concerning the importance of preserving rather than closing and destroying local church buildings. Direct each group to choose the most persuasive letter, and have a volunteer "editor" share it with the group as a whole.

Discuss with the students the statements they underlined on pages 82 and 83. Have them highlight or underline in color the main ideas that are highlighted here.

Presentation ___ min.

◆ Ask a volunteer to summarize *Catholic Teachings* on page 83. Have the young people highlight the last two sentences. Explain that the doors of a church are symbols of Jesus Christ. In the Prayer of Blessing of new church doors, the celebration emphasizes this symbolism:

> He is the Good Shepherd;
> he is the door through which
>   those who follow him
> enter and are safe, go in and go out, and find
>   pasture.

Tell the young people that in the late Middle Ages and during the Renaissance, the Church commissioned famous sculptors to design doors for churches and baptistries. Explain that Lorenzo Ghiberti (1378–1455) depicted the life of Christ and the four evangelists on the doors of the cathedral baptistry in Florence, Italy.

◆ Have volunteers explain the symbolism and use of the president's chair, the lectern, and the altar.

◆ Emphasize that because the altar represents Christ, we give it special reverence. Remind the students that the priest shows reverence to the altar at the beginning and at the end of the Eucharist.

A Place of Celebration

Our parish church serves multiple purposes, but the most important is the celebration of the Eucharist. Earlier in this book, when we described the celebration of the Eucharist, we spoke of gathering, storytelling, meal sharing, and commissioning. In each of these aspects, how does the church building itself help us to celebrate the Eucharist? How does the design or shape of the church serve these four functions?

Gathering The church is the place where we gather for worship. We gather to do something together. This fact makes the design of a church different from the design of a sports stadium or a movie theater, for example. Most large public spaces have a stage where the action takes place and an area set aside for the spectators or audience. In church there is no stage because at Mass there is no audience. We are all *doers*, and the entire assembly area is the stage.

If we visit an empty church, the gathering area will look strange. The space only looks "right" when it is being used. Visiting an empty church is something like visiting an amusement park during the winter when it is closed. We can imagine what the park looks like with lights flashing, music playing, crowded with happy people. But the park needs actual people and real activity to look right. And the nave of the church needs a worshiping assembly of people to look right.

From wherever we stand in the assembly area, our attention is drawn to three important pieces of furniture: the presider's chair, the lectern, and the altar. The presider's chair is positioned so that the priest is seen to be both a member of the assembly and the leader of the assembly. In the principal church of a diocese, the chair (*cathedra* in Latin) for the bishop gives its name to the entire building, the *cathedral*.

82

Storytelling The church must be designed for the proclamation of God's word. We must be able to hear and see well. Good acoustics (sound quality) and sight lines are very important for this function.

The readings are proclaimed from the *lectern*, or *ambo*, a reading stand upon which the lectionary is placed and from which we proclaim the word of God.

It may be hard to believe, but originally Catholics worshiped standing. Even today the standing posture indicates that the worshiper is alert and ready to follow in the footsteps of Jesus. Standing is a mark of both reverence and readiness.

In the fifteenth century, as the readings and sermon became longer, Christians began to sit for the Liturgy of the Word. Pews and fixed seating began

Point out the altar, the presider's chair, and the lectern or ambo

Ask, "Why is the altar anointed with oil?" (Because it is a symbol of Christ, the Anointed One.) Explain that when an altar is anointed, the bishop stands before it and says:

> We now anoint this altar.
> May God in his power make it holy,
> a visible sign of the mystery of Christ,
> who offered himself for the life of the world.

The bishop then pours chrism (oil) on the middle of the altar and on each of its four corners. It is recommended that he anoint the entire table of the altar with the chrism.

be used in churches at about the time that the printing press was invented. People in church began to line up like lines on a printed page to hear the word of God read to them from a printed book.

Meal Sharing As the liturgical action moves from storytelling to the sharing of our meal, our attention moves from the lectern to the altar. The altar is not an ordinary table. On the *altar* the sacrifice of the cross is made present under the sacramental signs. The altar is also the table of the Lord, to which we are all invited.

The altar, which is anointed with oil when a church is dedicated, also represents Christ, the Anointed One. As a sign of love for Christ, the priest greets the altar with an act of reverence at the beginning and end of the Eucharist.

In the thirteenth century Catholics did not receive Holy Communion frequently. Instead looking at the sacred Host after the consecration became the high point of the Mass. So Catholics began to kneel during the eucharistic prayer. As the practice of kneeling was extended, kneeling benches were introduced, often attached to the back of the chairs or pews.

Commissioning Following Communion we are dismissed and commissioned to take the gospel message from the church to our daily lives in the world. What happens in the church must be connected to our lives outside the church. This connection is made clearer when the design and furnishings of the church building are related to the community it serves.

Describe the many ways your parish church helps you to celebrate the liturgy.

CATHOLIC TEACHINGS

About Churches

The Eucharist not only remembers and makes present the past (the Last Supper) but it also makes present the future, our banquet with Christ in heaven. The church building that houses the Blessed Sacrament is a sign of this future banquet, the world to come. When we enter a church, we know that we are entering a very special, "heavenly" place, a symbol of the Father's house toward which we are journeying.

83

Conclusion ___ min.

◆ Explain to the young people that the church Francis rebuilt by hand still stands today, as does the universal Church he helped to renew.

◆ Ask, "What does it mean to say that a church building is 'related to the community it serves'?" Think about the ways your church building or parish facilities serve the community (for example, through adaptations made to serve those with disabilities).

◆ Discuss the thought provoker on page 83.

FORUM Assignment

✔ Read pages 84 and 85. Underline in pencil the statements that express six main ideas.

✔ Imagine that time travelers from the future have arrived in your parish church on a quiet afternoon. The travelers have never seen your church before but have time to walk around. As they do so, they transmit information to the Church members of the future. Make a list of everything the time travelers see.

Closing Prayer: Suggest that the group pray a litany of thanksgiving for all the parish churches in the area. As many as possible should be mentioned by name. For example, "For the parish church of St. Michael the Archangel, let us praise and thank the Lord."

FOR SESSION 3

• Prepare the volunteers for opening prayer.

FYI A small and neglected church played a major role in the conversion of Saint Francis of Assisi. One day, as he was praying, he heard a voice say, "Francis, rebuild my church." Francis answered, "Yes, Lord." Joyfully he began gathering stones to repair the little church. Only later did he realize that the Lord had meant him to rebuild not only that one church but the universal Church, the body of Christ on earth. Francis made the little church the headquarters of his new order. He died there in 1226.

SESSION 3

Objective: To become more familiar with the parish church as a place of prayer and worship.

Introduction ___ min.

Opening Prayer

Forum: Have the students gather in small groups with their time traveler lists. Direct them to take a few moments to compare their lists and to add to their lists if necessary. Then ask each group to appoint a "Church Checker" to review pages 84 and 85, calling out the items and areas in the parish church mentioned in the text (for example, baptistry, ambry, reconciliation chapel). Have the rest of the group circle these items on their own lists and add any that are missing. Remind the group that the circled items are the ones we will be learning more about in this session.

Ask the young people to share the statements they underlined on pages 84 and 85. Then have the students highlight or underline in color the statements that express the main ideas that are highlighted here.

Presentation ___ min.

◆ Draw attention to *Catholic ID* on page 85 for a discussion of vestments. Explain that the color of the vestments changes with the seasons. Ask the group to recall the colors of the liturgical seasons from their own observation. A complete explanation can be found on page 111 (Chapter 9).

◆ Ask, "What things in the parish church remind us of our Baptism?" (the baptismal font or pool, the blessed water, the paschal candle because of its association with the Baptisms at Easter and the candle we all receive at Baptism as a symbol of the light of Christ)

◆ Have a volunteer explain what the ambry is and what it contains. Have another volunteer explain what the three kinds of oil are and how each kind is used in the celebration of the sacraments.

◆ Ask, "How is Christ present in the Eucharist?" List the young people's responses on the board. Then have a volunteer explain the two reasons we reserve the Blessed Sacrament in the tabernacle.

St. Mary's Cathedral, San Francisco

A Place of Worship

Because the sacrament of Baptism is the spiritual door to the Church, the baptismal font or baptismal pool is usually located near the front door when possible. In fact one early Church custom was to build the baptismal pool completely outside the church, in a separate building near the entrance. This building was called the *baptistry*. It signified the absolute need for Baptism before celebrating the Eucharist with the assembly. Today as we enter the doors of the church, we dip our fingers into blessed water and make the sign of the cross, that sign in which we were baptized. Each time we gather as the body of Christ for Eucharist, we continue and renew the celebration of our Baptism.

In this baptismal area you will also see a niche in the wall or a little chest called the *ambry*. It contains three vessels of oil: the oil of catechumens, which is used to bless and strengthen those preparing for baptism; the oil of the sick, with which the priest strengthens and heals those who are ill; and the sacred chrism, which is used in celebrating the sacraments of Baptism, Confirmation, and Holy Orders. The word *Christ* means "anointed one." So being anointed with oil is a sign of the

84

special and strengthening presence of Christ, the Anointed One.

The reconciliation chapel, a small space designed for the celebration of the sacrament of Reconciliation (confession), is often located in the baptismal area. This reflects the historical connection between the sacraments of Baptism and Reconciliation. As we will see in Chapter 10, the sacrament of Penance or Reconciliation developed from the need of those Christians who had not been faithful to their baptismal promises and who had separated themselves from the community by grave sin.

Another important area of a Catholic church is the place set aside for the tabernacle. Sometimes this is a side chapel; sometimes it is a prominent place in the sanctuary. The *tabernacle* is the place in which the Eucharist is kept, or reserved. The word comes from the Latin for "tent" or "little house."

We have seen that Christ becomes present at the Eucharist in several ways. At different times during the eucharistic celebration, our attention is directed to these different ways in which Christ is really present: He is present in the gathered assembly and in the person of the priest.

◆ Emphasize the importance of the eucharistic chapel or place where the Eucharist is reserved and the reconciliation chapel. Ask, "Why is the reconciliation chapel often located near the baptismal area?" (If we are not faithful to our baptismal promises, we need the sacrament of Reconciliation.)

◆ Direct attention to the second full paragraph in the right-hand column on page 84. Note the use of the word *sanctuary*, which means "holy place" and refers here to the area around the altar. Explain that sometimes *sanctuary* refers to an ancient Church custom of providing "a safe place," a place free from violence. Because of the presence of the Blessed Sacrament, no violence was permitted in a church. This meant that those who were fearful of violence against them could take refuge there. Even lawbreakers were allowed this privilege. The civil authorities could not arrest them if they sought *sanctuary* in the church. This was the

e is present in the Scriptures. He is present ost especially under the forms of bread and ne. And as we are commissioned to out into the world, we find Christ esent there also.

arist is also present in the *Blessed crament,* that is, in the Eucharist served in the tabernacle. The Blessed crament is reserved in this way so at the eucharistic Bread may be taken those who are sick and to those who e dying. In addition the tabernacle s become the focus for the adoration Christ under the eucharistic species. atholics have a long tradition of aying before the tabernacle.

Bonus

The vestments worn by the priest at the liturgy have their roots in the earliest years of the Church. Originally they came from the way that ordinary people dressed. Today their function has changed. As powerful visible parts of our liturgy, they help us to celebrate the sacred mysteries of the Church. Like everything connected with the liturgy, vestments should be beautiful and well made because they are part of our worship of God.

Bonus

me churches are spacious enough to include a icharistic chapel, a space especially designed for ivate prayer and adoration. This quiet place mply yet beautifully emphasizes and honors the al presence of Christ in the Blessed Sacrament.

lamp or candle burning before the tabernacle dicates to Catholics that the consecrated Bread is esent there. Candles will also be found in other evotional areas and in the assembly area of the hurch. At every Mass candles are lit. Once they ere used primarily to give light for reading the criptures and celebrating the sacred action. Now at churches are fitted with electric lighting, ndles have lost much of their practical function. et their symbolic purpose remains.

he beautiful quality of candlelight reminds us Christ, the Light of the World. As a candle onsumes itself in the service of the liturgy, so ust we in the service of God and of others. A ndle is also a symbol of the continual presence God to us and of us to God.

Find time this week to make a visit to the Blessed Sacrament. In your prayer tell sus anything that is on your mind or in your heart.

85

Conclusion ___ min.

◆ Direct the students' attention to the thought provoker on page 85. Adapt this suggestion to your group's situation. You may want to suggest a visit to the prayer corner as an alternative or as an additional quiet time for prayer.

FORUM Assignment

✔ Read pages 86 and 87. Underline in pencil the statements that express three main ideas.

✔ Do you have a favorite statue or picture that helps you pray? If it is portable, bring it to the *Forum* tomorrow. Be prepared to explain what it means to you and how it helps you. If the object cannot be transported, write a brief description of it, and be prepared to say what it means to you.

Closing Prayer: Explain to the young people that Saint Nicholas of Flüe was a Swiss hermit who was a great peacemaker in the fifteenth century. He was known to everyone as "Brother Klaus." The following prayer, composed by this saint, recalls the exclamation of the apostle Thomas as he recognized the risen Jesus: "My Lord and my God!" (John 20:28). It is a good prayer to say when making a visit to the Blessed Sacrament. Pray these words together:

My Lord and my God,
take me from all that keeps me
from you.
My Lord and my God,
grant me all that leads me to you.
My Lord and my God,
take me from myself and
give me completely to you.

FOR SESSION 4

• recording of Gregorian chant with English translation

Church's way of giving a "time-out" to those who might need it, especially when the fairness of the system of justice was questionable.

Invite the young people to express their opinions on this concept. Ask, "Should it be revived for use in our country today?"

◆ Have the group review quietly the discussion of the last two paragraphs on page 85. Ask, "Why do you think candles are good symbols to use in prayer and during the Eucharist?" Invite the young people to recall times when they or members of their family have lit candles as a way of praying symbolically. (possible answers: during times of illness or death, when praying for a much-needed intention)

SESSION 4

Objective: To understand the reasons for different styles, arrangements, and decoration of churches; to realize where the principal beauty of a church is found.

Introduction ____ min.

Opening Prayer

Forum: Have the young people form small buzz groups to discuss the ways in which the statues or pictures they chose help them to pray. Have each small group choose a recording secretary to report their discussion to the group as a whole. Then invite the students to place their statues, pictures, or written descriptions in the prayer corner or another prominent area in the room.

Point out that physical objects can help us to pray. Ask, "What might happen if we have too many objects before our eyes?" (They might be distracting.) Explain that this session may help us to appreciate the balance needed.

Have the young people share the statements they think express the main ideas on pages 86 and 87. Then have them highlight or underline the statements that are highlighted here.

Presentation ____ min.

◆ Play a recording of Gregorian chant for which an English translation is provided. Direct the young people to close their eyes and experience the soothing sounds of the music. When the selection is finished, have them open their eyes. Ask, "How did the music affect you?" "How did it make you feel?"

Then write the English translation of the Latin words on the board. Play the music again, and ask the students to read the words in a prayerful manner. Ask, "Did knowing the meaning of the words help you to pray with the music?" "How was this different from listening the first time?"

Ask a volunteer to summarize the first paragraph under "Finding the Balance," on page 86. Ask, "Why do you think the bishops decided that liturgy should be celebrated in our own languages?"

Seeing, Hearing, Doing

Like our homes, church buildings can tell us so much just by the way they look. In some older churches, for example, you may find many paintings, statues, mosaics, and perhaps even several altars. Modern churches do not have these. Why are there such differences?

In the early days of the liturgy, when Latin was the spoken language of the congregation, both the ear and the eye had something to do. The ear listened to the meaning of the words, and the eye followed the sacred action. As Latin became less and less understood by the people in the congregation, their ears had less to do. So churches began to be more elaborately decorated to become feasts for the eyes.

In the early Middle Ages, a greater stress began to be placed on the sacrificial dimension of the Eucharist, and Holy Communion was received only by the clergy. Therefore the altar was moved farther away from the faithful and was placed against the wall.

From early times this wall had been decorated with a painting of the cross, the Lamb of God, or Christ in glory. These paintings now began to be placed on the altar itself. The altar was filled with statues or paintings: first the crucifixion, then the patron saint of the parish or town. Later other saints were added.

Finding the Balance

After the Second Vatican Council (1962–65), the bishops determined that the liturgy would once again be celebrated in our own languages. Once again we can understand Sacred Scripture and the prayers at Mass. As our ears became active again, we discovered that sometimes too many decorations in the church could distract us from concentrating on what we were hearing! Today we Catholics are looking for a balance of seeing, hearing, and doing.

86

Does this mean that newer churches are better than the older ones? Does this mean that churches should have no decoration at all? No, absolutely not. We will not strengthen the ear by starving the eye. No one wants to remove statues and decorations from our churches simply to get rid of them. Statues and beautiful objects of art, banners and flowers will always be an important part of the environment for our worship.

Many churches have stained-glass windows. In former times the pictures formed by the stained glass, in addition to bathing the assembly area with beautiful light, illustrated Bible stories for those who could not read. But stained-glass windows are not merely history lessons. Their artistic beauty reveals to us something of the beauty of God.

Around the walls of many churches, you will find the stations of the cross. This is a set of pictures, statues, or even simple crosses (numbered from one to fourteen) which mark incidents in the last journey of Jesus to the cross.

Scripture UPDATE

An image from the Bible that tells us about our union with Christ is that of a "building." Saint Peter told the first Christians, "Like living stones, let yourselves be built into a spiritual house to be a holy priesthood to offer spiritual sacrifices" (1 Peter 2:5). And in the preface for the dedication of a church we pray,

You continue to build your Church with chosen stones, enlivened by the Spirit, and cemented together by love.

What does it mean to you to be a "living stone"?

FYI In the early days of the Church, some Church leaders felt that pictures (called *icons*) should not be allowed in churches. "God is spirit," they reasoned, "and should not be portrayed in any way." They were called *iconoclasts* (image breakers). Other Church leaders reasoned that because God became Man in Jesus, the use of pictures and statues was allowed and even encouraged. It took the Second Council of Nicaea (A.D. 787), to resolve this issue in favor of icons.

Chancery Chapel, Diocese of Victoria (Texas)

his form of devotional prayer became popular the late Middle Ages. The desire of Christians follow in the footsteps of Jesus on his way to e cross had led to a long tradition of pilgrimage the Holy Land. Those who could not afford e expense of the long and dangerous trip to rusalem could, by praying the way of the cross, rticipate in the passion of Jesus in their own llages. Either individually or as a parish, we still ray the stations of the cross today, especially ring Lent. We go to each station and meditate an event of the passion. However, the church primarily a place for our liturgical worship. rsonal devotions, such as the stations of the oss, should not distract from the principal rpose of the assembly area.

There is a great variety in the way Catholic churches are decorated. Some have many statues; others have none. Some churches have marble altars and golden ceilings; others have simple wooden altars and plaster ceilings. When we visit the home of friends, we know that the warmth, hospitality, and friendship we experience there are more important than the cost or style of the furniture. In the same way, in a Catholic church the principal beauty is found in the hospitality of our assembly, our devotion to the Eucharist, and the love we carry forth to our brothers and sisters.

 Describe those things in your parish church that help you to pray.

87

FORUM Assignment

✔ Prepare your responses to *Things to Think About* and *Things to Share*.

✔ Imagine that you have been called in as a consultant to a new parish. They have not yet designed their church. They need your help in deciding what their church should look like inside and out. They also want your opinion on the name they might choose for their parish. What would you tell them they need? How would you plan their church? What name would you recommend?

Closing Prayer: Ask the students to form two lines, facing one another. With palms flattened and facing out, have them raise their arms and reach toward the person across from them and join hands palm to palm. Explain that they have just made a church with a peaked roof.

Invite the young people to repeat each line of Psalm 24:9–10:

Lift up your heads, O gates;
    rise up, you ancient portals,
    that the king of glory may enter.
Who is this king of glory?
    The LORD of hosts is the king of
        glory.

Then ask the young people to drop hands and conclude by recalling that Jesus is present with us and that we are temples of the Holy Spirit.

 **FOR SESSION 5**

• copies of handout *Standing Faithfully*, page 78C
• copies of *Chapter 7 Assessment*, page 89A
• copies of *Highlights for Home*, page 89B

Conclusion ___ min.

◆ If you chose to share the *FYI* with your group, ask, "How do images beautify and enhance our worship?" "What would our churches be like without images (statues, pictures, icons, stained-glass windows)?"

◆ Draw attention to the thought provoker on page 87. You might expand this discussion by asking, "Of all the things in our parish church that help you to pray, what helps you the most?"

◆ Ask the students to review the second column on page 87. Then ask, "What is the principal beauty of a Catholic church?" Explain the old saying "Beauty is in the eye of the beholder." To emphasize the beauty of the Catholic Church that can never change, have the young people highlight the last sentence on this page.

SESSION 5

Objective: To deepen an appreciation of the parish church building as a symbol of Catholic life and worship.

Introduction ___ min.

Opening Prayer

Forum: Have the young people form small groups to share their plans and ideas for a new parish. Direct each group to imagine that they are the "parish council." Each consultant should try to answer any questions the council members may have. After all members have shared their plans, each council should consolidate their ideas into one plan to present to the whole group. Each small group should choose one member to present the plan to the group as a whole.

Distribute the handout *Standing Faithfully*. Remind the young people that they are temples of the Holy Spirit. Allow a few minutes for the young people to write their responses to the "Reflection" questions. Remind them of their importance to all in the Church.

Presentation ___ min.

◆ Discuss *Things to Think About* and *Things to Share*. Remind the young people of the saying "Beauty is in the eye of the beholder." Ask, "If every parish needs the same things in its church, why is each parish church unique?" "Why wouldn't one parish just copy what another parish has done?" Explain that communities, just like people, are unique and need to express that uniqueness. Ask, "What makes your parish unique?" "What makes your parish church unique?"

◆ Direct attention to *On Line with the Parish*. Form a research committee to gather the photos suggested. You may want to plan a special display for the entire parish to enjoy on the anniversary of its founding or the feast of its patron. You may want to include the young people's scale models and the posters or booklets suggested in the last paragraph of *Life in the Spirit*.

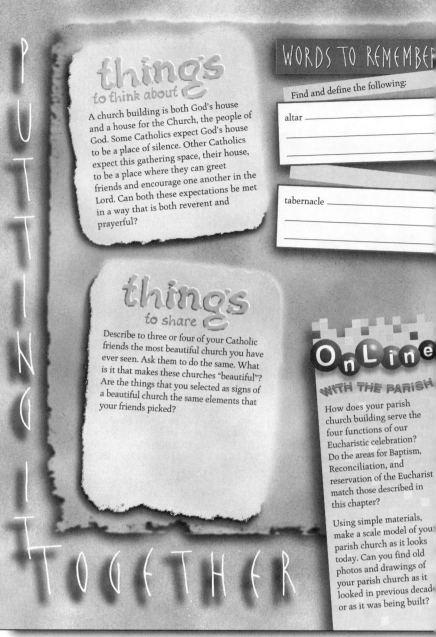

things to think about

A church building is both God's house and a house for the Church, the people of God. Some Catholics expect God's house to be a place of silence. Other Catholics expect this gathering space, their house, to be a place where they can greet friends and encourage one another in the Lord. Can both these expectations be met in a way that is both reverent and prayerful?

things to share

Describe to three or four of your Catholic friends the most beautiful church you have ever seen. Ask them to do the same. What is it that makes these churches "beautiful"? Are the things that you selected as signs of a beautiful church the same elements that your friends picked?

WORDS TO REMEMBER

Find and define the following:

altar _____

tabernacle _____

OnLine WITH THE PARISH

How does your parish church building serve the four functions of our Eucharistic celebration? Do the areas for Baptism, Reconciliation, and reservation of the Eucharist match those described in this chapter?

Using simple materials, make a scale model of your parish church as it looks today. Can you find old photos and drawings of your parish church as it looked in previous decades or as it was being built?

PUTTING IT TOGETHER

◆ Direct attention to *Words to Remember*. The definition of *altar* may be found on page 83; the meaning of *tabernacle* is discussed on page 84.

Assessment: Suggest that the students work independently to complete *Testing 1, 2, 3*. You may want to list the reference pages for each answer on the board. If time permits, have the students share their answers with the entire group.

If you are administering *Chapter 7 Assessment*, page 89A, allow the students ten minutes to complete the test.

◆ Encourage the young people to share *Highlights for Home*, page 89B, with their families.

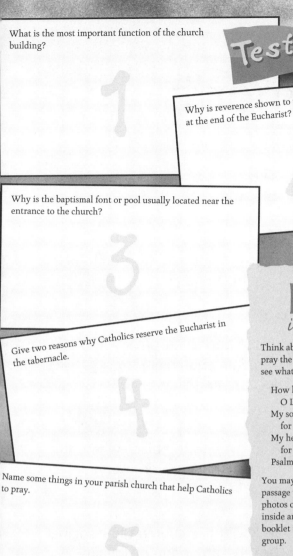

What is the most important function of the church building?

1

Why is reverence shown to the altar at the beginning and at the end of the Eucharist?

2

Why is the baptismal font or pool usually located near the entrance to the church?

3

Give two reasons why Catholics reserve the Eucharist in the tabernacle.

4

Name some things in your parish church that help Catholics to pray.

5

Life in the Spirit

Think about your parish church. Then pray the following prayer slowly, and see what meaning it has for your life:

How lovely your dwelling,
O LORD of hosts!
My soul yearns and pines
for the courts of the LORD.
My heart and flesh cry out
for the living God.
Psalm 84:2–3

You may want to illustrate this passage with several drawings or photos of your parish church, both inside and out. Make a poster or booklet to share with others in your group.

89

Testing 1,2,3

1. See page 82. Our parish church serves multiple purposes, but the most important is the celebration of the Eucharist.

2. See page 83. The altar represents Christ. As a sign of love for Christ, the priest greets the altar with an act of reverence at the beginning and end of the Eucharist.

3. See page 84. Because the sacrament of Baptism is the spiritual door to the Church, the baptismal font or baptismal pool is usually located near the front door when possible.

4. See page 85. The Blessed Sacrament is reserved in the tabernacle so that it may be taken to those who are sick and to those who are dying. In addition the tabernacle has become the focus for the adoration of Christ in the Blessed Sacrament.

5. Accept reasonable responses.

Conclusion ___ min.

Closing Prayer: Direct the young people's attention to *Life in the Spirit*. Ask them to pray the verses from Psalm 84 quietly. Then have them close their eyes as you play a recording of a song that celebrates the house of the Lord, dwelling with God, or a similar theme. Ask them to picture their own parish church as you play the song.

Evaluation: Do the young people appreciate their parish church as a beautiful symbol of faith? as the gathering place of the community around the Eucharist and the other sacraments? as the house of God? Do they understand what the principal beauty of the Catholic Church is?

Answers for Chapter 7 Assessment

1. i   2. d   3. b   4. a   5. f
6. e   7. g   8. h   9. c   10. See page 81.

Assessment

Choose the correct letter for the term that completes each of the statements below.

a. apse

b. basilica

c. devotion to the Eucharist

d. the early Christians

e. narthex

f. nave

g. president's chair

h. tabernacle

i. Jesus

1 _____ taught us that we must worship God in Spirit and in truth.

2 _____ met for worship in one another's homes.

3 A _____ was a building designed for public meetings in which Christians met for worship.

4 The _____ is a semicircular domed area in a church.

5 The _____ is a large open assembly area.

6 The _____ is a lobby, porch, or vestibule of a church.

7 Three important pieces of furniture in a church are the _____, lectern, and altar.

8 The _____ is the place where the Eucharist is kept, or reserved.

9 In a Catholic church the principal beauty is found in hospitality, _____, and the love we carry forth to our brothers and sisters.

10 Why do we need churches?

_____

_____

_____

_____

_____

_____

Highlights for Home

Focus on Faith

In one city where Catholic roots are strong, people often identify their neighborhood by naming their parish: "I live in Our Lady of Refuge." "I live in St. Philip's." The parish is our spiritual home, and the parish church symbolizes what "dwelling with God" means. The parish church is the place in which we share the family meal, the Eucharist. There we are fed with the Bread of Life and there the Blessed Sacrament is reserved in the tabernacle.

As you share this chapter on the church building with your son or daughter, note the last sentence on page 87. It reminds us that no matter what the style of the parish church, the true beauty of the church consists in the hospitality of the parishioners, their devotion to the Eucharist, and their sharing of love.

Conversation Starters

. . . . a few ideas to talk about together. . . .

◆ What do you particularly appreciate about your parish church? Do you have a favorite window, statue, or picture that you like to look at?

◆ How does the atmosphere of the church affect you when you pray alone? during a sacramental celebration?

Feature Focus

The *Scripture Update* feature on page 86 presents two sources for consideration: the Scripture passage from 1 Peter 2:5, in which we are called "living stones," and the preface for the dedication of a church. The verse from 1 Peter is "let yourselves be built." It seems to suggest that we have a choice. We *allow* ourselves to become a real part of this structure. The dedication preface hints at the only way this can be done: We must be "cemented together by love." Christian love is like cement—strong, binding, and lasting!

Reflection

Take a few moments to look at the collage of churches on pages 78 and 79. The variety of architectural styles illustrates that the Church takes all that is human and uses it for the service of God. Picture your own parish church. Place it, just for now, at the top of a high mountain. You see it from a distance and begin to walk the road toward it as you pray the following words:

Send your light and fidelity,
*   that they may be my guide*
And bring me to your holy mountain,
*   to the place of your dwelling,*
That I may come to the altar of God,
*   to God, my joy, my delight.*

Psalm 42(43): III, 3–4

SEASONS OF PRAISE

Adult Focus

"Seasons of Praise" invites us to recall the ways in which the prayer life of the Church is intimately connected with the cycle of nature: coming to life, flowering, dying, and rising once again. The major liturgical seasons of Lent-Easter, Advent-Christmas, and the periods of Ordinary Time provide an opportunity for us to grow in our understanding of the paschal mystery of Christ and the ways in which God is present in our lives.

In this chapter the young people are encouraged to explore the seasons of the Church year in which the Church unfolds the entire mystery of Christ from his incarnation until his ascension, Pentecost, and the anticipation of his return in glory. It is a mystery so rich that no one single prayer or liturgical celebration can ever completely express it. They will discover the grace and mystery of God's time of salvation in which the saving acts of his Son continue to happen in their lives today.

Catechism Focus

The theme of Chapter 8 corresponds to paragraphs 638–640, 1163–1171, 1361–1366, 2180–2188 of the *Catechism*.

Enrichment Activities

Medleys of the Seasons

The young people might enjoy putting together taped medleys of secular and spiritual songs on the following themes: nature's seasons, the seasons of our lives, the seasons of the Church year. Appropriate selections might include "Winter Grace" (from the album of that name, by David Haas and Jeanne Cotter, GIA); "All My Life's a Circle" by Harry Chapin; and "Summertime Blues" by Eddie Cochran.

Making Growth Charts

Using newsprint or long strips of wallpaper, have partners work together to make a teen-year variation on the growth charts by which children measure their changing height. Have them mark off their present height. In the space between that mark and the bottom, have them record and illustrate their growth as Catholics (for example, Baptism, First Eucharist, Confirmation, participation in retreats, ministries).

A Personal Church Season Calendar

Have the young people refer to the explanation of the Church seasons on page 190. Invite them to make their own Church year calendars. They may wish to include illustrations or photos of symbols that help them understand the meaning of these seasons.

Teaching Resources

	Overview	Opening Prayer Ideas	Materials
SESSION 1	**Discovery:** To appreciate the ways in which the liturgical year helps us to enter into the paschal mystery.	Write a prayer about being in touch with God through nature.	These will be needed for every session: texts, journals, Bible, highlighters or colored pencils. • objects for human camera activity
SESSION 2	**Exploring 1:** To explore the meaning of the Lord's Day.	Pray together Psalm 111:1–5. Reflect on its "clues" about ways to keep the Lord's Day holy.	• writing and art materials • copies of handout *Quite a Character* • bell (optional)
SESSION 3	**Exploring 2:** To explore Baptism as the key to understanding the season of Lent.	Proclaim Ephesians 4:1–6. Write the fifth verse in your journal and pray it often.	• thematic music • parish hymnals (optional) • long strips of drawing paper
SESSION 4	**Exploring 3:** To understand the Triduum and the ways we prepare for Easter.	Share a dramatic reading of John 20:11–18. Sing an Alleluia.	• duplicated chart forms (optional) • display area for *Forum* presentations
SESSION 5	**Putting It Together:** To recall the meaning of the liturgical year, the Lord's Day, and the Triduum.	Proclaim Ecclesiastes 3:1–8. Pray that today is filled with peace.	• copies of *Chapter 8 Assessment* • copies of *Highlights for Home*

Supplemental Resources

Videos
Seasons of Life
Sheed & Ward
P.O. Box 419492
Kansas City, MO 64141

Lent: A Time of Renewal
St. Anthony Messenger Press
1615 Republic Street
Cincinnati, OH 45210

**Faith and Witness Journal:
Liturgy & Worship**
For Chapter 8 see pages
32–35.

CHAPTER eight

Quite a Character

Some young people model themselves after a favorite professional athlete or popular musician. As people grow older, their tastes and values change. However, the most important thing about any young person never changes. He or she was marked at Baptism with the "character" of Jesus. The way we reflect that character is unique to each of us. Take the following *Quite a Character* test to see how you are doing in your life right now.

Choose a number between 1 and 5 to indicate how strongly you are reflecting each Jesus quality (5 = highest level, 1 = lowest level).

Jesus' Character Traits in Me	My Level of Reflection 1 2 3 4 5
Faithful to God's will	
Faithful to prayer/worship	
Compassionate to those in need	
Openness in sharing faith	
Forgiving toward others	
Healthy self-love	
Healthy friendships	
My total score =	

Add your total score. Decide for yourself how well you are reflecting Jesus' character traits. Choose one trait you will exercise this week. Describe how you will do that.

90C

Every day I will bless you;
I will praise your name forever.
Psalm 145:2

Seasons of Praise

Objective: To appreciate the ways in which the liturgical year helps us to enter into the paschal mystery.

Introduction ___ min.

Opening Prayer: Prepare construction paper pennants and print one of the following titles of poems by the poet Robert Frost on each pennant:

- "To the Thawing Wind"
- "A Prayer in Spring"
- "Putting in the Seed"
- "Stopping by Woods on a Snowy Evening"
- "Looking for a Sunset Bird in Winter"
- "Fireflies in the Garden"
- "In Time of Cloudburst"
- "The Wind and the Rain."

Display the pennants around the room. Invite the young people to choose one of the titles and write in their journals a poem or a prayer of their own describing an experience of being in touch with God through nature in the season that the title suggests to them. Explain that the poem or prayer should communicate the ways in which God speaks to us through the changing seasons of the year. (Make colored pencils and fine-line markers available for those who wish to use them.) To aid the writing process, you may want to play quiet instrumental music, such as *Songbirds of Spring* (Nature Recordings) or *Harboring the Holy* by Robert M. Hutmacher, OFM, (GIA). Allow about ten minutes for this activity. Tell the young people that those who wish to share their poems or prayers with the group may do so during the *Closing Prayer*.

Chapter Warm-up: Invite responses to the photographic collage on pages 90 and 91. Ask, for example, "Do you have a favorite season? What is it? Why is it your favorite?" "What do the changing seasons tell us about life? about God?" Read the following lines of Thomas Moore's prayer poem "God's Presence in Nature." Encourage a sharing of ideas about the reflections of God they find in nature.

Thou art, O God, the life and light
    Of all this wondrous world we see,
Its glory by day, its smile by night,
    Are but reflections caught from Thee.
Where'er we turn, Thy glories shine,
And all things fair and bright are Thine!

Presentation ___ min.

◆ Have someone read aloud the opening question on page 92. Invite reflection on the seasons of the young people's lives. Ask, "Which part of the cycle of life—coming to life, growing, flowering, dying, being born again—are you in now?" Explain that the cycle may refer to our entire lives from birth to physical death to cycles we go through repeatedly as we grow and change.

◆ Ask volunteers to read pages 92 and 93. Then have the young people underline in color or highlight the main ideas that are highlighted here.

◆ Have the young people form small groups. Give each group a three-dimensional object to observe in detail—for example, an ornate crucifix, a statue, a decorative vase, a flower arrangement. Direct the group leaders to place the object in the center of a table. Explain that each person should imagine that she or he is a camera and should sit at a different angle to and a different distance from the object. He or she may not move, nor may the object be moved. Have each person close one eye and "take a sixty-second exposure" of the object, focusing on every detail that can be seen from that one point of view. When the minute is up, the leader writes a three-dimensional description of the object based on what each "camera" saw. Then invite one or more of the group leaders to present their three-dimensional portraits.

Point out to the young people that our celebration of the liturgical year enables us to "walk around," or get different angles on, the mystery of Christ from his incarnation to his return in glory.

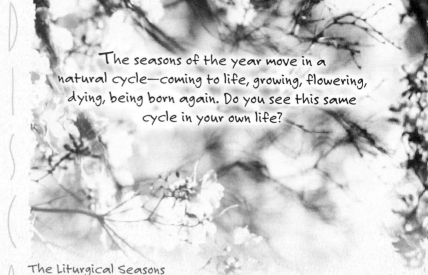

The seasons of the year move in a natural cycle—coming to life, growing, flowering, dying, being born again. Do you see this same cycle in your own life?

The Liturgical Seasons

Our life of prayer in the Church follows the same beautiful cycle of coming to life, growing, flowering, dying, being born again. Just as the seasons give variety to nature, the seasons of the liturgical year (the Church's year) give variety to the liturgy. Our life of prayer has its seasons also.

The two principal seasons of the liturgical year are formed around the two great feasts of Easter and Christmas. First we will explore the season of Easter and its preparation period, Lent. Then we will look at the season of Christmas and its preparation time, Advent. Finally we will explore Ordinary Time, the period between the Lent-Easter season and the Advent-Christmas season.

We can see a certain parallel with the birth, life, death cycle of the natural year. We can think of two great moments, birth and death, separated by the ongoing experiences of growing and changing. The Church year, then, has two main seasons, Lent-Easter and Advent-Christmas, separated by two seasons of Ordinary Time.

The seasons of the Church year do not exist simply for the sake of variety or change; they serve a much deeper purpose. As we have learned, each time we celebrate the liturgy, we celebrate the paschal mystery of Christ. In the liturgical year, the Church unfolds the entire mystery of Christ. This mystery is so complex and rich in meaning that no one single prayer or liturgical celebration can ever express it adequately.

For example, let's say that your mom or dad buys a car which you hope might be yours someday (now this takes some imagination!). You want to take a photograph of it to send to a friend. Where are you going to stand to take the picture? From the side, the picture won't show the lines of the hood and grille. If you stand in front, the picture won't show the fender wells. There is no way a flat piece of photographic film can fully capture the beauty of the three-dimensional object. Perhaps the best you can do is to walk around the car and take pictures from various angles and perspectives.

The liturgical year helps us to "walk around" the paschal mystery. During the course of a year, we view it from different angles, in different lights. Within the cycle of a year, the Church unfolds the whole mystery of Christ, from his incarnation and birth until his ascension, the day of Pentecost, and the expectation of his return in glory.

92

◆ Invite volunteers to serve as a trio or quartet of liturgical singers. If possible, play a recording of the African-American spiritual "Were You There." Then have a volunteer in the back of the room hold up cue cards with the following "Were You There" questions to be sung by the group. Direct the young people to reflect quietly about their response to each question.

• Were you there when Jesus Christ was born?
• Were you there when Jesus was baptized?
• Were you there when they shared the Last Supper?
• Were you there when they crucified my Lord?
• Were you there when he rose from the dead?

As we celebrate the mystery of Christ, we are not merely recalling past events. When we celebrate in memory of Jesus, our liturgical remembering (anamnesis) makes the mystery present.

The liturgy enables us to pass from our past-present-future concept of time into God's time of salvation, so that the grace and mystery of the event remembered are in some way made present. When we hear the passion of Christ proclaimed on Good Friday and sing "Were You There When They Crucified My Lord?" the answer is *yes!* You were there! You are there now! You do not have to feel disappointed that all the wonderful events of our faith happened long before you were born. These wonderful events of Christianity are happening now, *today*.

Before we look at the various seasons of the liturgical year, we will look at the word that gives us the key to understanding why we have a liturgical year in the first place. That word is *today*.

A prayer from the psalms that we often find in the liturgy is:

Oh, that today you would hear his voice:
Do not harden your hearts....
Psalm 95:7–8

The liturgical year, with its various feasts and seasons, helps us to keep our hearts open *each day* to the voice of God in our lives and in our world.

Throughout the liturgical year we experience for ourselves what Saint Paul described: "Behold, now is a very acceptable time; behold, now is the day of salvation" (2 Corinthians 6:2). These wonderful events of Christianity are happening now, *today*.

93

FORUM Assignment

✔ Read pages 94 and 95. Underline in pencil the sentences that express six main ideas.

✔ Using any method you prefer, make up a "Dream Sunday" schedule. Indicate what you would do from the time you wake up until you turn in at night. Indicate where you would like to be and who, if anyone, would be with you. Just be sure your "Dream Sunday" pleases both you and Jesus.

Closing Prayer: Gather around the prayer table. Play the nature recording or instrumental music used in the *Opening Prayer*. Invite the young people to share, on a voluntary basis, their poems or prayers in response to Robert Frost's titles. Close by praying together Psalm 145:2 on page 91.

Conclusion ___ min.

◆ Read aloud or have a student who is prepared to do so present this brief reflection:

Oh, that today you would hear God's voice in the beauty of bird song or the howling of the wind . . . in the greeting of a parent or a call from a friend . . . in the crying of a child or the whisper of the aged . . . in the words of Scripture or the lyrics of an inspired song . . . in your own voice praying or in unbroken silence. Oh, that today you would hear God's voice.

FOR SESSION **2**

- writing and art materials
- copies of handout *Quite a Character*
- bell for *Closing Prayer* (optional)

Objective: To explore the meaning of the Lord's Day.

Introduction ___ min.

Opening Prayer

Forum: Choose a student host to conduct a TV talk show on the theme "Dream Sundays." Have the host invite participants to share their schedules and explain why they think their choices would also please Jesus. Members of the audience may question or comment on any of the dreams that are being shared. The host summarizes the kinds of activities, places, and companions chosen. If time allows, he or she might write on the board categories of activities, such as prayer or worship, entertainment, resting or relaxing, music or sports, "hanging out" with friends, visiting the sick or elderly, and getting in touch with nature.

Presentation ___ min.

◆ Have volunteers share the statements they underlined on pages 94 and 95. Ask all to underline the key statements that are highlighted here.

◆ Conduct a three-minute brainstorming session in which you challenge the young people to come up with as many meaningful ways as they can think of to complete the statement: "Sunday is _____."

(Among those to be included from the text are: the key to the liturgical year, the Lord's Day, a day to gather for worship, the day of Christ's resurrection.) Have two volunteer recorders alternately write the responses on the board as quickly as possible.

◆ Have the young people form small groups of "resurrection messages makers." Provide writing and art materials for the young people to use to produce any of the following: teleprompter scripts, radio ad scripts, bumper stickers, posters or banners, billboard designs. Direct the students to come up with appealing messages that will remind people of the resurrection in the midst of a world that is often filled with messages of frustration, disappointment, suffering, and death. Ask the message makers to consider these questions:

The Lord's Day

When most Catholics think of the major feasts of the liturgical year, they usually think of Christmas and Easter. But the *original* Christian feast day is Sunday. Sunday is the key to the whole liturgical year.

At the time of Jesus, Sunday was called "the first day of the week." The other days were simply numbered in order: the second day, the third day, and so on. The only day given a special name was the seventh day, the Sabbath. Each of the four gospels mentions explicitly that the resurrection of Jesus took place on "the first day of the week"—that is, Sunday.

The name for Sunday came originally from the Romans, who gave each day of the week a name honoring either a heavenly body or one of the gods (for example *Sun*day for the sun). The early Christians renamed the first day of the week, the Sun's Day, and called it the Lord's Day. In English the day is still called "Sunday"; "the Lord's Day" is only used in the context of religion. In some other modern languages, however, the very name on the calendar is literally "the Lord's Day": *domenica* in Italian, *domingo* in Spanish. All of these come from the Latin word for "Lord," *dominus*. But whatever we name it, this day is our primary holy day because this day was chosen by God to transform history! This is the day Christ rose from the dead.

The Christian celebration of Sunday has a different focus from the Jewish sabbath. Jews rest on the sabbath because God rested on the seventh day: "God blessed the seventh day and made it holy, because on it he rested from all the work he had done in creation" (Genesis 2:3). The Christian Sunday is primarily a day to assemble for worship. At first the Christian Sunday was a workday like the other days of the week; only later did it take on the Jewish characteristic of a day of rest.

The Sunday assembly for Eucharist is at the very heart of the meaning of Sunday. As we sit at the eucharistic table—with Jesus, with the disciples, with all those who believed in the resurrection throughout ages past, and with all those who will

believe in ages to come—past, present, and future become one. We come to the table of the One who died in the past and taste the future banquet of heaven. We sing of our confidence in life:

Dying you destroyed our death,
rising you restored our life.

We sing of our freedom:

Lord, by your cross and resurrection
you have set us free.

In which eucharistic acclamation do we proclaim our faith that Christ will come again?

94

• How can you help people to believe that everything will turn out right in the end?

• How will you communicate that Jesus has conquered sin, grief, loss, and death?

Allow as much time as possible for this project. Share the results today or in Session 3.

...ay of Resurrection

...hat we think about Sunday depends on what we ...ink about the resurrection. Do you believe in the ...surrection? You will surely answer yes to that ...uestion. But what if we ask, "Do you believe in the ...surrection not only as a historical event but also ...s happening *now*?"

...hat does it mean to believe that the resurrection ...s now? Consider this: Have you ever watched ...he tape of a sporting event on television already ...nowing that your favorite team had won ...he game? Knowing the ending can take the ...xcitement out of a ball game, but it can certainly ...ive you confidence and hope at those times when ...our team seems to be losing. Or have you ever ...vatched a movie that you have seen before? In ...pite of all the twists and turns of plot, you already ...now that everything turns out all right in the ...nd. In the same way, the resurrection tells us that ...verything will turn out more than "all right" for ...s. The resurrection tells us that sorrow will be

overwhelmed by joy, loss by victory, and death by new life. This is the role the resurrection of Jesus plays in our daily lives.

There are times when life can be discouraging and the world disappointing. There are times when we look around us and see so much pain and violence that we are tempted to wonder: Is death winning the battle? But in the midst of all that is evil in the world, the resurrection is God's great cry of triumph. The resurrection is our proof that life has a happy ending. The risen Jesus is our proof that loving and forgiving one another even as God loves and forgives us is a road that leads, not to death, but to life. The resurrection lets us know that God is in charge. Sin and evil will never win in the end. God's love and God's life will triumph.

CATHOLIC TEACHINGS

About Sunday

The teaching of the Church is clear. The most important way Catholics praise God and honor the risen Christ is by participating in the Eucharist, our source of strength and joy. This is the obligation of every Catholic. This means that, except for a serious reason, we must worship God at the liturgy. Another way to celebrate Sunday is to share strength and joy with others through visiting the sick, the infirm, and the elderly. Our Sunday celebration can be enriched by spending time with our families and by setting aside extra quiet time for prayer and reading.

Spending leisure time well is important for everyone. "Traditional activities (sports, restaurants, etc.), and social necessities (public services, etc.), require some people to work on Sundays, but everyone should still take care to set aside sufficient time for leisure" (*Catechism*, 2187).

Conclusion ___ min.

◆ Have someone read aloud *Catholic Teachings* on page 95. Emphasize that although some people have to work on Sundays, God wants all of us to find a way to be with him in prayer and leisure for whatever time is available to us.

FORUM Assignment

✔ Read pages 96 and 97. Underline in pencil the sentences that express four main ideas.

✔ Reflect on the character traits of Jesus listed on the handout *Quite a Character*, and complete the test. Be prepared to share some of your insights.

Closing Prayer: Form a circle around the prayer table. Have a text open to page 95 with its illustration of "Christ is risen." If possible, have a volunteer ring a bell throughout the memorial acclamation. Sing any familiar version of the following verse:

> Dying you destroyed our death, rising you restored our life. Lord Jesus, come in glory.

FYI Whenever we need reassurance that bad news is not the last word in our lives, we should tune in to the voice of a fourteenth-century saint. Julian of Norwich was a wise and holy woman who wrote her prayer conversations with Jesus. During one prayer session Jesus seemed to say to Julian, "You shall see for yourself that all manner of things shall be well." When Julian wondered how that could happen when there is so much evil in the world, Jesus seemed to answer, "Since I have brought good out of the worst-ever evil, I want you to know, by this, that I shall bring good out of all lesser evils, too."

FOR SESSION 3

- thematic music such as album *By Cross and Water Signed* by M.D. Ridge (OCP)
- parish hymnals (optional)
- illustrations of Jesus
- duplicated pictograph instructions (optional)
- long strips of drawing paper, markers

SESSION 3

Objective: To explore Baptism as the key to understanding the season of Lent.

Introduction ___ min.

Opening Prayer

Forum: If possible, display illustrations of Jesus and contemporary pictures of young people and others who reflect the character of Jesus. Have a student coordinator call on volunteers to share their responses to the handout *Quite a Character*. You may wish to have the coordinator write on the board those Jesus traits on which the young people score highest and lowest. Ask the young people to discuss why certain qualities seem to be more difficult for young teens to exercise. They may also share their chosen traits and tell how they plan to exercise them.

Presentation ___ min.

◆ Call attention to the photographs on pages 96 and 97. Ask volunteers to draw a connection between the photographs and something Jesus teaches us about death and growth. Point out that water, a symbol of Baptism, is prominent in the photo and is necessary for all life and growth. Encourage recognition that the grain of wheat must die and be buried in the soil before it can rise again as golden wheat. Discuss with the young people how and why we have to "die" to old ways that we have outgrown and to sinful habits before we can move on to a new and "more golden" stage of life in Christ.

◆ Have volunteers share the key ideas they underlined on pages 96 and 97. Then have them highlight or underline in color the statements that are highlighted here.

◆ For this activity have the young people work alone or with a partner. Play thematic music quietly in the background while the young people work. The title song and "The Seed That Falls on Good Ground" from the album *By Cross and Water Signed* by M.D. Ridge (OCP) would be appropriate.

The Lenten Retreat

You probably already know a lot about the liturgical season of Lent. *Lent is the time of preparation for the celebration of Easter. It begins on Ash Wednesday and extends to Holy Thursday. Lent is like a retreat. It is a time of prayer, fasting, and almsgiving (which means sharing what we have with the poor).*

When you hear the word *Lent,* what picture comes to mind? Penance, purple, fish, ashes, fasting, sacrifice, giving up movies? These are the images many Catholics associate with Lent. But your idea of Lent will be closer to the Church's meaning of the season if the first thing that comes to your mind is an image of new life—of Baptism. Baptism provides the key to Lent.

We have seen that in the fourth and fifth centuries, the Church developed liturgies to assist people who wanted to become Christians. The final forty days of this faith journey, the final "forty-day retreat" before Baptism, became what we now call Lent. Lent is the time for the catechumens to continue their preparation for Baptism, Confirmation and Eucharist. It is a time for those of us who are already baptized to reaffirm what this sacrament means in our lives today.

When was the last time you thought about your Baptism? For some Christians, Baptism is an event that happened long ago and does not have much impact on what they do today. But Baptism, as we have seen, changes us so radically that we are different, "marked" forever. Baptism gives us the spiritual mark that we call *character*. We are "characterized" by the life of Jesus that we find in the gospels. Once we are baptized, the promises of our Baptism should influence our decisions for the rest of our lives.

When we understand Baptism as the focus of Lent, the things we choose to give up can be more clearly understood. We saw that the ritual sacrifices in the Old Testament found their meaning in joyful union with God, not simply in the death of an animal or the destruction of something. Similarly our Lenten sacrifices are not a negative giving up of something. Rather, they direct us to a positive goal, joyful union with God.

96

Making Lenten Pictographs

A pictograph uses symbols to communicate a message. Design a pictograph using symbols, numbers, and a few key words to communicate the following messages:

- Baptism is the key to Lent.
- Lent can be seen as a forty-day retreat or faith journey.
- Baptism marks us forever with the "character" of Jesus.
- During Lent the Spirit tells us, "Give it up! Move on!"

Encourage everyone to review pages 96 and 97 before making their pictographs. Distribute markers and long strips of drawing paper. Display the completed pictographs.

ying and Rising

aptism is both a dying and a rising. Saint Paul says,
", then, we have died with Christ, we believe that
e shall also live with him" (Romans 6:8). The
nitential aspect of Lent, the "giving something
" part, is related to the dying aspect of Baptism.
t the "dying" is not an end in itself. We need to
ep our eyes fixed on the "rising" that Baptism
ers us.

t death, in whatever form it comes, is never
sy. Sometimes we resist change in our lives, even
ange for the better. Jesus promises us that life
ill spring out of death: "Unless a grain of wheat
lls to the ground and dies, it remains just a grain
f wheat; but if it dies, it produces much fruit"
ohn 12:24). The intention of the farmer is not to
ll the seed. Yet in order to grow, the seed must
range its life-form. It cannot remain the same
d seed!

ere is another example. When you were in the
rst grade, you were at the bottom of the heap;
verybody else was older and seemed stronger and
marter. They could write cursive, multiply, and
new the capitals of all fifty states. Now, however,

you are older and stronger and smarter. But just
when it seems that you are at the top, it is time for
you to move on. You have to start over again in
high school, and once again everyone else is older
and stronger and smarter.

What if you would decide that you don't want to
give up being at the top of the heap, that you want
to stay where you are, where you are comfortable?
You would probably be told, "Give it up! Move on!"

Sometimes we get attached to something that
keeps us from moving on. We can get caught at a
particular stage of growth in our Christian lives.
But during Lent we may hear the voice of the Spirit
tell us, "Give it up! Move on!"

The moving on does not have to be a big thing.
Rather, it is like the seed that needs to be planted—
something good in itself, but only in its proper
time. For most of us, moving on involves letting go
of something *good* in order to get *an even greater
good*. It means planting small seeds and looking
forward to a good harvest.

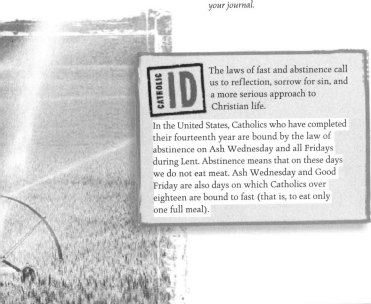 *Is there something now that keeps you from
moving on in your faith? Write about it in
your journal.*

CATHOLIC ID

The laws of fast and abstinence call
us to reflection, sorrow for sin, and
a more serious approach to
Christian life.

In the United States, Catholics who have completed
their fourteenth year are bound by the law of
abstinence on Ash Wednesday and all Fridays
during Lent. Abstinence means that on these days
we do not eat meat. Ash Wednesday and Good
Friday are also days on which Catholics over
eighteen are bound to fast (that is, to eat only
one full meal).

97

Conclusion ___ min.

◆ Invite the young people to use the
thought provoker on page 97 as a
journal exercise to help them come to
know themselves better.

◆ Have a volunteer summarize *Catholic
ID* on page 97. Then ask another person to clarify the difference between
fasting and abstinence.

FORUM Assignment

✔ Read pages 98 and 99. Underline in
pencil the sentences that express four
main ideas.

✔ Using any materials available to you,
make up or assemble one of the following to illustrate the symbols and
rituals of the Triduum ("three days"):
a three-dimensional display, a collage
or banner, a poem set to music. Be
prepared to share your work with the
group.

Closing Prayer: If possible, sing
"Unless a Grain of Wheat" by
Bernadette Farrell (OCP), which may be
found in the parish hymnal. Or you
may wish to have two student lectors
proclaim John 12:24–26 from the
Bible. All respond, "Jesus, we are your
followers."

FYI Marriage is not the only time when a
Catholic says "I do." Each year at Easter
we renew our baptismal promises. The
promises come in two parts: First, we say "I do"
to rejecting Satan and sin; then we reaffirm our
Catholic beliefs. By rejecting the empty promises
of Satan and accepting once again our faith in
Jesus Christ, we reveal our true identity.

FOR SESSION 4

• display area for *Forum* presentations
• duplicated chart forms (optional)

SESSION 4

Objective: To understand the Triduum and ways we prepare for Easter.

Introduction ___ min.

Opening Prayer

Forum: Have a place prepared for the display of the young people's Triduum illustrations. You may wish to display a paper streamer with the message "The Three Days: Easter Is Coming!" Have a student host invite participants to display and explain their illustrations. Encourage the group to offer comments or ask questions.

Presentation ___ min.

◆ Ask volunteers to share the main ideas they underlined on pages 98 and 99. Then have them highlight or underline in color the statements that are highlighted here.

◆ Print the terms *Lent* and *Triduum* on the board. Call for definitions of these key words. Explain that the former is from the Middle English word *lenten*, meaning "spring."

◆ Duplicate or put on the board the following chart:

The Triduum

The Holy Day   The Ritual

How We Prepare

Have the young people work with partners to fill in their charts using the information on pages 98 and 99. (The completed charts should show that the Holy Thursday ritual is the Mass of the Lord's Supper, which includes the washing of the feet; the Good Friday liturgy, which includes the reading of the Passion and adoration of the cross; the Easter Vigil liturgy, which includes blessing the new fire, lighting the paschal candle, singing Alleluias and the Easter Proclamation, and initiation of catechumens. We prepare for all three by fasting, praying, and reflecting on the meaning of the Triduum.)

The Triduum

Did you know that the oldest Christian feast is Sunday? Jesus rose on the Sunday after the Passover, and, remembering this, Christians began to celebrate the Sunday closest to the Jewish Passover with special solemnity. This "Christian Passover" became what we now call Easter.

The Christian Passover soon became the special time to celebrate the sacrament of Baptism, the sacrament of our passing over from death to life in Christ. As the rites and celebrations surrounding Christian initiation grew and developed, the Christian community found that one twenty-four-hour day was simply not enough time to experience the mystery, and the celebration was extended to three days. Today we call this celebration the *Triduum*, from the Latin word meaning "three days."

The Triduum took hundreds of years to develop into the three-day celebration we know today. Saint Augustine speaks of the Triduum of Christ crucified, buried, and risen. In Augustine's time the Triduum was Good Friday, Holy Saturday, and Easter Sunday. About two hundred years later, an evening Liturgy of the Lord's Supper became a part of the Holy Thursday celebration in Rome. The Triduum was then extended to include not only Friday but also the evening before Friday. The three-day observance now begins with the Mass of the Lord's Supper in the evening on Holy Thursday and ends with evening prayer on Easter Sunday.

The solemn liturgies of the Triduum are the most important liturgies of the Church year. The washing of the feet after the gospel of Holy Thursday is followed by the reading of the Passion and the adoration of the cross on Good Friday. At the Easter Vigil, the darkness and grief of Good Friday is broken by the blessing of the new fire and the paschal candle, the singing of the Easter Proclamation, the first sounds of the "Alleluia," and the sacramental initation of the catechumens.

These are ceremonies we can experience at no other time during the year. As we participate in them each year, they teach us the meaning of Christ's life, death, and resurrection, not in words alone, but in symbols and rituals: in fire, in water, in darkness, in light, in walking, in kneeling, in standing again. Describing these ceremonies or reading about them can never equal being there.

FYI In the Middle Ages when most people were unable to read, the Church often used music and drama to explain the liturgical "moment." For example, in Lent the joyful Alleluia was never heard. In some places to dramatize its absence the word was printed on a ball and thrown out the church door on Ash Wednesday, the first day of Lent! At the Easter vigil, the Alleluia was greeted with the extended ringing of bells every time it was sung.

reparing for Easter

takes a special kind of attention and alertness to ter into these mysteries. How can we come to ese events fully aware and prepared? The Church commends that we fast, especially on Good Friday nd, where possible, Holy Saturday as well. This sting is very different from dieting. The purpose f fasting is not to lose weight; its purpose is to gain sight into the mysteries of the Triduum. It is a fast awareness. It creates a hunger that can be satisfied nly by the best of foods: our Easter Eucharist, hich we share with those who join us at our ucharistic table for the very first time.

Catholics eighteen years of age and under are not obliged to fast, but even younger Catholics can prepare, through prayer and simple acts of love and selflessness, to celebrate the Triduum with an open heart and a clear mind. If we have prepared well, as we stand at the foot of the cross on Good Friday and look up at Jesus dying for us, all our doubts and questions—Why did my baby sister die? Why did my parents have to get divorced? Why does my dad drink so much? Why didn't our team win? Why don't I have more friends?—fade into one question. We simply ask, "Jesus, how much do you love me?" And he stretches wide his arms on the cross and answers, "This much."

As a group, plan ways you will prepare during Lent this year to celebrate the Triduum together in your parish.

Scripture UPDATE

A scriptural theme that can be followed throughout the Triduum is the symbol of the Lamb of God. On Holy Thursday the reading recalls the Passover lamb (Exodus 12: 1–8). On Good Friday Isaiah describes "the suffering servant" who is compared to a lamb (Isaiah 53:7). At the Easter Vigil the proclamation reminds us:

> This is our passover feast,
> when Christ, the true Lamb, is slain. . . .

On Easter Sunday this triumphant song praises the victorious Lamb:

> A Lamb the sheep redeems: Christ,
> who only is sinless,
> Reconciles sinners to the Father.

99

✔ Read pages 100 and 101. Prepare your responses to *Things to Think About* and *Things to Share*.

✔ Review all the photographs in Chapter 8. Choose one and write a one-paragraph explanation to describe how the image helps you to appreciate the Church's seasons of praise.

Closing Prayer: Direct the young people to stand in two lines that inter-sect to make a cross. Have them link arms and pray together:

> We adore you, O Christ, and we bless you; because by your holy cross you have redeemed the world.

Then invite the young people to form a circle. Read aloud the last stanza of Hopkin's poem "Easter."

> Seek God's house in happy throng;
> Crowded let His table be;
> Mingle praises, prayer and song,
> Singing to the Trinity.
> Henceforth let your souls always
> Make each morn an Easter Day.

Conclusion ____ min.

◆ Invite the young people to do the following journal exercise based on the closing paragraph on page 99. Reflect on the questions we might ask Jesus as we stand at the foot of the cross on Good Friday. Write the questions that ring true in your life and any other questions you would ask Jesus.

◆ Use the thought provoker on page 99 to initiate planning for a group celebration of the Triduum.

◆ Ask a volunteer to read *Scripture Update* on page 99. If time allows, sing any familiar version of "Lamb of God."

FOR SESSION 5

- Prepare volunteers for opening prayer.
- copies of *Chapter 8 Assessment*
- copies of *Highlights for Home*
- list of parish projects (optional)

SESSION 5

Objective: To recall the meaning of the liturgical year, the Lord's Day, and the Triduum.

Introduction ___ min.

Opening Prayer

Forum: If possible, have the young people arrange their desks and chairs in a circle. Invite a volunteer host to open the discussion by describing the *Forum Assignment*. Then have the host call on members of the group to indicate which photograph in the text they chose and to share their one-paragraph explanation. You may also want to have the host ask participants to describe what kind of art they would have used to illustrate Chapter 8 and why.

Discuss *Things to Think About* and *Things to Share*.

Presentation ___ min.

◆ Call attention to the *Words to Remember* on page 100. The description of *Lent* may be found on page 96; the explanation of the *Triduum* appears on page 98.

Assessment: Suggest that the students work with partners to complete *Testing 1, 2, 3*. If time allows, have the partners share their responses with the group.

If you are administering *Chapter 8 Assessment*, page 100A, allow about ten minutes for the students to complete the test.

◆ Have a volunteer read *On Line with the Parish*. If possible, present the group with a list of specific tasks that the parish liturgy committee needs help with during the Church year. You may also want to find out whether the young people might participate in decorating the church for a particular season or feast.

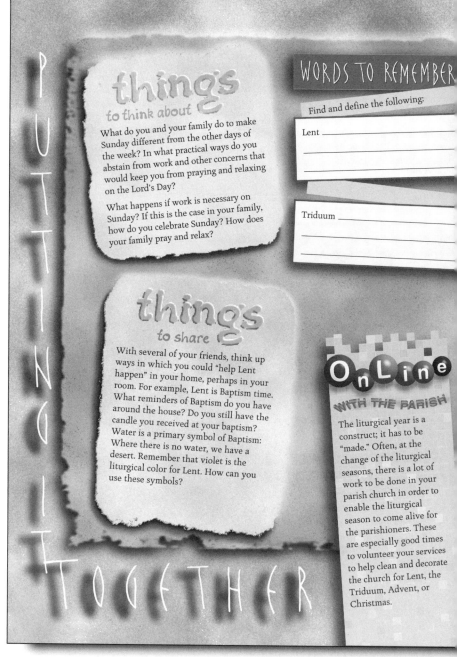

things to think about

What do you and your family do to make Sunday different from the other days of the week? In what practical ways do you abstain from work and other concerns that would keep you from praying and relaxing on the Lord's Day?

What happens if work is necessary on Sunday? If this is the case in your family, how do you celebrate Sunday? How does your family pray and relax?

things to share

With several of your friends, think up ways in which you could "help Lent happen" in your home, perhaps in your room. For example, Lent is Baptism time. What reminders of Baptism do you have around the house? Do you still have the candle you received at your baptism? Water is a primary symbol of Baptism: Where there is no water, we have a desert. Remember that violet is the liturgical color for Lent. How can you use these symbols?

WORDS TO REMEMBER

Find and define the following:

Lent _____

Triduum _____

OnLine WITH THE PARISH

The liturgical year is a construct; it has to be "made." Often, at the change of the liturgical seasons, there is a lot of work to be done in your parish church in order to enable the liturgical season to come alive for the parishioners. These are especially good times to volunteer your services to help clean and decorate the church for Lent, the Triduum, Advent, or Christmas.

Conclusion ___ min.

◆ Remind the young people to share the *Highlights for Home*, page 101, with their families.

Closing Prayer: Have a volunteer read aloud the first paragraph of *Life in the Spirit*. Ask the young people to reflect on the prayer during a brief period of silence. Then offer the prayer aloud together.

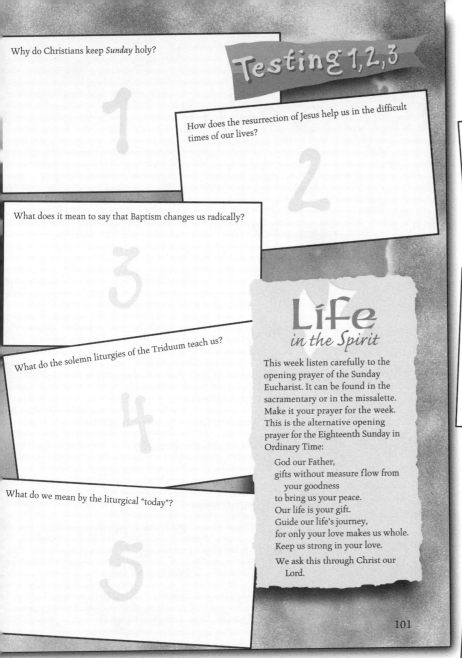

Why do Christians keep *Sunday* holy?

How does the resurrection of Jesus help us in the difficult times of our lives?

What does it mean to say that Baptism changes us radically?

What do the solemn liturgies of the Triduum teach us?

What do we mean by the liturgical "today"?

Testing 1, 2, 3

Life
in the Spirit

This week listen carefully to the opening prayer of the Sunday Eucharist. It can be found in the sacramentary or in the missalette. Make it your prayer for the week. This is the alternative opening prayer for the Eighteenth Sunday in Ordinary Time:

God our Father,
gifts without measure flow from
   your goodness
to bring us your peace.
Our life is your gift.
Guide our life's journey,
for only your love makes us whole.
Keep us strong in your love.
We ask this through Christ our
   Lord.

101

Testing 1,2,3

1. See page 94. Christians keep Sunday holy because Sunday is the day Christ rose from the dead. Sunday is primarily a day to assemble for worship.

2. See page 95. The resurrection tells us that sorrow will be overwhelmed by joy, loss by victory, and death by new life. The resurrection is our proof that loving and forgiving one another leads to life and lets us know that God's love and life will triumph.

3. See page 96. Baptism changes us so radically that we are different, "marked" forever. We are "characterized" by the life of Jesus that we find in the gospels. Once we are baptized, the promises of our Baptism should influence our decisions for the rest of our lives.

4. See page 98. The solemn liturgies of the Triduum teach us the meaning of Christ's life, death, and resurrection, not in words alone, but in symbols and rituals.

5. See page 93. By the word *today* we mean that the wonderful events of Christianity are happening now. The liturgy enables us to pass from our past-present-future concept of time into God's time of salvation, so that the grace and mystery of the event remembered are in some way made present.

Evaluation: Do the young people understand the meaning of the liturgical year, the Lord's Day, and the Triduum? Do they appreciate the baptismal focus of Lent?

Answers for Chapter 8 Assessment

1. d   2. c   3. d   4. a   5. a
6. d   7. a   8. b   9. d   10. See page 99.

Assessment

1 The liturgical year
- **a.** unfolds the mystery of Christ.
- **b.** follows a cycle of birth, life, and death.
- **c.** has ten main seasons.
- **d.** both a and b

2 When we celebrate in memory of Jesus,
- **a.** we live in the past.
- **b.** we live in the future.
- **c.** he is present to us today.
- **d.** none of the above

3 Sunday is
- **a.** the original Christian feast.
- **b.** the Lord's Day.
- **c.** the day of Christ's resurrection.
- **d.** all of the above

4 For Christians Sunday is
- **a.** primarily a day of worship.
- **b.** primarily a day of fasting.
- **c.** primarily a day of rest.
- **d.** just like the Jewish Sabbath.

5 The resurrection of Jesus
- **a.** is our proof that life has a happy ending.
- **b.** has no meaning for us.
- **c.** should not be celebrated every year.
- **d.** meant sin had triumphed.

6 Lent is a time for
- **a.** remembering our Baptism.
- **b.** praying, fasting, giving alms.
- **c.** letting go of some things.
- **d.** all of the above

7 By our Baptism we are
- **a.** marked with the character of Jesus.
- **b.** not changed.
- **c.** freed from making sacrifices.
- **d.** denied free will.

8 Triduum refers to
- **a.** three days before Christmas.
- **b.** three-day celebration of the paschal mystery.
- **c.** a town in ancient Rome.
- **d.** days at the beginning of Lent.

9 Celebrating the Triduum
- **a.** involves symbols and rituals.
- **b.** recalls Christ's death and resurrection.
- **c.** begins on Holy Thursday.
- **d.** all of the above

10 How can we best prepare for Easter?

_____

_____

_____

_____

Highlights for Home

Focus on Faith

In a Christmas sermon (1625), the English poet John Donne observed "Now God comes to thee, not as in the dawning of day, not as in the bud of the spring, but as the sun at noon to illustrate all shadows . . . all occasions invite his mercies, and all times are his seasons." When we as Catholics actively connect with the Church's liturgical year, we experience the truth of "all times are his seasons."

Each liturgical season (Advent-Christmas, Lent-Easter, Ordinary Time) links us with the unfolding mysteries of Christ's life. Each Sunday calls us to be present once again at the key event in salvation history: the resurrection of Jesus from the dead. The Lord's Day reminds us that he has overcome death—and so will we.

Family life is deeply enriched when we focus on and participate fully in the Church year.

Conversation Starters

. . . . a few ideas to talk about together . . . .

◆ What is our favorite part of the liturgical year? Why?

◆ How might we make our Sundays a more joyful, peaceful, or loving celebration of Christ's resurrection?

◆ What forms of fasting might we pledge ourselves to during Lent or at other times when we want to gain spiritual insight?

Feature Focus

The *Catholic Teachings* feature on page 95 focuses on our obligation to participate in the liturgy on Sundays. The Eucharist is the heart of our Catholic faith. When we go forth from the Mass to live the Eucharist, we may spend the Lord's Day in restful leisure, visit the sick, share time with family members, or spend quiet time in the presence of Jesus in meditative prayer or spiritual reading.

Reflection

Ask yourself, "What season of the Church year are we celebrating right now?" "How can we make this time a season of praise in our lives?"

Ask the Holy Spirit to help you be present to Jesus during this particular season. Sit in silence. When you are ready, pray Psalm 145:2:

Every day I will bless you;
I will praise your name forever.

YEAR OF GLORY

Adult Focus

During the "great fifty days" of the Easter season, we welcome with the risen Lord the neophytes (newly initiated Christians) into the family of faith. This period of mystagogy (learning about and reflecting on the paschal mystery) deepens our commitment to Christ and his Church. In stories from the Acts of the Apostles, we hear once again how the early disciples followed Jesus' example of healing, teaching, and evangelizing. And we are reminded that their stories are to be repeated in our lives.

The triumphal Easter season culminates in Pentecost with our celebration of the coming of the Holy Spirit. The liturgy makes Pentecost present to us now, and we grow in our understanding of the Holy Spirit's work in our lives today not only through the liturgy but also through reflection on the Scriptures and our own lives and experiences.

During the Advent and Christmas seasons, we express our longing for the coming of Christ and the fulfillment of God's kingdom in our midst. Ordinary Time celebrates the mystery of Christ not in one specific aspect, such as his birth or resurrection, but in all its aspects. It also encourages us to make the most of our "ordinary time" to grow spiritually and become faithful disciples of Jesus Christ.

Catechism Focus

The theme of Chapter 9 corresponds to paragraphs 731–737, 1095, 1163, and 1168-1171 of the *Catechism*.

Enrichment Activities

Interviewing Neophytes

The young people might enjoy interviewing several neophytes from their own or other parishes. Suggest that they use audiotape or videotape to record the neophytes' responses to questions about their experiences of the catechumenate, the Easter Vigil, and mystagogy. They might also ask what attracted the neophytes to the Church, how they interacted with their sponsors, and what they now enjoy most about being Catholics.

Collecting Angel Stories

Most teens are very interested in the role angels play in our lives. They might be encouraged to put together a collection of angel stories taken from the Scriptures (such as Luke 1:26–38; Matthew 2:13–15, Acts 12: 1–11), from literature (*A Month by Month Guide to Entertaining Angels* by Father Mark Boyer, ACTA Publications; *A Dictionary of Angels* by Gustav Davidson), and from the media (*Touched by an Angel*).

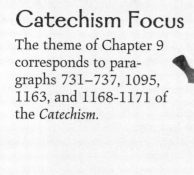

Teaching Resources

Overview	Opening Prayer Ideas	Materials
SESSION 1 **Discovery:** To appreciate the "great fifty days" of the Easter season.	Pray antiphonally Ecclesiastes 3:1–8. Write a refrain for the song "Turn, Turn, Turn."	These will be needed for every session: texts, Bibles, highlighters or colored pencils, journals. • copies of handout *Holy Spirit, Is That You?* • recording of "Turn, Turn, Turn" by Pete Seeger (optional)
SESSION 2 **Exploring 1:** To explore the meaning of Pentecost and the gift of the Holy Spirit.	Compose a prayer to the Holy Spirit, using images from the text. Example: "Holy Spirit, Breath of God, inspire us."	• Catholic magazines, newspapers • *How Excellent: Songs for Teens*, Vol. 1, (GIA) (optional) • parish missalettes or hymnals (optional)
SESSION 3 **Exploring 2:** To understand that Advent and Christmas express our longing for God's reign.	Proclaim and reflect on 1 Corinthians 4:5. Decide on one way to heed this Advent message.	• samples of songs and poems • missalettes • symbols of God's kingdom • *Prophets of Hope*, album, (OCP) (optional) • sample Advent calendar (optional)
SESSION 4 **Exploring 3:** To explore the relationship between Ordinary Time and our spiritual growth.	Make a drawing that illustrates Psalm 119:105. Let it be your prayer for Ordinary Time.	• copies of journal assignment (optional)
SESSION 5 **Putting It Together:** To recall and appreciate the seasons of the Church year and our participation in them.	Make up prayerful gestures to accompany Psalm 117. Pray it together.	• samples of liturgical music • copies of *Chapter 9 Assessment* • copies of *Highlights for Home* • recording of "Turn, Turn, Turn" (optional) • guest speaker from liturgy committee (optional)

Supplemental Resources

Videos

By Way of the Heart: The Sacredness of the Ordinary
Paulist Press
997 Macarthur Blvd.
Mahwah, NJ 07430

Seasons of Life
Sheed & Ward
P.O. Box 419492
Kansas City, MO 64141

Faith and Witness Journal:
Liturgy & Worship

For Chapter 9 see pages 36–39.

CHAPTER nine

Holy Spirit, Is That You?

The Holy Spirit probably won't make an appearance as "tongues of fire" or "a driving wind" in your everyday life. But the Spirit is present—guiding, inspiring, and breathing life into you as a follower of Jesus. Give examples of how the Spirit has come to you in the following ways.

In the presence of a person . . .

In a scientific or natural wonder . . .

In a song or a poem . . .

In a prayer . . .

In a story . . .

In these other ways:

A Year of Glory

Praise the LORD, all you nations!
Give glory, all you peoples!
The LORD's love for us is strong;
the LORD is faithful forever.
Hallelujah!

Psalm 117

103

Objective: To appreciate the "great fifty days" of the Easter season.

Introduction ___ min.

Opening Prayer: If possible, play any recording of Pete Seeger's folk song "Turn, Turn, Turn." It has been recorded by several artists and is widely available. Ask the young people to form two groups, and have them alternate in praying aloud Ecclesiastes 3:1–8.

Explain that the liturgical year gives us the opportunity to turn to Jesus in every season. Pray the following litany, asking the group to respond to each petition: "Jesus, you are the reason we celebrate this season."

• During the Advent season, when we are thinking about the gifts we will receive at Christmas, help us not to strain family relationships during this hectic time. Help us to turn to you, Jesus, and to pray:

• During Christmas, when we want to party constantly with our friends, help us to spend quality time with both family and friends and to rejoice as we turn to you:

• During Ordinary Time, when life may seem boring or routine, help us to make it interesting by finding ways to help others. Help us to turn to you in gratitude and pray:

• During Lent, help us to live our baptismal promises by remembering the poor, the hungry, and the homeless in prayer and action. As we encounter your sufferings in others, help us to turn to you and remember:

• During the Easter season, we tend to think about the new clothes we want to buy. Help us to rejoice in our new life in you and to remember this greatest of gifts as we turn to you and pray:

• During Ordinary Time after Pentecost Sunday, when we are bogged down with end-of-school activities and excited about summer plans, help us to find the Holy Spirit in our everyday lives and to turn to you as we pray:

Presentation ___ min.

◆ Invite responses to the photograph on pages 102 and 103. Explain that the photo shows a sculpture of the risen Christ by the Italian artist Pericle Fazzini. It is displayed in the pope's audience hall in the Vatican. Ask: "What message does it communicate?" "What feelings does it evoke about Jesus?"

◆ Have volunteers review pages 104 and 105. Ask the young people to underline in color or highlight the main ideas highlighted here.

◆ Print the terms *neophyte* and *mystagogy* on the board. Call first on students whose names begin with *n* or *m* to define the terms. (*Neophytes* are newly initiated Christians who have experienced Baptism and Eucharist at the Easter Vigil. *Mystagogy* is a time of learning about and reflecting on the mysteries of Catholic faith. It begins during the fifty-day Easter season, when the neophytes deepen their understanding of the paschal mystery.

◆ Have the young people form three groups. Tell them that in this activity they will be "Cycle Makers." Give the following assignments on index cards:

• *Group A:* Design a chart or symbol illustrating the cycle of Lent, Easter season, and Pentecost.

• *Group B:* Design a chart or symbol illustrating the three purposes of the cycle of readings in the Gospel of Luke and the Acts of the Apostles.

• *Group C:* Design a chart or symbol that illustrates how we are to continue the cycle started by Jesus and continued by his first disciples.

Distribute drawing materials. Allow about ten minutes for this project. Have one person from each group explain the completed charts.

"There is a season, turn, turn, turn . . .
And a time for every purpose under heaven."©
(Song lyrics adapted from Ecclesiastes 3:1)

How do these words suggest that we live in a world of time, of change, of new beginnings?

The Great Fifty Days

We human beings need change. Yet we often don't like sudden changes. We like predictable changes. Usually we like to know ahead of time that a change is coming so that we can prepare for it. The seasons of the Church year are seasons of change and seasons of preparation.

That's what Lent does—it prepares us for the great events of the Triduum. Now we will follow this great event to its fulfillment in the Easter season and at Pentecost.

104

◆ Read together the song lyrics at the top of page 104. Explain that the author lived three centuries before Jesus. Ecclesiastes was pessimistic about the ability of human beings to act at the right time to achieve God's purposes. He had not heard the good news, so he could not share our privilege of celebrating the triumph of Jesus over sin and death. He missed out on the beauty of the liturgical year and the opportunity to grow in holiness by uniting ourselves with Jesus in every season.

the heart of our Christian life is the belief that ...d has radically changed the universe through the ...schal mystery of Jesus. We call this radical change ...vation. It is the focus of our Easter celebration.

...ster, after all, is not just one more feast among ...ers. Easter is "'the Feast of feasts,' the 'Solemnity ...solemnities'" (Catechism, 1169). Easter is so ...portant that we cannot even begin to celebrate ...adequately in one day. It takes a week—and ...en more; it takes a "week of weeks." It takes ...ty days, a Pentecost (from the Greek word ...eaning "fifty"). Each day of these fifty days ...Easter.

...the Easter Vigil we received new members ...to our community through the sacraments ...initiation. During their time of preparation, ...e catechumens learned about the sacraments ...om outside," as it were. Now, as neophytes ...ewly initiated Christians), they experience ...e sacraments of Baptism and Eucharist "from ...thin" the community.

...r the neophytes (and for us as well) this fifty-day ...ason of Easter is the time of mystagogy. Mystagogy ...a time for learning about and reflecting on the ...ysteries of faith. The Easter season is a time for ...e community and the neophytes to grow in their ...derstanding of the paschal mystery. It is a time to ...ake the paschal mystery part of our lives through ...editation on the gospel, sharing in the Eucharist, ...d doing good works.

...ystagogy is something like the process of being ...opted. Imagine this: You have just been adopted ...to a new family. One day your new parents say, ...low that you're a member of the family, we ...ant to tell you more about us and what you've ...tten yourself into! Let's look at some family ...ctures together." So you look at pictures of ...andparents, of aunts, uncles, and cousins. You ...scover that your picture will soon be in the ...bum, too. You are now part of a whole family ...story and family system.

So it is with the newly baptized. They have not only "put on Christ"; they have also put on his body, the Church. They have joined a new family. And they (and we) take time during these fifty days to learn who that family, that Church, is. We find the picture of the birth and early growth of the Church in the Acts of the Apostles.

The Story Continues

The Acts of the Apostles forms one story with the Gospel of Luke. If you compare the way the two parts of this story (Luke 1:1–4 and Acts 1:1–2) begin, it is clear that Luke/Acts is meant to be read as a unit. Luke/Acts is a very special form of writing. The author wants to show three things: (1) the life and deeds of Jesus, (2) how his life and deeds were continued in the lives and deeds of the first disciples, and (3) how his life and deeds are to be continued by us in the Church today.

In Luke's Gospel we see Jesus healing the sick; in Acts we see Peter doing the same. In the gospel we see Jesus brought before the high priest to be interrogated; in Acts we see the same thing happening to Peter. The death of Stephen, the first martyr, parallels the death of Jesus. Stephen prays, "Lord, do not hold this sin against them" (Acts 7:60) as Jesus had prayed "Father, forgive them, they know not what they do" (Luke 23:34).

Why did Luke write in this way? He wanted to show us that what Jesus did during his lifetime, the first disciples also did during theirs, and we—today's disciples—are to do during ours! As we hear readings from the Acts of the Apostles proclaimed at each Mass during the great fifty days, we might ask ourselves these questions: "Is this our Church family today?" "Are we a healing Church?" "Are we a forgiving Church?" The stories in Acts are not simply stories of long-ago people and places, not simply faded pictures in some unknown photo album. They are our stories, our pictures. The challenge of the great fifty days of Easter is to continue the story of Luke/Acts today, in our Church and in our lives.

105

FORUM Assignment

✔ Read pages 106 and 107. Underline in pencil the sentences that express five main ideas.

✔ Complete the handout *Holy Spirit, Is That You?* Be prepared to share your responses. Bring audio or visual aids if you choose.

Closing Prayer: Have Psalm 117 printed on a poster displayed behind the prayer table. Invite the groups to gather in a semicircle in front of the table. Ask the young people to raise their arms in a victory gesture like that of the risen Jesus in the photo on pages 102 and 103. Then direct them to pray the psalm in "victory voices."

Conclusion ___ min.

◆ Ask the young people to look again at the opening illustration on pages 102 and 103. Invite them to read the psalm verse to themselves. Then ask these questions:

• Why might this psalm make a good theme song for the great fifty days?

• Why do you think our Church year can be called a "year of glory"?

FOR SESSION **2**

• tape or CD player
• drawing paper or posterboard, scissors, glue, Catholic magazines, newspapers
• *How Excellent: Songs for Teens,* Vol. 1, GIA (optional)
• parish missalettes or hymnals (optional)

SESSION 2

Objective: To explore the mean-ing of Pentecost and the gift of the Holy Spirit.

Introduction ___ min.

Opening Prayer

Forum: Have a tape or CD player available for those who wish to share excerpts from songs. Direct a student host to invite participants to share selected responses to the handout *Holy Spirit, Is That You?* Have the host ask the participants why they think the Spirit was present to them in these var-ious ways. Examples may be listed on the board to illustrate the Spirit's com-ing in our daily lives. Participants should also be encouraged to question one another on how they recognize when the Spirit is guiding, inspiring, or breathing life into them.

Presentation ___ min.

◆ Have volunteers share the state-ments they underlined on pages 106 and 107. Ask all to underline the key statements highlighted here.

◆ Challenge the young people to write captions for each of the photographs on pages 106 and 107. Explain that the captions should indicate ways in which the Holy Spirit is present to us and in us. Invite volunteers to share their completed work.

◆ Have the young people form small groups of "Spirit Communicators." Distribute large sheets of drawing paper or half sheets of posterboard, markers, scissors, glue, and Catholic and secular magazines and newspa-pers. Invite each group to produce a visual aid that illustrates the three primary sources of our understand-ing of the work of the Holy Spirit. (Tell them to refer to page 106 for review if necessary.)

Encourage the young people to incorporate in their collages or other artwork symbols of the Holy Spirit such as breath, air, wind, and fire. While they are working, you may want to play thematic music such as "Lord, Send Out Your Spirit" by Jeanne Cotter from the album *How Excellent: Songs for Teens*, vol. 1 (GIA).

Have the young people display and comment on their completed work.

The First Pentecost

On the final day of our fifty-day celebration of Easter, we celebrate Pentecost. As with each feast and each liturgical season of the year, its meaning is best understood by looking at the Scripture readings. The readings for Pentecost speak of the sending of the Holy Spirit. The word *spirit* is a translation of the Hebrew word *ruah*, which means "breath," "air," or "wind."

In the second reading for Pentecost, we read about the descent of the Holy Spirit upon the disciples: As they were gathered together, they heard a noise like a strong wind (*ruah*). "Then there appeared to them tongues as of fire.... And they were all filled with the holy Spirit and began to speak in different tongues, as the Spirit enabled them to proclaim" (Acts 2:3–4). Right away we begin to see the gifts and graces of the Spirit at work in the Church.

In the gospel for Pentecost, we read John's account of Jesus giving the Holy Spirit. On the evening of the first day of the week, "Jesus came and stood in their midst and said to them, 'Peace be with you.... As the Father has sent me, so I send you.' And.... he breathed [*ruah*] on them and said to them, 'Receive the holy Spirit'" (John 20:19–22). Sins are to be forgiven! The gifts of peace and reconciliation are given to the Church.

We do not need to ask *when* the Holy Spirit is given: on Pentecost (as in Luke), on Easter Sunday (as in John), or on Good Friday when Jesus bowed his head and "handed over the spirit" (John 19:30). The liturgy is not concerned with retelling the past. The liturgy combines all these accounts in order that we might reflect and ask ourselves: "How does the Holy Spirit act in the Church today?" "How does the Spirit come to me?" The liturgy makes Pentecost present to us now, today.

Our understanding of the work of the Holy Spirit today comes from three sources. The first is the witness of the Scriptures, which we have briefly explored. The second is the public prayer of the Church, the liturgy. The third is our own lives and experience.

106

FYI Pope John XXIII was seventy-seven years old when he became the leader of the Roman Catholic Church. He was talking with a good friend about ways the Church should respond to the many problems that were afflicting the world. Suddenly, out of the blue, he knew the answer. "My soul was illu-mined by a great idea," he said. That great idea was the Second Vatican Council, which brought about many positive changes in the Church and the world. As soon as the idea came to him, Pope John felt "a profound sense of joy and hope." He knew he was following the Holy Spirit's lead.

Pentecost Today

...t us consider the prayer of the Church. In ...charistic Prayer IV we speak directly to God ...d recall Jesus' sending us the Holy Spirit:

And that we might live no longer for ourselves
but for him,
he sent the Holy Spirit from you, Father,
as his first gift to those who believe,
to complete his work on earth
and bring us the fullness of grace.

What can we learn from this prayer? First we learn that the Holy Spirit is not the possession of an exceptional few. The Holy Spirit is given to *every* Christian, to all who believe. "First gift" does not mean that we first believe in Jesus and then the Holy Spirit is given to us as a reward for our good act. No, the Holy Spirit is God's free gift, given before any good work of ours.

We also learn here that the gift of the Holy Spirit is a gift of *mission*. When Jesus gave the Holy Spirit, he told the disciples, "As the Father has sent me, so I send you" (John 20:21). What the Father gave Jesus to do, the risen Lord commissions us to continue. This is the message of Pentecost. This is the work of the Holy Spirit. This is the work of a lifetime.

The Holy Spirit works with each one of us for the good of all. How is the Spirit breathing life into you?

Scripture UPDATE

The Holy Spirit equips us for our mission by giving us seven gifts, or *charisms*. The gifts of the Holy Spirit are wisdom, understanding, right judgment, courage, knowledge, reverence, and wonder and awe in the presence of the Lord. The source of these traditional names is Isaiah 11:2–3.

The gifts of the Spirit do not work automatically, of course. It is up to us to develop these gifts and to use them for our own spiritual growth and for the service of God and others.

107

FORUM Assignment

✔ Read pages 108 and 109. Underline in pencil the sentences that express six main ideas.

✔ Find or write a song or a poem that expresses our longing for the way things ought to be—for example, peace not war, love not hate, joy not sorrow, light not darkness. Be prepared to share this expression of human longing for the completion of God's plan.

Closing Prayer: Invite the young people to gather at the prayer table. Light a battery-operated candle. Sing any familiar Spirit song from the parish missalette or hymnal, such as the traditional "Come, Holy Spirit."

Conclusion ___ min.

◆ Discuss with the young people times when they may have followed the Spirit's lead.

◆ If time allows, use the thought provoker on page 107 as a journal exercise. Invite the young people to describe in writing the ways the Spirit is breathing life into them.

◆ Have someone summarize *Scripture Update* on page 107. To help the students remember the seven gifts of the Holy Spirit, have them draw a circular chart, divided into seven segments, in their journals. Direct them to inscribe the name of one of the gifts on each segment. Then read the names of the seven gifts aloud together.

FOR SESSION 3

- samples of songs and poems
- drawing materials
- parish missalettes
- symbols of God's kingdom
- *Prophets of Hope*, album (OCP)
- sample Advent calendar

SESSION 3

Objective: To understand that Advent and Christmas express our longing for God's reign.

Introduction ___ min.

Opening Prayer

Forum: Have available several examples of songs and poems that express our longing for the signs of God's kingdom among us, such as, "'Hope' is a thing with feathers" by Emily Dickinson; "Mending Wall" by Robert Frost; "Easter" by Gerard Manley Hopkins; "A Divine Image" by William Blake; "City of God" by Dan Schutte, S.J.; "We Are the World" by Lionel Ritchie; "World Peace Prayer" from the album *Come and Journey* (Haugen, Haas, Jon, and Cas, GIA). Direct a student host to invite each participant to share his or her expression of this longing. If time allows, have the young people share some of the above examples of poems and songs. The host concludes by praying: "Lord, we long for your coming among us."

Presentation ___ min.

◆ Invite volunteers to share the main ideas they underlined on pages 108 and 109. Then have them highlight or underline in color the statements highlighted here.

◆ Call on someone to retell the story recounted in the opening paragraph on page 108. Encourage the young people to learn this story by heart as a reminder of how completely Jesus shared ordinary human life with us.

◆ Ask a volunteer to read aloud the prophecy from Isaiah 11:6. Then tell the following true story:

In County Louth, Ireland, there is a beautiful seventeen-foot-high cross. It was carved in the tenth century by an unknown artist. Among the inscriptions on the cross is Isaiah 11:6. However, the artist did not choose to carve a lamb or a leopard to illustrate Isaiah's prophecy of peace and universal tolerance. He carved instead two contented cats. One cat is being hugged by a mouse. The other has three little birds perched on its paw.

Distribute drawing materials to partners. Invite them to make original sketches that illustrate Isaiah 11:6 for

Advent and Christmas

During World War II, when the United States and Japan were at war, the Japanese took over the Philippines. American missionaries working there were sent to prisoner-of-war camps. In one camp the guards allowed their prisoners to gather for prayer. Every day during the Lenten and Easter seasons, they prayed before a crucifix hung on the wall. When Advent came, they set up a small manger scene. On Christmas Day the figure of the infant Jesus was placed in the manger. One day a sister was praying at the manger scene. A Japanese guard posted nearby pointed first to the crucifix, then to the figure of the baby. "Same one?" he asked her. "Yes," she replied. "The same One." The guard's face saddened. "I am sorry," he said.

During Advent we go back to the beginning. We do not forget that we are celebrating the same Jesus who died and rose for us but we remember also that he chose to share ordinary human life with us. He chose to become one of us and to experience life as we do: its joys, sorrows, disappointments, hopes. He is indeed "the same One."

108

Advent is a time of joyful expectation. Joyful expectation! What do we expect, and why are we joyful? The answer to these questions is given in the Scriptures proposed for the season.

From the First Sunday of Advent until December 16, the readings express the hope and longing for that day when the plan of God will be complete. We dream of how things ought to be and long for the day when Christ will come again in glory. From December 17 to December 24, the readings direct our attention to the birth of Jesus.

The prophet Isaiah sets the tone for Advent. He voices the hope and longing of God's people, wandering far away from home, in exile in a foreign land. They want to return home. They dream of the day when God's rule will prevail and wars will end. God's people long for the time when all hatred and prejudice will cease, when the streets will be safe and children will not live in fear:

> Then the wolf shall be a guest of the lamb,
>   and the leopard shall lie down with the kid;
> The calf and the young lion shall browse
>   together,
>   with a little child to guide them.
> Isaiah 11:6

The Kingdom Among Us

How and when will this all come about? We do not know. Asked by the Pharisees when God's reign would come, Jesus replied, "The coming of the kingdom of God cannot be observed, and no one will announce, 'Look, here it is,' or, 'There it is.' For behold, the kingdom of God is among you" (Luke 17:20–21).

today's world. (They may use any of God's creations, including human beings.) While the young people are working, play thematic music such as "Canticle of Creation," "Prophets of Hope," and "Rejoice in the Kingdom" from the album *Prophets of Hope* by Trisha Watts (OCP). Have the young people share their completed works. You may wish to display them in the prayer corner or another appropriate place.

◆ Explain that the custom of making Advent calendars for children was brought to America by Catholics from Germany. These unusual calendars were often shaped like houses with twenty-five numbered doors on them. This custom is still practiced today. Each day during Advent the child opens a door and discovers a symbol or a scene depicting the Advent-Christmas season. Behind door twenty-five, which is larger than the others, is a nativity scene. Have the students work in small groups to make Advent calendars for younger

Christmas is the season when we pray fervently for the final revelation of God's mysterious plan. We pray for an end to war, hunger, and injustice. We pray, *Marana tha!* "Come, Lord Jesus!"

Have you ever noticed how often at Mass we pray for the coming of Christ? Can you recall a few examples?

Although we pray for Christ to come again, Christmas teaches us to live in the present. Our attention is not fixed on a baby's birth long ago, nor does fear of the end of the world keep us awake at night. Christ comes now. The Spirit of Jesus is offered to us always, in the events of each day. It is in the present that we find Jesus, not yesterday, nor tomorrow, but today.

Madonna of the Streets, Raphael, 1514

ow can the kingdom be among us when the world so full of sin and violence? To see the kingdom, e need a special kind of light: faith. The light of dvent (as symbolized in the Advent wreath and in the other beautiful lights we see at this time of ear) little by little replaces the darkness of doubt d discouragement. By the light of faith, we see e kingdom.

hristmas, then, is a celebration of light—the ght of Christ, the Word made flesh. In the birth Jesus, the invisible God becomes visible. In the fe of Jesus, we see God's plan for the world nfold. This plan is revealed gently and quietly, ven as God gently and quietly appeared among s in the stable at Bethlehem.

our lives, too, God's plan is usually revealed ently and quietly: in a quiet moment of prayer, the stillness after the loss of a friend, in those inutes at night before we fall asleep. Little by ttle we are to grow into the likeness of Christ. Only when Christ is formed in us will the ystery of Christmas be fulfilled in us" *Catechism*, 526).

CATHOLIC TEACHINGS

About Angels

Angels appear often in the stories we hear during the Advent and Christmas seasons. What does the Church believe about angels? We believe that angels are spirits created by God to be his servants and messengers. Angels assure us that God is concerned about us. Even their names speak of God: *Gabriel* means "strength of God," *Raphael* means "God's healing," and *Michael* means, "Who is like God?"

The whole Church benefits from the help of the angels, and each of us here on earth has an angel "as protector and shepherd" to guide us on the path of life (*Catechism*, 334, 336).

FORUM Assignment

✔ Read pages 110 and 111. Underline in pencil the sentences that express six main ideas.

✔ Choose one of the four gospels and scan the stories of Jesus that take place "in between" his birth, death, and resurrection. Choose one story that appeals to you. Be prepared to tell the story and share what it reveals to you about Jesus in "ordinary time."

Closing Prayer: Have the young people place on the prayer table symbols of God's coming kingdom (light, hope, joy, peace). Invite all to gather around the table and make the following response to the petitions offered by two leaders:

1: Come to make our darkness light.
2: Come to fill our hearts with love.
1: Give us joy that lasts forever.
2: Give us peace that binds us together.
1: Be our hope, our strength, our courage.
2: Be our friend, our guide, our leader.

Close with the Sign of the Cross.

109

children. Direct them to use symbols or scenes of the coming of God's kingdom among us, such as lambs, doves, lights, bells, and musical notes.

Conclusion ___ min.

◆ Distribute missalettes to help students respond to the thought provoker on page 109. Some examples are the memorial acclamations; Our Father; Holy, Holy, Holy; and Advent prayers and hymns.

◆ Have a volunteer summarize *Catholic Teachings* on page 109. Tell the young people that Gallup polls indicate that seventy-five percent of teens in America believe in angels. Many enjoy popular TV shows and movies about angels. If time allows, invite students to share their ideas or stories about angels who protect and guide us. Clarify any mistaken ideas. (For example, people do not become angels when they die.)

FOR SESSION 4

• Prepare volunteers for opening prayer
• journal assignment duplicated (optional)
• Bibles

Objective: To explore the relationship between Ordinary Time and our spiritual growth.

Introduction _____ min.

Opening Prayer

Forum: Distribute Bibles and have the group gather in a storytelling circle. Two student hosts alternate in calling on participants to share their chosen stories of Jesus in "ordinary time." Whenever questions arise about the meaning or context of the stories, the young people may use their Bibles to clarify these concerns. The hosts might also record on the board names of stories chosen by the group, as well as the number of times certain stories are chosen. (This information may be used in planning prayer services, retreats or gospel reflections.)

Presentation _____ min.

◆ Have volunteers share the key concepts they underlined on pages 110 and 111. Then have them highlight or underline in color the statements highlighted here.

◆ Do a two-minute brainstorming session in which students supply as many accurate completions of the following statement as they can: "Ordinary Time in the Church year is _____." (Possible responses: outside the seasons of Advent-Christmas and Lent-Easter; a time for non-thematic Scripture readings; a time to get to know Jesus better through gospel readings from Mark, Matthew and Luke; not an inferior or second-rate time of the year.)

◆ If possible, have the students separate their desks from one another so that each person has a "reflection space." Give the following journal assignment:

• Write a reflection on the theme "Making the Most of My Ordinary Time."

• Describe at least one important goal you are (or could be) working toward in your life right now.

• Tell how you are practicing and honing the skills required to meet your goal.

• Describe how your faith in Jesus has influenced your goal and helped you to make the most of your ordinary, everyday time.

Ordinary Time

What is Ordinary Time? If we take *ordinary* to mean "usual, average, of inferior quality or second-rate," it will be hard to get excited about Ordinary Time. However, these days are not ordinary in that sense. *Ordinary* here means "not seasonal." *Ordinary Time is the time that lies outside the seasons of Lent-Easter and Advent-Christmas.* In Ordinary Time, the Church celebrates the mystery of Christ not in one specific aspect but in all its aspects.

During the *seasons* of the Church year, the readings from Scripture are chosen according to the theme of the season: Lent, Baptism; Easter, resurrection; the great fifty days of Easter, Acts of the Apostles; Advent, Isaiah and joyful expectation; Christmas, God's taking flesh. During Ordinary Time the readings are not chosen according to a theme. Rather, in Ordinary Time we read from the various books of the Bible from beginning to end in a continuous fashion. This is the key to understanding Ordinary Time.

Christ prayed that the Holy Spirit would enable us to carry on the work that the Father gave him. In order to do this, in order to carry on the work of Christ, we must know Christ. To know Christ, we must know the Scriptures, for, as Saint Jerome said, "Ignorance of the Scriptures is ignorance of Christ."

In Ordinary Time we concentrate for an entire year on the life and work of Jesus Christ as proclaimed in one of the Gospels, either Matthew, Mark, or Luke. (John's Gospel is read principally during the liturgical seasons.) As we meet Christ in the Scriptures, we come to know him better. Knowledge of the Scriptures is knowledge of Christ.

Everyday Growth

Ordinary Time enables us to hear the whole gospel—not just the "big stories" of birth, death, and resurrection, but all the "in between" stories, parables, and teachings. Our Christian life is not just Christmas and Easter. It is all the days in between, the ordinary days. And perhaps that is what makes it difficult.

We all enjoy the wonderful and the spectacular, the miraculous and the exceptional. Yet when we look around us and see people who have accomplished great things, we seldom find that these accomplishments occurred overnight. Think of the hours and years of practice that go into becoming an accomplished musician or a fluent translator or a computer expert. Obviously these skills were not acquired overnight.

110

Allow as much time as possible for this activity. Some young people may want to extend their time by completing the reflection at home. Others may be asked to share their reflections during the *Closing Prayer*.

◆ Invite responses to the photographs on pages 110 and 111. Ask: How is the value and purpose of ordinary time illustrated? What connections can you draw between the farmer in the picture and the farmer in Jesus' parable of the kingdom (Mark 4:4–8)?

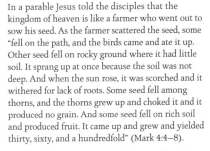

...e hardest part of following Jesus is simply ...t, for the most part, it is so terribly ordinary! ...tting up every morning and going to school, ...ating others with respect and fairness, doing ...mework and chores every night, practicing a ...usical instrument day after day, showing up for ...orts practice night after night—these things ...m so ordinary, so routine, and possibly even ...ring. However, we know that the truly valuable ...ings in our lives are achieved just that way: ...le by little, day after day.

In a parable Jesus told the disciples that the kingdom of heaven is like a farmer who went out to sow his seed. As the farmer scattered the seed, some "fell on the path, and the birds came and ate it up. Other seed fell on rocky ground where it had little soil. It sprang up at once because the soil was not deep. And when the sun rose, it was scorched and it withered for lack of roots. Some seed fell among thorns, and the thorns grew up and choked it and it produced no grain. And some seed fell on rich soil and produced fruit. It came up and grew and yielded thirty, sixty, and a hundredfold" (Mark 4:4–8).

Scholars who know about such things tell us that at the time of Jesus, a return of a hundredfold was not an exceptional harvest. It is only an average-to-good harvest. Jesus tells us that the harvest is "ordinary." For the most part God is not revealed in the spectacular or the sensational. Rather, the miracle of the kingdom is found in our daily efforts and everyday growth. We take up our cross daily and allow God's Spirit to help us grow gradually into the likeness of Jesus.

 What does Ordinary Time of the Church year teach us about our lives?

 CATHOLIC ID White, red, green, violet—what do these liturgical colors mean? Red (the color of fire) symbolizes the Holy Spirit, and is used on Pentecost and for the sacrament of Confirmation. Red (the color of blood) is also used on days when we celebrate the passion of Jesus (on Passion Sunday and Good Friday) and on the feasts of martyrs. White, the color of joy and victory, is used for the other feasts of the Lord, Mary, and the other saints. White is also used for the seasons of Easter and Christmas. Violet is used for the seasons of Lent and Advent. Green, the color of life and hope, is used during Ordinary Time.

111

FORUM Assignment

✔ Read pages 112 and 113. Prepare your responses to *Things to Think About* and *Things to Share*.

✔ Make or design a symbolic decoration for any season of the Church year. Decide whether your decoration is more fitting for a church or a home. Keep in mind what you have learned about the "year of glory."

Closing Prayer: If time allows, distribute Bibles and have the young people silently read Mark 4:3–9. (Or, have someone retell the parable using the text, page 111.) Then invite a few volunteers to share their journal reflections on "Making the Most of My Ordinary Time." Encourage the young people to become the rich soil that produces an "ordinary harvest."

Conclusion ___ min.

◆ Call for responses to the thought provoker on page 111. Be certain that the young people recognize Ordinary Time as a time in which to know Jesus better.

◆ Have a volunteer review *Catholic ID* on page 111. Some students may want to make charts of the liturgical year using seasonal colors. Display the charts for other groups in the parish.

 **FOR SESSION 5**

- samples of various styles of liturgical music (See suggestions.)
- copies of *Chapter 9 Assessment*
- copies of *Highlights for Home*
- recording of "Turn, Turn, Turn" (optional)
- Invite a liturgy committee representative. (optional)

SESSION 5

Objective: To recall and appreciate the seasons of the Church year and our participation in them.

Introduction ___ min.

Opening Prayer

Forum: If possible, play the theme song from Session One, "Turn, Turn, Turn" by Pete Seeger, or any other appropriate music as an introduction. Prepare a space where the young people can display their symbols for the seasons of the Church year. A student host invites each participant to display and explain his or her work. The decorations may be displayed in seasonal groups, or according to their usage in church or home. Then ask the young people to discuss their responses to *Things to Think About* and *Things to Share*.

Presentation ___ min.

◆ Call attention to the *Words to Remember* on page 112. The explanation of *neophyte* and *mystagogy* can be found on page 105.

Assessment: Suggest that the students work with partners in writing answers to *Testing 1, 2, 3*. If time allows, have the partners share their responses with the group. If you plan to administer *Chapter 9 Assessment*, page 113A, allow about ten minutes for its completion.

◆ Have a volunteer read *On Line With the Parish*. If possible, have a representative of the parish liturgy committee present to encourage the young people to participate in these Advent activities.

Conclusion ___ min.

◆ Call on someone to read aloud *Life in the Spirit*. Take a survey of the kind of liturgical music or particular songs that the young people favor. If time allows, put together a "Top Ten Liturgical Chart" based on their suggestions. To give the group an example of a music style they may not be familiar with, play one or more of the following:

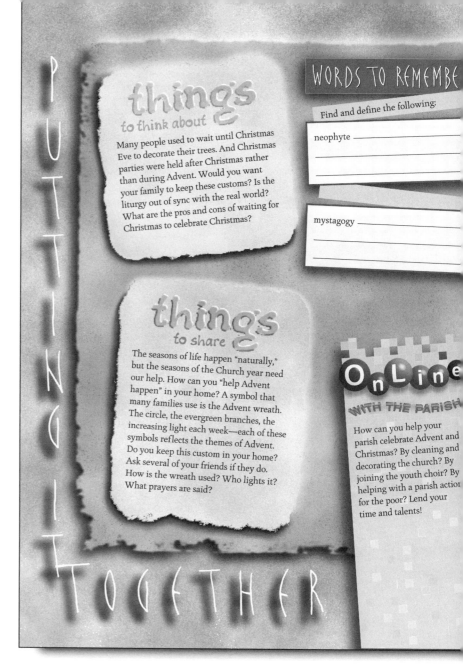

things to think about

Many people used to wait until Christmas Eve to decorate their trees. And Christmas parties were held after Christmas rather than during Advent. Would you want your family to keep these customs? Is the liturgy out of sync with the real world? What are the pros and cons of waiting for Christmas to celebrate Christmas?

things to share

The seasons of life happen "naturally," but the seasons of the Church year need our help. How can you "help Advent happen" in your home? A symbol that many families use is the Advent wreath. The circle, the evergreen branches, the increasing light each week—each of these symbols reflects the themes of Advent. Do you keep this custom in your home? Ask several of your friends if they do. How is the wreath used? Who lights it? What prayers are said?

WORDS TO REMEMBER

Find and define the following:

neophyte _____

mystagogy _____

OnLine WITH THE PARISH

How can you help your parish celebrate Advent and Christmas? By cleaning and decorating the church? By joining the youth choir? By helping with a parish action for the poor? Lend your time and talents!

• "Kyrie Eleison" from *Many* and *Great* by the Iona Community (GIA);
• "Spiritus domini" from *Chant* by the Benedictine Monks of Santo Domingo de Silos (Angel);
• "Gloria, Gloria" from *Taize-Cantate* (GIA).
• "Cordero de Dios" from *Misa Criolla*, (Philips).

Have the group proclaim energetically, "To sing is to pray twice!" Then sing any familiar seasonal hymn or psalm response.

◆ Remind the young people to share the *Highlights for Home*, page 113B, with their families.

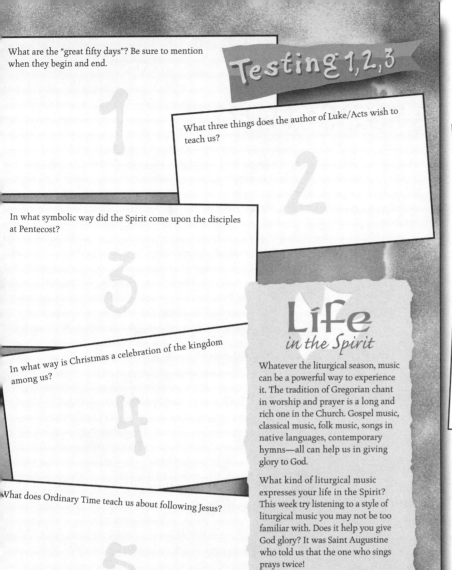

What are the "great fifty days"? Be sure to mention when they begin and end.

Testing 1,2,3

What three things does the author of Luke/Acts wish to teach us?

In what symbolic way did the Spirit come upon the disciples at Pentecost?

In what way is Christmas a celebration of the kingdom among us?

What does Ordinary Time teach us about following Jesus?

Life in the Spirit

Whatever the liturgical season, music can be a powerful way to experience it. The tradition of Gregorian chant in worship and prayer is a long and rich one in the Church. Gospel music, classical music, folk music, songs in native languages, contemporary hymns—all can help us in giving glory to God.

What kind of liturgical music expresses your life in the Spirit? This week try listening to a style of liturgical music you may not be too familiar with. Does it help you give God glory? It was Saint Augustine who told us that the one who sings prays twice!

113

Testing 1,2,3

1. See pages 105 and 106. The "great fifty days" is the celebration of Easter, the Easter Season. It begins on Easter Sunday and ends on Pentecost Sunday, the final day of the fifty-day Easter celebration.

2. See page 106. The author of Luke/Acts wishes to teach us these three things: (1) the life and deeds of Jesus, (2) how his life and deeds were continued in the lives and deeds of the first disciples, and (3) how his life and deeds are to be continued by us in the Church today.

3. See page 106. The Spirit came upon the disciples at Pentecost in the symbols of wind and fire.

4. See page 109. Christmas is a celebration of the kingdom among us because it is the celebration of the Word made flesh. In the life of Jesus, we see God's plan for the world unfold. This plan unfolds in our own lives, too, gently and quietly. At Christmas, we also pray for the final revelation of God's plan.

5. See pages 110 and 111. Ordinary Time teaches us that following Jesus is ordinary. We learn that the truly valuable things in life are accomplished little by little. We learn that the miracle of the kingdom is found in our daily efforts and everyday growth.

Evaluation: Do the young people understand the meaning of the Easter, Advent-Christmas seasons and Ordinary Time? Are they aware of the Holy Spirit's presence in their lives and their need to come to know Jesus better during their own "ordinary times"?

Answers for Chapter 9 Assessment

1. b 2. b 3. a 4. b 5. d
6. c 7. b 8. c 9. a 10. See pages 110–111.

Assessment

 1 The "great fifty days" is
a. Ordinary Time.
b. the Easter season.
c. Advent.
d. Lent.

 2 Mystagogy is
a. a time of reflecting on Advent.
b. a time for the neophytes to learn more about the Church.
c. the season of Easter.
d. the Lenten retreat.

 3 Saint Jerome said, "Ignorance of the Scriptures is ignorance of _____."
a. Christ.
b. the first disciples.
c. politics of Israel.
d. geography of Palestine.

 4 At Pentecost we celebrate
a. the birth of Jesus.
b. the descent of the Spirit.
c. the birth of the Spirit.
d. Saint Peter's birthday.

 5 We understand the Spirit's work
a. through the Scriptures.
b. through the liturgy.
c. through our own experiences.
d. all of the above

 6 During Advent we
a. prepare for Easter.
b. celebrate Christmas.
c. long for Christ's coming.
d. focus on the cross.

 7 Christmas celebrates
a. the risen Christ.
b. the Word made flesh.
c. the paschal mystery.
d. the Eucharist.

 8 The Church teaches that angels
a. have wings.
b. are human.
c. protect and guide us.
d. wear white robes.

 9 Ordinary Time means
a. not seasonal.
b. second-rate time.
c. the season after Advent.
d. the season after Lent.

10 Describe the purpose of Ordinary Time.

_____
_____
_____
_____
_____
_____

CHAPTER 9: Year of Glory

Highlights for Home

Focus on Faith

In *The Spiritual Life of Children*, Robert Coles interviews a fourth-grader who wonders how "the Holy Ghost comes down." The boy recalls how a bird had once flown up close to him and then flew off. He wonders if the bird might have had a message for him. He consults an uncle who is a priest. The boy reports, "He told me never to forget that God has his own way of reminding us of him—that he's around!"

One of the ways God has of reminding us Catholics of the Holy Spirit's presence is the liturgical year. Not only at Pentecost but throughout the Church year, the Holy Spirit "comes down" to inspire and guide the disciples of Jesus. Ordinary Time (outside the seasons of Lent-Easter and Advent-Christmas) offers us the opportunity each year to grow in our knowledge of and love for Jesus as we reflect on the Gospels of Matthew, Mark, and Luke. By attending to the Scriptures, the liturgy, and our prayer life, we come to understand how the Holy Spirit works in us.

Conversation Starters

. . . . a few ideas to talk about together . . . .

◆ How might we make the neophytes in our parish feel more at home in our faith community?

◆ What can I do to become more aware of the Holy Spirit's presence in my ordinary life?

◆ How will we pray and work for the coming of God's kingdom?

Feature Focus

The *Catholic Teachings* feature on page 109 focuses on the meaning and significance of angels in our lives. Catholics believe that angels are God's servants and messengers. Out of love for us, God has given each person an angel whose mission is to protect, shepherd, and guide us in this life.

Reflection

Among the Church's treasures is a beautiful prayer to the Holy Spirit composed in the thirteenth century by an unknown writer. In a restful place, slowly pray the following verses. Then close your eyes and feel the breath of the Holy Spirit.

Come, Father of the poor
Come, giver of all gifts
Come, light of every heart.

Give goodness its reward
Give safe journey through death
Give joy that has no end.
(Amen, Holy Spirit. Amen.)

THE SACRAMENT OF RECONCILIATION

Adult Focus

In Mark's Gospel (Mark 2:1–12) there is a dramatic account of a paralyzed man being lowered by his friends through a roof to be laid at the feet of Jesus. What did the paralytic want of Jesus? Healing. What is the first thing Jesus said to him? "Child, your sins are forgiven." The greatest evil, the greatest sickness, the greatest paralysis we can have in our lives is sin. God's forgiveness, then, is the first and greatest gift Jesus gives the paralyzed man—and us.

One of the most profound ills of our age, which our young people face daily, is the denial of sin. If there is no sin, there is no need of forgiveness, conversion, or reconciliation. Therefore, we must provide opportunities for our young people to experience their need for God's forgiving and unconditional love. They need moments when they recognize that if they first reach out and touch "the hem of his garment" in prayer they will be healed, moments when they are encouraged to turn from sin and turn for home where a loving father awaits them.

This chapter explores the sacrament of Reconciliation, Jesus' gift of healing to his Church. It is a sacrament that restores and supports the life of our souls. It is a sacrament that continually turns us towards home and the welcoming love of the Father.

Catechism Focus

The theme of this chapter corresponds with paragraphs 1422–1497 of the *Catechism*.

Enrichment Activities

Computer Connection

Have the students use a word-processing software program, such as *The Writing Center*™, to compose a newsmagazine article recapping an imaginary interview with the lost son, his father, his brother, and a neighbor attending the celebration of his return (Luke 15:11–32). Have the young people form news teams. To conduct the interviews, one team member should ask questions from a prepared script for each of the characters. The characters may wear costumes and be photographed when interviewed. The photos can be scanned into the final articles when the students take their work to the computer. If students are using *The Writing Center*™, have them set up their articles to appear in a two-or-three column layout and include the scanned-in photos. Have the news teams print and present the news articles to the entire group.

A Story of Forgiving Love

If possible, show the segment from the video *Jesus of Nazareth* in which Jesus tells the parable of the lost son. It appears on the second of the three tapes, right after the miraculous catch of fish. The film beautifully blends Peter's resentment of the still unconverted Matthew, the tax collector, with Jesus' gentle and wry telling of how God extends forgiveness.

This three-tape video is an invaluable addition to any religion library.

Teaching Resources

	Overview	Opening Prayer Ideas	Materials
SESSION 1	**Discovery:** To discover that through the sacrament of Reconciliation our relationship with God and with the Church is restored.	Pray together the Our Father. Have volunteers suggest gestures to express each petition.	These will be needed for every session: texts, Bibles, highlighters or colored pencils, journals. • five masks made from construction paper; colors: red, green, yellow, blue, purple • container of water
SESSION 2	**Exploring 1:** To explore the development of the rites of the sacrament of Reconciliation.	Quietly read the story of the healing of the paralytic (Luke 5:17–26). Encourage a few moments of quiet reflection.	• copies of sentences for the *Forum Assignment*
SESSION 3	**Exploring 2:** To examine the communal rite of Reconciliation.	Listen to a recording of *Amazing Grace*. Sing or pray aloud the verse that begins: "Through many dangers, toils, and snares . . ."	• lectionary, *Book of Rites*, volume 1 • copies of handout *Oh, What a Web!* • recording of *Amazing Grace;* copies of words for verse 2 (optional)
SESSION 4	**Exploring 3:** To understand the need for continual conversion of heart; to examine the individual rite of Reconciliation.	Invite volunteers to role-play the parable of the lost son (Luke 15:11–31).	• two small stones for each person • basket
SESSION 5	**Putting It Together:** To recall and apply the main ideas of the chapter.	If possible, play the recording of "Earthen Vessels"(GIA). Provide a copy of the words from *Glory and Praise,* volume 1. Have the group pray the words quietly as they listen to the music.	• words of Psalm 27:7–9 on board or newsprint • copies of *Highlights for Home* • copies of *Chapter 10 Assessment*

Supplemental Resources

Videos

Pardon and Peace: Sacrament of Reconciliation
Franciscan Communications/
St. Anthony Messenger Press
http://www.american
catholic.org

Jesus of Nazareth
Ignatius Press
P.O. Box 1339
Ft. Collins, CO 80522

Faith and Witness Journal: Liturgy & Worship

For Chapter 10 see pages 40–43.

CHAPTER ten

Oh, What a Web!

Oh, what a tangled web we weave,
When first we practice to deceive!

from "Lochinvar" by Sir Walter Scott

Sometimes people get caught up in the web of selfishness and sin. Before we celebrate the sacrament of Reconciliation, we are asked to take some time to unravel the selfish situations in which we and others have become involved. We do this by examining our conscience.

Look at the photograph of the spider's web on this page. Imagine you are the spider who has had a change of heart. You begin to unravel the web strand by strand. On the reverse side of this page, write questions young people might ask themselves to help identify selfish entanglements. The following examples will help you get started.

Love of God

◆ Do I use God's name with profanity or with respect?

Love of Neighbor

◆ Have I gossiped about someone or spread false rumors?

Love of Self

◆ Have I given in to peer pressure and done something I know is wrong? Have I done this just to be popular?

114C

The Sacrament of Reconciliation

Lord, you are kind and forgiving,
most loving to all who call on you.
Psalm 86:5

115

Objective: To discover that through the sacrament of Reconciliation our relationship with God and with the Church is restored.

Introduction ___ min.

Opening Prayer: Before the session begins, have volunteers make simple masks with colored construction paper. There should be one mask for each of the following colors: red, green, yellow, blue, and purple. Have on hand a large tub or bowl of water. Give a colored mask to five volunteers.

To begin the prayer activity, use the following script:

> As we get older and wiser, we may discover that the ways of selfishness and sin wear many colorful disguises. These disguises prevent us from showing our best qualities in order to reflect God's love.

Ask each volunteer to take a turn coming forward, holding the mask in front of his or her face. As each does so, read the appropriate line of the script below:

- I am the red mask of unjustified anger.
- I am the green mask of jealousy.
- I am the yellow mask of fearing to do what's right.
- I am the blue mask of iciness to others.

- I am the purple mask of false pride.

Invite the group to respond to each line by naming aloud certain times when the negative thought or action mentioned prohibited someone from showing the true colors of God's love.

Then ask the young people to gather around the container of water. Have a volunteer read Ephesians 4:20–32. Ask those with the masks to tear them into confetti-like pieces. Have them cast these pieces into the water to symbolize the intention to get rid of the old self. Read aloud the following petitions. Ask the group to respond to each petition by praying, "Lord, help us to show our true colors."

- Help us to reflect the red fire of your love.
- Help us to remember that green is a symbol of growth and trust in your love.
- Help us to walk always in the yellow light of your guidance.
- Help us to mend our icy ways and to remain your true-blue friend.
- Help us to remember that purple symbolizes the sacrament of your forgiveness, the sacrament of Reconciliation.

114–115

Presentation ____ min.

◆ Invite the young people to return to their seats and to open their texts to pages 114 and 115. Ask them to focus on the photographs as they read together Psalm 86:5. Ask, "What might the hands reaching up symbolize?" (Possible responses: calling on God for forgiveness, asking for mercy, praising God for the gift of forgiveness) Explain that the "lifting up of hands" is an ancient prayer gesture. It is spoken of in the psalms, and many Christians today still lift their hands up when they pray. It is a gesture of both petition and praise.

Direct attention to the water in the photograph. Ask, "Of what sacrament does the symbol of water remind us?" (Baptism) Ask, "What does the symbol of water have to do with the sacrament of Reconciliation?" (Possible responses: water is a sign of cleansing, and Reconciliation gives us the opportunity to become "clean" again; Reconciliation also gives us the opportunity to confess that we have not kept the promises we made at Baptism, and to be forgiven.) Explain that we will learn more about the Baptism-Reconciliation connection later in the week.

◆ Direct attention to the forgiveness story at the top of page 116. Discuss the two questions following the story. Ask the young people to recall similar stories of hurt followed by forgiveness in their own or others' lives. (Remind them to protect confidentiality by changing names and places if necessary.) Stress the importance of forgiveness with another example from the teaching of Pope John Paul II:

> The former country of Yugoslavia had been divided by a devastating war between two groups of people, the Croats and the Serbs. Sarajevo was the capital city, and it suffered severely during this war. This ancient, beautiful city was divided by ethnic hatred. Former neighbors and friends became enemies. Many innocent people were killed. Children playing in parks were shot at because they were on the "wrong side" of an ethnic divide. When the war ended, Pope John Paul visited Sarajevo and begged the people to rebuild their city on "the courage of forgiveness."

Remind the group that the pope is passing on the teaching of Jesus and not just his own opinion.

Some people were shocked when they learned that Pope John Paul II had gone to the jail cell of the man who tried to assassinate him. They were even more shocked when they found out that the pope forgave the man. Why do you think the pope did this? Are forgiveness and mercy so important in our lives?

Christ and the Samaritan Woman at the Well, Paolo Veronese, sixteenth century

Rich in Mercy

When the writers of Sacred Scripture wanted to describe their experience of God's love and mercy, they used some very dramatic imagery. The prophet Micah, for example, said that God "will cast into the depths of the sea all our sins" (Micah 7:19). When God forgives and removes our sins, he is described as putting them "as far as the east is from the west" (Psalm 103:12). Our God is truly a God of compassion!

Jesus knew this and wanted us to experience this forgiveness of God even more in our lives. Only God can forgive sins, and this is why Jesus, God's only Son, came among us. He wanted to free us from sin, to heal our wounded and broken natures. Who else but Jesus told the stories of the lost sheep and the prodigal son (Luke 15:1–7, 11–32)? He wanted us to know how much God loves us.

After Christ's resurrection the early Church community recognized what he had done for them. By offering his life for us on the cross, Jesus had redeemed us. He had reconciled us to God and to one another. This means that in Christ we were brought back into friendship again with God. We first share in this reconciliation and forgiveness at Baptism. But our rebirth in the waters of Baptism does not mean that we will never sin again. As we struggle to live a life of holiness, we do sin.

116

Ask some or all of the following questions:

• What do you think the pope meant by "the courage of forgiveness"?

• Why does forgiveness take courage?

• If a member of your family was shot or killed, would you be willing to forgive?

• Is the pope asking too much of the people of Sarajevo? Why or why not?

• Can you think of similar situations in which forgiveness takes courage? (Possible response: victims of violence need courage to forgive those who violated them and their rights.)

◆ Explain that being forgiven ourselves can help us to forgive others. Ask, "In what sacrament do we experience being forgiven?" (in the sacrament of Reconciliation) Explain the concept of the "domino" effect. Imagine a row of dominoes placed on end, one behind the other, like a line of toy soldiers.

r this reason we need to be healed again. We ed to turn to Jesus, who is really the sacrament God's forgiveness. How do we do this? Jesus ntrusted his Church with the mission of healing d forgiveness, especially in the sacraments. In e Eucharist we share in Christ's Body and Blood, ven for us and shed for the forgiveness of sins. In e Eucharist we realize and share in the peace hrist gave to us.

sus did not stop there, however. He gave to his ostles and their successors the power to forgive ns. On Easter night Jesus appeared to his apostles d breathed on them. He said, "Receive the holy pirit. Whose sins you forgive are forgiven them, nd whose sins you retain are retained" (John 0:22–23). This same Holy Spirit makes our hearts eady to receive God's forgiveness. And we do this a most wonderful way in a special sacrament.

ctually we may know this sacrament by many ames. We call it the *sacrament of Reconciliation* ecause through it our relationship to God and to e community of the Church is restored. The acrament is also called the sacrament of *Penance*. Ve have seen how penance (conversion, turning round) is our lifelong task. The sacrament of enance celebrates our continuing conversion, ur turning from selfishness and sin to e Spirit of love and generosity. The vord *penance* can also mean that part of he sacrament in which the priest asks s to say certain prayers or to perform ome other action to help atone for ur sins.

Church documents usually call the acrament *Penance* and those going o the sacrament *penitents*. For many ears most Catholics called the acrament *Confession. Confession*, owever, names only one part of he sacrament and not the most mportant part at that. *Reconciliation* ames what is most important, what Jesus does. Sinners are

brought back to God and to the community. They are reconciled. The *sacrament of Reconciliation* is the name used in the rite itself.

The sacrament of Reconciliation is a beautiful celebration of love and forgiveness. It is sad that few people take the time to understand what it really offers us. The sacrament is never meant to make us feel false guilt or to become overly concerned with sin. Nor is the sacrament meant to make us blame ourselves for things beyond our control. The Church teaches us that it is meant for healing what is broken, for setting free that which is bound up. In addition this sacrament is not just intended for the times when we commit serious, or mortal, sin. Whenever we confess our venial sins, we are strengthened and grow in God's grace.

Only when we are more mature, perhaps, can we grow in our appreciation of what is really happening in this special sacramental moment. Let's look more closely at Reconciliation, part of its fascinating history, and its celebration in the life of the Church. Let's experience in a deeper way why this sacrament is not something to be feared but something in which to rejoice.

117

Ask a volunteer to read the parable of the unforgiving servant (Matthew 18:23–35). Ask, "What importance does Jesus place on mercy and forgiveness in our lives?" Ask, "How did the servant interfere with the domino effect?" "What is Jesus' opinion of what the man did?"

FORUMAssignment

✔ Read pages 118 and 119. Underline in pencil the statements that express six main ideas.

✔ Imagine that you are a penitent at a time when canonical penances were given. You want desperately to be forgiven so that you can join the community for the Eucharist again. In your journal, write a letter to your bishop about your sorrow and your need for forgiveness.

Closing Prayer: Have the group read together the exchange of Peter and Jesus about forgiving others (Matthew 18:21–22). Point out that Jesus was trying to teach his followers that their forgiveness must be without limit. Pause for a moment of quiet reflection on the following questions: "When have I been forgiven? When have I forgiven others?" Then pray:

God the Father, God the Son, and God the Holy Spirit, help me to uncover what is false and deceptive in me. Help me to ask for forgiveness. Help me to forgive others freely and without limit. Amen.

FOR SESSION 2

- Prepare volunteers for the opening prayer.
- copies of sentences for *Forum Assignment*

(If possible, have a set of dominoes lined up and invite someone, at the appropriate moment, to start the "effect".) To make the line fall, there is no need to knock each domino down. You need only knock down the first domino. It will then fall against the second, knocking it down. That will knock down the third. The whole line will come down because one domino was knocked over. In the sacrament of Reconciliation, the domino effect is a positive one: Because we have been forgiven, we can forgive others who are standing with us in the line of life.

Conclusion ___ min.

◆ Have the students read pages 116 and 117. Have them highlight or underline in color the key ideas highlighted on these pages. Discuss the importance of each of the statements.

SESSION 2

Objective: To explore the development of the rites of the sacrament of Reconciliation.

Introduction ___ min.

Opening Prayer

Forum: Ask the young people to form small groups to share their letters to the bishop asking for reconciliation with the community through canonical penance. In the large group, ask for volunteers to read the letters. Then, ask the students to form pairs to role-play *Celtic penance* as described in the text, taking turns being a penitent and a monk. Remind the students that the penance given was usually an exercise of the virtue most opposite to the vice confessed.

Discuss the statements the young people underlined. Have them highlight the key concepts highlighted on pages 118 and 119.

Presentation ___ min.

◆ Write on the board the term *canonical penance.* Have the young people review the ritual way the Church helped a sinner to repent, convert, and rejoin the community.

In your discussion of canonical penance, remind the young people of the Church's importance in the lives of the early Christians. Explain that a person's entire life revolved around the Church. If someone committed a serious sin, the entire population of the town or village would be affected. Emphasize that even though sin is a personal choice, it hurts the entire community. Ask, "Why is it fitting that the rite of penance is a liturgical celebration?"

◆ Write on the board the term *Celtic penance* beside the term *canonical penance.* Have the young people chart the differences between these two ways in which Reconciliation was celebrated in the past.

canonical penance	Celtic
for grave public sins	for all sins
celebrated once	repeatable
with whole parish	private
community had liturgical rites	no liturgical rites

A Reconciling Church

Jesus called the Church to be a community of reconciliation and forgiveness. It is in his name and through his power that this forgiving and healing work continues in the Church. The ways in which the Church has answered this call have changed and developed over the centuries. We have seen how all our sins are forgiven when we are plunged into the death and resurrection of Jesus at Baptism. But what about sins committed after Baptism?

In the early Church these sins were forgiven by prayer, almsgiving, fasting, self-denial, and especially by the Eucharist. However, there were times when baptized Christians committed grave, public, and scandalous sins. Were these Christians still welcome at the Eucharist? Some process of conversion, repentance, and reconciliation had to take place first. The Church developed a ritual way to help the sinner repent, convert, and rejoin the community. This was called *canonical penance* because it was celebrated according to the *canons* (laws) of the Church. It was also modeled on the rite of Baptism, the first call to repentance.

The sinner came to the bishop, and they talked privately. Then, at Sunday Eucharist, the bishop prayed for the penitent and laid his hands on the sinner in a gesture of blessing and healing. A penance was given. The time of penance was long, often lasting several years or even the rest of the person's life.

Finally the day came for reconciliation. At Mass, after the readings and the homily, the penitent approached the bishop, they exchanged a kiss of peace, and the penitent was embraced once again as a member of the community. The penitent received the Eucharist and was reconciled with the community and with God.

This rite of penance was public. It involved the entire community, and it was a liturgical celebration. However, it was only for serious public sins and could be celebrated only once in a person's lifetime.

118

Later Developments

How did this public practice of the rite of Penance change? To help us understand this, we turn to fifth-century Ireland and Celtic monks. The Celts (the race of people who inhabited the island) had different Church structure than that found in other countries. Their Christian life was organized around monasteries rather than cathedrals. Celtic monastic practices soon influenced the Church at large.

Celtic monks were accustomed to going to a holy person to ask for advice in overcoming their sins, just as today we might go to a doctor to ask for help and advice in overcoming a physical illness. Christians in fifth-century Ireland would seek out a holy person, tell their sins, and ask for healing. The "medicine" consisted of "healing by opposites." If one was a glutton, this could be healed by fasting. If one was lazy, this could be healed by rising early for prayer. This practice is called *Celtic penance.*

Celtic penance was very different from the canonical penance practiced in the rest of Europe. Canonical penance was only for grave public sins; Celtic penance was for all sins. Canonical penance was celebrated only once; Celtic penance was repeatable. Canonical penance involved the whole parish and was accompanied by liturgical rites; Celtic penance was a private affair.

Scripture UPDATE

The gospels clearly show that forgiveness of sins is central to the message of Jesus. Frequently in the gospels we see Jesus forgiving sins. He taught us to pray "Forgive us our trespasses, as we forgive those who trespass against us." And with his dying breath, he forgave even those who had nailed him to the cross.

◆ Emphasize with the group that the Holy Spirit has continually guided the Church in its understanding of the sacrament of Reconciliation throughout history. Explain that, in the next two sessions, we will learn about the two ways the Church liturgically celebrates the sacrament of Reconciliation.

w did Celtic change ? Eur?

During the seventh century Irish missionaries brought the practice of Celtic penance to Europe, and it eventually became the ordinary way that people celebrated the sacrament of Reconciliation. Confession was made to a priest who had the power to forgive sins in God's name. The penance the sinner was to perform was greatly reduced; for example, in place of "fasting for ten years," the penance might have been "say six Our Fathers."

The sacrament came to be seen in terms of a trial before a judge. The priest acted as judge. It was important to confess sins accurately, for a judge must have accurate knowledge on which to base his decision. The focus was on the judgment itself, the pronouncement of absolution. _Absolution is pardon, or being set free, from sin._ This understanding of the sacrament was common until the time of the Second Vatican Council.

In all of this, it is wonderful to see how the Spirit of God has continually guided the Church in its understanding of the sacrament of Reconciliation throughout history.

Read these passages from Luke's Gospel: 5:17–26; 7:36–50; 15:1–17. What is the attitude of Jesus toward the sinner? Is Jesus judge or healer?

119

Conclusion ___ min.

◆ Have volunteers read each of the stories of Jesus' forgiveness listed in the thought provoker on page 119. Ask the young people to respond to the questions in their journals. Ask volunteers to recount the Scripture stories mentioned in the FYI, and then ask, "How is the priest fulfilling the ministry of Jesus?"

FORUM Assignment

✔ Read pages 120 and 121. Underline in pencil the statements that express five main ideas.

✔ Choose one of the following ideas. Illustrate it with a drawing, a short poem, or an appropriate photograph. Be prepared to share your choice.

- Jesus calls us to wholeness, to maturity.
- Sin is a failure to grow.
- Jesus came that we might have life and have it more abundantly.

Closing Prayer: Invite the young people to look at the photo of the river on pages 114 and 115 or the photo on page 119 as you read aloud the verses of the blessing in _FYI_. Encourage the young people to add their own verses.

At the end of the blessing, invite the young people to exchange a sign of peace.

FOR SESSION 3

- lectionary, the _Book of Rites_, Volume 1
- copies of the handout _Oh, What a Web!_
- recording of _Amazing Grace_; copies of words for verse 2 (optional)

FYI The following verses are taken from the Celtic Blessing of Peace-Healing.

- Deep peace, a quiet rain to you;
- Deep peace, an ebbing wave to you!
- Deep peace, pure red of the flame to you.
- Deep peace, pure green of the grass to you.
- Deep peace, pure brown of the earth to you.
- Deep peace, pure blue of the sky to you.
- Deep peace of the quiet earth to you,
- Deep peace of the sleeping stones to you,
- Deep peace of the Son of Peace to you,
- Deep peace, deep peace!

SESSION 3

Objective: To examine the communal rite of Reconciliation.

Introduction ___ min.

Opening Prayer

Forum: Invite the young people to share their illustrations or writings about sin and Jesus' call to reconciliation.

Have the students discuss the statements they underlined on pages 120 and 121. Have them highlight or underline in color the statements highlighted on these pages.

Presentation ___ min.

◆ Remind the young people of the four parts of the celebration of the Eucharist. Ask, "How many parts does the sacrament of Reconciliation have?" (four) "What are these parts?" (gathering, storytelling, sacramental action, commissioning) Write these parts on the board, leaving room for more writing under each one. Ask the young people to fill in this chart with information about each part. For example:

gathering
minister of hospitality greets us
introductory rites: hymn
liturgical greeting
prayer offered by priest

◆ Explain that within the communal rite of Reconciliation individual and private confession to a priest is always provided. Ask, "Why do you think this private and individual confession is included in the communal rite?"

◆ Draw attention to the photograph on page 120. Explain that the hand is raised because, when a priest gives absolution, he raises his hand in a sign of blessing and prayer over the person to be absolved. As he does so, he prays the prayer of absolution given on page 121. When he comes to "of the Son" he makes the sign of the cross in blessing over the person absolved.

The Communal Rite

The Second Vatican Council looked at this history of the various forms in which the Church has exercised the power to forgive sins. It revised the rites for Reconciliation to express more clearly what the sacrament really means and what it really does. These rites show that the sacrament is clearly a liturgical act. Like the Eucharist, Reconciliation celebrates the paschal mystery of Christ. Like the Eucharist, it consists of four parts: gathering, storytelling, the sacramental action, and commissioning.

There is no "one way" to celebrate this sacrament. Here is a general description of the *communal* celebration of the sacrament of Reconciliation.

Gathering The community gathers at the appointed time. There is a minister of hospitality at the door of the church to welcome us and to distribute any materials we may need to participate in the sacrament. The introductory rites usually include a hymn, a liturgical greeting, and a prayer by the priest to gather the assembly together.

Storytelling Once we are gathered, we tell the stories of God's love and mercy that are recorded in the Bible. The shape of this part of the rite is modeled on the Sunday Eucharist.

In hearing these stories of God's love, we come to see how much we are loved and to realize how little we have loved in return. The difference between these two loves—*how much* God has loved us and *how little* we have loved him—is called the "sense of sin." This is an important part of the sacramental process. It is the word of God that helps us to know our sinfulness.

Sin must be understood in relation to love. God has loved us so much, and we have so often failed to return that love. When we examine our lives in the light of the message of Jesus, we find that Jesus calls us to wholeness, to maturity. He came that we might have life and have it abundantly. For the Christian sin is not merely breaking

120

the rules; it is the failure to grow. Sin is being today just as you were yesterday. Sin is the failure to respond to the love God has shown us in Christ Jesus.

After we have heard how much God loves us, we examine our lives to see how well we have loved God and our brothers and sisters in return. We examine our conscience in the light of the Scriptures. Together we express our sorrow in an Act of Contrition. Then we each confess our sins to a priest in private and hear the proclamation of God's forgiveness (absolution): "I *absolve* you." ("I pardon your sins.")

 In what ways do the Scriptures help us prepare for Reconciliation?

The Sacramental Action This prayer of absolution is the central prayer and sign of the sacrament of Reconciliation. As we have seen, the key prayer of each sacrament is usually a prayer blessing God in the form of a berakah. The sacrament of Reconciliation is an exception to this rule. The central prayer is not a berakah but a declaration: "I absolve you from your sins."

For a sin to be mortal, the Church teaches that three conditions must be met:

- It must involve a grave and serious matter.
- We must have full knowledge that what we are doing is mortally sinful.
- We must freely and fully consent to it.

We have responded to the word of God by confessing our sins and receiving God's forgiveness. Now we celebrate this forgiveness, for it is God's response to *our* word. This part of the celebration might include a hymn, a proclamation of praise and thanksgiving for God's mercy, the Lord's Prayer, the kiss of peace, a song of thanksgiving, and a concluding prayer.

Commissioning The communal rite of Reconciliation concludes with prayers, blessings, and dismissal.

his declaration is expanded to mention the Father, the Son, and the Holy Spirit, for as we have seen, all liturgical prayer is prayer to the Trinity. The prayer of absolution mentions the principal effects of the sacrament: forgiveness, pardon, and peace.

The prayer of absolution that we hear each time we celebrate the sacrament is this:

God, the Father of mercies,
through the death and resurrection
  of his Son
has reconciled the world to himself
and sent the Holy Spirit among us
for the forgiveness of sins;
through the ministry of the Church
may God give you pardon and peace,
and I absolve you from your sins
in the name of the Father, and of the Son,†
and of the Holy Spirit.

Our response is "Amen."

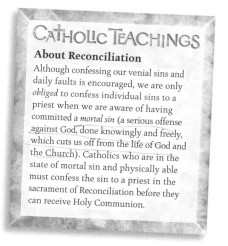

CATHOLIC TEACHINGS
About Reconciliation
Although confessing our venial sins and daily faults is encouraged, we are only *obliged* to confess individual sins to a priest when we are aware of having committed a *mortal sin* (a serious offense against God, done knowingly and freely, which cuts us off from the life of God and the Church). Catholics who are in the state of mortal sin and physically able must confess the sin to a priest in the sacrament of Reconciliation before they can receive Holy Communion.

121

Reconciliation, we should talk to a priest or trustworthy adult about it. Jesus wants us to be honest so that he can forgive us through the ministry of the priest. Jesus does not want us to be upset and anxious over things that are not sins!

Note: The group may want to invite a priest to celebrate a communal rite of Reconciliation with them. This would be an opportunity for the young people to prepare the celebration by choosing the readings and appropriate hymns.

Conclusion ___ min.

◆ Have a volunteer read aloud the prayer of absolution on page 121. Encourage the young people to listen carefully to it. Ask, "What feelings do these words evoke in you? Why?" Then ask the young people, "What principal effects of the sacrament of Reconciliation are mentioned in this prayer?" (forgiveness, pardon, peace)

FORUM Assignment

✔ Read pages 122 and 123. Underline in pencil the statements that express main ideas.

✔ Complete the handout *Oh, What a Web!* Be prepared to discuss your questions.

◆ Draw attention to *Catholic Teachings* on page 121. If you wish, share the information on mortal sin detailed in the *FYI*. A detailed explanation of mortal and venial sin may be found in Chapter 4 of *Morality: A Course on Catholic Living,* William H. Sadlier's *Faith and Witness* program.

◆ Ask for responses to the thought provoker on page 120. You may want to write the young people's responses on the board. Emphasize that it is the word of God that helps us to know our sinfulness, that helps us to develop a "sense of sin." You may want to stress that we sometimes need guidance on what a sin is and what it is not. Explain that sometimes we can get too worried about sin and become scrupulous or unnecessarily concerned about it. This is the opposite of what Reconciliation is intended to give us—the peace of Christ. If we find we are overly anxious and nervous when preparing for the sacrament of

Closing Prayer: Recite or sing together the Lamb of God as we do at every Eucharist.

 **FOR SESSION 4**

- two small stones for each person
- basket

121

SESSION 4

Objective: To understand the need for continual conversion of heart; to examine the individual rite of Reconciliation.

Introduction ___ min.

Opening Prayer

Forum: Ask the young people to form buzz groups to discuss the handout *Oh, What a Web!* Invite them to learn from each other and to add anything to their own sheets that would make the sets of questions more complete for an examination of conscience. Suggest that the Ten Commandments and the Beatitudes are helpful guides. Ask each group to appoint a recording secretary to list what the group thinks are the five most significant questions for each panel. After calling the groups together, ask the secretaries to read the questions. Appoint a committee to put all the questions together into a small booklet. Keep the booklet in the prayer corner for future reference.

Presentation ___ min.

◆ Introduce the work of the Holy Spirit in relation to the sacrament of Reconciliation by explaining the origin of the word *contrite*. Write the word on the board, and explain that it comes from two Latin words: *com,* meaning "intensely" and *terere,* meaning, "to grind." Explain that when we feel contrition, we might describe it as something "grinding" in us. Sometimes these feelings of regret, irritation, or guilt are signs that the Spirit is calling us to conversion and contrition.

To illustrate this point, give each student two small stones. Tell them that stones are naturally very dull. But if they are placed in a tumbler and made to *grind* against each other (recalling the root meaning of *contrition*), they become very shiny and beautiful. Allow the young people to keep the stones on their desks until the *Closing Prayer.*

◆ Read aloud Ezekiel 36:26–28. Explain that in this passage Ezekiel compares the human heart to a stone. He promises the people that God will remove their stony hearts and replace them with natural hearts. This is a symbol of the process of conversion.

Conversion of Heart

Catholics celebrate Reconciliation even when they have less serious sins to confess. Why? Because this sacrament is a great help to what Jesus wants for all his followers: conversion of heart.

In the life of the Church, the primary moment of conversion is the moment of Baptism. Yet conversion is not limited to that moment. It is the work of a lifetime. As followers of Christ we are called to a continual conversion of heart. One big "turning toward" God at Baptism is not enough for a full Christian life. We must continually turn toward God, as a growing plant continually turns toward its source of light, growth, and energy.

Conversion, our everyday turning away from evil and toward good, is not something we are expected to do on our own. Conversion is a grace of the Holy Spirit. Under the Spirit's guidance we are led to right thinking and good action. And with the help of the Spirit, we find the honesty to admit our failings and the courage to promise to do better. The sacrament of Reconciliation keeps us on track in our own individual work of conversion. It helps us to stop and reflect on how far we have come, and it helps us to resolve to continue the journey.

122

When the Fathers of the Church explained Baptism, they imagined an individual in the midst of a shipwreck. How to be saved in the midst of a raging sea? Grab a plank! This first plank is the sacrament of Baptism. When they taught about the sacrament of Reconciliation, they called it "the second plank" (*Catechism*, 1446). As Christians we need both to keep us afloat.

The Individual Rite

The individual rite of Reconciliation is another way the Church gives us to celebrate this sacrament. There are two important elements to this rite. As we learn about them, imagine yourself preparing to receive the sacrament. How would each of these elements apply to you?

The first element is human action: contrition, confession, and satisfaction (doing one's penance). The second element is God's action: the forgiveness of sins through the Church. Both our human actions and God's action are equally essential.

Contrition *Contrition* is sorrow for having sinned, detestation for the sin committed, and also a firm decision not to sin again. Before Reconciliation we should take time to make an examination of conscience and to ask ourselves if we really are sorry for our selfish actions and wrong choices.

Confession Confessing our sins to a priest is an essential part of this sacrament because the priest forgives sin in the name of Jesus Christ and the Church. Our sins are personal, but they are never private. We, the Church, are the body of Christ in the world. Sin affects the whole body of Christ. Just as in physical illness, when one part is in pain, the whole body suffers. The priest represents Christ and his body, so it is his task and joy to welcome sinners, as Jesus did, and to restore them to their rightful place in the body of Christ.

◆ Explain the ways that the sacrament of Reconciliation helps us to grow in our Christian lives. Ask, "What are the two important elements of this sacrament?" (human action and God's action) Then ask the students to explain what this human action entails. (contrition, confession, satisfaction)

◆ Ask a volunteer to explain what *contrition* is. (sorrow for having sinned, detestation of the sin committed, and a firm decision not to sin again) Ask, "Why is the decision not to sin again a part of contrition?" (Possible response: Without this decision, we would not be taking our own actions or the sacrament of Reconciliation seriously.) Explain that it is wrong to think of the sacrament of Reconciliation as a revolving door or a "license" to sin again. We may indeed sin again, but we cannot take sin lightly. We must do all we can to avoid it.

ometimes people worry about what the priest
inks of them when they tell him their sins. They
magine that the priest sees them at their worst.
ctually the very opposite is true. *Everybody* sins,
ut only *some* sinners are moved to do penance.
hen you tell your sins to the priest and express
our desire to repent, the priest sees you at your
est. The priest sees you, not in your sinning, but
your repentance.

atisfaction *Satisfaction* is simply repairing, in
me way, the harm our sins have done. Returning
r paying for stolen goods, for example, is one
bvious way of making satisfaction for the sin
f stealing.

his kind of satisfaction is usually included in
e *penance* given. A penance can be prayer, an
ffering, works of mercy, service to a
eighbor, voluntary self-denial, sacrifices,
nd most of all a patient acceptance of the
rdinary circumstances of our lives.

Reconciliation Now we turn to God's
ction in the sacrament of Reconciliation:
he forgiveness of sins. Through this

forgiveness, as Pope John Paul II explained, we are
reconciled with self, God, the entire Church, and
"with all creation" (*Catechism*, 1469). Reconciliation
is a sacrament of peace and comfort, a sacrament
sealed in the conversational tones of a human voice:
"I absolve you. . . . Go in the peace of Christ."

 The symbol of the sacrament of Reconciliation is the symbol of language. How would you explain this statement?

CATHOLIC ID The priest is strictly forbidden to use *in any way* anything he hears in the sacrament of Reconciliation. He can never, *never*, NEVER tell anyone what sin you confessed. If he does so, he himself commits a mortal sin. This obligation and promise is called the *seal of confession*. That is, the priest's lips are sealed, and he cannot reveal your sin or your identity.

123

◆ Draw attention to the thought provoker on page 123. Explain that the essential sign of the sacrament is the absolution spoken by the priest.

FORUM Assignment

✔ Read pages 124 and 125. Prepare your responses for the questions in *Testing 1, 2, 3.*

✔ You have been asked by your pastor to write a TV or radio ad, or to design a billboard or magazine ad, encouraging parishioners to celebrate the sacrament of Reconciliation. He wants everyone to know that the individual rite is celebrated on Saturday afternoons or when the need arises.

Closing Prayer: Ask the young people to place the two small stones they received at the beginning of the session on their desks. Direct them to think of one or two burdens they are bearing in their lives right now. Encourage them to see these stones now as symbols of these burdens.

Before you walk among the students to collect the stones, say something like: "Jesus told us that he would always be with us, that he would help us to bear our burdens. When I stop at your desk, place your burdens in the basket." Then stop at each one's desk and say: "(Name), give your burdens to Jesus." When all the burdens have been collected, ask the group to open their books to page 115 and read together Psalm 86:5. Put the basket of stones in the prayer corner. Invite the young people to use it as a reminder to pray for one another.

◆ Introduce the element of *confession* by asking, "Why do we confess our sins to a priest? Why don't we confess them privately to God?" (possible response: Our sins are not private. They affect the whole body of Christ. The priest represents both Christ and his body, the Church.)

◆ Ask a volunteer to explain *satisfaction.* Point out that the penance we are given in the sacrament helps to satisfy our human need for justice, to "make up for" what we have done wrong. When we have made satisfaction in some way, we are ready to move on and do better. Ask, "Have you ever had to make satisfaction for something in your everyday life? How did you feel about it?"

◆ Have a volunteer summarize *Catholic ID.* Ask, "Why would you think the seal of confession would be necessary?"

 **FOR SESSION 5**

• copies of *Chapter 10 Assessment*
• copies of *Highlights for Home*

SESSION 5

Objective: To recall and apply the main ideas of the chapter.

Introduction ___ min.

Opening Prayer

Forum: Have the young people take turns presenting their ads encouraging parishioners to celebrate the sacrament of Reconciliation.

Discuss the first set of questions in *Things to Think About.* Ask, "Do you think that knowing the priest is bound by the seal of confession is an encouragement to individuals to speak freely in this sacrament?"

Presentation ___ min.

◆ Discuss the *Things to Think About* question about communal and individual celebration preferences. Remind the group that individual confession is a part of the communal celebration of the sacrament.

◆ Direct attention to *Things to Share.* Encourage the young people to find out ways other Christian communities seek God's forgiveness and celebrate Reconciliation.

◆ Have a volunteer summarize *On Line with the Parish.* You may want to suggest that the young people plan a communal celebration for other youth groups within the parish.

◆ Direct attention to *Words to Remember.* Ask volunteers to define each word. The definition for *Reconciliation* may be found on page 117; the definition for *absolution* may be found on page 120.

Assessment: Suggest that the young people work in pairs to write answers for *Testing, 1, 2, 3,* using the individual answers they have prepared. If time permits, have the partners share their answers with the entire group.

If you are administering *Chapter 10 Assessment,* page 125A, allow about ten minutes for the students to complete the test.

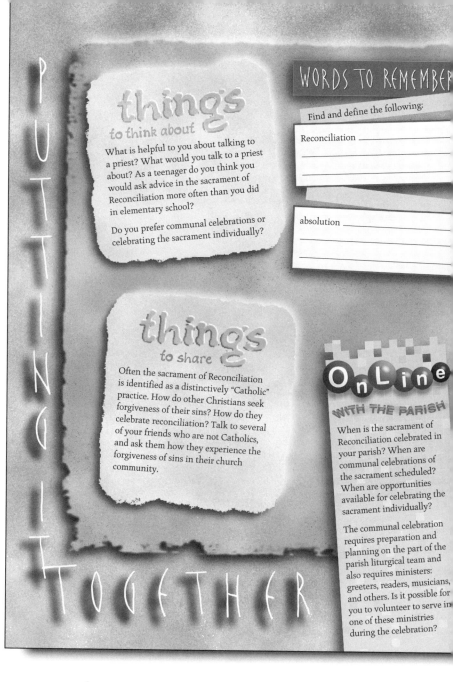

PUTTING IT ALL TOGETHER

things to think about

What is helpful to you about talking to a priest? What would you talk to a priest about? As a teenager do you think you would ask advice in the sacrament of Reconciliation more often than you did in elementary school?

Do you prefer communal celebrations or celebrating the sacrament individually?

things to share

Often the sacrament of Reconciliation is identified as a distinctively "Catholic" practice. How do other Christians seek forgiveness of their sins? How do they celebrate reconciliation? Talk to several of your friends who are not Catholics, and ask them how they experience the forgiveness of sins in their church community.

WORDS TO REMEMBER

Find and define the following:

Reconciliation _____

_____

_____

absolution _____

_____

_____

OnLine WITH THE PARISH

When is the sacrament of Reconciliation celebrated in your parish? When are communal celebrations of the sacrament scheduled? When are opportunities available for celebrating the sacrament individually?

The communal celebration requires preparation and planning on the part of the parish liturgical team and also requires ministers: greeters, readers, musicians, and others. Is it possible for you to volunteer to serve in one of these ministries during the celebration?

Conclusion ___ min.

Closing Prayer: In Psalm 27, we are encouraged to seek the face of God. Because we are created in the image and likeness of God, when we seek God, we find ourselves. When we seek the face of God, we also face our best selves. Reconciliation enables us to look at ourselves realistically and to face God and others with love.

Ask the group to pray together Psalm 27:7–9.

Close by praying one of the prayers suggested in *Life in the Spirit:* the Jesus Prayer, the Hail Mary, or the Our Father.

◆ Encourage the young people to share *Highlights for Home,* page 125B, with their families.

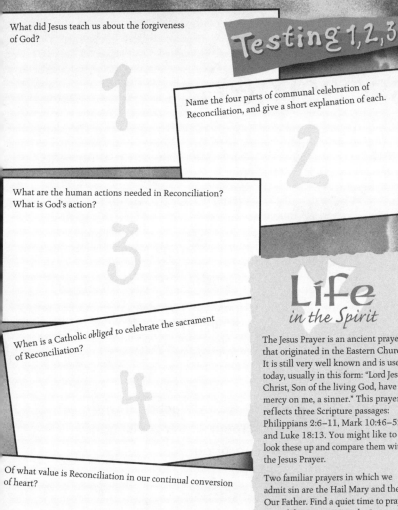

What did Jesus teach us about the forgiveness of God?

Testing 1, 2, 3

Name the four parts of communal celebration of Reconciliation, and give a short explanation of each.

What are the human actions needed in Reconciliation? What is God's action?

When is a Catholic *obliged* to celebrate the sacrament of Reconciliation?

Of what value is Reconciliation in our continual conversion of heart?

Life in the Spirit

The Jesus Prayer is an ancient prayer that originated in the Eastern Church. It is still very well known and is used today, usually in this form: "Lord Jesus Christ, Son of the living God, have mercy on me, a sinner." This prayer reflects three Scripture passages: Philippians 2:6–11, Mark 10:46–52, and Luke 18:13. You might like to look these up and compare them with the Jesus Prayer.

Two familiar prayers in which we admit sin are the Hail Mary and the Our Father. Find a quiet time to pray one of these prayers or the Jesus Prayer this week. Ask for the grace of forgiving and being forgiven.

125

Testing 1,2,3

1. See page 116. Jesus wanted us to experience the forgiveness of God in our lives. He wanted to free us from sin, to heal our wounded and broken natures. He wanted us to know how much God loved us. He taught us this through the parables of the lost sheep and the prodigal son.

2. See pages 120–121. Accept specific descriptions.

3. See page 122. The human actions needed in the sacrament of Reconciliation are contrition, confession, and satisfaction. God's action is the forgiveness of sin through the Church.

4. See page 121. A Catholic is obliged to celebrate the sacrament of Reconciliation when he or she is aware of having committed a mortal sin. Catholics who are in the state of mortal sin must confess the sin to a priest in the sacrament of Reconciliation before they can receive Holy Communion.

5. See page 122. The sacrament of Reconciliation keeps us on track in our own individual work of conversion. It helps us to stop and reflect on how far we have come, and it helps us to resolve to continue the journey.

Evaluation: Do the young people understand the purpose of the sacrament of Reconciliation? Do they appreciate its history? Do they understand its role in their lives of faith?

Answers for Chapter 10 Assessment

1. CA   2. CE   3. CA   4. CE   5. CA
6. c   7. c   8. d   9. b   10. Entire chapter.

Assessment

For each of the following statements use this code for identification.

- Write CE for statements about Celtic penance.
- Write CA for statements about canonical penance.

1 _____ refers to ways of celebration according to the laws of the Church.

2 _____ consisted in healing by opposites.

3 _____ often lasted several years.

4 _____ meant for all sins, not just public sins.

5 _____ was accompanied by liturgical rites.

Choose the letter beside the best answer.

6 Pardon, or being set free, from sin is called
  a. penance.
  b. confession.
  c. absolution.
  d. Celtic penance.

7 Which of the following statements is true?
  a. Baptism means we will never sin again.
  b. Forgiveness meant nothing to Jesus.
  c. Sin affects the whole body of Christ.
  d. Conversion is something we do all on our own.

8 What is God's action in the sacrament of Reconciliation?
  a. contrition
  b. confession
  c. satisfaction
  d. the forgiveness of sins

9 The sign of the sacrament of Reconciliation is
  a. bread and wine.
  b. words of absolution.
  c. oil.
  d. water.

10 Name one important thing you have learned about the sacrament of Reconciliation. How has it helped you to appreciate this sacrament?

_____

_____

_____

Highlights for Home

Focus on Faith

Jesus understood human life "from the inside out." In the Letter to the Hebrews, we read that "we do not have a high priest who is unable to sympathize with our weaknesses, but one who has similarly been tested in every way, yet without sin" (Hebrews 4:15). In Jesus is revealed the compassion of God. He often reassured sinners, "Your sins are forgiven. Go in peace."

In the sacrament of Reconciliation, we encounter Christ and are offered the same reassurance today. In our battle with the sins of everyday life—envy, jealousy, meanness of spirit, anger, pride— the sacrament of Reconciliation gives us another chance to turn to God in our need for continual conversion, to turn to God who heals our brokenness.

From the early Church to today, it is clear that forgiving and being forgiven are essential to Christian life. For Jesus himself taught us to pray: "Forgive us our trespasses as we forgive those who trespass against us."

Conversation Starters

. . . . a few ideas to talk about together . . . .

◆ What would you say is the attitude toward sin today in society as a whole? among your friends? in your family?

◆ How hard do you find it to admit when you are wrong? Can you recall a time when doing so helped heal a friendship?

◆ How can you grow in your appreciation of the sacrament of Reconciliation?

Feature Focus

The *Catholic ID* on page 123 reminds us of the obligation of the priest to honor the seal of confession. This obligation is a great reassurance to us, because we can be sure that everything we say to the priest is totally confidential. Protected by the seal of confession, Catholics through the ages have celebrated Reconciliation without fear of gossip or scandal.

Reflection

Take a quiet moment to look at the photograph on pages 114 and 115. The many colors interspersed with the water may remind you of the story of Noah, a story that began with a flood of water and ended with a rainbow: symbol of the covenant, symbol of reconciliation.

Imagine yourself sitting beside this quiet pond. How is the rainbow of your life reflected in the waters of Baptism? Are the colors fading a bit in the routine of daily life? Renew the covenant now. Pick up three stones from the beach. Pray, "God, forgive me" and throw a stone into the pond. Let forgiveness ripple through your life. Pray, "Help me to forgive others," and toss the next stone into the pond. Pray, "Help me to forgive myself," and plop the last stone in. Watch it disappear.

125B

THE ANOINTING OF THE SICK

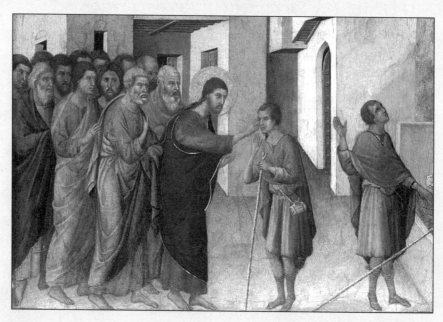

Adult Focus

The question "Why me?" in the face of illness and suffering may not be as self-pitying as it sounds. It is often more possible to tolerate difficult situations if we can sense deeper meaning behind them. Viktor Frankl was able to survive the devastation of a concentration camp by writing a book in his head. That book became the core of his philosophy and one of the most important written in the twentieth century: *Man's Search for Meaning*.

The search for meaning begins at an early age and never ends. As toddlers, our young people gazed at the green grass and the blue sky and asked, "Why?" Now they ask, "Why do people suffer?" "Why do people die?"

This chapter will not answer these questions. But it will introduce the young people to the great gift of the sacrament of the Anointing of the Sick, in which Jesus Christ, through his Church, strengthens and brings peace to the suffering. This sacrament is an instrument of healing of the soul and also of the body, if God so wills. At the last stages of life, this sacrament, together with Penance and Eucharist as Viaticum, prepares us for the final journey, the passage from death to eternal life.

Catechism Focus

The theme of this chapter corresponds to paragraphs 1500–1525 of the *Catechism*.

Enrichment Activities

Ministers to the Sick

You may want to ask someone in your parish who ministers to the sick to speak with your group. This person may be a eucharistic minister, or someone delegated by the parish to visit the sick in homes or in hospitals in order to maintain a link with the parish community. If you have a hospice for the dying in your community, invite one of the volunteers to share with your group the work of this special group. Have the young people prepare a list of questions to ask this minister or volunteer.

Praying with the Sick

Plan a prayer service to film and send on videotape to a nursing home or rehabilitation center. Encourage the young people to choose a joyful, upbeat theme. Responses should be simple so that those in the center may join you in praying. Consider using traditional hymns if you are going to send the video to a nursing home.

CHAPTER 11

Teaching Resources

	Overview	Opening Prayer Ideas	Materials
SESSION 1	**Discovery:** To discover that Jesus and his Church are signs of God's healing.	Look at the photo on pages 126–127. Open your Bibles to Psalm 23 and pray it together.	These will be needed every session: texts, Bibles, highlighters or colored pencils, journals. • handout *A Spiritual Safety Net* • videos mentioned in Session 1
SESSION 2	**Exploring 1:** To explore the historical development of the rites that the Church uses to continue the healing ministry of Jesus.	Ask volunteers to take turns reading the parable of the Good Samaritan (Luke 10:29–37).	• index cards (one for each person) • recording of "On Eagle's Wings" by Michael Joncas
SESSION 3	**Exploring 2:** To understand the changes suggested by the Second Vatican Council and the celebration of the Anointing of the Sick during Sunday liturgy.	Ask a volunteer to read the cure of Simon's mother-in-law (Luke 4:38–39). Pray in silence for all those in our own families who are sick.	• index cards (two for each student) • net made for Session 2
SESSION 4	**Exploring 3:** To explore the sacrament of the Anointing of the Sick as a ritual that makes present the Church as a community of healing and support.	Ask two volunteers to take turns reading the healing of a paralytic (Luke 5:17–26). Take a moment to pray for those in hospitals who are without friends or family to support them in their illness.	• large pieces of cardboard, butcher paper • magazines and scissors • construction paper • blank audiocassette and cassette recorder
SESSION 5	**Putting It Together:** To deepen understanding of the sacrament of the Anointing of the Sick.	Ask two volunteers to take turns reading the healing of the centurion's slave (Luke 7:1–10). Take a moment to pray for those who are sick and cannot afford medical insurance or medical care.	• copies of *Chapter 11 Assessment*, page 138A • copies of *Highlights for Home*, page 138B

Supplemental Resources

Pamphlets: *Catholic Youth Update*
• "For Our Healing: The Sacrament of the Anointing of the Sick"
• "Jump-Starting Your Future: Getting Control of Your Habits"

St. Anthony Messenger
1615 Republic Street
Cincinnati, OH 45210
See video suggestions in Session 1.

Faith and Witness Journal: Liturgy & Worship

For Chapter 11 see pages 44–47.

CHAPTER eleven

A Spiritual Safety Net

Just as people invest in medical insurance policies as economic safety nets in case of illness or medical emergencies, we should invest our time in planning a spiritual safety net for such a time. Read the questions below. Discuss the topics with your family and friends. Consider your plans for spiritual health an important safety net to have in place in healthy times as well as in times of illness.

1. In Sirach 6:16 we read that a loyal friend is a life-saving remedy. What qualities should a person have in order to be considered a life-saving remedy?_____

_____

_____

_____

_____

2. What spiritual attitudes or habits can you develop now to prepare you to do what God wants in both sickness and health?_____

_____

_____

_____

_____

3. How will reflecting on the Scriptures help you flex spiritual muscle at all times? What are your favorite readings that comfort you when your spirit sags?_____

_____

_____

_____

_____

4. What can you do to develop a supportive atmosphere at home, in school, in your neighborhood? How can you tone things down when they reach a fever pitch? How can you pump supportive energy into attitudes weakened by indifference?_____

_____

_____

_____

_____

Even when I walk through a dark valley,
    I fear no harm for you are at my side....
You anoint my head with oil;
    my cup overflows.

Psalm 23:4–5

The Anointing of the Sick

CHAPTER 11

Objective: To discover that Jesus and his Church are signs of God's healing.

Introduction ___ min.

Opening Prayer: Invite the young people to imagine that they are sitting or walking with Jesus in a quiet place. They are sharing with him their questions, concerns, and fears about the existence of illness and pain in the world. Have the young people write their reflections in their journals. You may wish to share the following young person's prayer with the group:

> Jesus, there were many times throughout your life when you experienced the same emotions I feel now. Often I forget the fact that you were once a young person like each of us. You worried about the problems facing society, even though they may have been different from the ones we face. You loved your family and friends. You laughed when something brought you joy. Many times you felt pity for those who were suffering, and you even cried at Lazarus's tomb. When you were taken away by those who wanted to convict you, all your friends left you, and you were alone. It probably was difficult for you to explain to those around you that you were the son of God, and you felt discouraged.
>
> Dear Jesus, help each of us to remember these things. Help us to understand and to have insight. Each of us is a special sign of God's love. Help us to see that in each of us, and never let us be afraid to show our emotions, especially the love that we have for you! Thanks for showing us that it is okay to feel the way we do!
>
> *Elizabeth*
> Holy Cross High School
> Marine City, Michigan

Have the young people look at the photo on pages 126 and 127 as you read Psalm 23:1–4 from the Bible. Ask, "Why might we compare experiencing physical suffering with walking through a dark valley?" "How does knowing that Jesus is with us give us comfort and support?"

Presentation ___ min.

◆ Ask a volunteer to read the introductory paragraph on page 128. Remind the young people that pain, suffering, and death are the effects of original sin.

Have a different volunteer read each paragraph on page 128. Ask the young people to highlight the last two sentences on this page.

◆ Have the young people form buzz groups to discuss ways that we exercise our responsibilities for personal health and safety. Ask the young people to include the dangers of exercise addiction and couch potato-ism. Point out that we need to maintain a balance between exercise and relaxation. Suggest that including prayer in exercise or relaxation time is a healthy way to deepen our friendship with God.

◆ Ask a volunteer to read the first paragraph on page 129. Emphasize that it is everyone's responsibility to learn about our bodies so we can care for them and seek appropriate help when we experience pain. Our studies will also help us dispel myths or false teachings about suffering and illness.

◆ Have a volunteer read the last two paragraphs in the left column on page 129. Discuss people who have given us good example in the face of suffering. You may wish to show one of the following videos:

- *Tyler, A Real Hero* is a film about a college athlete whose life was changed dramatically by a paralyzing accident.
- *Encounter with Garvan Byrne* is a film about a twelve-year-old boy who suffered from painful bone cancer. In the film he shares his insights about the meaning of life and his deep faith in Jesus.

Both videos are available from:
Ignatius Press
P.O. Box 1339
Ft. Collins, CO 80522

- Have the young people read the healing of Peter's mother-in-law (Mark 1:29–31) and the healing of the paralytic (Mark 2:1–12). Then ask the students to work in small groups to prepare eyewitness accounts of those whose lives were changed by Jesus' healing touch. Have one person in each group act as a reporter interviewing the eyewitnesses for a nightly news feature.

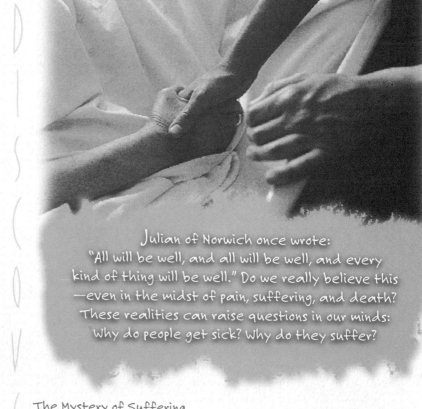

Julian of Norwich once wrote: "All will be well, and all will be well, and every kind of thing will be well." Do we really believe this —even in the midst of pain, suffering, and death? These realities can raise questions in our minds: Why do people get sick? Why do they suffer?

The Mystery of Suffering

People have asked questions like these since the beginning of time!

There is no easy answer to the mystery of illness. It is one of those big questions whose answer is discovered bit by bit through our lived experience.

It is also a dangerous question because we can easily jump to overly simplified (and consequently, wrong) answers: "He got sick because he was bad." "She is ill because God wants her to suffer." It is very dangerous to think in this way, for such thinking leads to false conclusions about suffering and false conclusions about God.

We know that God created us out of love, and that creation is holy and good. Suffering and illness do not exist because God wants them to exist. But if they do not come from him, where do they come from?

Sometimes, but not always, they come from our own ignorance and poor decisions. We have the responsiblity to care for our bodies, to be attentive to proper nourishment, exercise, rest, and relaxation. Pain is often a message from the body telling us that something is wrong, that something needs to be corrected or cared for.

128

man illness can urge us to learn more about
functions of the body through the study of
mistry, biology, physiology, and other sciences.
so doing, perhaps we can help others someday.
n more important, illness is a call to learn more
ut our inner selves, about life and its meaning.

know that one of the hardest things about being
k is the sudden end to our ordinary activities at
ool, with friends, in sports, and so on. Much of
way we think about ourselves is tied up with
at we can do. When our health is taken away, we
d that we cannot do very much! Then we begin to
nder who we really are.

faith gives us a new way of seeing illness. In
d's eyes we are more than what we do, more
n our accomplishments. The world often judges
ple by how much money they make, by how
ny things they have. Illness can remind us that
d loves us for who we are, not for what we have
what we do.

Jesus Heals a Blind Man,
Duccio di Buoninsegna,
thirteenth century

Jesus and Healing

We know about God's love and concern for the
sick because we can see it made visible in Jesus.
On almost every page of the gospels, we see Jesus
bringing health and wholeness to those who are
ill and suffering.

Look, for example, at the first chapter of Mark's
Gospel. After Jesus called the first disciples, he cured
a man with an unclean spirit; then he cured Peter's
mother-in-law, who was in bed with a fever. Mark
continues: "When it was evening, after sunset, they
brought to him all who were ill or possessed by
demons. The whole town was gathered at the door.
He cured many who were sick with various diseases,
and he drove out many demons" (1:32–34). Mark
tells us that Jesus' reputation as a healer spread so far
and wide that "it was impossible for Jesus to enter a
town openly. He remained outside in deserted places,
and people kept coming to him from everywhere"
(Mark 1:45).

All this takes place in just the first chapter of
Mark's Gospel! Jesus has hardly begun his ministry,
but already he is known as someone who
heals the sick and cares for them.

Jesus himself is a visible sign of God's
desire for our health and wholeness. Jesus
"spoke to them of the kingdom of God,
and he healed those who needed to be
cured" (Luke 9:11). When we see Jesus in
this way as a sign of God's healing, we
are well on our way to understanding the
Church as a sign of healing. The Church
exercises this ministry in many ways and
celebrates it in the sacrament of the
Anointing of the Sick.

129

FORUM Assignment

✔ Read pages 130 and 131. Underline
in pencil the statements that express
six main ideas.

✔ Complete the handout *A Spiritual
Safety Net.*

Closing Prayer: Invite the young people to look at the artwork on pages 128
and 129 as you pray a spontaneous
litany of petition. Ask the group to
respond, "Jesus, bring your healing
touch to our world" after each petition.
You may wish to begin by praying the
following petitions:

• Jesus, help us to act in kindness and
compassion when we hear a friend is
ill.

• Jesus, help our health care workers to
act with compassion, not indifference.

Conclusion ___ min.

◆ Ask volunteers to read "Jesus and Healing" on page
129. Have the young people highlight the statements
highlighted here.

• Distribute copies of the handout *A Spiritual Safety
Net.* Have a volunteer read the directions. Ask for
volunteers to make a net to use for prayer and *Forum*
discussions in the four remaining sessions for this
chapter.

FOR SESSION **2**

• index cards (one for each person)
• recording of "On Eagle's Wings" by Michael Joncas
• net made by volunteers

Objective: To explore the historical development of the rites that the Church uses to continue the healing ministry of Jesus.

Introduction ___ min.

Opening Prayer

Forum: Have a volunteer act as a "television talk-show host" to facilitate discussion of the questions on the handout *A Spiritual Safety Net.* Distribute index cards and have the young people write one or two actions that would help people to develop and promote a spiritually supportive environment in school. Have the volunteers display the net, and attach the index cards to it. Keep the net in your designated prayer space.

Discuss the statements that the young people underlined on these pages. Have them highlight the statements highlighted here.

Presentation ___ min.

◆ Point out the last paragraph on page 130. Invite the group to think of the ways we still use oil in the care of our bodies and as a healing ointment today. You may want to ask a volunteer to list these on the board. (Possible responses: as sunscreen, as bath oil, as ointment for sore muscles) Emphasize that we still use oil to "heal and strengthen and preserve."

◆ Ask a volunteer to read aloud the passage from the Letter of James (James 5:13–15) in the first column. Stress that this is an early account of the community involved in prayer for healing. Suggest that volunteers look up and read these accounts of healing in the early Church: Acts 5:12–16; Acts 9:32–35; and Acts 14:8–10.

Ask, "Who is healing in these passages?" (Peter, Paul, and Barnabas) Stress that the author of Acts wanted to emphasize that these leaders of the Church had received the power and authority of Jesus himself. This is when healing took place.

Healing in the Early Church

Jesus' desire to heal the sick did not stop when he ascended into heaven. He had told his disciples to continue this work: "So.... they anointed with oil many who were sick and cured them" (Mark 6:12–13).

In the Letter of James, we read of the way in which one early Christian community continued this healing work of Jesus. "Is anyone among you suffering? He should pray. Is anyone in good spirits? He should sing praise. Is anyone among you sick? He should summon the presbyters of the church, and they should pray over him and anoint [him] with oil in the name of the Lord, and the prayer of faith will save the sick person, and the Lord will raise him up. If he has committed any sins, he will be forgiven" (James 5:13–15).

James tells us that prayer is necessary in every situation in our lives: when we are well, when we are sick, and at every moment in between. Look at the passage from the Letter of James again. Prayer is mentioned in every verse. It is in this context of prayer that James tells us of his community's practice of praying for the sick. The sick person calls for the priests. When they arrive, they pray. The phrase "pray over" the sick person suggests a laying on of hands, the ancient sign of blessing. They anoint the sick person with oil.

The community of that time would have been familiar with the use of oil as a common medicine. People rubbed oil on their bodies as an ointment to heal and strengthen and preserve. In the story of the Good Samaritan, we read that when the Samaritan found the man who had fallen prey to robbers, he bandaged the man's wounds and poured oil on them (Luke 10:34).

130

◆ Direct attention to the *Scripture Update* on page 131. Ask volunteers to look up and read each of the Scripture passages listed there. Explain that the Church has always been concerned about the sick as we see in the Acts of the Apostles and the letter of James. Later, many monasteries set aside a section of the guest house as an infirmary for the sick of the area. These were the first hospitals. Saints of every age have been concerned for the sick. Some of these saints are: John of God, Camillus de Lellis, Vincent de Paul, Frances of Rome, and Margaret of Scotland. Some religious congregations were founded especially to help the sick, like the Little Company of Mary, the Alexian Brothers, the Dominican Sisters of the Sick Poor, and the Missionaries of Charity, founded by Mother Teresa. You may want to suggest that volunteers research these saints and congregations.

...ealing and Anointing

...e rites that the Church uses to continue the ...aling ministry of Jesus have changed and ...veloped through the centuries, just as the "rites" ...edical doctors use to cure and heal have changed. ...ing to the doctor in times past was a different ...perience from a visit to the doctor today.

...hen Saint Francis of Assisi suffered from severe ...ins in his eyes, the doctor heated metal axheads in ...ire and, when they were red-hot, pressed them to ...ancis's temples so that the burning irons would ...aw the pain out of his eyes. When we consider the ...mmon medical practices of those times, we see ...hy one would put off going to the doctor as long as ...ssible! If the disease didn't kill you, the doctor ...obably would.

...the same time period, when priests and teachers ...plained the meaning of the rites of anointing, ...ey drew a parallel between physical healing by ...edical doctors and spiritual healing administered ...the Church. Many good things can be learned ...om this analogy. But one bad effect it had was ...at the Church's anointing was put off as long as ...ssible, just as going to the doctor was put off ...til the sick person was at death's door. The ...cramental anointing (*unction* in Latin) came to be ...called *Extreme Unction*, the last anointing. The ...crament for the *sick* became a sacrament only for ...e *dying*. The priest's final absolution of our sins ...d this anointing at the time of death came to be ...lled the *last rites*.

OI stands for Oleum Infirmorum
(*Latin for* Oil of the Sick).

The focus of the sacrament then changed from physical healing to spiritual healing, to the forgiveness of sins. The public, liturgical rite of the early Church became a private ceremony. Often only the priest and the dying person were present. Extreme Unction had become more private than public, more fearful than joyful, and more dreaded than celebrated. For many Catholics, when the priest arrived with the holy oil for the last rites, it was a sure sign of death.

Catholics experienced Extreme Unction in this way from the Middle Ages until the Second Vatican Council in this century. Following the liturgical reforms of this Council, Extreme Unction became once again the sacrament of the Anointing of the Sick as we know it today.

 Take a moment to think of those "among you" who are sick. Pray for them now.

Scripture UPDATE

As we have seen, Luke's Gospel and the Acts of the Apostles together form one work. Luke sets out to show how the mission of Jesus is continued in the work of the apostles and in the Church community through the ages. Read these parallel healing stories: Luke 5:17–26 and Acts 3:1–10. How does the Church today continue this healing ministry?

FYI

Rose Hawthorne Lathrop was the youngest daughter of the American writer Nathaniel Hawthorne and Sarah Peabody Hawthorne. In 1871, Rose married George Parsons Lathrop, and they lived in New York City. Their son, Francis, died of diphtheria at the age of five. Both Rose and her husband converted to Catholicism ten years later. Through a Passionist priest, Rose learned the plight of a young seamstress suffering from cancer in a home for the destitute. Rose determined to help poor cancer sufferers. After training at a cancer hospital, she began her work in one of the poorest parts of the city.

131

Conclusion___ min.

◆ Explain to the young people that after the death of her husband, Rose Hawthorne Lathrop made her first vows as a Dominican sister. Her congregation was founded as the "Servants of Relief for Incurable Cancer," but is now popularly known as "the Hawthorne Dominicans."

◆ Ask a volunteer to summarize the history of the sacrament of healing under its various names.

FORUM Assignment

✔ Read pages 132 and 133. Underline in pencil the statements that express five main ideas.

✔ Imagine that someone in your family, or a friend of yours, becomes ill. What would you say to persuade him or her to receive the sacrament of the Anointing of the Sick the next time your parish celebrates it? Write a dialogue between you and the sick person.

Closing Prayer: Call attention to the thought provoker on page 131. Take time to pray a short litany for the sick people known to your group. The response might be, "Lord, heal him (her) and bring him (her) peace."

You may want to end the prayer by having the young people listen to a recording of a song offering encouragement and hope. "On Eagle's Wings" by Michael Joncas from the album *On Eagle's Wings*, (OCP) is a suggestion.

FOR SESSION 3

• index cards (two for each student)
• net made for Session 2

SESSION 3

Objective: To understand the changes suggested by the Second Vatican Council and the celebration of the Anointing of the Sick during Sunday liturgy.

Introduction ___ min.

Opening Prayer

Forum: Have the young people work in pairs to role-play a young person trying to convince a family member to participate in a communal celebration of the Anointing of the Sick. Then discuss what the young people's responses would be if they became ill and were encouraged to participate in a parish celebration.

Presentation ___ min.

◆ Discuss with the young people the statements they underlined for "Not Just for the Dying," on page 132.

◆ Have the young people form small groups to be TV or radio-commentator teams. Ask them to explain to listeners or viewers each part of the Anointing of the Sick as it takes place at a Sunday liturgy. In their commentaries, they may also want to include a discussion of the changes in the celebration of the sacrament made after the Second Vatican Council.

◆ Have the young people discuss the statements they underlined for "Celebration of Anointing." Ask them to highlight or underline in color the main ideas highlighted on these pages.

◆ If time permits, plan and celebrate a prayer session for those who are ill. The following suggestions may be helpful.

Gathering Prayer: The group may wish to make up their own prayer, or use the following:

Father,
the cross of Jesus Christ, your Son,
is now a sign of life and victory.

We gather to pray for the sick
who share in his suffering.
Give them courage and healing.

We ask this through Christ our Lord.
Amen.

Not Just for the Dying

To remove the atmosphere of hesitation and fear that surrounded Extreme Unction, the Second Vatican Council made three important changes.

First, it was important to teach that this sacrament is not just intended for the dying, that it is primarily a sacrament of healing for all Christians who are seriously ill. It can be received more than once—each time, in fact, that a Christian becomes seriously ill, and again if the illness worsens. So the Council suggested that we call this sacrament not Extreme Unction but the sacrament of the *Anointing of the Sick.*

Second, this sacrament of healing was restored to its liturgical (public) setting. No longer was it to be considered a private action between the priest and the sick person. The community's role of prayerful support was restored, and the celebration of the Anointing of the Sick within the Eucharist was encouraged.

Third, the focus of the sacrament was directed once again toward *healing.* In anointing the hands of the sick, the priest leads the community in prayer:

> May the Lord who frees you from sin
> save you and raise you up.

We pray that our sick brothers and sisters will be raised up to share in the life of the resurrected Jesus—both physically and spiritually.

Celebration of Anointing

The celebration of the sacrament may take various forms: It may take place at a Sunday or weekday Mass in a parish church, in the home of the sick person, in the hospital, or in an emergency situation. Here is a general description of the way the sacrament is celebrated at the Sunday liturgy.

Gathering The parish Eucharist begins as usual. Sometimes the sick, along with the whole congregation, are blessed with baptismal water. In Baptism we died with Christ; the suffering that these sick persons are now experiencing is part of that dying.

132

Storytelling We then read from the Sacred Scriptures and hear how Christ has conquered suffering and death by his own death and resurrection. Usually the readings assigned for the Sunday are appropriate because nearly every page of Scripture speaks of God's desire for our health and healing.

The homily relates the readings to the Christian meaning of suffering. Those who are ill or suffering can freely and lovingly choose to unite their sufferings with the sufferings of Christ. Following the homily we join in a litany of intercession for the sick, for the parish, and for the needs of the world.

Imposition of Hands Those to be anointed are invited to come forward. With silent and intense prayer to the Holy Spirit, the priest lays his hand on the head of each person. This is one of the key symbolic actions of the sacrament. The gesture indicates that this particular person is the object of the Church's prayer. It is a sign of blessing. Most important, it was Jesus' own gesture of healing: "At sunset, all who had people sick with various diseases brought them to him. He laid his hands on each of them and cured them" (Luke 4:40).

Storytelling: The group may choose a favorite passage from the gospels on the theme of healing. The following are suggestions:

• Mark 2:1–12 (healing for the paralytic)
• Luke 7:18b–23 (the healings of Jesus)
• John 5:1–9 (cure at the pool of Bethesda)

Prayers of Intercession: Draw the young people's attention to the net used in Session 2. Remove the cards that are on it. Then give each person an index card. On the card, ask the young people to write down people who are sick, not identified by individual name, but by group: for example, those suffering from cancer, those suffering from Alzheimer's disease.

vocation The priest blesses God for the gift of Olive oil reminds us of the suffering of Jesus the Garden of Olives (Luke 22:39–46). The oil lessed by the bishop of the diocese on Holy ursday. It is this blessing that makes the oil ramental. Sometimes the priest blesses the oil the time of anointing. He prays:

God of all consolation,
you chose and sent your Son to heal the world.
Graciously listen to our prayer of faith:
send the power of your Holy Spirit, the Consoler,
into this precious oil, this soothing ointment,
this rich gift, this fruit of the earth.

Bless this oil † and sanctify it for our use.

Make this oil a remedy for all who are anointed
    with it;
heal them in body, in soul, and in spirit,
and deliver them from every affliction.
We ask this through our Lord Jesus Christ, your
    Son,
who lives and reigns with you and the Holy Spirit,
one God, for ever and ever.
Amen.

Anointing with Oil Next we see the essential rite of the sacrament. The priest anoints each sick person with the oil. He makes the sign of the cross first on the person's forehead and then on the palm of each hand. He prays that God in his love and mercy will "raise" the sick person to health. We all respond, "Amen."

Look again at the blessing of the oil of the sick. What does the prayer say about God? About oil? What does it ask for the sick?

CATHOLIC TEACHINGS

About Viaticum

In addition to the sacrament of the Anointing of the Sick, the Church provides another great gift to those who are close to death: the Eucharist. Holy Communion given to the dying is called *Viaticum,* a word from Latin that literally means "with you on the way." Communion has a special significance when received at the close of life. "It is the seed of eternal life and the power of the resurrection" (*Catechism,* 1524).

133

Closing Hymn: End with an appropriate hymn of peace and encouragement, or a recording of a song with the theme of hope and courage.

Conclusion ___ min.

◆ Draw attention to the thought provoker on page 133. Ask three different volunteers to answer the three questions posed.

◆ Ask a volunteer to summarize *Catholic Teachings* on page 133.

FORUM Assignment

✔ Read pages 134 and 135. Underline in pencil the statements that express six main ideas.

✔ Compose a personal message to a person who is ill. Use some of the ideas on pages 134 and 135 to explain what you consider this person contributes to the parish and the Church. Ask the person for prayers for yourself, your family, and your friends.

Closing Prayer: Ask the young people to turn to page 187 to find the traditional prayer for those who have died. Lead the group in the prayer, "Eternal rest grant unto them, O Lord."

For the prayer, ask each person to read one group from her or his list, and then attach the card to the "Prayer Network." A suggested response is "May the Lord bless you and keep you and give you strength."

Final Prayer: This prayer is taken from the Liturgy of Anointing.

Father in heaven. . .
    grant [the sick we have prayed for]
        comfort in [their] suffering.

When they are afraid, give [them]
        courage,
when afflicted, give [them] patience,
when dejected, afford [them] hope,
and when alone, assure [them] of the
        support of your holy people.

We ask this through Christ our Lord.
Amen.

Just in case... some pronunciation helps

Viaticum . . . . *vi-**ah**-tih-kum*

FOR SESSION 4

- large pieces of cardboard, butcher paper
- magazines and scissors
- construction paper
- blank audiocassette and cassette recorder

SESSION 4

Objective: To explore the sacrament of the Anointing of the Sick as a ritual that makes present the Church as a community of healing and support.

Introduction ___ min.

Opening Prayer

Forum: Ask the young people to gather in small groups. Have them share their encouraging words, and have them ask one another for help in refining and "polishing." Then, according to your preference, have them share their words of encouragement with the sick in one or more of the following ways:

• Make a large greeting card out of cardboard covered with butcher paper. Each young person may write an encouraging note on the card and sign the note (first names only).

• Make a large mural with colorful pictures and encouraging messages on it. Send it for display to a hospital or nursing home.

• Each young person may make an individual card for a nursing-home or rehabilitation-center resident, or for a child in a hospital. They should use simple language if the card is intended for a child.

• The words of encouragement may be recorded on a cassette tape. The tape may then be given to a eucharistic minister or parish visitor to play for sick or homebound parishioners on the next visit. Your group may want to add a favorite song to their words of encouragement.

Presentation ___ min.

◆ Have the students discuss the statements they underlined on these pages. Then have them highlight or underline in color the statements highlighted here.

◆ Explain that in the sacrament of the Anointing of the Sick both the community and the sick are signs to each other. Ask the following questions:

• What do the sick bring to the community? (They witness to our baptismal promises to die and be buried with Christ, offering their suffering in union with Christ's, for the good of the Church and the salvation of the world.)

Following the Gospel and homily at next Sunday's Mass, we will celebrate the sacrament of the Anointing of the Sick. Volunteers are needed to help our infirm parishioners. Call the parish office.

An Exchange of Signs

In the liturgy signs are given and signs are received. The care and concern of the Christian community is a sign to the sick person of the Lord's own great concern for the bodily and spiritual welfare of the sick. We who are the body of Christ must continue to proclaim the kingdom of wholeness and salvation in word and deed.

The celebration of the sacrament of the Anointing of the Sick is a ritual moment that makes visible and present to the sick and to the whole community who we are as Church: a community of healing and support. That is why the whole parish community is invited to come together in prayerful support of those among us who are in special need.

The sick, in return, offer a sign to the community: In this sacrament they give witness to their promises at Baptism to die with Christ and be buried with him. They tell the community that they are prepared to offer their suffering, in union with Christ's, for the good of the whole Church and the salvation of the world.

This exchange of signs between the sick and the healthy members of the community is at the heart of the sacrament. The sick are assured in the ritual that their suffering is not useless, that it is a sharing in the saving work of Jesus. Their sins are forgiven. At the same time the Church asks the Lord to lighten their suffering, to give them peace and courage, and to save them.

134

The sick are recognized as productive members of the community of faith, contributing to the welfare of us all by associating themselves freely with Christ's passion and death. The sick embody for us the words of Paul to Timothy:

> If we have died with him
> we shall also live with him. . . .
> 2 Timothy 2:11

For All Ages

Who can receive anointing? How sick does one have to be in order to be anointed? The Church tells us that the sacrament is for those whose health is seriously impaired by sickness or old age. One does *not* have to be in danger of death. The sacrament is most fruitful when the person being anointed is well enough to participate fully in it.

A person can be anointed before surgery when a serious illness or disability is the reason for the operation. In this case it is preferable to celebrate the sacrament even before the person goes to the hospital.

• What does the Church ask the Lord to do for the sick? (to lighten their suffering, to give them peace and courage, and to save them)

◆ Direct attention to the section "For All Ages" beginning on page 134. Ask, "Who can receive anointing?" You may want to list the answers on the board.

◆ Ask a volunteer to explain this statement found on page 135 in reference to the sacrament of Anointing of the Sick: "But some form of healing does take place. It is not always physical healing; sometimes it is a healing of the spirit." Ask another volunteer to give some examples of "healing of the spirit," suggesting that these can be found in the last paragraph on page 135.

ere are times when old age and the fear and
eliness that can sometimes come with it need to
brought to the healing presence of Christ in this
rament. At the same time it is important to avoid
ntifying illness with certain age groups. Today
do not automatically equate high numerical age
h fragile health, weakness, or inactivity.

e sacrament is for all ages and all types of illness.
k children who have sufficient use of reason to
strengthened by the sacrament can be anointed.
sons with the disease of alcoholism or suffering
m other addictions can be anointed, as can those
o suffer from various mental disorders.

t the big question is, "Does it work?" Does the
k person experience healing? The answer is
. The sacrament is the prayer of the Church,
e body of Christ. Christ himself has assured us
at whatever we ask the Father in his name will
granted.

ple who have been anointed are eager to tell of
healing that they experienced. And often the
ries they tell are of wonderful, unexplainable
aling. Sometimes, for others, the stories are less
ectacular. But some form of healing does take
place. It is not always physical healing; sometimes
it is a healing of the spirit. The sacrament is never
a substitute for the work of doctors and nurses,
drugs and hospitals. God's healing power also
works through the hands and intelligence of
medical professionals.

In the sacrament we pray that the sick be healed
in body, in soul, and in spirit. God knows more
than we do what healing the sick person might
need most: that a wound be healed, that a fear turn
to confidence, that loneliness disappear, that
bafflement in the face of all the whys—Why me?
Why suffering? Why now?—may turn into
understanding. Ultimately we pray that the
sacrament of the Anointing of the Sick will give us
a better understanding of the mystery of a loving
God who raised his crucified Son, bearing his
victorious wounds, to be with the Father in glory.

 Describe what you think is meant by spiritual healing.

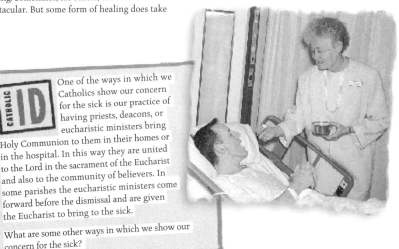

One of the ways in which we Catholics show our concern for the sick is our practice of having priests, deacons, or eucharistic ministers bring Holy Communion to them in their homes or in the hospital. In this way they are united to the Lord in the sacrament of the Eucharist and also to the community of believers. In some parishes the eucharistic ministers come forward before the dismissal and are given the Eucharist to bring to the sick.

What are some other ways in which we show our concern for the sick?

135

Conclusion ___ min.

◆ Draw attention to *Catholic ID* on page 135. Take this opportunity to acquaint the young people with the work of parish groups who help the sick. Perhaps the Saint Vincent De Paul Society collects blankets or brings food and clothing to the homebound. Other groups may sew or make bandages for the sick. There may be a phone network to support the sick in prayer, or a group of people who are involved bringing meals to the sick and homebound.

FORUM Assignment

✔ Read pages 136 and 137. Prepare your answers for *Testing 1, 2, 3*. Be prepared to share them with the group.

✔ Prepare your responses for *Things to Think About* and *Things to Share*.

Closing Prayer: Explain that the following "Prayer for All Needs" was written by Saint Clement of Rome. Pause briefly after reading each line, and ask the group to repeat it reverently.

We beg you, Lord,
to help and defend us.

Deliver the oppressed.
Pity the insignificant.
Raise the fallen.
Show yourself to the needy.
Heal the sick.

May every nation come to know
that you alone are God,
that Jesus is your Child,
that we are your people, the sheep that you pasture.
Amen.

◆ Emphasize with the young people that through this sacrament we are strengthened to unite ourselves more closely to the passion of Christ. Our suffering is transformed into and becomes a participation in the saving work of Christ. Help the young people realize that for those who suffer from terminal illness and will not recover this sacrament will help them give witness with dignity and peace.

Note: The Church's teaching about moral issues at times of sickness and death are addressed in Chapter 8 of *Morality: A Course on Catholic Living*, William H. Sadlier's *Faith and Witness* Program.

FOR SESSION 5

• copies of *Chapter 11 Assessment*, page 138A
• copies of *Highlights for Home*, page 138B

135

SESSION 5

Objective: To deepen understanding of the sacrament of the Anointing of the Sick.

Introduction ___ min.

Opening Prayer

Forum: Form small groups to discuss the questions posed in *Things to Think About* and *Things to Share*. Ask for a volunteer from each group to summarize the small group's discussion for the group as a whole.

Presentation ___ min.

◆ Direct the students' attention to *Words to Remember*. The definition for *Anointing of the Sick* can be found on page 132; the definition for *Viaticum* can be found on page 133.

◆ Discuss together *On Line with the Parish*. You may want to write a group letter to the pastor or liturgy committee, expressing the group's willingness to help with the next scheduled celebration of the sacrament of the Anointing of the Sick. The group may also want to plan a long-term project, perhaps to announce the celebration with a poster or to enhance it with a banner.

The group may also want to compose a prayer for the sick of the parish and have it published in the parish bulletin as a reminder to all the parish to support its infirm members. This prayer can help invite all parishioners to celebrate the sacrament with the sick the next time it is offered.

Assessment: If time permits, have the students share their answers they have written for *Testing 1, 2, 3* with the entire group.

If you are administering *Chapter 11 Assessment*, page 137A, allow the students about ten minutes to complete the test.

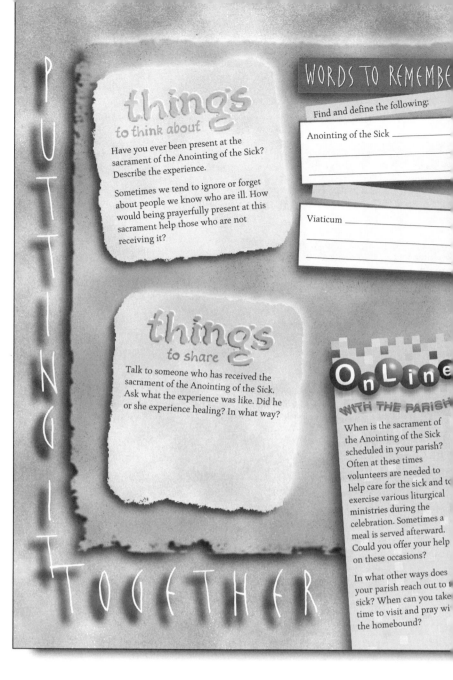

PUTTING IT TOGETHER

things to think about

Have you ever been present at the sacrament of the Anointing of the Sick? Describe the experience.

Sometimes we tend to ignore or forget about people we know who are ill. How would being prayerfully present at this sacrament help those who are not receiving it?

things to share

Talk to someone who has received the sacrament of the Anointing of the Sick. Ask what the experience was like. Did he or she experience healing? In what way?

WORDS TO REMEMBER

Find and define the following:

Anointing of the Sick _____

_____

Viaticum _____

_____

OnLine WITH THE PARISH

When is the sacrament of the Anointing of the Sick scheduled in your parish? Often at these times volunteers are needed to help care for the sick and to exercise various liturgical ministries during the celebration. Sometimes a meal is served afterward. Could you offer your help on these occasions?

In what other ways does your parish reach out to the sick? When can you take time to visit and pray with the homebound?

Conclusion ___ min.

◆ Encourage the young people to share *Highlights for Home*, page 137B, with their families.

Closing Prayer: First ask the group to copy the prayer given in *Life in the Spirit* into their journals. Then have the young people read the prayer together in a reverent way. You may want to end the session with a recording of "Day by Day," from the musical *Godspell*. The lyrics for this song are based on the prayer by Saint Richard of Chichester.

How do we know about God's love and concern for the sick? Give two examples from the gospels.

1

List three ways in which the sacrament of the Anointing of the Sick is different from Extreme Unction.

2

What different forms of celebration may the sacrament of the Anointing of the Sick take?

3

Who can receive this sacrament? How sick does a person have to be to receive it?

4

How does a communal celebration of the sacrament of the Anointing of the Sick benefit the whole parish?

Testing 1,2,3

Chapter 11·Session 5

Life
in the Spirit

The prayer below was written by Saint Richard of Chichester, an English bishop who cared for the poor and the needy. Use it as a prayer of thanksgiving and as a prayer of discipleship, asking for the grace to follow Jesus each day, in sickness and in health!

Thanks be to you, Lord Jesus Christ,
for all the benefits and blessings
which you have given to me....
O most merciful friend, brother, and redeemer,
may I know you more clearly,
love you more dearly,
and follow you more nearly.

137

Testing 1,2,3

1. See page 129. We know about God's love and concern for the sick because we can see it made visible in Jesus. Throughout the gospels, we see Jesus bringing health and wholeness to the suffering. Accept descriptions of two accounts of Jesus' healing.

2. See pages 131–132. The focus of Extreme Unction was spiritual healing, the forgiveness of sins; it was private and only for the dying. The focus of Anointing is physical and spiritual healing; it is a public, liturgical rite and can be received more than once.

3. See page 132. The celebration may take place at a Sunday or weekday Mass in a parish church, in the home of a sick person, in the hospital, or in an emergency situation.

4. See pages 134–135. The sacrament is for those whose health is seriously impaired by sickness or old age. It is for all ages and all types of illness, including sick children who have sufficient use of reason and those who suffer from addiction or various mental disorders.

5. See page 134. The celebration of the sacrament is a ritual moment that makes visible and present to the sick and to the whole community who we are as Church—a community of healing and support.

Evaluation: Do the young people understand the Church as a community of healing and support for the sick? Do they understand the history of the sacrament of the Anointing of the Sick? Do they appreciate the sacrament as a sign of both physical and spiritual healing?

Answers for Chapter 11 Assessment

1. b   2. b   3. d   4. c   5. a
6. d   7. b   8. a   9. d   10. See page 134.

137

Assessment

1 Jesus' desire to heal the sick _____ when he ascended into heaven.

a. stopped completely
b. did not stop
c. was of no concern to his disciples
d. had no meaning

2 Illness should remind us that

a. God is punishing us.
b. God loves us for who we are.
c. we are basically lazy.
d. we are useless.

3 The name *Extreme Unction* means

a. "anointing with oil."
b. "physical healing."
c. "spiritual healing."
d. "the last anointing."

4 Most of the time during Extreme Unction _____ were present.

a. relatives and friends
b. the physician, the priest, and the patient
c. only the priest and the dying person
d. none of the above

5 During the liturgical celebration of Anointing, the priest anoints with oil _____ of the sick person.

a. the forehead and each hand
b. the hands, lips, and eyes
c. the lips, eyes, and forehead
d. the eyes, ears, and heart

6 The word *Viaticum* means

a. "the last anointing."
b. "Jesus' healing touch."
c. "anointing with oil."
d. "with you on the way."

7 Viaticum is _____ the dying.

a. the sacrament of Reconciliation for
b. Holy Communion given to
c. the last anointing of
d. the laying on of hands over

8 The Second Vatican Council suggested that the sacrament

a. be called Anointing of the Sick.
b. is intended for the dying.
c. be considered a private action.
d. include final absolution of our sins.

9 Healing in the early Church included

a. anointing with oil.
b. laying on of hands.
c. forgiveness of sins.
d. all of the above

10 Explain the meaning of the exchange of signs between the sick and the healthy members of the community during the Anointing of the Sick. Write your response on the reverse side of this page.

Highlights for Home

Focus on Faith

Our bodies are fragile compositions which can break down and suffer from diseases like cancer and heart disease to injuries from accidents. These more devastating assaults on our bodies test our endurance and our faith. In times like these we have the assurance that God is with us as comforter and healer. The Church is the visible sign of his presence.

In times of illness and suffering, the sacrament of the Anointing of the Sick offers hope and comfort, strength and courage. The sacrament was once reserved for the dying; now it is celebrated for the living. It can be received more than once, each time, in fact, that a Christian becomes seriously ill. And it is always directed toward *healing*. We pray with the Church that our sick brothers and sisters will be "raised up" to share in the life of the risen Jesus — both physically and spiritually.

Conversation Starters

. . . . a few ideas to talk about together . . . .

◆ Am I comfortable around sick people? How can I remember to think of them as part of the faith community?

◆ How do I support the sick members of my parish? In prayer? In celebrating the Sacrament of Anointing when my parish schedules it? With cards or phone calls?

Feature Focus

The *Scripture Update* on page 131 reminds us that the healing ministry of the Church originated with Jesus, continued through the apostles, and now is an integral part of our mission today. You might want to consider the many ways the healing ministry of the Church touches your life and the life of the community around you. From large hospitals to mobile clinics, the Church tries to be a sign of healing for physical as well as spiritual ills.

Reflection

Take a moment to look at the photograph on pages 126 and 127. Then read the verse of Psalm 23 that it illustrates. This psalm is the well-known one which begins, "The LORD is my shepherd."

Have you ever heard the saying, "The only way out is through"? The key word is *through*. We will get through the dark valley because we are with the shepherd who is not walking far ahead of us, but, as the psalmist has written—at our side. Whenever we walk through the dark valley, we are not alone. Whatever the darkness—illness, lack of employment, a rift with a friend—we can trust that healing and a cup overflowing with mercy await us. "I can get through this, for you are at my side."

THE SACRAMENT OF HOLY ORDERS

Adult Focus

When Joseph Cardinal Bernardin died in 1997, he was remembered as a leader and teacher of gentleness and strength, a shepherd who sought justice at great cost to himself, a reconciler of opposing groups, and a wise mentor to his fellow priests. One person summed it up, saying, "He was a priest in the image of Christ."

This was a very appropriate description of Cardinal Bernardin; it is also close to being a definition of the priesthood itself. In the sacrament of Holy Orders, a man is called to share in a unique way Jesus' mission of "sanctifying, teaching, and building the Christian community." The ordained priest "becomes—in the Church and for the Church—a real, living, and faithful image of Christ, the priest" (*Directory on the Ministry and Life of Priests*, Vatican Congregation for the Clergy, 1994).

The ordained ministers of the Church are bishops, priests, and deacons. Bishops, who have the primary ministry to teach, govern, and sanctify, receive the fullness of the priesthood. They share their ministry with the priests and deacons whom they ordain by the laying on of hands. From the earliest days of the Church the ordained ministry has thus literally been handed on from the apostles, of whom our bishops today are the successors. It is through this succession that our faith has been preserved and strengthened through the centuries. Our young people need the security of knowing and appreciating that the Church is built on the solid rock of a faith consistently upheld by the teaching, governing, and sanctifying work of those ordained to be priests "in the image of Christ."

Catechism Focus

The themes of Chapter 12 correspond to paragraphs 1533–1536 and 1544–1588 of the *Catechism*.

Enrichment Activities

Write Requests

Several weeks before beginning this chapter, have the young people write to a variety of religious orders of priests, diocesan seminaries, and diocesan diaconate programs for vocational materials. Many addresses can be found in *The Official Catholic Directory*, available in most rectories.

Guest Speakers

Consider inviting a diocesan priest, a religious order priest, a seminarian, or a permanent deacon to speak to your group or to participate in a panel discussion. A good resource in regard to finding guest speakers is your diocesan director of vocations. Ask your pastor how you might contact him or her. Make a list of possible guests, and involve students in the process of planning and inviting. You may want to ask your guests to share videos of their ordinations.

Interviews

Have selected students prepare and conduct, by regular mail or E-mail, interviews with priests or permanent deacons who serve as chaplains of the following: police or sheriff departments, hospitals or emergency services, professional sports teams, prisons, state or federal legislatures, or the armed services. Students may want to invite these men to be guest speakers.

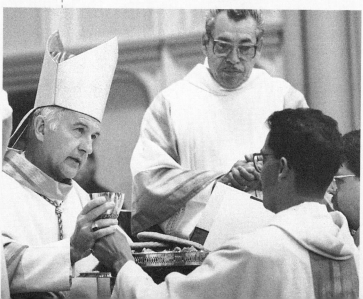

Teaching Resources

	Overview	Opening Prayer Ideas	Materials
SESSION 1	**Discovery:** To discover that in Holy Orders a man shares in the priesthood in three essential ways: ministry, divine worship, and authority.	Pray together a shortened form of the Litany of the Saints.	These will be needed for every session: texts, Bibles, highlighters or colored pencils. • copies of Closing Prayer (optional)
SESSION 2	**Exploring 1:** To explore the role of the bishop in the Church, to appreciate the liturgical rite of the ordination of a bishop.	Pray together the words of Saint Anselm, a bishop and doctor of the Church: Lord, while here on earth let me know you better, so that in heaven I may know you completely.	• construction paper and other materials for making bishop's crest • copies of handout *Following in Christ's Footsteps* • recording of song celebrating Jesus the Good Shepherd
SESSION 3	**Exploring 2:** To explore the connection between the roles of bishop and priest; to appreciate the liturgical rite of the ordination of a priest.	Reflect on the words of Saint John Vianney: "Prayer is honey making everything sweet; like the sun it melts the cold snow away."	• videotape of a priest's ordination (optional)
SESSION 4	**Exploring 3:** To explore the role of the deacon in the Church; to appreciate the liturgical rite of the ordination of a deacon.	Read together Acts 6:1–7 and share your reflections.	• posterboard for charts
SESSION 5	**Putting It Together:** To increase awareness of Holy Orders as the sacrament through which the mission and authority Christ gave his apostles continues in the Church.	Pray together the words of Saint Jerome, priest and doctor of the Church. Good Samaritan, come help me. I am like the sheep gone astray. Good Shepherd, come seek me and bring me home safe.	• copies of *Chapter 12 Assessment* • copies of *Highlights for Home*

Supplemental Resources

Video
The Changing Sacraments,
"Clerical Clarence: Priesthood"

Pamphlet
Catholic Youth Update, "What
Being a Priest Is All About"

St. Anthony Messenger Press/
Franciscan Communications
http://www.americancatholic.org

**Faith and Witness Journal:
Liturgy & Worship**

For Chapter 12 see pages
48–51.

CHAPTER twelve

Following in Christ's Footsteps

You are a reporter for a weekly news show. Your producer has given you an assignment. She wants a fifteen-minute segment about the role of a priest. The producer wants to make sure you cover three important areas: ministry, divine worship, and authority. She wants a "human interest" angle, too—something personal about this particular priest. (For example, when did he realize that he was being called by God to become a priest, to follow in Christ's footsteps in a unique and different way?)

This sheet is your "prep sheet." For each category, prepare two or three important questions to ask Father during your interview.

Ministry	Divine Worship
Authority	**Personal Information**

The Sacrament of Holy Orders

*How beautiful upon the mountains
    are the feet of him who brings glad tidings,
Announcing peace, bearing good news.*
Isaiah 52:7

Objective: To discover that in Holy Orders a man shares in the priesthood in three essential ways: ministry, divine worship, and authority.

Introduction ___ min.

Opening Prayer: Invite the young people to look at the photograph on pages 138 and 139. Read together Isaiah 52:7. Remind the group that we are all called by our Baptism to announce peace and to bear good news to others.

The priests of the Church are called to commit themselves to this work in a special way. This photograph shows an ordination ceremony at the moment when the Litany of the Saints is prayed over the candidates for the priesthood. At this moment, the entire Church in heaven and on earth is united in prayer for these men who have answered Christ's call to the ordained ministry. Pray the form of the litany below, calling on these saints to give guidance to those who are now serving in the priesthood.

The response for each of the following petitions is, "Pray for us."

Holy Mary, Mother of God,
Saint Michael,
Saint John the Baptist,
Saint Joseph,
Saint Peter and Saint Paul,
Saint Stephen,
Saint Francis Xavier,
Saint John Vianney,
All holy men and women,

Then you may want to sing together the last verse of the traditional hymn, "Faith of Our Fathers."

Faith of our fathers! We will love
Both friend and foe in all our strife:
And preach thee, too, as love knows how,
By kindly deeds and virtuous life.
Faith of our fathers, holy faith!
We will be true to thee till death.

Presentation ___ min.

◆ Draw attention to the statement at the top of page 140 and the question following it. Write the word *essential* on the board and record responses under it. To stimulate more thought at both "macro" and "micro" levels, rephrase the statement to read, "The pope is essential to the life of the parish. Why?" Help the group to see the relationship between their answers to these questions and their answers to the original question.

◆ Have the young people read page 140 silently. Then play a game of "What Is the Question?" You may divide the group into two teams if you wish. Read the statements below, and ask the group members to come up with the correct question for the statement. Make up additional statements as time permits.

- They consecrate each Christian for the common priesthood of the faithful. (What are the sacraments of Baptism and Confirmation?)

- It is the sacrament through which the mission and authority Christ gave his apostles continues in the Church. (What is Holy Orders?)

- They are the episcopate, the presbyterate, and the diaconate. (What are the three ranks of Holy Orders?)

- This word means "priest." (What is a *presbyter*?)

- They are ministry, divine worship, and authority. (What are the three essential ways a man shares in the priesthood of Christ?)

◆ Have three volunteers read "Ministry," "Divine Worship," and "Authority" on page 141. Then have the group highlight or underline in color the statements highlighted here.

◆ You may want to expand upon the meaning of *presbyterate* by supplying this historical context: When a local Church was founded, it was usually founded by an apostle or a leader, like Paul, who was called an *apostle* even though he was not one of the original Twelve. Once the local Church became established, the apostolic leaders moved on. But they chose and left behind local Church officers, whom they had

The priesthood is essential to the life of the Church. Why do you think this is so?

The Call to Holy Orders

Each of us was called at Baptism to share in the priesthood of Christ. We share in his priesthood by living out our baptismal promises and by continuing Christ's work on earth. The sacraments of Baptism and Confirmation consecrate each Christian for the common priesthood of the faithful. We are not ordained ministers, but we are called to share the good news of Christ and to carry on his mission in the world.

Some, however, are called to share in Christ's priesthood in a unique way as his ordained ministers. In the sacrament of Holy Orders, men are consecrated for a special life of sacramental ministry to the body of Christ, the Church. What makes the ordained ministry different?

140

Holy Orders is the sacrament through which the mission and authority Christ gave his apostles continues in the Church. The sacrament includes three ranks, or orders:

- the episcopate (bishops)
- the presbyterate (priests)
- the diaconate (deacons).

In this chapter we will look at each of these orders and examine the ways in which each is celebrated in the liturgy of the Church. In general, however, we can say that in Holy Orders a man shares in the priesthood in three essential ways: ministry, divine worship, and authority.

ordained by the laying on of hands. These men were called by a number of different titles: *pastor* (which means "shepherd"), *teacher*, *presbyter* (priest or elder) or *bishop* (overseer). The words seem to have been used interchangeably because official titles had not yet been determined. Gradually the title of *bishop* was used only for the successors of the apostolic leaders. The title *presbyter* was used for the other local officers.

Note: Refer to *Creed: A Course on Catholic Belief*, Chapter 12, for a more extensive presentation of this topic.

Note: For a clear statement and explanation of the question "Who can receive the sacrament?," see *Catechism*, 1577–1580.

Ministry Before Christ ascended into heaven, he gave his apostles this mandate:

Go, therefore, and make disciples of all nations, baptizing them in the name of the Father, and of the Son, and of the holy Spirit, teaching them to observe all that I have commanded you. And behold, I am with you always, until the end of the age.
Matthew 28:19–20

Those ordained to ministry today have the same mandate: to bring the gospel to all people and to baptize them in the name of the Trinity.

All ministry is service, and Jesus made quite clear that his ministers were to be the servants of the Church. At the Last Supper he washed the feet of his apostles, symbolically demonstrating their call to service. He told them that he "did not come to be served but to serve" (Mark 10:45).

We read in the Acts of the Apostles that after Jesus Christ ascended to his Father and after the coming of the Holy Spirit, the apostles led the early Church in two ways:

They traveled through the known world preaching the good news of salvation through Jesus Christ.

They taught and passed on to the early followers of Jesus their lived memories of his words and actions, especially of his death and resurrection.

With great power the apostles bore witness to the "resurrection of the Lord Jesus" (Acts 4:33).

Divine Worship At the Last Supper Jesus gave the Church his own Body and Blood in the Eucharist and told his apostles to "do this in memory of me" (Luke 22:19). The ordained ministers of the Church celebrate the Eucharist and the other sacraments with the people of God.

Priests share in Christ's priesthood to the highest degree in the Eucharist. In this divine worship they act in the person of Christ himself. They proclaim and offer to the Father Christ's paschal mystery, for "in the sacrifice of the Mass they make present again and apply, until the coming of the Lord, the unique sacrifice of the New Testament" — Christ himself (*Catechism*, 1566).

Clearly it is in the holy Eucharist that the whole ministry of the priest draws its strength.

Authority Ordained ministers share in the authority of Jesus Christ. In the gospel we see Jesus sending his disciples out to teach, to baptize, to heal, and to forgive with this authority.

After the resurrection the Church grew very rapidly as more and more people joined the Christian community. The apostles chose others to help them in their work of teaching and leading the Church in worship and service. The apostles laid their hands on them and prayed that the Holy Spirit would strengthen them. In time these successors of the apostles, as we will see, were called bishops. Bishops in turn ordained priests to help them in the work of ministry. The authority of bishops and priests comes, not from themselves, but from Jesus Christ.

"No one can give himself the mandate and the mission to proclaim the Gospel. The one sent by the Lord does not speak and act on his own authority, but by virtue of Christ's authority" (*Catechism*, 875).

Holy Orders is the sacrament through which the mission given by Christ to the apostles continues in the Church today. The sacrament confers an indelible mark. As in the sacraments of Baptism and Confirmation, this unique sharing in the priesthood of Christ is given only once; it cannot be repeated. One who is ordained is ordained forever.

141

✔ Read pages 142 and 143. Underline in pencil the statements that express six main ideas.

✔ Imagine that, in preparation for his *ad limina* visit to the pope, your bishop has appointed a panel of consultants. You are one of them. What needs of your local church do you think your bishop should bring to the pope's attention? If you have ideas for meeting some of these needs, the bishop would like to hear your solutions.

Closing Prayer: Lead the group in the following prayer for priests. Allow time for them to mention priests they might know personally, or priests in challenging work.

Lord Jesus Christ,
  we place in your hands the priests of the world, especially. . . .
Offer them to the Father in the joy of the Holy Spirit.
Help them to minister with joy and energy.
Help them to lead us in worship.
Help them preach the gospel with their lives and counsel their brothers and sisters with your authority.
Help them follow in the footsteps of the saints.
We ask this in your name, Lord Jesus.
(All): Amen.

Conclusion ___ min.

◆ Ask a volunteer to summarize the last paragraph on page 141. Ask the students to open their Bibles to Psalm 110, verse 4. This psalm verse is often associated with the priesthood. Explain that Melchizedek was an ancient king and priest of Jerusalem who blessed Abraham. Because he "brought out bread and wine," (Genesis 14:18) to Abraham (perhaps in a gesture of hospitality), Melchizedek was associated by teachers in the early Church with Christ and the priesthood.

◆ Be sure to stress the highlighted statement that priests share in Christ's priesthood to the highest degree in the Eucharist. It is important to understand that the priest acts in the person of Christ himself.

FOR SESSION 2

• construction paper and other materials for bishop's crest
• copies of handout *Following in Christ's Footsteps*

SESSION 2

Objective: To explore the role of the bishop in the Church; to appreciate the liturgical rite of the ordination of a bishop.

Introduction ___ min.

Opening Prayer

Forum: Have the young people form small groups. Ask the members of each group to consolidate their concerns and whatever solutions they may suggest into one list. Ask each group to appoint a member to be on the "bishop's panel of consultants." Ask the panel to sit at the front of the room when presenting the needs, concerns, and solutions to the group as a whole.

Discuss with the young people the statements they underlined on pages 142 and 143. Have them highlight or underline in color the statements highlighted on these pages.

Presentation ___ min.

◆ Draw attention to the statement in the last paragraph of column one: "Our bishops today are successors to the apostles, for they share to the fullest extent in the grace of Holy Orders." Another way of saying this is to say that the bishop enjoys "the fullness of the priesthood." A priest teaches, governs, and sanctifies God's people under the authority of the local bishop; the local bishop is the chief teacher, the chief governor, and the chief sanctifier (or priest).

◆ To summarize the ritual of ordination of a bishop, you might like to ask these questions:

• What is the visible sign of the ordination of a bishop? (the principal ordaining bishop laying his hands on the head of the bishop-elect)

• What prayer is part of this sign? (the prayer of consecration)

• What oil is used in the ordination of a bishop? (the same oil used in the sacraments of Baptism and Confirmation) You may want to add that this oil is called *sacred chrism*.

• What does the bishop's ring symbolize? (fidelity to the Church)

A new bishop receives the ring, symbol of fidelity.

The Apostolic Call

Jesus knew that he could not do his work for the kingdom alone. He needed helpers to carry out his mission of preaching God's love, healing the sick, and reconciling sinners. In the Gospel of Luke, we read that before choosing his apostles, Jesus spent the whole night in prayer: "In those days he departed to the mountain to pray, and he spent the night in prayer to God. When day came, he called his disciples to himself, and from them he chose Twelve, whom he also named apostles" (Luke 6:12–13).

These apostles, as we know from the accounts given in the Acts of the Apostles, did carry out the work of Jesus. They were the first missionaries. They founded and guided local churches. When the need arose, they met together to consider the best decision to make for the life and growth of the Church.

In time the apostles ordained others to follow in their footsteps. From one generation to the next, new apostolic leaders have been called and ordained to service in the Church. Our bishops today are successors to the apostles, for they share to the fullest extent in the grace of Holy Orders. Bishops teach, govern, and sanctify with the authority of Christ. In his local church the bishop is the chief teacher, the chief governor, and the chief priest. The bishop is the leader of the local church, whether that local church is the church of New York, the church of Los Angeles, the church of Tulsa, the church of Paris, the church of Bangkok, or the church of Rio de Janeiro.

But the responsibilities of a bishop are not confined to his own local church. The bishop is also responsible, under the leadership of the bishop of Rome, the pope, and together with all the other bishops, for the teaching, governance, and sanctification of the entire Church throughout the world. Bishops often meet together to discuss current issues facing the Church and the world. Bishops also meet regularly with the pope on an individual basis. In this way the pope and each bishop can confer about the particular needs of a local church. This visit to the pope is called the *ad limina* visit. This term literally means "to the doorstep" in Latin. The bishop is invited to the pope's doorstep because the life and welfare of each local church is vital to the whole body of Christ.

The Ordination of a Bishop

A bishop is ordained by other bishops. Only bishops can lay hands in ordination of a newly chosen bishop. The ordination takes place during the Eucharist, after the reading of the gospel. First a mandate, or letter, from the Holy Father is read, confirming the ordination of the new bishop.

142

◆ Explain that it is a Church tradition for every bishop to have a crest or a coat-of-arms. The coat-of-arms shows an emblem symbolizing the chief concerns of the bishop. It also includes a motto (in Latin) expressing the prayerful goal of the bishop. This custom originated in the Middle Ages, when kings, bishops, and knights were identified by their coats-of-arms.

You might like to ask a volunteer to find out what your bishop's coat-of-arms or crest looks like and what its particular symbols mean. Help the group translate, if necessary, his motto.

Note: The following activity is optional.

◆ As a reminder of the bishop's role as chief teacher, governor, and priest for his diocese, have the young people work in small groups to make a bishop's crest. Use the following directions:

Receiving the miter

The miter is a traditional headcovering worn by the bishop during liturgical ceremonies. The word *miter* comes from a Latin word meaning "headband." As a symbol of his office, the miter has come to signify the role of the bishop as a "herald of truth," the principal teacher of the gospel in his diocese. During the liturgy the miter is removed whenever the bishop speaks to God in prayer.

...en the people of the local church are asked to give ...eir consent to the ordination. The congregation ...ually responds with enthusiastic applause. A ...mily is given by the principal ordaining bishop. He ...en asks the newly chosen bishop, or bishop-elect, a ...ries of questions. By his answers the bishop-elect ...clares his readiness to serve his people.

...ring the Litany of the Saints, the bishop-elect ...ostrates himself; that is, he lies facedown on the ...oor as he asks the help of the Church in heaven. ...ostration is an ancient symbol of humble and ...cere prayer.

...e principal ordaining bishop prays that the Lord ...ll anoint his servant, the bishop-elect, "with the ...llness of priestly grace." This bishop, in complete ...ence, lays his hands on the head of the bishop-...ect. The other bishops present then do the same. ...is ritual action, along with the prayer of ...nsecration, is the visible sign of the ordination ...a bishop.

...hile the Book of the Gospels is held above the ...w bishop's head, the principal ordaining bishop ...fers the prayer of consecration. The new bishop's ...ead is anointed with oil, the same oil used in the ...craments of Baptism and Confirmation. The Book ...the Gospels, which symbolizes the bishop's role ...s teacher and preacher of the word of God, is then ...ven to the new bishop.

He is also given a ring as a symbol of fidelity to the Church. He receives the miter and, with these words, the crosier, or pastoral staff:

> Take this staff as a sign of your pastoral office:
> keep watch over the whole flock
> in which the Holy Spirit has appointed you
> to shepherd the Church of God.

The new bishop is then invited to take his seat in the chair of the bishop, the *cathedra,* and all the bishops exchange the sign of peace.

At the end of the Eucharist, the new bishop himself may give the solemn blessing. He may say:

> Lord God,
> now that you have raised me to the order of bishops,
> may I please you in the performance of my office.
> Unite the hearts of people and bishop,
> so that the shepherd may not be without the support of his flock,
> or the flock without the loving concern of its shepherd.

All respond, "Amen."

The new bishop then blesses the people.

 Who is the bishop of your diocese? What are some ways you can support your bishop?

143

Conclusion___ min.

◆ Ask a volunteer to summarize *Catholic ID* at the top of page 143.

◆ Draw attention to the thought provoker on page 143. Elicit suggestions from the group about ways you can support your bishop.

FORUM Assignment

✔ Read pages 144 and 145. Underline in pencil the statements that express six main ideas.

✔ Complete the handout *Following in Christ's Footsteps.* Be prepared to share your questions with the group.

Closing Prayer: Say together the prayer at the end of the right column on page 143 for your own bishop. Ask the group to pray it together. Insert the name of your local bishop and change the "I" and "my" to "he" and "his" as needed.

Close with a recording of a song celebrating Jesus the Good Shepherd, who is the bishop's model and guide. One suggestion might be "Like a Shepherd," by Bob Dufford, S.J., from the album *A Dwelling Place* (OCP).

- Draw an outline of the crest and divide it into three sections.
- In one section, draw a symbol of the bishop's role as chief teacher of the diocese.
- In another section, draw a symbol of the bishop's role as chief governor of the diocese.
- In the last section, draw a symbol of the bishop's role as chief priest of the diocese.

Explain to the group that they will find symbols in "The Ordination of a Bishop" on pages 142 and 143. The ordination ceremony uses symbols of the bishop's role in these areas.

You may want to save your crests for display during the bishop's next visit to your parish. Or, you may want to write a group letter to your bishop to express your support for his work. Enclose the crests, with an explanation of their meaning, as a gift.

FOR SESSION 3

- videotape of a priest's ordination (optional)

Objective: To explore the connection between the roles of bishop and priest; to appreciate the liturgical rite of the ordination of a priest.

Introduction ___ min.

Opening Prayer

Forum: Have one half of the group role-play reporters asking questions and one half role-play priests being interviewed. Ask a volunteer producer and a volunteer director to listen to the interviews and make any necessary edits based on the information on pages 144 and 145. Then have the young people switch roles with two different volunteers as producer and director.

Discuss the statements the young people underlined. Have them highlight or underline in color the statements highlighted on these pages.

Presentation ___ min.

◆ If a videotape of a priest's ordination is available, show it to the young people now.

After viewing the celebration, discuss the training and preparation a man makes before ordination day. If possible, invite a seminarian from the diocesan seminary to explain his courses of study and the steps he will take before being ordained.

◆ You may want to put a chart on the board to explain the differences between a religious priest and a diocesan priest.

religious	diocesan
professes vows of poverty, chastity, and obedience	makes a promise of celibacy
serves anywhere in the world as assigned by superiors	serves in a particular diocese, promising obedience to the bishop of his diocese

Additional information about the college of bishops and the priesthood may be found in Chapter 13 of *Creed: A Course on Catholic Belief* in William H. Sadlier's *Faith and Witness* Program.

The Priesthood of Christ

There are many bishops and many priests, but there is only one priesthood, the priesthood of Christ. Saint Paul explained that Jesus Christ is the one priest, the one mediator between God and the human race:

> For there is one God.
> There is also one mediator between God and the human race,
> Christ Jesus, himself human,
> who gave himself as ransom for all.
> 1 Timothy 2:5–6

The unique sacrifice of Jesus Christ on the cross is made present in the Eucharist. In the same way the one priesthood of Christ is made present in the priesthood of his ministers: our bishops, priests (presbyters), and deacons. This priesthood is the means that Christ chose to build up and lead the Church. Through the ordained ministry of bishops and priests, the presence of Christ as head of the Church is made visible. Through the sacrament of Holy Orders, bishops and priests are ordained to bring this unique presence of Christ to us.

Priests and bishops act not only in the name of Christ but also in the name of the whole Church, especially at the Eucharist, in which they present the entire body of Christ to God. It is because they represent Christ that they also represent the body of Christ, the Church. To share in the priesthood of Christ means to share in the work of Christ as mediator between God and the human race. It is the work of the priest, in all that he does, to serve the people of God.

In this work the priest is a coworker with the bishop. In Holy Orders priests are united with the bishop in the priesthood of Christ. The priest is consecrated and ordained to preach the gospel, to celebrate the sacraments, and to guide the members of the body of Christ. He does this under the authority of his bishop.

When he is ordained, the new priest makes a promise of obedience to the bishop of the local church in which he will serve. At the end of the ordination rite, the bishop and the new priest exchange the sign of peace. Both actions are signs

144

that the priest and his bishop are united in working for the kingdom of God. The bishop needs priests to help him and considers the priests of his diocese his "co-workers, his sons, his brothers and his friends" (*Catechism*, 1567).

 What do you think is the main work of a priest? Why is it essential to the Church?

The Ordination of a Priest

The ordination of a priest is very much like the ordination of a bishop. The essential rite of the sacrament—the laying on of hands and the prayer of consecration—is the same except that after the bishop lays hands on the candidate, the other priests present also lay their hands on him. This is a sign of their unity, of working together for the kingdom.

The rite of the ordination of a priest takes place during the Eucharist, after the reading of the gospel. The candidate is called forward and presented to the bishop. After the bishop is assured that the candidate is prepared for the priesthood, the bishop says:

◆ Ask the young people to write a caption for each of the photos on pages 144 and 145. Ask the young people what the essential signs of ordination are. Have them imagine themselves as photographers planning to take a series of pictures at an ordination. What moments would they consider to be the most important to photograph?

◆ Discuss the thought provoker on page 144. Emphasize that, through the sacrament of Holy Orders, bishops and priests are ordained to bring the unique presence of Christ to us. Point out that the ways they do this are described in the last three paragraphs of "The Priesthood of Christ."

◆ Draw attention to the *Scripture Update* on page 145. Ask a volunteer to find and read the Scripture passage suggested. Ask, "What does it mean to welcome our priests and bishops today?"

We rely on the help of the Lord God and our Savior Jesus Christ, and we choose this man, our brother, for priesthood in the presbyteral order.

e consent of the people is then given, usually by ful applause.

e bishop gives a homily explaining that the ndidate "is to serve Christ the Teacher, Priest, d Shepherd in his ministry which is to make own body, the Church, grow into the people God, a holy temple." The bishop then asks e candidate, in a series of questions, if he is ling to carry out the duties of a priest. The ndidate answers, "I am, with the help of God."

e candidate promises obedience to the bishop of e local church under whom he will serve. After e bishop leads a prayer for the candidate, the ndidate prostrates himself during the Litany of e Saints. The bishop asks God the Father to pour t upon the candidate the blessing of the Holy irit and the grace and power of the priesthood.

en, in silence, the bishop lays his hands on the ndidate's head. Still in silence, all the priests o are present also lay their hands upon the ndidate. The bishop, extending his hands over e candidate, offers the prayer of consecration. ese two actions—the laying on of hands lowed by the prayer of consecration—are the sential signs of ordination.

*Scripture*UPDATE

In Luke's Gospel we read that Jesus sent out the Twelve to minister to the people. Take the time to read Luke 9:1–6 to discover what the apostles were commissioned to do and what power and authority they were given.

The new priest is invested with the stole and chasuble as symbols of the priesthood. Next the bishop anoints the palms of the new priest's hands with chrism, the same oil used in Baptism and Confirmation. After the gifts of bread and wine are presented, the bishop gives the paten and chalice to the new priest with these words:

> Accept from the holy people of God the
> gifts to be offered to him.
> Know what you are doing, and imitate
> the mystery you celebrate:
> model your life on the mystery of the
> Lord's cross.

Then the bishop and the newly ordained exchange a sign of peace, and the celebration of the Eucharist continues.

Describe what is happening in each picture.

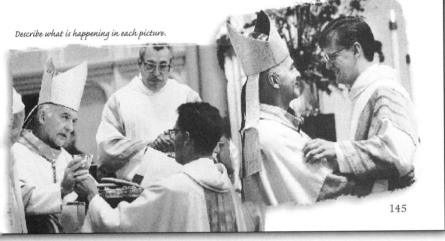

145

FORUMAssignment

✔ Read pages 146 and 147. Underline in pencil the statements that express four main ideas.

✔ Make a chart outlining the roles of the priest and the deacon in the sacraments. To organize your chart, write *Sacraments* at the top of the first column and list the sacraments below. Remember to include Matrimony and Holy Orders. Write *Priest* at the top of the second column, and *Deacon* at the top of the third. List the activities and role of the priest and deacon for each sacrament.

Closing Prayer: Explain that Saint Ignatius Loyola was ordained a priest after a career in the military. The following is a prayer he wrote. As a former soldier, he often used the metaphor of battle to express his love for God. Ask the group to pray each verse after you.

> Lord, teach me to be generous.
> Teach me to serve you as you
>   deserve.
> Grant me, O Lord, to give to you
>   and not to count the cost;
> To fight for you and not to mind the
>   wounds;
> To toil and not to seek for rest;
> To labor, but to ask for no reward
>   except the knowledge
>   that I do it for you, O Lord.

FOR SESSION 4

• posterboard for charts

Conclusion ___ min.

◆ As a summary, you may want to share this profile of a parish priest. At its conclusion, ask the group to complete the profile.

Father Jerry's bishop assigned him to St. Columba's parish. Each day at 7:30 A.M., he offers Mass. He has a small office in the rectory where he prepares his Sunday homily. The phone on his desk rings constantly: a funeral must be arranged; a young couple wants to speak with a priest about marriage; a teacher at school would like him to speak with her class about the sacrament of Reconciliation. Often Father Jerry visits the sick in the hospital and is on call for emergencies. On different nights of the week there are meetings with the parish council, the soup kitchen team, and the parish school committee. . . .

SESSION 4

Objective: To explore the role of the deacon in the Church; to appreciate the liturgical rite of the ordination of a deacon.

Introduction ___ min.

Opening Prayer

Forum: Have the students gather in small groups to present their charts. Ask them to help one another to fill in or add to their charts as needed. Ask each group to choose one person's chart to represent the group.

Have the students discuss the statements they underlined on these pages. Then have them highlight or underline in color the statements highlighted here.

Presentation ___ min.

◆ Draw the group's attention to *Catholic Teachings* at the top of page 147. Explain that, through the long history of the Church, the diaconate gradually lost its role as a distinct ministry. It became one of the ordained ministries on the way to ordination. All deacons became priests. The Second Vatican Council restored the diaconate as a permanent ministry for those who are called to it, not only for those planning to be priests.

◆ Ask the group if they know any deacons. List the names on the board. (Leave them there for use during the *Closing Prayer*.) Refer to the last paragraph in the left-hand column on page 146 and ask, "What do deacons do?" After the group responds, ask if they can recall being present when a deacon was giving service in any of these ways. If a deacon serves in your parish, ask the young people if they can add specific examples of what a deacon does by using the parish deacon's ministry as an example.

◆ Ask, "How is the ordination of a deacon similar to that of a priest or bishop?" (It takes place at the Eucharist, the candidate is called forward after the reading of the gospel, the bishop is assured of his worthiness, and the people show acceptance by applause. The candidate is questioned by the bishop and the Litany of the Saints is prayed. The bishop lays hands on the candidate and prays the prayer of consecration.)

Ordained for Service

The word *deacon* comes from a Greek word meaning "to serve." The first deacons were called to serve by providing food for the poor of the early Church. We read in the Acts of the Apostles that the Church in Jerusalem was growing so quickly that the daily distribution of food was not being taken care of properly. Some groups were complaining of neglect. So the apostles met with the community and said, "'It is not right for us to neglect the word of God to serve at table. Brothers, select from among you seven reputable men, filled with the Spirit and wisdom, whom we shall appoint to this task...' The proposal was acceptable to the whole community" (Acts 6:2–5).

The first deacon chosen was Stephen, "a man filled with faith and the holy Spirit" (Acts 6:5), who is now honored as the patron saint of all deacons. To carry out his task, Stephen was given wonderful gifts from God. He was "filled with grace and power" (Acts 6:8), and no one could deny "the wisdom and the spirit with which he spoke" (Acts 6:10). When Stephen was brought before the religious judges to defend himself against false charges, the officials "saw that his face was like the face of an angel" (Acts 6:15). This means that they recognized Stephen to be "like an angel" — a true messenger from God.

Like Stephen, deacons today carry God's message to us and share in the mission of Christ through the grace of Holy Orders. They are marked with an indelible spiritual character that conforms them to Christ, "who made himself the 'deacon' or servant of all" (*Catechism*, 1570). Deacons today may perform their service to the Church in many ways: in assisting the bishops and priests in the liturgy, above all in the Eucharist; in the distribution of communion; in assisting at and blessing marriages; in the proclaiming of the gospel and in preaching; in presiding over funerals; and in works of service and charity. In all these tasks the deacon is guided first of all by the bishop of the local church and then by the pastor of the parish in which he serves.

146

The Ordination of a Deacon

The ordination of a deacon is similar to that of a bishop or priest except that at a deacon's ordination only the bishop lays hands on the candidate. This symbolizes the deacon's special attachment to the bishop in the tasks of his service.

The ordination of a deacon, like that of a bishop and a priest, takes place at the celebration of the Eucharist. After the reading of the gospel, the candidate is called forward, the bishop is assured of his worthiness, and the people assent to ordination by enthusiastic applause. In his homily the bishop explains the role of a deacon: "He will draw new strength from the gift of the Holy Spirit. He will help the bishop and his body of priests as a minister of the word, of the altar, and of charity. He will make himself a servant to all."

If an unmarried deacon intends to remain celibate, or if he intends to be ordained to the priesthood at a future time, he now makes a promise of lifelong celibacy. *Celibacy* means remaining unmarried for the sake of the kingdom of God.

Next the candidate is questioned by the bishop, who asks if the deacon-elect is willing to be ordained for ministry and if he is resolved to carry out its responsibilities. The candidate answers, "I am, with the help of God."

After the Litany of the Saints, the bishop lays his hands, in silence, on the candidate's head. Then, with his hands extended over the candidate, the bishop prays the prayer of consecration.

Ask, "How is the ordination of a deacon different from that of a bishop or priest?" (Only the bishop lays hands on the candidate to show the deacon's special attachment to the bishop of the diocese.)

Ask, "What are the deacon's special vestments?" (the dalmatic and the stole) You may want to ask a volunteer to find a picture of the deacon in a dalmatic (a short squared-off robe) and stole.

◆ Draw the group's attention to the chart on page 147. Have the young people form three groups, "Bishops," "Priests," "Deacons." Read sections of the chart at random. If a section refers to bishops, this group should stand. If to priests, the priest group will stand, and so on. Sometimes only one group will stand, sometimes all three.

deacon is given a deacon's stole and the special
con's vestment called the dalmatic. He wears
stole, not around his neck as a priest does, but
gonally across his chest. Now vested as a deacon,
newly ordained minister kneels before the
hop and receives from him the Book of the
spels. The bishop instructs the new deacon:

Receive the Gospel of Christ,
whose herald you now are.
Believe what you read,
teach what you believe,
and practice what you teach.

e whole Church rejoices in the ordination of a
w servant, a new herald, a new messenger, a new
ephen for our times.

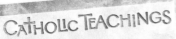 *In what ways is a deacon to be a servant
and a herald?*

ere is a brief summary of Holy Orders to help you recall the main ideas of this chapter.

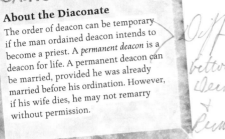

Cozy Chart

CATHOLIC TEACHINGS

About the Diaconate

The order of deacon can be temporary if the man ordained deacon intends to become a priest. A *permanent deacon* is a deacon for life. A permanent deacon can be married, provided he was already married before his ordination. However, if his wife dies, he may not remarry without permission.

Three Ranks	Who Ordains?	Essential Signs	Ministry
bishop (episcopate)	Only a bishop can ordain another bishop, a priest, or a deacon.	the laying on of hands and the prayer of consecration	successor to the apostles leader of his local church chief teacher, governor, and priest for his diocese
			in union with the pope and the other bishops, responsible for the teaching, governance, and sanctification of the entire Church
priest (presbyterate)	A priest is ordained by a bishop, usually the bishop of his diocese.	same as above	coworker with the bishop in preaching the gospel, celebrating the sacraments, and guiding the members of the body of Christ
deacon (diaconate)	A deacon is ordained by the bishop of his diocese.	same as above	assists the bishops and priests in works of service and charity and, in the liturgy, proclaiming the gospel and preaching

147

FYI A man thinking about becoming a deacon feels a strong desire to live the gospel as deeply as possible in his own life, and wants to help others to do so. He is usually a dependable helper in his parish. Most dioceses have programs designed for those studying to become deacons. If a man wanting to become a deacon is married, he must have the understanding and support of his wife in his decision.

The term "lay deacon" is incorrect because the deacon is truly ordained and is a member of the clergy of a particular diocese. He is not obliged to wear clerical clothing, and he is usually expected to receive his financial support from his secular occupation.

Conclusion ___ min.

◆ Ask, "What would you advise your father (or another male member of your family) if he wanted to become a deacon?" You might want to remind the group that the wives and families of deacons make certain sacrifices of the deacon's personal time with them. The whole family joins in the deacon's gift of self.

FORUM Assignment

✔ Read pages 148 and 149. Prepare your answers to *Things to Think About* and *Things to Share*.

✔ It is ten years from now. Your best friend has just graduated from college. He tells you he wants to become a priest or a permanent deacon. Prepare a conversation in which you discuss with your friend the reasons for his decision and your reaction to his choice. As a friend, will you support his decision?

Closing Prayer: Pray together this prayer for deacons.

Lord Jesus, ...
Be with these servants,
  your deacons . . . . ,
Under the leadership of our bishop,
help them be strong friends and
  helpers to our priests.
May they share the reward of the
  good and the faithful.
We ask this in your name, Lord Jesus.
Amen.

FOR SESSION 5

• copies of *Chapter 12 Assessment*
• copies of *Highlights for Home*

147

SESSION 5

Objective: To increase awareness of Holy Orders as the sacrament through which the mission and authority Christ gave his apostles continues in the Church.

Introduction ___ min.

Opening Prayer

Forum: Ask the young people to work in pairs to share their roleplaying of the two friends discussing the one friend's choice of a vocation to the priesthood. When the pairs have finished sharing, ask each for a summary. Make the point that sometimes we must follow God's call even if others do not support our decisions.

Presentation ___ min.

◆ Direct attention to *Things to Think About* on page 148. Stress that people who do things for others need to be in touch with God for their own strength and also for sensitivity to others' needs. People of prayer know that they can call on God for help. Then discuss the question in *Things to Share.*

◆ Direct the students' attention to *Words to Remember.* The definition for *Holy Orders* can be found on page 140; the definition for *deacon* can be found on page 146.

◆ Discuss *On Line with the Parish.* If a thank-you celebration is not possible, perhaps the group would like to send a card or letter of thanks to the pastor, priests, and deacons of the parish. You may want to send this card or letter to the men in connection with a special feast day meaningful to the parish or on the anniversaries of their ordinations.

Assessment: Suggest that the young people work in pairs to discuss their answers for *Testing 1, 2, 3.* If you are administering *Chapter 12 Assessment,* page 149A, allow about ten minutes for the students to complete the test.

Conclusion ___ min.

◆ Direct attention to *Life in the Spirit.* Remind the group that Pope John XXIII was the pope who convened the Second Vatican Council, the council which helped renew the liturgy that we have been studying.

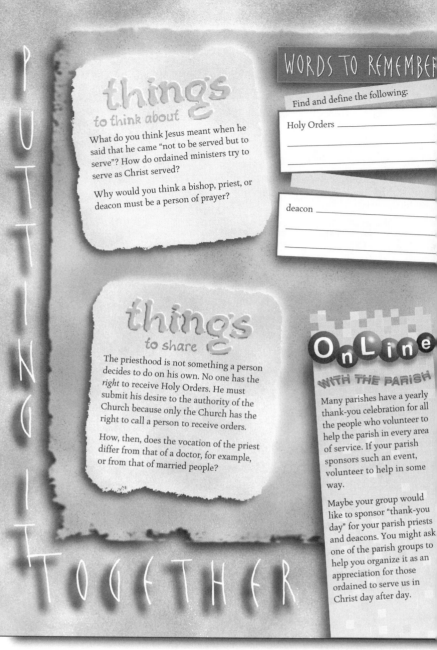

PUTTING IT TOGETHER

things to think about

What do you think Jesus meant when he said that he came "not to be served but to serve"? How do ordained ministers try to serve as Christ served?

Why would you think a bishop, priest, or deacon must be a person of prayer?

things to share

The priesthood is not something a person decides to do on his own. No one has the *right* to receive Holy Orders. He must submit his desire to the authority of the Church because only the Church has the right to call a person to receive orders.

How, then, does the vocation of the priest differ from that of a doctor, for example, or from that of married people?

WORDS TO REMEMBER

Find and define the following:

Holy Orders _____

deacon _____

OnLine WITH THE PARISH

Many parishes have a yearly thank-you celebration for all the people who volunteer to help the parish in every area of service. If your parish sponsors such an event, volunteer to help in some way.

Maybe your group would like to sponsor "thank-you day" for your parish priests and deacons. You might ask one of the parish groups to help you organize it as an appreciation for those ordained to serve us in Christ day after day.

Closing Prayer: Formulate a prayer session using the quote from Pope John and the psalm in *Life in the Spirit* in this way:

All: Say the quotation from Pope John.
Reader 1: Read the verse from Psalm 143.
All: Repeat the quotation from Pope John.
Reader 2: Read the verses from Psalm 121.
All: Repeat the quotation from Pope John.

◆ Encourage the young people to share *Highlights for Home*, page 149B, with their families.

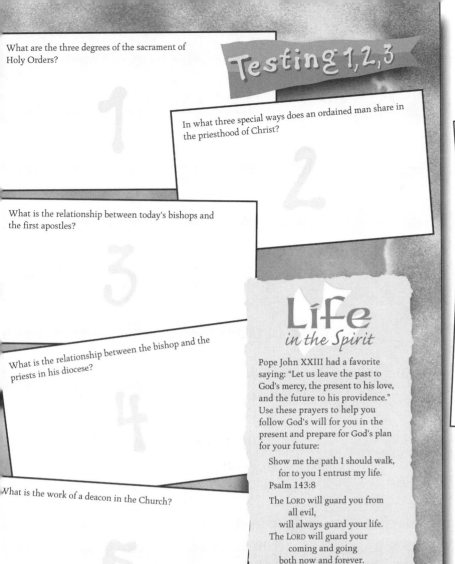

What are the three degrees of the sacrament of Holy Orders?

Testing 1,2,3

In what three special ways does an ordained man share in the priesthood of Christ?

What is the relationship between today's bishops and the first apostles?

What is the relationship between the bishop and the priests in his diocese?

What is the work of a deacon in the Church?

Life in the Spirit

Pope John XXIII had a favorite saying: "Let us leave the past to God's mercy, the present to his love, and the future to his providence." Use these prayers to help you follow God's will for you in the present and prepare for God's plan for your future:

Show me the path I should walk,
   for to you I entrust my life.
Psalm 143:8

The LORD will guard you from
   all evil,
   will always guard your life.
The LORD will guard your
   coming and going
   both now and forever.
Psalm 121:7–8

149

Testing 1,2,3

1. See page 140. The sacrament of Holy Orders includes three ranks, or orders: the episcopate (bishops); the presbyterate (priests); the diaconate (deacons).

2. See pages 140–141. The three special ways are: ministry (service); worship (They celebrate the Eucharist and the other sacraments with the people of God.); authority (Jesus sent his disciples to teach, to baptize, to heal and to forgive with his authority.)

3. See page 142. The apostles ordained others to follow in their footsteps. Our bishops today are successors to the apostles, for they share to the fullest extent in the grace of Holy Orders. They teach, govern, and sanctify with Christ's authority.

4. See page 144. In Holy Orders, priests are united with bishops in the priesthood of Christ. The priests preach the gospel, celebrate the sacraments, and guide the members of the body of Christ under the authority of the bishops. Priests and bishops are united in working for the kingdom of God.

5. See page 146. Deacons assist bishops and priests in the liturgy; in the distribution of Communion; in assisting at and blessing marriages; in proclaiming the gospel and in preaching; and in works of service and charity.

Evaluation: Do the young people understand the purpose of the priesthood and its three orders? Do they appreciate the symbolism of the rite of ordination? Do they understand that bishops, priests, and deacons are following in the footsteps of Christ through ministry, divine worship, and authority?

Answers for Chapter 12 Assessment

1. c   2. b   3. d   4. a   5. b
6. d   7. c   8. a   9. c   10. See page 142.

149

Assessment

1 The sacrament of Holy Orders
   a. is given to anyone who wishes.
   b. is given more than once.
   c. is given only once.
   d. none of the above

2 A bishop is ordained
   a. by the pope alone.
   b. by other bishops.
   c. by the people of the diocese.
   d. by the priests of the diocese.

3 _____ is an ancient symbol of humble and sincere prayer.
   a. The miter
   b. The bishop's ring
   c. The bishop's staff
   d. Prostration

4 The bishop is given _____ as a symbol of fidelity to the Church.
   a. a ring
   b. a miter
   c. a staff
   d. the Book of the Gospels

5 The _____ symbolizes the bishop's role as teacher and preacher of the word of God.
   a. staff
   b. Book of the Gospels
   c. miter
   d. ring

6 The essential signs of ordination are the laying on of hands and
   a. the stole and chasuble.
   b. the exchange of the sign of peace.
   c. the Litany of the Saints.
   d. the prayer of consecration.

7 If the man being ordained intends to become a priest, the order of deacon is
   a. permanent.
   b. invalid.
   c. temporary.
   d. indelible.

8 In Holy Orders a man shares in the priesthood in three essential ways: ministry, _____, and authority.
   a. divine worship
   b. teaching
   c. healing
   d. none of the above

9 Circle the letter beside the phrase that does *not* describe a deacon's task.
   a. blessing marriages
   b. distributing Holy Communion
   c. ordaining other deacons
   d. preaching

10 Explain briefly the responsibilities of a bishop. Write your response on the reverse side of this page.

Highlights for Home

Focus on Faith

Bishops, priests, and deacons are ordained to bring the good news of salvation to us. In this chapter, your son or daughter learned the vital importance to the Church of our ordained ministers. This chapter also introduced them to the beauty and symbolism of the rites of ordination.

It is hoped that in this chapter the young people also glimpsed the beauty of a life dedicated to God in the Church. For beautiful are the hands that baptize our children, offer the Eucharist, and anoint the sick among us. Beautiful the voice that preaches the gospel, assures us of God's forgiveness, and asks us to repeat wedding vows. Beautiful the life given to the service of God's people.

Conversation Starters

. . . . a few ideas to talk about together . . . .

◆ Do we take the ministry of the priests of our parish for granted? What can we do to show priests our appreciation and support?

◆ Do we consider it our responsibility to pray for priestly vocations? What words can we pray?

Feature Focus

Catholic ID on page 143 explains that the miter, the traditional headcovering worn by the bishop during liturgical ceremonies, symbolizes the bishop's role as a "herald of truth." The bishop is the principal teacher of the gospel, the main messenger of the good news of Jesus Christ.

Reflection

Saint Francis de Sales (1567–1622) was ordained a priest during the time when many Catholics were joining the churches of the Protestant Reformation. Through his tireless efforts he re-established Catholicism in Switzerland. In 1602, he was appointed Bishop of Geneva. As the shepherd of his diocese, he counseled many people and helped them to see that through their own unique calling they could deepen their friendship with God.

Reflect on his words of advice:

Go courageously to do whatever you are called to do.
   Go simply.
If you have any fears, say to your soul:
   "The Lord will provide for us. . . ."
The apostles were mostly unlearned fishermen,
   but God gave them learning enough
   for the work they had to do.

Trust in him, depend on his providence, fear nothing.

THE SACRAMENT OF MATRIMONY

Adult Focus

The focus of this chapter is to encourage the young people to move beyond a romantic conception of marriage that focuses on a beautiful wedding and a hazy idea that "love will keep us together." It explores the sacrament of Matrimony as a lifelong commitment between a baptized man and a baptized woman whom God has brought together. Through the marriage covenant, they become one. By God's grace, they mirror for others the relationship between Christ and his beloved Church. By their free gift of self they are united in body, heart, and soul. Their indissoluble union and openness to having children is a sign of God's faithful love present in them and in the Church.

Our young people need to recognize that this exalted yet seemingly "ordinary" sacrament requires long-range preparation and self-discipline. The chapter provides them with a useful questionnaire to discern which interpersonal skills they need to develop in order to establish healthy relationships.

The young people are encouraged to pray for married and engaged couples, as well as for themselves, for they are members of the domestic Church (the family), and may one day be called to seek their own holiness in the sacrament of Matrimony.

Catechism Focus

The theme of Chapter 13 corresponds to paragraphs 1601–1605, 1638–1645, 1652, 2331 and 2335 of the *Catechism*.

Enrichment Activities

Marriage Medleys

To encourage the young people to discern popular songs that extol or describe true love, invite them to put together taped medleys. They might intersperse Christian rock, pop, and spiritual music dealing with faithful love, friendship, and marriage. If possible, make available to them the album *United As One*, Volumes 1 and 2 (OCP). The medleys may be used in class or at a youth retreat.

Anniversary Action Plans

Recognizing a married couple on their anniversary year after year is a sign of the Christian community's support for their gift of faithfulness. Suggest that the young people compile "Anniversary Action Plans" for all married couples in their extended families (as well as others of their choice). Have them list anniversary dates and one affirming action such as: making a greeting card, serving a meal, offering a service (free babysitting or praying a rosary for the couple's intentions).

Teaching Resources

Overview	Opening Prayer Ideas	Materials
SESSION 1 **Discovery:** To discover the meaning and importance of the sacrament of Matrimony.	Look at the photo on pages 150–151. Pray together the verse from Scripture on page 51. Then ask a volunteer to read aloud 1 John 4:7–12.	These will be needed every session: texts, Bibles, highlighters or colored pencils, journals. • album *Companions on the Journey* (Carey Landry, OCP) • videos listed in *Chapter Warm-up*
SESSION 2 **Exploring 1:** To explore the sign of Matrimony and the process of preparation.	Ask two volunteers to take turns reading John 2:1–11, the story of the miracle at Cana. Pray a Hail Mary together and ask Mary to watch over engaged and newly married couples.	• writing materials • copies of parish bulletin
SESSION 3 **Exploring 2:** To explore the characteristics of real love; to deepen understanding of the celebration of Matrimony.	Ask two volunteers to take turns reading 1 Corinthians 13:1–7. During the prayerful reading, pray for all married couples.	• cassette player, CD player, VCR • assorted art materials • copies of handout *Happily Ever After?* • song on the theme of faithful love
SESSION 4 **Exploring 3:** To explore needed skills for marriage readiness.	Read together Ruth 1:16–17. Explain that this is a passage that is often related to marriage. However, as written, Ruth is speaking to her mother-in-law, Naomi.	• large purse or briefcase
SESSION 5 **Putting It Together:** To deepen appreciation for the sacrament of Matrimony.	Have the young people form two groups in order to pray the verses of Psalm 128 alternately. Note that in the *New American Bible*, the psalm is titled, "The Happy Home of the Just."	• friendship sayings • bowl of blessed water • *Chapter 13 Assessment*, page 161A • *Highlights for Home*, page 161B

Supplemental Resources

Pamphlets: *Catholic Youth Update*
• "Finding 'Forever' Friends"
• "Marriage Insurance: Never Too Soon to Invest"
• "Marriage: Supernatural and Sacramental"

St. Anthony Messenger Press
1615 Republic Street
Cincinnati, OH 45210

Videos (See those listed on page 150–151.)

Faith and Witness Journal: Liturgy & Worship

For Chapter 13 see pages 52–55.

Happily Ever After?

Write a thoughtful response to each of these letters to "The Marriage Counselor."

Dear T.M.C.,

Joe and I are getting married soon. There's only one problem. He wants to be the boss. I think we should be equal partners. Do you think we can live happily ever after?

Hopeful in Houston

Dear Hope,

_____

_____

_____

_____

Sincerely, T.M.C.

Dear T.M.C.,

Should I get engaged to Teresa? I really love her. We are both Catholics, and we pray together sometimes. We enjoy hiking, dancing, and just being together. But my parents are divorced. I'm afraid Teresa and I will wind up the same way.

Doubtful in Dubuque

Dear Doubtful,

_____

_____

_____

_____

Cordially, T.M.C.

Dear T.M.C.,

Help! My wedding date is only two weeks away. I just found out my sweetheart doesn't want any children—ever! Should I let this discovery ruin everything? Or should I go ahead and hope for the best? Please respond by EXPRESS MAIL!!!

Frantic in Frankfurt

Dear Frantic,

_____

_____

_____

_____

Advisedly, T.M.C.

The Sacrament of Matrimony

God is love,
and whoever remains
in love remains in God.
1 John 4:16

Objective: To discover the meaning and importance of the sacrament of Matrimony.

Introduction ___ min.

Opening Prayer: Invite the young people to look at the photograph on pages 150 and 151 as you share the following account.

> In an essay on youth, Pope John Paul II points out that the origin of all vocations—including marriage—is the call to become "a free gift for others." He tells the story of a young Polish student who hungered after holiness. The student knew that he was not called to holy orders or religious life. So "he sought a companion for his life and sought her on his knees, in prayer." When he later recognized the woman who would be his wife, he saw her as having been sent to him by God.

Invite the young people to write a prayer to Jesus seeking his help in finding and becoming a good and loving marriage partner or friend. Assure the group that sharing of this reflection will be on a voluntary basis.

While the young people are writing their prayers in their journals, you might choose to play quietly in the background the title song from the album *Companions On the Journey* by Carey Landry (OCP).

Chapter Warm-up: You may wish to show one of the following videos to help the young people understand the importance of self-respect and respect for others.

- William H. Sadlier's *Power Surge Videos:* "Friends," "Integrity," and "Self-Image." (See address on guide cover.)
- Dr. James Dobson's *Life on the Edge Series:* "Finding God's Will for Your Life," "The Keys to a Lifelong Love," and "Emotions: Can You Trust Them?" These tapes are made available by Ignatius Press, P.O. Box 1339, Ft. Collins, Colorado 80522.

Presentation ___ min.

◆ Have someone read aloud the introductory quote and opening question at the top of page 152. Seek a few responses clarifying the difference of importance between the wedding event and the vocation of marriage.

◆ Ask volunteers to read pages 152 and 153. Have all underline in color or highlight the key concepts highlighted here.

◆ Have the young people form "Sacrament of Matrimony Defense Teams." Give the following case histories on index cards. Explain that each team is to dialogue on the assigned case and prepare a defense of the sacrament to be presented to the entire group.

• *Team 1:* Tom and Kerry say that it is "nobody's business" but their own whether they get married or not. They insist that it is their right to simply live together and have children whenever they feel like it. If things don't work out, they can always go their separate ways. Tom and Kerry say they have no obligation to society or to the Church when it comes to marriage. What response would you make to this couple?

• *Team 2:* Meg and Renaldo want to be married in the Catholic Church. However, they disagree with many Catholic teachings about the sacrament of Matrimony. "If we don't choose to have children, or if we decide we want a divorce later on, that's up to us," says Renaldo. Meg adds, "I don't see why the Church gets so involved in marriage anyway. It only complicates things."
What response would you make to this couple?

• *Team 3:* A young Catholic couple, P.J. and Sarah, are very much in love. They have been dating for six months and want to be married as soon as possible. They are pressuring their pastor to "speed up" a

A wise priest counsels a young couple: "Remember, a wedding lasts an hour; a marriage lasts a lifetime." What do you think this means?

The Sacrament of Matrimony

Weddings are beautiful ceremonies. Whether large or small, weddings are intended to be celebrations of love; and as many people say, love makes the world go round. But is this simple understanding of love enough to make a marriage last? Is there more to marriage than the feeling of romance we see so often in movies, on television, and in the books and magazines we read? What are we to think as Catholics and members of the Church, the body of Christ? Let's take a long look at the wonder and mystery of marriage.

152

marriage preparation course so their wedding can be celebrated before the end of the year. When their pastor explains that the course requires six months' preparation, P.J. and Sarah are discouraged and upset. They wonder if they should go ahead and get married in a civil ceremony.

What response would you make to this couple?

Allow about ten minutes for group preparation. Then have the "Marriage Defense Teams" give their responses.

iously the civil authorities think there is more
arriage than movies or television portray. Take
United States, for example. Each year thousands
en and women obtain a civil license from the
e in which they want to be married, and each
e has special requirements that must be fulfilled
marriage is to be considered legal. These may
ude an age requirement or even the taking of a
d test as a check to keep society free from
municable diseases. Then every couple must
for a marriage license—which may be easier to
han a driver's license!

y is the state so interested in
riage? Because marriage is
mportant for society. In
society is built on
riage and the family.
as a society must
w when two people
promising to share
onsibility for rearing
dren, owning property,
paying taxes. Without
rriage and family life,
ety would fall apart in
1s. The state wants to
e sure that all is well
those who want to be
ried. Healthy marriages
1 a healthy society
rywhere in the world.

after thinking about
ance and society, is there
ething more we should know about marriage?
Catholics marriage is something much greater.
Church teaches us that marriage between two
tized persons is more than a legal arrangement,
e than a contract, and more than romance.
rriage is a sacrament and was raised to that
nity by Christ. In the *sacrament of Matrimony*,
aptized man and a baptized woman commit
mselves to each other as partners for the whole
ife. This partnership is a sacred covenant that
rors the relationship that Christ has with
Church.

In marriage we realize in a particular way that we
were created by God out of love and that men and
women were meant for one another. In the very
first book of the Bible, we read that God said, "It is
not good for the man to be alone" (Genesis 2:18). In
the Christian ideal of marriage, a man and a woman
are equal partners, devoted to each other in true
love, committed to each other's good, and ready to
find God at the very center of their love for each
other. Such a love cannot help but be open to new
life—to the procreation and education of children.
So important is this marriage in the
Lord that the Church calls the
family the domestic Church.

How does this come about? In
the sacrament of Matrimony,
a man and woman commit
themselves totally to each
other in Christ. They vow
to love and help each
other for the rest of
their lives and to share
this love with their
children. Therefore the
marriage covenant is a
blessing and a gift to the
couple, to their children,
to the Church, and to the
whole world.

As we shall see, this is a
sacrament filled with great joy
and love. But it is also a serious
and solemn obligation. Not everyone
is ready to make such a commitment. It takes time,
hard work, and deep dedication before two people
are ready to walk down the aisle of a church and
speak the vows of marriage to each other. Let's
explore the most important aspects of marriage
from the Catholic point of view and then look at
the beautiful celebration of this sacrament.

153

FORUM Assignment

✔ Read pages 154 and 155. Underline
in pencil the sentences that express
six main ideas.

✔ The task is to prepare *questions* for
which the following are answers:

- Healthy marriages mean a healthy
society.
- "What God has joined together, no
human being must separate."
- Catholics must marry in the presence of a priest or deacon and two
witnesses.
- A free, faithful, and permanent
commitment.

Closing Prayer: Read aloud the following prayers, pausing at the places
indicated. Invite the young people to
repeat these words.

Jesus, teach us the meaning of true
love. (*Pause.*) Give us the wisdom to
know the difference between love
and infatuation, (*Pause.*) between
false friends and faithful companions. (*Pause.*) Give us a deep respect
for marriage (*Pause.*) and a desire to
help others who are struggling with
their commitment to this lifelong
vocation.

Conclusion ___ min.

◆ Inside a sketch of two large wedding rings drawn
on the board, print "sacrament of Matrimony." Call for
a definition of this term. (A sacred covenant uniting a
baptized man and a baptized woman as partners for
the whole of life. Matrimony mirrors the relationship
between Christ and the Church.) Have volunteers
come forward to surround the rings with words and
phrases describing the Christian ideal of marriage
(equal partners, true love, commitment to each
other's good, finding God at the center of their mutual love, sharing love with children, a covenant and
a blessing, a gift to the Church and the world).

FOR SESSION 2

- writing materials
- copies of parish bulletin

SESSION 2

Objective: To explore the sign of Matrimony and the process of preparation.

Introduction ___ min.

Opening Prayer

Forum: Choose someone to be the "Oracle" who holds all the answers. The "Oracle" calls randomly on individuals saying, for example: "The answer is healthy marriages mean a healthy society. What is the question?" The person called on replies: "Why is the state so interested in marriage?"

The "Oracle" can ask several people to respond to the same answer since more than one question might be possible. Continue until all the answers have been given questions.

Presentation ___ min.

◆ Have volunteers share the statements they underlined on pages 154 and 155. Ask all to underline in color or highlight the key statements highlighted here.

◆ Conduct a brainstorming session in which the young people provide as many accurate definitions for Matrimony as they can come up with in three minutes. Invite two recorders to alternate writing the responses on the board. (Possible definitions: a sacrament, a life-giving sign of grace, a public act, a lifetime commitment, a valid marriage union for Catholics, a sign of Christ's love for his Church, a sign of a married couple's faithful love)

Call on volunteers to clarify the respective roles of the priest and the bride and groom. (The former is the Church's official witness. The latter are the ministers of the sacrament.)

◆ Present the following "What if. . .?" situation. Have the young people role-play a family conference discussing the situation.

A Life-giving Sign of Grace

People are often amazed when they realize that Scripture uses the marriage covenant as a symbol of God's love for his people. God is always faithful. The prophet Hosea knew this and compared God to a faithful husband and Israel to a loving bride. These are Hosea's words:

> I will espouse you to me forever:
>   I will espouse you in right and in justice,
>   in love and in mercy;
> I will espouse you in fidelity,
>   and you shall know the LORD.
> Hosea 2:21–22

In the New Testament Jesus says: "What God has joined together, no human being must separate" (Matthew 19:6). In his letter to the Ephesians, Saint Paul compared this union of marriage to the love of Christ and the Church. Just as Christ loves his body, the Church, so husband and wife must love each other.

154

A sacrament is a sign given to us by Christ throu which we share in God's grace—God's own life. The sacrament of Matrimony is a life-giving sign grace, not just at the wedding ceremony when t wedding vows are made, but for the whole time the marriage, for a lifetime during which the vo are lived out by a man and a woman.

Like each of the sacraments, the sacrament of Matrimony is a public act. Standing before God a the community of the Church, a man and woma speak vows of love and commitment. The priest deacon who accepts these vows is the Church's official witness. There must also be two other witnesses. For a Catholic marriage to be considere valid, Catholics must marry in the presence of a priest or deacon and two witnesses. Unless otherwise dispensed, or excused, from this by the local bishop, any other marriage by Catholics would be considered invalid.

It is a surprise to many Catholics that the bride and groom themselves are the ministers of the sacrament. When the marriage vows are pronounced, the couple begins a whole new way of life. They are no longer two; they are one. The grace of this sacrament will enable them to put aside selfishness and to be open to each other in mutual support and generosity. The sacrament w strengthen them to approach an unknown futur

What if your favorite cousin got engaged but was reluctant to get involved "in those weird Pre-Cana classes"? What if you, because of what you have learned about the Catholic way of preparing for the sacrament of Matrimony, could help your cousin by explaining the "whats" and "whys" of the preparation process?

Allow about ten minutes for the activity.

◆ Have someone read aloud *Catholic ID* on page 155. If possible, read any banns currently appearing in the parish bulletin, and write the names of engaged couples on the board.

see that marriage vows must be made not only freely but also faithfully. When we marry, we promise fidelity to one person with a permanent commitment. We do not stand before God and the Church and say that we are only going to try this out for a while!

Most dioceses sponsor special preparation courses that are required before marriage. These are called Pre-Cana classes, reminding us of Christ's first miracle at the wedding feast in Cana of Galilee (John 2:1–11). In any event, marriage preparation takes time. Most parishes require six months' advance notice. As one parish bulletin stated: See the pastor before you rent the reception hall!

So much can go into planning the wedding celebration. But such a celebration will be empty if the bride and groom are not prepared. Marriage is a big step, perhaps the greatest step in life. If we prepare well, we will give ourselves the best chance of being successful and happy. And that is exactly what God and his Church want for us all.

Think about important events in your life that have taken preparation on your part. Why is preparation for marriage so important?

h its joys and sorrows. It will help them to build eir family life on the rock foundation of faith in rist. A man and woman will be able to do this y if they are ready to give themselves to each er freely in the Lord.

etting Ready

hen a couple decides to marry, it is because they ve decided to spend the rest of their lives together. ey become engaged and announce their intention marry. When one or both of them Catholic, they meet with the parish est, deacon, or other minister to gin a time of preparation. The rament of Matrimony requires ecial preparation because this serious mmitment is made for life. The couple st know of marriage's responsibilities, allenges, and graces. No one must enter to marriage lightly or without thought.

e priest or deacon will help the couple determine whether or not they truly are e to marry to be certain that nothing or one holds them back from making a free mmitment in love. He will help them to

CATHOLIC ID

The banns of marriage are customary in the Church. The word *banns* means "proclamations" or "announcements." For three weeks before a wedding, the parish prints in the weekly bulletin or announces at Mass the names of the bride and groom and the date of the wedding. Because we are a community, we need to know when our sisters and brothers in faith are taking this decisive step in their lives. When you read or hear the banns of marriage, pray for those entering into this beautiful sacramental commitment.

155

Conclusion ___ min.

◆ Call on volunteers to respond to the thought provoker on page 155.

FORUM Assignment

✔ Read pages 156 and 157. Underline in pencil the sentences that express six main ideas.

✔ Find three examples in music, poetry, greeting cards, or videos of expressions of true love — the kind of love on which a lasting commitment in marriage can be founded. Be prepared to share your examples.

Closing Prayer: Ask the young people to read 1 Corinthians 13. Allow a few minutes for them to write their reflections in their journals. Then invite volunteers to offer their own petitions for engaged couples in the parish.

FYI When married couples who have taken Catholic marriage preparation courses are surveyed, here are some of the things they say:

• "The best preparation is presented by a team including a priest, parish staff, and married couples who share their own experiences."

• "The most helpful topics are the five C's: communication, commitment, conflict resolution, children, and Church."

• Those couples with the highest expectations of the course derived the greatest benefits.

What might you add to the five C's?

FOR SESSION 3

• cassette/CD player, VCR
• assorted art materials
• copies of handout *Happily Ever After?*
• *United As One* album or other music

Objective: To explore the characteristics of real love; to deepen understanding of the celebration of Matrimony.

Introduction ___ min.

Opening Prayer

Forum: If possible, have a cassette and CD player as well as a VCR available for student use. Have the young people conduct the *Forum* as a TV talk show on the theme "Recognizing Real Love." Two co-hosts invite members of the audience to share their examples of expressions of true love in music, poetry, greeting cards, or videos. The co-hosts question participants about ways they can tell the difference between real love (on which a lasting marriage can be built) and false love (which dies when romance evaporates or infatuation runs its course). When all have participated, the co-hosts summarize key ideas expressed.

Presentation ___ min.

◆ Have volunteers share the key concepts they underlined on pages 156 and 157. Then have them highlight or underline in color the statements highlighted here.

◆ Print *indissoluble bond* on the board. Ask the young people to define the term. (a bond formed in Matrimony that can never be broken) Challenge the young people to name at least three reasons why some people are incapable of honoring an indissoluble bond. (They get married before they are ready; they are immature; they fail to work at marriage; they remain self-centered; they fail to pray and trust in God.)

◆ Call on volunteers to respond to the thought provoker on page 157. Briefly review the eight elements.

◆ Have a volunteer summarize *Catholic Teachings* on page 157. Emphasize that the Church values both the loving intimacy expressed in a married couple's sexual relationship and the children who are a sign of their covenanted love.

Real Love

What is real love? Certainly the feelings of love sometimes just happen. Such feelings are natural and beautiful gifts from God. They help to make us more human, more caring of others. But a commitment to love cannot be based on feelings alone because feelings come and go. The love needed in marriage must be a love based on a firm decision, a free choice. No other love will do. But this type of love is not easy. This love keeps on loving even when things get tough and we say to ourselves, "I don't feel like it." This is the love we vow when we say, "I promise to be true to you in good times and in bad, in sickness and in health. I will love you and honor you all the days of my life."

Catholics can never take the attitude that "we can always divorce if it doesn't go well." We believe that the sacrament of Matrimony forms an *indissoluble bond*—a bond that can never be broken. Real love based in Christ is not here one day and gone the next; real love is forever. Saint Paul once wrote that real love "bears all things, believes all things, hopes all things, endures all things. Love never fails" (1 Corinthians 13:7–8).

156

Sadly, some people cannot make this type of commitment in Christ. Others try too early or when they are immature. Others fail to work at marriage. But such a beautiful understanding of marriage is real. Such marriages are possible.

Celebrating Matrimony

Like every other sacrament Matrimony reveals something of the paschal mystery, the death and resurrection of Christ. When two Catholics celebr[ate] the sacrament of Matrimony, they celebrate their willingness to imitate and encounter Christ in the lives of service, in the dyings and risings, sorrows and joys of family life.

The meaning of Catholic marriage is expressed in the rite of marriage. The sacrament of Matrimony has the same basic shape as all the other sacrament[s]: gathering, storytelling, the sacramental action (in Matrimony, the exchange of vows, preferably with the eucharistic meal), and commissioning. It is mo[st] fitting that the rite of marriage be celebrated with[in] a nuptial Mass. In this way the bride and groom uni[te] themselves to the self-offering of Christ in the Eucharist. It is also fitting that they receive the Bo[dy] and Blood of Christ in Holy Communion, which seals their union in Christ.

Gathering The priest or deacon usually greets the bride and groom, welcoming them and their families and friends in the name of the Church.

FYI Together with their pastor, Alan and Lynn carefully planned their nuptial liturgy. They included a blessing of their parents. They reflected on several possible Scripture readings before choosing those which best expressed their vision of marriage. As their theme, they chose the lines: "Your people shall be my people, and your God my God" (Book of Ruth 1:16). Alan and Lynn also chose liturgical music that helped them focus on the meaning of Christian marriage. Why do you think it is important for the couple to participate in the planning of the liturgy for their wedding?

...rytelling The couple often selects the ...ipture passages from the rite that correspond to ... religious meaning they wish to express in ...ir wedding. The readings will sometimes have ...eference to creation, for husband and wife are ...rting something new: a new relationship, a new ...ily, a new domestic church. The readings will ...netimes refer to the two becoming one. They ...l often refer to the unselfish love stressed by ...us in the gospels.

...change of Vows It is the bride and groom ...o, by their free consent and mutual vows, are ... ministers of the sacrament. The pledging of ...vs must be *witnessed* by a priest, the Church's ...icial witness, and two other people, usually ... maid of honor and the best man. The free consent ...he couple and the presence of a priest and two ...nesses are the essential signs of the sacrament. ...e bride and groom stand before the congregation ...d vow "to give themselves, each to the other, ...tually and definitively, in order to live a covenant ...aithful and fruitful love" (*Catechism*, 1662).

...d is faithful "no matter what." In order for the ...ple to be a sign of this divine love, they must ...lect God's faithful love in three ways: in *unity* ...body, heart, and soul; in *indissolubility*, that is, ...long faithfulness; and in *openness to having* ...dren. These three qualities are essential to ...ristian marriage.

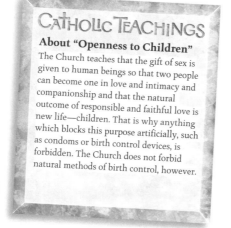

CATHOLIC TEACHINGS

About "Openness to Children"

The Church teaches that the gift of sex is given to human beings so that two people can become one in love and intimacy and companionship and that the natural outcome of responsible and faithful love is new life—children. That is why anything which blocks this purpose artificially, such as condoms or birth control devices, is forbidden. The Church does not forbid natural methods of birth control, however.

Meal Sharing As we have seen, when two practicing Catholics exchange their vows, they usually do so in the context of the Eucharist at a nuptial Mass. All that marriage says about union with Christ in sacrificial love is said even more eloquently in the Eucharist.

Following the Lord's Prayer the priest extends his hands over the couple and invokes the Holy Spirit upon them. The Holy Spirit is the seal of their covenant and an ever-present source of love and strength.

Commissioning The blessing at the end of Mass is directed especially to the bride and groom. One blessing asks that the peace of Christ may always be in their home, that they will live in peace with all people, and that they will always bear witness to the love of God in this world.

Recall a wedding liturgy in which you have participated. Can you describe the main elements based on the outline given here?

157

FORUM Assignment

✔ Read pages 158 and 159. Underline in pencil the sentences that express two main ideas.

✔ Complete the handout *Happily Ever After?* Be prepared to share your work.

Closing Prayer: Play one of the following songs (or any other on the theme of faithful love):

* "United As One" by Owen Alstott from the album of that title, Vol. 1 (OCP)

* "Wherever You Go" by Gregory Norbet/Weston Priory (album as above)

* "First Corinthians 13" from the album *Like A Seal On Your Heart: Music for the Christian Wedding* (OCP).

Invite volunteers to respond to the music by offering petitions for married or engaged couples they know. All respond:

May they be united as one.

Conclusion ___ min.

◆ Have the young people form small groups of "Nuptial Mass Illustrators." Distribute posterboard, newsprint, construction paper, markers, rulers, scissors, and glue to each working area. Give the following assignment:

Design one of the following to illustrate the parts of the nuptial Mass and how they fit together: a poster, a collage, a chart, a mobile, an original work of imagination. Include all eight parts of the liturgy. Illustrate them any way you choose.

Allow fifteen minutes for this activity. Display the completed works.

FOR SESSION 4

* "mail bag" (large purse or briefcase)

SESSION 4

Objective: To explore needed skills for marriage readiness.

Introduction ___ min.

Opening Prayer

Forum: Have participants fold their handout sheets twice (as in a business letter) and drop them in a "mail bag" (a large purse or briefcase). Then ask a designated delivery person to re-distribute the letters. Have each person read aloud the responses from "The Marriage Counselor." He or she is then free to contrast these responses with his or her own. When all have shared responses, the host summarizes the Catholic point of view on each of the three imaginary situations.

Presentation ___ min.

◆ Have volunteers share the key concepts they underlined on pages 158 and 159. Then have them highlight or underline in color the statements highlighted here.

◆ Write the following statement on the board: "Marriage is a union of two compatible but often very different people." Ask the young people to consider the married people they know well. In responding to the following, they should not name the couples they are describing but may generalize about the age group and approximate number of years the couple has been married.

• How can you tell that this couple is compatible?
• What important differences have you noticed?
• How do you think this couple deals with their differences?

Discuss with the young people why airing differences, sharing decisions, and revealing deep feelings may help the couple to remain united.

◆ Have the young people form small groups to work with the questionnaire on page 159. Read the introduction and directions aloud. Suggest that the young people work individually in their journals for the first three to five minutes. Then encourage them to share ideas and solutions. After a brief group session, call on volunteers to identify those interpersonal skills that are

most difficult for them (or for the majority in their group). Identify ways of practicing the needed skills (everything from counting slowly to three before responding to criticism, to volunteering to help out with young children).

◆ Discuss with the young people the positive and negative ways the media presents love and sexuality. Stress the importance of remembering that these expressions do have a deeper meaning to those who share in respectful love. Share with them the *FYI* story that reminds us of the truth and strength of a loving relationship.

Are You Ready for Marriage?

The correct answer to the question above is, of course, no. Readiness for a lifelong commitment demands a certain maturity, an ability to care for and support a family, and an awareness of the challenges and responsibilities that joining one's life to another's demands. Still most of you are, whether you know it or not, preparing for marriage right now.

As we grow through life, we become aware of our own unique characteristics. Some of these we can do nothing about. The color of our hair and eyes is based on genetics, not personal preference. Other characteristics, however, even if based on inborn tendencies, are not fixed forever. We can make decisions about our personality traits. We can decide, for example, to be kind, to be more patient, to listen to others, to keep our promises. In other words, we can begin now to decide what kind of person we want to become, what kind of interpersonal skills we want to learn.

The vocation of marriage requires interpersonal skills. Marriage is a union of two compatible but often very different people. Two unique personaliti must learn to make important decisions together to discuss their differences of opinion, to allow themselves to reveal deep feelings to the other. This is not easy for anyone!

ScriptureUPDATE

The Church provides a variety of Scripture readings for the rite of marriage. Find the passages listed here. Then choose one. What does it tell you about the sacrament of Matrimony?

1 Corinthians 12:31—13:8 1 John 4:7–12
Ephesians 5:2, 25–32

158

e following questionnaire is a sample the kinds of questions engaged couples e asked. Such a questionnaire can lp the couple to become more aware of eir own personalities and their ability communicate with others. You have bably used these skills in friendships, in oups or teams you might belong to, or in oup projects in school. Everyone needs

these skills. Those who work on developing their interpersonal skills are headed toward satisfying friendships and, in time, a good marriage.

You may want to write your personal responses to these questions in your journal and then share your ideas and solutions in small groups. Check those skills you wish to improve.

MY INTERPERSONAL SKILLS

- ☐ **A**m I a good listener? How do I show this?

- ☐ **H**ow do I deal with criticism?

- ☐ **D**o I show respect for others in my speech, saying "please," "thank you," and "pardon me"?

- ☐ **D**o I talk over problems with the person or persons directly involved?

- ☐ **W**hat is my reaction when my plans are upset for some reason?

- ☐ **H**ave I learned to play with and watch over young children safely?

- ☐ **D**o I apologize when I've made a mistake or caused a problem?

- ☐ **D**o I spend money wisely?

- ☐ **H**ow do I treat the elderly persons I meet?

- ☐ **W**hat do I do when I am angry? How do I solve the problem?

- ☐ **D**o I speak with adults respectfully and courteously?

- ☐ **D**o I give positive feedback? Do I affirm others and thank them when I am grateful for their help or support?

- ☐ **D**o I look for ways to help others when I can?

- ☐ **I**f I have a serious problem or need, do I talk it over with an adult I can trust?

How do you think developing interpersonal skills can prepare you for marriage?

159

Conclusion ___ min.

◆ Call for brief responses to the thought provoker on page 159.

◆ Have a volunteer read aloud *Scripture Update* on page 158. Let the young people know that they will be looking at these readings during the *Closing Prayer.*

FORUM Assignment

✔ Read pages 160 and 161. Prepare your responses to *Things to Think About* and *Things to Share.*

✔ Write a list of "Ten Rules for Finding and Keeping Good Friends." Reflect on ways good friendships prepare young people for marriage.

Closing Prayer: Have the young people form three prayer groups. Assign one of the three readings from *Scripture Update* to each group. Have them read and reflect silently on what their readings tell them about the sacrament of Matrimony. Then have each group proclaim one or two verses as follows: 1 Corinthians 13:4; Ephesians 5:29–31; 1 John 4:12.

FYI To remove a tumor in the young woman's face, the surgeon had to cut a nerve. Now her mouth was crooked like a clown's with a goofy expression. She asked if it would always be that way, and the surgeon said "Yes." Her young husband said, "I like it. It is kind of cute." The surgeon watched as the husband bent over to kiss his wife. "I can see how he twists his own lips to accommodate to her, to show her that their kiss still works. . ." the surgeon later wrote. He knew that he was in the presence of a true and faithful love.

FOR SESSION 5

- bowl or font of holy water
- copies of *Chapter 13 Assessment*
- copies of *Highlights for Home*
- posters on true friendships (optional)

Objective: To deepen appreciation for the sacrament of Matrimony.

Introduction ___ min.

Opening Prayer

Forum: Before the session begins, print on posters the following sayings or write them on the board. You might choose to display around the room wise sayings about friendship such as these:

- "Hold a true friend with both your hands." (Nigerian proverb)
- "The only way to have a friend is to be one." (Ralph Waldo Emerson)
- "To get the full value of a joy, you must have somebody to divide it with." (Mark Twain)
- "The best mirror is an old friend." (George Herbert)

Begin by having two co-hosts call on volunteers to share one or two of their "Ten Rules for Finding and Keeping Good Friends." A master list may be kept on the board for possible duplication. Have the students share in a brief discussion on ways good friendships prepare them for marriage. Then discuss *Things to Think About* and *Things to Share.*

Presentation ___ min.

◆ Call attention to *Words to Remember* on page 160. The description of the *sacrament of Matrimony* can be found on page 154; the definition of *indissoluble bond* is on page 156.

Assessment: Suggest that the students work with partners in writing answers to *Testing 1, 2, 3.* If time allows, have the partners share their responses with the group.

If you are administering *Chapter 13 Assessment,* page 161A, allow about ten minutes for its completion.

◆ Have a volunteer read *On Line With the Parish.* Be prepared with information about the kind of marriage preparation offered in your parish. Encourage the young people to share this information with those who may need it.

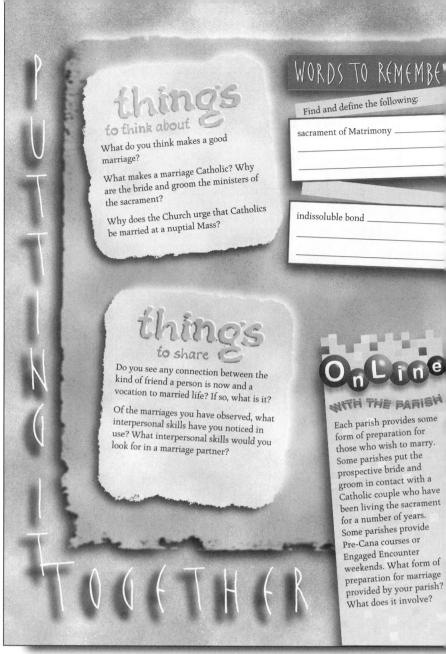

PUTTING IT TOGETHER

things to think about

What do you think makes a good marriage?

What makes a marriage Catholic? Why are the bride and groom the ministers of the sacrament?

Why does the Church urge that Catholics be married at a nuptial Mass?

things to share

Do you see any connection between the kind of friend a person is now and a vocation to married life? If so, what is it?

Of the marriages you have observed, what interpersonal skills have you noticed in use? What interpersonal skills would you look for in a marriage partner?

WORDS TO REMEMBER

Find and define the following:

sacrament of Matrimony _____

indissoluble bond _____

OnLine WITH THE PARISH

Each parish provides some form of preparation for those who wish to marry. Some parishes put the prospective bride and groom in contact with a Catholic couple who have been living the sacrament for a number of years. Some parishes provide Pre-Cana courses or Engaged Encounter weekends. What form of preparation for marriage provided by your parish? What does it involve?

Conclusion ___ min.

◆ Encourage the young people to share *Highlights for Home,* page 161B, with their families.

Closing Prayer: If possible, have a bowl or font of blessed water available for the blessing on page 161. Have the young people read *Life in the Spirit* silently before gathering at the prayer table. Invite all to extend their right arms forward toward others in the prayer circle in a gesture of blessing. Pray aloud the *Blessing for a Family or Household.* Then have the young people bless themselves with the holy water.

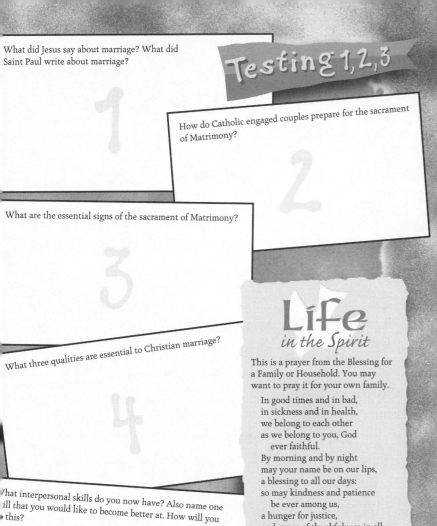

What did Jesus say about marriage? What did Saint Paul write about marriage?

How do Catholic engaged couples prepare for the sacrament of Matrimony?

What are the essential signs of the sacrament of Matrimony?

What three qualities are essential to Christian marriage?

What interpersonal skills do you now have? Also name one skill that you would like to become better at. How will you do this?

Testing 1,2,3

Life
in the Spirit

This is a prayer from the Blessing for a Family or Household. You may want to pray it for your own family.

In good times and in bad,
in sickness and in health,
we belong to each other
as we belong to you, God
   ever faithful.
By morning and by night
may your name be on our lips,
a blessing to all our days:
so may kindness and patience
   be ever among us,
a hunger for justice,
and songs of thankfulness in all
   we do.
We ask this through Christ our Lord.

Catholic Household Blessings and Prayers

161

Evaluation: Do the young people understand the meaning and importance of the sacrament of Matrimony? Do they understand the need for maturity, faith, and preparation before accepting the responsibility of a lifelong commitment?

Testing 1,2,3

1. See page 154. Jesus said, "What God has joined together, no human being must separate" (Matthew 19:6). Saint Paul compared the union of marriage to the love of Christ and the Church. Just as Christ loves his body, the Church, so husband and wife must love each other.

2. See page 155. They meet with the parish priest, deacon, or pastoral minister to begin a time of preparation. They attend special preparation courses called Pre-Cana classes.

3. See page 157. The essential signs of the sacrament are the free consent of the couple and the presence of a priest and two witnesses.

4. See page 157. The three qualities essential to Christian marriage are unity of body, heart, and soul; indissolubility, lifelong faithfulness; openness to having children.

5. See page 159. Accept reasonable responses.

Answers for Chapter 13 Assessment
1. a   2. c   3. b   4. a   5. b
6. d   7. c   8. d   9. a   10. See pages 156–157.

161

Assessment

 1 Marriage is important
a. to the Church and society.
b. as a political tool.
c. to the couple alone.
d. economically.

 2 The sacrament of Matrimony involves
a. unbaptized persons.
b. only a legal contract.
c. a covenant between a baptized man and a baptized woman.
d. none of the above

 3 Saint Paul compares marriage
a. to a court case.
b. to the love of Christ and the Church.
c. to a business deal.
d. to a Baptism.

 4 Catholic marriage vows require
a. the witness of a priest or deacon.
b. a doctor's certificate.
c. that the children be present.
d. all of the above

 5 The ministers of Matrimony
a. are the priest and deacon.
b. are the bride and groom.
c. are the wedding party.
d. are not necessary.

 6 Marriage preparation is
a. required by most dioceses.
b. only for certain couples.
c. a recognition of Matrimony's challenges and responsibilities.
d. both a and c

 7 An indissoluble bond
a. is water solvent.
b. is only a legal term.
c. can never be broken.
d. has nothing to do with marriage.

 8 Married couples reflect God's faithful love in
a. their unity of body and soul.
b. their lifelong faithfulness.
c. their openness to children.
d. all of the above

 9 Interpersonal skills are
a. needed in marriage.
b. not needed by youth.
c. unimportant.
d. none of the above

10 Describe the process of celebrating a nuptial Mass.

_____

_____

_____

CHAPTER 13: The Sacrament of Matrimony
Highlights for Home

Focus on Faith

In a culture of quick change, temporary relationships, and the ready availability of divorce, society no longer provides the unqualified support that once strengthened spouses and families. Because we want our young people to be prepared for a good marriage, if that is their call from God, Chapter 13 helps them to take a clear-eyed look at what the sacrament of Matrimony is all about. In the eyes of the Church this beautiful sacrament unites a baptized man and a baptized woman in a lifelong covenant of love before God. As ministers of the sacrament to one another, they pronounce their vows before the community and are "united as one." By their gift of self to each other, their openness to having children, and their acceptance of the indissolubility of marriage, they are a sign of God's grace active in them. Christ is in them helping them to love each other" with a tender and powerful love" (*Catechism*, 1642).

Conversation Starters

. . . . a few ideas to talk about together . . . .

◆ Can you think of ten characteristics of a good marriage?

◆ What interpersonal skills can I work on to prepare for a marriage in which these characteristics are present?

Feature Focus

The *Catholic ID* feature on page 155 explains the custom of announcing a couple's intention to marry in the parish. Printed in the weekly bulletin, these "banns" (or proclamations) inform us about who is to be married and when the wedding will take place. As members of the faith community, we offer our prayers for those who are about to celebrate the lifelong sacrament of Matrimony.

Reflection

When a baptized couple marry in the Church, they promise each other, "I will love you and honor you all the days of my life." Perhaps you, too, will make that promise one day to the man or woman you believe God wants you to marry. To prepare for that day, ask yourself:

• How well am I doing at loving and honoring the members of my immediate family right now?

• Why is it often difficult to love and honor the people we live with, day in and day out?

• What improvements are needed in my actions or attitudes? When will I begin?

Adult Focus

By her complete acceptance of God's will, her total cooperation in her son's work of redemption, and her adherence to every prompting of the Holy Spirit, "The Virgin Mary is the Church's model of faith and charity" (*CCC*, 967). The Church rightly honors Mary with special devotion, especially with four principal titles: Mother of God, Virgin, the Immaculate Conception and the Assumption. Because of her singular vocation, she is solemnly honored on January 1, December 8, and August 15. These liturgical feasts express her relationship to the Church and to all humanity: she is mother to us all "in the order of grace" (*CCC*, 968).

Mary continually intercedes for us before God. But hers is not the only voice raised on our behalf. The entire communion of saints intercedes for us. We do not worship or adore Mary or the saints. However, we do ask for their prayers, support and intercession with God as we attempt to walk the path of holiness. Our young people need to know that, as part of the communion of saints, they are surrounded and cherished by holy friends, and guarded and loved by the Mother of God. It is a realization that strengthens our faith and enlivens our hope on our journey to eternal life.

Catechism Focus

The theme of Chapter 14 corresponds to paragraphs 490–507, 964–971, 946–948, 2673–2679 of the *Catechism*.

Enrichment Activities

Making a Pilgrimage

Plan a group pilgrimage to a Marian shrine or a retreat center dedicated to Mary. Include plans for a picnic, Christian music concert or sing-along, and praying the rosary. The young people might invite a youth group from a different parish to join them for this day-long or weekend outing.

Viewing Videos

Invite a few volunteers to preview with you selected segments from the following videos. We suggest showing to the entire group a ten-minute segment from "The Road to Sainthood" in which the process of canonization is explained and illustrated. (See *Passion of the Saints*, Volume III. Fast-forward to the second half of this 100-minute video.) You may also wish to show "Saints for All Seasons" included in the third volume of *Saints' Gallery*.

Both series are available from:
Videos with Values
7315 Manchester Road
St. Louis, Missouri 63143

Teaching Resources

	Overview	Opening Prayer Ideas	Materials
SESSION 1	**Discovery:** To discover our connection with the communion of saints.	Reflect on and sing "Song of the Body of Christ" by David Haas. Celebrate our belonging to the communion of saints.	These will be needed every session: texts, Bibles, highlighters or colored pencils, journals. • skein of yarn • "Song of the Body of Christ" from *Glory Day* (GIA)
SESSION 2	**Exploring 1:** To explore the three types of liturgical celebrations of the life of Mary and the lives of the saints; to explore the process of canonization.	Pray Hebrews 12:14. Reflect on one or more ways to strive for holiness.	• graph paper or drawing paper, rulers, pencils • index cards, markers • sheets of posterboard covered with aluminum foil
SESSION 3	**Exploring 2:** To explore the role that Mary, as mother of Jesus and his first disciple, plays in our salvation and our devotion.	Reflect on Luke 1:49. Name the great things God has done for you and your family.	• display of Marian art, craft, literature and music (optional) • video "Madonna" (optional) • duplicated copies of group assignments (optional) • *Christ, Be Our Light* album by Bernadette Farrell (OCP)
SESSION 4	**Exploring 3:** To explore the meaning and richness of the Hail Mary and the Rosary.	Pray the Hail Holy Queen on page 188 in the text.	• writing and drawing materials • copies of handout *Nine Days of Prayer* • icon or statue of Mary
SESSION 5	**Putting It Together:** To deepen understanding of and appreciation for Mary and the saints.	Pray aloud and then quietly reflect on Romans 8:31–35.	• parish calendar • parish hymnal • copies of *Chapter 14 Assessment* • copies of *Highlights for Home*

Supplemental Resources

Videos
The Madonna
Palisades Home Video
P.O. Box 2794
Virginia Beach, VA
23450–2794

Communion of Saints
Paulist Press
997 Macarthur Blvd.
Mahwah, NJ 07430

Faith and Witness Journal: Liturgy & Worship

For Chapter 14 see pages 56–59.

CHAPTER fourteen

Nine Days of Prayer

A novena is a traditional prayer practice commemorating the nine days the followers of Jesus spent praying with Mary as they waited for the coming of the Holy Spirit on Pentecost Sunday. (The word *novena* comes from the word "nine" in Latin.)

Usually a novena is made for a particular intention. It can be made privately or with others. It can be prayed for nine consecutive days or once a week for nine consecutive weeks (for example, nine consecutive Fridays).

Make a novena to Mary. Pray to her for nine consecutive days under nine of her special titles. You may want to take these titles from the Litany of the Blessed Virgin Mary on page 188, or you may use titles you already know. A sample has been started for you. Begin to plan your prayers here and continue on the back of this sheet.

The First Day

Our Lady of Good Counsel,
help us and guide us when we face
difficult situations.

The Second Day

Title:

Prayer:

The Third Day

Title:

Prayer:

SESSION 1

Mary and the Saints

*Lord, this is the people that
longs to see your face.*
Solemnity of All Saints

163

---

*Objective: To discover our connection with the
communion of saints.*

Introduction ___ min.

Opening Prayer: Invite the young people to look at
the artwork on pages 162 and 163. If possible, begin
by playing "Song of the Body of Christ" from the
"Glory Day" video by David Haas (St. Anthony
Messenger Press) or from the album *Glory Day* (GIA).
As the song progresses, encourage the group to sing
the chorus. Then ask the general group to respond to
each acclamation with the prayer on page 162.

> Together with all believers, we belong to the body
> of Christ.
> With all God's holy people who have died and
> gone on before us, we belong to the body of
> Christ.
> May Mary and the entire communion of saints be
> our companions on the journey of faith.

Continue the group's prayer with the following
activity to demonstrate that the communion of saints
is a network of support and companionship on our
journey of faith.

1. Ask the group to stand in a circle.

2. Designate one person as the beginner. Ask this
person to think of a saint, say the saint's name
aloud, and give a short biographical statement
about the saint. An example statement is "Saint
Joseph was the foster-father of Jesus." Ask the
group to respond: "(Saint's name), support us on
our journey of faith." Then this first person should
hold tightly to the end of a skein of yarn, and, still
holding the end, gently throw the skein across the
circle to a person on the opposite side.

3. Each person who catches the skein should say a
saint's name aloud and give a short statement
about the saint. After the group responds, the
catcher should hold a section of the string tightly
and throw the skein to another person.

4. Repeat this process until everyone standing in the
circle is part of the network. Then all take one step
backward to tighten the net. The prayer can conclude with one person (the teacher or the appointed leader) saying, "Mary and all the saints,
your shining lives are examples for us to follow. We
ask you to continue to support us on our journey
of faith." All respond: Amen.

Presentation ___ min.

◆ Have a volunteer read the introductory paragraph on page 164. Discuss the question about asking in prayer for Mary and the saints' intercession.

◆ Ask volunteers to read pages 164 and 165. List on the board the four images used to describe our union in holiness with the saints: communion of saints, household of God, body of Christ, and family. Ask all to highlight or to underline in color the key concepts highlighted here.

◆ Discuss the thought provoker on page 165. Draw a house framework on the board. Write on the frame strengths the young people suggest that they can use to build up the communion of saints. Then ask the young people to draw a framework in their journals. Have them write their own individual strengths as well as strengths they think they need to work on.

◆ Ask a volunteer to find and read John 15:1–5. This is the passage of the vine and the branches. Explain that Jesus compared himself to the vine because a vine is the main source of life for the branches. In order for the branches to have life, they must stay connected to the vine. The saints became saints and bore fruit in their lives, not on their own power, but because they stayed connected to the vine, Jesus.

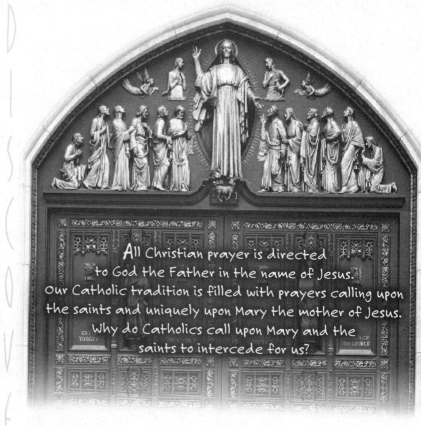

All Christian prayer is directed to God the Father in the name of Jesus. Our Catholic tradition is filled with prayers calling upon the saints and uniquely upon Mary the mother of Jesus. Why do Catholics call upon Mary and the saints to intercede for us?

The Communion of Saints

Sometimes on headstones in a cemetery, there is a request: "Please pray for me," or "Pray for the repose of the soul of…." We find such inscriptions in the early Christian cemeteries, too.

On the tombs of the martyrs, however, the inscriptions are different: They ask the martyrs to pray for us! These inscriptions are our earliest evidence of Christian prayer to the saints. From the beginning Christians have called upon Mary and the saints to intercede with God for them.

You remember that old saying: The way we pray shows what we believe. And how do we pray about the saints? In the preface for Masses on saints' days, we thank God because:

You renew the Church in every age
by raising up men and women outstanding
   in holiness,
living witnesses of your unchanging love.
They inspire us by their heroic lives,
and help us by their constant prayers
to be the living sign of your saving power.

164

As a reminder that we, too, want to stay connected to Jesus, Mary, and all the saints, make a "Communion-of-Saints Vine." Give each group member three green leaves (you might want to cut them in the shape of grape leaves, as this brings in a eucharistic dimension). Ask the young people to write the name of a saint (their patron or any saint they may choose) on one leaf. On the second leaf, ask them to write the name of a "fruit" their chosen saint bore. For example, Saint Francis of Assisi bore the fruit of peace. On the third leaf, ask them to write their own names. On the back of that leaf, ask them to write what good fruit they are bearing now. (Remind them that noting our good fruit, or good points, is often harder than noting our weak points!) If they need help, remind them that friendliness, helpfulness, cheerfulness, kindness, and fairness are all good fruits to write on the leaf.

Using a rope clothesline or string or yarn for the vine, help the young people attach their leaves to it. Drape the vine in a prominent place, perhaps over a set of windows or a doorway.

You may want to end this activity with a recording of a song on the theme of the saints, unity, the body of Christ, or the vine and the branches.

honor the saints because of their example
their intercession. They show us how to
ow Christ, and they help us by their prayers.

e holiness of the saints is a reflection of God's
iness. In the sacraments the Father shares his
iness with us through the Son and the Holy
rit. Through the sacraments we enter into a
ly communion" and share, in union with the
nts, God's life. Our union with God's holiness
d with his holy ones (the saints) is called the
munion of saints.

hen we use the title Saint, we normally think
:hose men and women of exceptional holiness
ose lives we see in movies or read about in
oks. It is important to remember that we too
e called to be saints. Saint Paul, in his Letter to
e Ephesians, wrote: "So then you are no longer
rangers and sojourners, but you are fellow
izens with the holy ones and members of the
usehold of God" (Ephesians 2:19).

*From the tombs
of the martyrs, the
catacombs, Rome*

nited in Holiness

ie doctrine of the communion of saints has very
iportant consequences for our daily lives. Think
. what it means—we are united with the saints in
common holiness!

or example, think of your physical body. When you
:ercise and strengthen your arms, your whole body
:nefits. When you do aerobics to strengthen your
ngs and your heart, your whole body benefits. So
is with the body of Christ. "Since all the faithful
rm one body, the good of each is communicated
. the others" (*Catechism*, 947).

ecause we are members of the same body of
hrist, all the good works, the merits, and the
aces of the saints are communicated to us. What
i encouragement this can be as we struggle and
ten fail in our efforts to follow Jesus. The
immunion of saints assures us that *together*
e form one family in Christ. In the family of
hristians, as in a human family, the good of one
ember is shared with the whole family. When
ur mother wins the lottery, the whole family
ets rich!

In America it is
important to emphasize this collective or
communal dimension of our salvation because
our culture places great emphasis on *individual*
accomplishment. This attitude, however, does not
apply to salvation or holiness. When it comes to
holiness and sanctity, we are all in this together.
We are one body, one family, one community in
Christ. God's holiness is a *shared* gift.

What, then, does holiness mean for each one of
us? As individuals, we each respond to God's grace
in our own way and as best we can. We grow in
holiness through a continual process of turning
our lives toward God. We keep trying to empty
ourselves of selfishness and sin in order to allow
God's Spirit to fill us and to work in us. The saints
have accomplished this to such a degree that when
we look at their lives, we see and understand what
Saint Paul meant when he wrote, "I live, no longer
I, but Christ lives in me" (Galatians 2:20).

The communion of saints is both a tremendous
responsibility and a source of great hope. Our
responsibility is to follow Christ faithfully, as
members of his body. Our hope is that we,
together with all the saints, will share eternally
in his final victory.

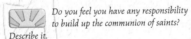

*Do you feel you have any responsibility
to build up the communion of saints?
Describe it.*

165

✔ Read pages 166 and 167. Underline
in pencil the sentences that express
six main ideas. Consider the process
of canonization as one main idea.

✔ Plan a simple way of observing the
feast days of your family members'
and friends' patron saints. Then discuss with the adults of your family
the saints to whom they have particular devotion. Include in your discussion ways these saints reflected the
light of God's love to others.

Closing Prayer: Call attention to the
illustration of a saint's tombstone on
page 165. Ask each young person
to remember one person in their
extended family or in the parish who
has died. In their journals, have
them sketch a simple memorial plaque
for that person. Under the plaque,
have them write or paraphrase a
scriptural quote expressing faith in the
resurrection.

Encourage the group to pray regularly
for any friends or loved ones who have
died. Remind them that the dead
remain with us in the body of Christ
and the communion of saints. They are
always a part of our lives.

Conclusion ___ min.

◆ Before you ask the following question, tell the
group, "I am going to ask you a question, and I will
give you the answer ahead of time. The answer is YES.
Now for the question: 'Can you be a saint?'" Ask,
"How do you know?" Ask the young people to skim
through page 165 and find encouragement to walk in
the footsteps of the saints. (Note especially the quota-
tions from Saint Paul and the second paragraph in the
right hand column.)

FOR SESSION 2

• index cards, markers
• sheets of posterboard covered with aluminum foil

SESSION 2

Objective: To explore the three types of liturgical celebrations of the life of Mary and the lives of the saints; to explore the process of canonization.

Introduction ___ min.

Opening Prayer

Forum: Begin the *Forum* by explaining that, to prepare for the celebration of certain holidays, many home shows discuss special recipes and certain traditional customs well in advance of the actual day. Suggest the use of this format to enable the young people to share their ways of observing feast days of patron or favorite saints. Have co-hosts ask their guests to share ways these faith-filled ancestors reflected the light of God's love to others.

Presentation ___ min.

◆ Have volunteers share the statements they underlined on pages 166 and 167. Ask all to underline the key statements highlighted here.

◆ Share the following fictional case with the group. Call on volunteers to describe the process the parishioners should follow, step by step.

> The people of St. Thomas Parish are determined to have one of their members recognized as a saint. She is Sister Maria Gonzalez, a missionary who spent forty years working among the poor in Latin America. Through her letters over the years and through testimony given by those she served, the pastor of St. Thomas has proof of Sister Maria's heroic self-sacrifice. She risked her life several times to save others, and died while caring for those afflicted by an epidemic. What advice can you give the pastor and people of St. Thomas? How should they proceed in this matter?

(Responses should include the following: Call on an expert in Church matters to study Sister Maria's life; have the expert produce a report on the faith and good works of Sister Maria; submit this report to the bishop; cooperate with the continuing investigation into her holiness; encourage the bishop to submit the

Celebrating the Saints

Devotion to Our Lady and the saints goes back to the earliest days of the Church. It is a rich tradition. We have seen how the liturgical year celebrates the birth, life, passion, death, and resurrection of Jesus. The liturgical year also celebrates the life of Mary and the lives of the saints.

Liturgical celebrations are divided into three degrees. The most important days are called *solemnities*. For example, the days we celebrate the Trinity, Our Lord, or the Holy Spirit—Trinity Sunday, Christmas, Easter, Pentecost—are solemnities. In addition, we celebrate eight solemnities in honor of Mary or the saints each year. These include the solemnities of Mary, the Mother of God (January 1); Joseph, patron of the universal Church (March 19); John the Baptist (June 24); and the Apostles Peter and Paul (June 29). Why would you think these celebrations are given the rank of solemnity?

Second in order of importance is that of *feast*. This rank includes, among others, the feasts of apostles and evangelists; the feast of the angels and archangels (September 29); the feast of the first martyr, Stephen (December 26); and the feast of the Holy Innocents (December 28).

The final rank is *memorial*. On memorial days we celebrate the *memory* of a saint. Just as you might mark the birthdays of your friends on your calendar, the Church marks the birthdays of individual saints. However, there is one important difference. The Church does not celebrate the day the saints were born on earth but marks instead the day on which they were born into eternal life—that is, the day on which they died. It is their passage into new and eternal life that we celebrate, affirming that Christ's victory over death became fully real in their lives.

166

Reflections of the Holy

What does it mean when we call someone a *saint*? The word means "holy." In order to understand the holiness of the saints, we must start with the realization that only God is holy. We pray in the Glory to God at Mass:

For you alone are the Holy One,
you alone are the Lord,
you alone are the Most High,
Jesus Christ....

If we call anyone other than God "holy," it is because this person reflects God's holiness. When we honor a saint's achievements, we are not honoring what the saint did; rather, we are honoring what God did through the saint. Holiness is achieved, not by doing great things, but by allowing God's greatness to work in us.

The Church is aware that millions and millions of Christians have lived holy lives and that they now share in the happiness of God's life in heaven. These are all saints in the general sense of the word. However, in order to recognize the holiness of particular saints in a formal way, the Church has instituted the process called *canonization*. In order for a holy person to be canonized, an expert in Church matters must study the holy person's life.

Saint Frances Xavier Cabrini

Blessed Katharine Drexel

Saint Charles Lwanga

final results of Sister Maria's case to the Congregation for the Causes of Saints in Rome. Keep track of any miracles attributed to her intercession. Pray that she will one day be a canonized saint.)

◆ Invite the young people to look at the art on pages 166 and 167. Share with them the way each saint reflected the holiness of God.

- Blessed Katharine Drexel shared the gospel with Native Americans and African Americans.

- Saint Frances Xavier Cabrini founded many schools, hospitals, and orphanages for immigrants in the United States.

- Saint Charles Lwanga encouraged others to resist immorality and was martyred for his courageous faith.

- Blessed Juan Diego, through his sharing of his encounter with Mary, gave hope to the oppressed Indians of Mexico.

ter this report of faith and good works is given the bishop, more investigation is done. The ...al results are then sent to the Congregation ...r the Causes of Saints in Rome. The holy ...rson may then be beatified and given the title "Blessed."

...sually, three miracles (often healings of the sick) ...ributed to the holy person's intercession are ...quired before formal declaration of sainthood. ...en the pope, in a beautiful and solemn ceremony, ...nonizes the saint, declaring that this holy person ...truly a saint and extending veneration of this ...wly canonized saint to the whole Church.

...ch year we celebrate well-known saints—saints ...ch as Saint Francis of Assisi, Saint Thérèse of ...sieux, Saint Joseph, and the special patron saint ...f our diocese or parish. We also celebrate those ...ints who worked for God and his people on ...merican soil: Blessed Kateri Tekakwitha, Saint ...aac Jogues and the North American Martyrs,

Pope John Paul II has added a large number of saints and "blesseds" to the Church's calendar. They include the Vietnamese martyrs Saint Andrew Dung-Lac and Companions; the Korean martyrs Saints Andrew Kim, Paul Chong and Companions; and Blessed Juan Diego, the native Mexican who was privileged with the vision of Our Lady of Guadalupe. The previous pope, Pope Paul VI, canonized the martyrs of Uganda, Saint Charles Lwanga and Companions. Celebrating the saints reminds us that holiness is not restricted to one time or place. Saints come from all over the world.

The diversity in the lives of the saints teaches us that all Christians are called to holiness by imitating Christ in their particular circumstances. Often, by learning the life stories of the saints, we find that they faced spiritual challenges similar to the ones we face in our own lives. As we learn from them, these great heroes and heroines become our role models in the Christian life.

Blessed
Juan Diego

Saint
Andrew Kim

Blessed
Kateri Tekakwitha

167

CATHOLIC ID

Do you have a patron saint? The Church encourages Catholics to be given the name of a saint when they are baptized as infants. Parents are not required to name their child after a saint, but it is an excellent tradition. A patron saint serves as an example of Christian life, and the child who is given a saint's name is assured of the saint's intercession.

Catholics may also choose another saint's name when they are confirmed. They do this in order to have another personal example of the Christian life to imitate. Today, however, some Catholics keep their baptismal names when they are confirmed in order to emphasize the connection between Baptism and Confirmation.

FORUM Assignment

✔ Read pages 168 and 169. Underline in pencil the sentences that express the main ideas.

✔ Using the Internet or the library, find a poem, story, painting, icon, statue, song, or play that honors Mary. Be prepared to share it with the group and tell why you find it appealing.

Closing Prayer: Refer again to the pictures of the saints on pages 166 and 167. Appoint a leader to say the name of each saint pictured there, and ask the group to respond, "Pray for us." Encourage the group to add saints' names from their memorial wall or other favorite ones. Then sing or pray together the words of the traditional hymn "For All the Saints."

> For all the saints
> who from their labors rest,
> Who thee by faith
> before the world confessed
> Thy name, O Jesus,
> be forever blest.
> Alleluia! Alleluia!

• Saint Andrew Kim helped missionaries to enter Korea and gave his life for the spread of the good news of Christ.

• Blessed Kateri Tekakwitha chose a life of chastity, prayer, and service.

Conclusion ___ min.

◆ Ask a volunteer to read aloud *Catholic ID* on page 167. Distribute index cards and markers. On the cards, have the young people write the names of their patron saints. For each saint, add a statement to explain one way this saint reflected the light of God's love to others. Have the young people display the cards on sheets of posterboard covered with aluminum foil. Then tape the edges of the posterboard sheets loosely together to make a reflective memorial wall. Display the wall in your group's prayer space.

FOR SESSION 3

• display of Marian art, craft, literature and music (optional)

• video *The Madonna* (optional)

• duplicated copies of group assignments (optional)

• *Christ, Be Our Light* album by Bernadette Farrell, OCP (optional)

Objective: To explore the role that Mary, as mother of Jesus and his first disciple, plays in our salvation and our devotion.

Introduction ___ min.

Opening Prayer

Forum: If possible, prepare a display of Marian art, literature, and craft. To complement the more unusual icons in the text, exhibit prints, icons or Christian art book illustrations of well-known works. Possible literary and musical works to include are: "A Christmas Carol" by G.K. Chesterton and "The Mantle of Mary" by Patrick O'Connor (poems); "Hail Mary: Gentle Woman" by Carey Landry from the album *I Will Not Forget You* (OCP) and "Magnificat" on the Taizé album *Sing to God* (GIA). Have a student host invite participants to share their chosen works and explain their appeal (personal or communal). If time allows, the *Forum* might close with an excerpt from the video *The Madonna*.

Presentation ___ min.

◆ Invite responses to the Marian art on pages 168 and 169. Why is it important for members of a universal Church to picture Mary in many different racial and ethnic representations? How might the representations on these pages help Native-American, African-American, and Asian-American Catholics to feel more at home in the Church? If you were an artist, how would you most like to depict Mary?

◆ Have volunteers share the key concepts they underlined on pages 168 and 169. Then have them highlight or underline in color the statements highlighted here.

◆ Print the term *immaculate conception* on the board. Call for explanations of its meaning. (Be certain the young people understand that the term applies to Mary's freedom from sin from the moment of her conception. The Church believes that this singular grace and privilege was bestowed by God on Mary because of her singular vocation to be the Mother of Jesus and his first disciple.)

Some of the many cultural representations of the Blessed Virgin Mary in art

Mary, Mother of Jesus

Throughout this book we have emphasized that our prayers, sacraments, and devotions begin and end with Jesus Christ, the Son of the Father. We must never lose sight of this most basic fact. But through the centuries those who have loved and served Jesus have also shown a love and devotion to Mary, his mother. Mary is the first of the disciples and the model for all Christians.

Mary has been honored in many ways through the centuries. However, everything that can be said about Mary, all the honor given to her, is due to two important facts: She is the mother of Jesus, and she is his first disciple. By understanding these two relationships, we can understand the role Mary plays in our salvation and in our devotion.

First of all, we honor Mary because of her relationship to Jesus: She is his mother. Mary does not draw our attention to herself; she always points to Jesus. Each of the honors given to Mary is best understood in relation to Christ. We can see this in the four principal privileges for which the Church

168

has traditionally honored Mary: Mother of God, Virgin, the Immaculate Conception, and the Assumption.

What we believe about Mary is based on our understanding of Jesus. For example, when the second Council of Ephesus (A.D. 431) proclaimed Mary the Mother of God, it was discussing who *Jesus* was. The child that Mary bore in her womb was divine and therefore Mary, the mother of that child, is indeed the Mother of God. The title *Mother of God* is a statement about Mary, about her first and greatest privilege, but it is first and foremost a statement about Jesus. We celebrate the Solemnity of Mary, Mother of God on January 1.

We call Mary *Virgin* because the Church has always believed and taught that Jesus was conceived by the power of the Holy Spirit.

Because God chose Mary to be the Mother of the Savior, it is fitting that she was the first to be saved. We believe that she was redeemed and free from all sin from the very beginning of her life—that is, from the moment of her conception.

FYI Debbie was seventeen when she went on a pilgrimage to the Marian shrine in Lourdes to pray for a cure. When she saw so many other pilgrims who were terminally ill or disabled, Debbie wanted to help them. She pushed their wheelchairs and tried to cheer them up. As for herself and her own illness, she prayed that Mary would stand by her, no matter what happened. Debbie told her friends, "Mary just makes it so easy for you to give of yourself." Although Debbie was not physically healed, she now knew that she, like Jesus, could serve others through her own suffering.

call this privilege the *immaculate conception.*
e celebrate the Solemnity of the Immaculate
nception on December 8.

e believe that when Mary's life on earth was over,
d took her into heaven body and soul. This
rticipation in the resurrection and ascension of
r son is called the *assumption* of the Blessed Virgin.
e celebrate the Solemnity of the Assumption on
gust 15.

ary, First Disciple of Jesus

e second reason we honor Mary is her relation to
e Church: Mary is the first member of the Church,
e model disciple. Genuine devotion to Mary is
lanced between Mary, Mother of God and Mary,
e model disciple. The first emphasizes God's
oice; the second emphasizes Mary's response.

hat does it mean to be a disciple? To be a disciple
Jesus, we must follow his example in doing the
ll of his Father. Jesus taught us to pray "Your will
done." Jesus himself was a perfect example of
is prayer. Throughout his life, from birth to
ath, he did the will of his Father.

the garden, on the night before his death on the
oss, Jesus prayed, "Father, if you are willing, take
is cup away from me; still, not my will but yours
done" (Luke 22:42). The prayer of Christ's
sciples must be this same prayer: "Not
y will but yours be done."

o one has prayed this or lived this
ore perfectly than Mary. When the
gel asked her to become the Mother
God, she replied, "May it be done
me according to your word" (Luke
38). Because Mary listened so
refully to the word of God, she is
le to help us listen to God's word
our own lives. As Mary helped
hers listen to Jesus, she can
lp us listen to him, too.
t the wedding at Cana,
was Mary who noticed
at the wine was
nning out. After she

told Jesus about this, she instructed the servants,
"Do whatever he tells you" (John 2:5). They
listened to Jesus, did as he asked, and the water
became wine. The miracle at Cana began with
Mary. Mary shows herself to be the perfect
disciple—one who, like Jesus, always seeks the
will of God.

In her discipleship Mary is an ideal for each of us.
She is all that the Church is and hopes to be. We
are the Church. We, too, are disciples. Mary, as
Mother of God, bore Jesus in her womb and gave
him birth. Today we, the Church, bear Christ in
our bodies by Baptism and Eucharist. We are to
bring forth Christ to our world by word and
example. This is how we live as Jesus' disciples.
Mary's virginity is the model for our own single-
minded devotion to Christ. Mary's sinlessness is
a model for the Church. Mary's assumption into
heaven is also our destiny as disciples of Jesus.

 What does Mary's life say to you about discipleship?

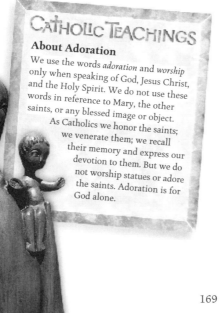

CATHOLIC TEACHINGS

About Adoration

We use the words *adoration* and *worship*
only when speaking of God, Jesus Christ,
and the Holy Spirit. We do not use these
words in reference to Mary, the other
saints, or any blessed image or object.
As Catholics we honor the saints;
we venerate them; we recall
their memory and express our
devotion to them. But we do
not worship statues or adore
the saints. Adoration is for
God alone.

169

Conclusion ___ min.

◆ Call on volunteers to respond to the
thought provoker on page 169. (Mary's
life tells us that disciples place God's
will above their own. They pray often,
listen carefully to the word of God, and
do whatever Jesus tells them.)

◆ Have someone read aloud *Catholic
Teachings* on page 169. Be certain the
young people understand that God
alone is adored or worshiped. Although
these words are used loosely in our
society ("I just adore your new car"; "I
worship that rock idol;"), we should
practice using them only when we are
referring to acts of honoring God.

 **FORUM Assignment**

✔ Read pages 170 and 171. Underline
in pencil the sentences that express
five main ideas.

✔ Make a one-decade rosary. Use any
available materials, such as: beads,
rounded buttons, small shells, knot-
ted twine, pasta shapes, string, or
fishing line. If possible, add a small
crucifix to one end and a medal of
Mary to the other.

◆ Form small groups of "Scripture Searchers." Write
the following chart on the board or duplicate copies
for the young people. Ask the group to find and read
these Scripture passages about Jesus and Mary. Write
a brief summary of each. Then compare the examples
of Jesus and Mary. Fill in the chart with your findings.

Scripture

My Findings on Jesus and Mary

Luke 1:38 and Luke 22:42

John 2:5 and John 15:14

Allow about ten minutes for this activity. Have group
leaders share their findings. (The first two passages
show how Mary and Jesus say yes to God's will rather
than their own. The second set of passages show that
Mary and Jesus teach others to do what Jesus requires
of us.)

Closing Prayer: If possible, play the recording of
"Magnificat" by Bernadette Farrell from the album
Christ, Be Our Light (OCP). If the song is in your parish
hymnal, have the lyrics available for the group to sing
along. Should the music be unavailable, have two
groups pray antiphonally Luke 1:47–55. If time allows,
have the young people consider how Mary's Song calls
us to be disciples of Jesus.

FOR SESSION 4

• writing and drawing materials
• copies of handout *Nine Days of Prayer*
• icon or statue of Mary

Objective: To explore the meaning and richness of the Hail Mary and the rosary.

Introduction ___ min.

Opening Prayer

Forum: Have a volunteer "host" invite participants to display their one-decade rosaries and to describe the process they used to make them. The host may emphasize that carrying a rosary in a pocket, purse, traveling bag, or car has long been a custom among Catholics around the world. The one-decade rosary is easy to carry and simply requires the person to use the same ten beads to pray each of five different mysteries. The host might ask the young people about people in their extended families who pray the rosary regularly.

Presentation ___ min.

◆ Have volunteers share the key concepts they underlined on pages 170 and 171. Then have them highlight or underline in color the statements highlighted here.

◆ Form small groups of "Mary Communicators." Have writing and drawing materials available. Give the following assignment:

> Your task is to communicate the Hail Mary, either in part or in its entirety, to an audience of young people who are unfamiliar with the prayer. How will you teach the prayer in a way that will appeal to your peers? Here are a few ideas: write a respectful rap version; find a familiar melody to use for the prayer; present it in some artistic fashion with attractive lettering and symbols. Or, the young people may come up with completely original ways of communicating the prayer. Allow fifteen minutes for this project which will be shared during the *Closing Prayer*.

◆ Invite the young people to look at the art on page 170 as you read the account of Mary's visit (Luke 1:39–45). Then ask them to hold their own rosaries as you review the process of praying this traditional prayer. Then have the group offer together one decade, the second joyful mystery, Mary's visit to her cousin. While they are offering their vocal prayer, suggest that they use the art on page 170 to help them focus on the mystery of the Visitation.

Hail Mary, full of grace,
the Lord is with you!
Blessed are you among women,
and blessed is the fruit of your
womb, Jesus.
Holy Mary, Mother of God,
pray for us sinners,
now and at the hour of our death.
Amen.

The greeting "Shout for joy" is addressed not only to Mary but also to us. And why? Because the Lord is with us, too, our midst. The presence of the Lord fill Mary—and us—with favor, blessing, a grace.

The second greeting of the Hail Mary that of Elizabeth: "Most blessed are yo among women, and blessed is the fru of your womb" (Luke 1:42). Mary is always seen in relation to her son. As Jesus is the source of every blessing, Mary, who bore Jesus in her womb ar brought him forth to the world, is indeed worthy to be called blessed. Sh is the model and example for us all. Fo we, by our acceptance of God's will in our lives, show Christ to our world. We too become both blessed and a source of blessing.

The Hail Mary

The most common prayer to Mary, the one all Catholics know by heart, is the Hail Mary.

The prayer consists of two greetings and a petition. The two greetings are taken from the first chapter of Luke's Gospel. The first is the greeting of the angel Gabriel (Luke 1:28); the second, that of Mary's cousin Elizabeth (Luke 1:42).

The greeting of the angel Gabriel reminds us of the Book of Zephaniah: "Shout for joy, O daughter Zion!... The LORD your God is in your midst" (Zephaniah 3:14, 17). In the Hail Mary we pray, "Hail Mary, full of grace, the Lord is with you." The word we translate as "Hail" is the same word Zephaniah used: "Rejoice" or "Shout for joy." In Gabriel's greeting to Mary, it is as if he were saying to her, "Shout for joy, O highly favored one! The Lord is in your midst." When we say "Hail Mary," then, it is helpful to remember that this greeting is a joyful reminder of God's goodness and favor: Shout for joy!

170

The Visitation (detail), Domenico Ghirlandaio, 1491

FYI Christian monks in the second century used beads or pebbles found in the Egyptian desert to count their prayers. The rosary as we know it originated in the twelfth century when devotion to Jesus and Mary was very popular. The word "bead" comes from the Middle English *beda*, meaning "prayer." The word *rosary* comes from the Latin *rosarium*, meaning "rose garden."

e second half of the Hail Mary
traditional prayer of petition
ose origins are lost in history.
it we ask that Mary will
ercede for us "now and at the
ur of our death."

s important to remember that,
en we call upon Mary and the
nts, we are asking them to pray
us, to intercede with God for
. All prayer is ultimately
dressed to God—the Father, the
n, and the Holy Spirit. When
e ask the intercession of Mary
d the saints, we are not "going
ound" God at all. In placing our
eds before Our Lady and the
ints, we are asking them to
esent our needs to God, the
urce of all good.

In what way is Gabriel's greeting to Mary a eeting to us, the Church, as well?

he Rosary

here came a time when many
hristians no longer knew the
salms by heart, so they began
meditate on the life of Jesus
hile reciting the Hail Mary or the
ord's Prayer. Eventually this practice was called
raying the rosary. By the fifteenth century it had
ecome a popular devotion.

he rosary can be prayed alone or with others.
Usually we start with the Apostles' Creed, one Our
ather, three Hail Marys, and one Glory to the
ather. Following this introduction, we begin our
editation on the mysteries. Meditation—thinking
nd praying about the wonderful events of our
alvation—is at the very heart of the rosary.

ach decade of the rosary is made up of one Our
ather, ten Hail Marys, and one Glory to the Father.
t the beginning of each decade, we select the

Scripture UPDATE

Most of the mysteries of the rosary come from the gospel accounts in the Scripture. The *joyful mysteries* are the annunciation, visitation, nativity, presentation, and finding in the temple. The *sorrowful mysteries* are the agony in the garden, scourging, crowning with thorns, carrying of the cross, and crucifixion. The *glorious mysteries* are the resurrection, ascension, descent of the Holy Spirit, assumption of Mary, and coronation of Mary. These last two mysteries are based on tradition.

These mysteries are not obligatory. We are free to meditate on any mystery or event in the life of Jesus or his mother. We need not pray all five decades of the rosary at once. Some Catholics carry the rosary with them and pray a few decades when they can during the day. Some families pray the rosary at the beginning of a car trip. It is a common practice to pray the rosary before going to sleep.

mystery on which we are going to meditate. Then we think of this event in the life of Jesus or in the life of his mother while praying the ten Hail Marys. We usually end the Rosary with a centuries-old prayer to Mary, the Hail, Holy Queen.

Say a decade of the rosary now. Choose a mystery for meditation, and end the decade by praying the Hail, Holy Queen.

171

✔ Read pages 172 and 173. Prepare your responses to *Things to Think About* and *Things to Share*.

✔ Complete the handout *Nine Days of Prayer*.

Closing Prayer: Gather around the prayer table. Have an attractive icon or statue of Mary placed in the center. Invite the young people to share their projects as "Mary Communicators." Close by praying the Hail Mary together.

Conclusion ___ min.

◆ Discuss responses to the thought provoker on page 171. (The Church is full of grace and the Lord is present among us.)

◆ Call on someone to summarize *Scripture Update* on page 171. Encourage the young people to learn gradually the names of the fifteen mysteries by heart. Also encourage them to consider what other events in the lives of Jesus and Mary they might want to commemorate while praying the rosary.

◆ Distribute the handout and ask a volunteer to read the directions. Explain that completing the handout is part of the *Forum Assignment*. Make sure everyone understands the assignment.

FOR SESSION 5

- parish calendar
- parish hymnal
- copies of *Chapter 14 Assessment*
- copies of *Highlights for Home*

Objective: To deepen understanding of and appreciation for Mary and the saints.

Introduction ___ min.

Opening Prayer

Forum: Have the young people gather in small groups. Ask them to discuss their novena plans together. Allow them time to suggest changes or improvements. Together with the entire group decide when the novena will begin. You may want to plan the novena so that it will end on a Marian feast day. You may want to plan a group prayer for each day of the novena, and then give time for each one to pray privately the novena prayer written on the handout sheet. Then plan a longer Marian prayer service for the last day of the novena.

Presentation ___ min.

◆ Call attention to the *Words to Remember* on page 172. The description of the *immaculate conception* can be found on pages 168 and 169; the explanation of the *communion of saints* can be found on page 165.

◆ Have a volunteer summarize *On Line with the Parish*. Have a parish calendar on hand for the group to use. Seek responses to the parish questions. (Be prepared with an explanation of when the title is celebrated and what is done on that day. If possible, the group may want to help plan the next celebration.) Suggest that the young people learn more about and pray to their saints.

Assessment: Suggest that the students work with partners in writing answers to *Testing 1, 2, 3*. If time allows, have the partners share their responses with the group.

If you are administering *Chapter 14 Assessment*, page 172A, allow about ten minutes for its completion.

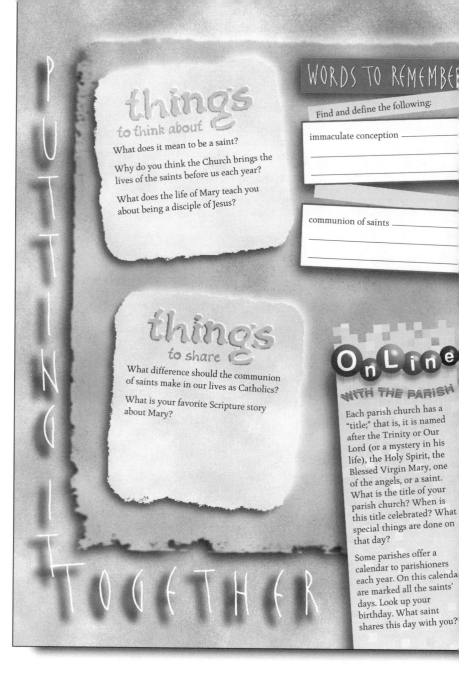

PUTTING IT TOGETHER

things to think about

What does it mean to be a saint?

Why do you think the Church brings the lives of the saints before us each year?

What does the life of Mary teach you about being a disciple of Jesus?

things to share

What difference should the communion of saints make in our lives as Catholics?

What is your favorite Scripture story about Mary?

WORDS TO REMEMBER

Find and define the following:

immaculate conception ___

communion of saints ___

OnLine WITH THE PARISH

Each parish church has a "title;" that is, it is named after the Trinity or Our Lord (or a mystery in his life), the Holy Spirit, the Blessed Virgin Mary, one of the angels, or a saint. What is the title of your parish church? When is this title celebrated? What special things are done on that day?

Some parishes offer a calendar to parishioners each year. On this calendar are marked all the saints' days. Look up your birthday. What saint shares this day with you?

Conclusion ___ min.

◆ Remind the young people to share *Highlights for Home*, page 173B, with their families.

◆ Have a volunteer summarize *Life in the Spirit* on page 173. Briefly brainstorm any Marian names in the state or the diocese in which the students live. Then pray together the Litany of the Blessed Virgin Mary on page 188. If time allows, close with a traditional song such as "Immaculate Mary" from the parish hymnal.

Describe the three levels of liturgical celebration.

How do we become holy?

What happens in the process of canonization?

Name and explain one of the four principal privileges for which the Church honors the Blessed Mother.

What is the prayer of petition in the Hail Mary?

Life in the Spirit

It has long been a Catholic custom to honor Mary by naming special places for her. The original name of Los Angeles, for example, is Nuestra Señora de los Angeles, "Our Lady of the Angels." Sometimes places, usually churches or religious houses, are named both in honor of Mary and in gratitude for one of God's gifts in her, as in her titles, Queen of Heaven or Mother of God.

Find the Litany of the Blessed Virgin Mary on page 188. Each invocation calls on Mary using one of her special titles. Pray the litany now together. If possible, share it and pray it with your family.

173

Testing 1,2,3

1. See page 166. The most important days are called *solemnities*. The feast of Mary, the Mother of God on January 1 is an example. The more important days are *feasts*. We celebrate the feast of Saint Stephen on December 26. The final level is a *memorial*. We celebrate the days on which certain saints died.

2. See page 166. Holiness is achieved by allowing God's greatness to work in us.

3. See pages 166 and 167. Accept specific steps presented on these pages.

4. See pages 168 and 169. Accept explanations of one of the following four privileges: Mother of God, Virgin, the Immaculate Conception, and the Assumption.

5. See pages 170 and 171. The second half of the prayer is considered the prayer of petition: "Holy Mary, Mother of God, ... hour of our death. Amen."

Evaluation: Do the young people understand why and how we celebrate Mary and the saints? Are they familiar with the Blessed Mother's four privileges? Do the young people understand the meaning of the words of the Hail Mary and the reasons Catholics are encouraged to pray the rosary?

Answers for Chapter 14 Assessment
1. b 2. d 3. d 4. b 5. b
6. b 7. d 8. a 9. d 10. See page 171.

Assessment

 1 The communion of saints
- **a.** is the Eucharist.
- **b.** is our union with God's holiness and with his holy ones.
- **c.** includes only holy people.
- **d.** means eternal life.

 2 Images of our unity include
- **a.** the household of God.
- **b.** the body of Christ.
- **c.** the Christian family.
- **d.** all of the above

 3 The saints
- **a.** intercede for us.
- **b.** have nothing to do with us.
- **c.** share their graces with us.
- **d.** a and c

 4 Solemnities are
- **a.** serious discussions.
- **b.** the most important days on the Church calendar.
- **c.** just like feasts and memorials.
- **d.** Vatican Councils.

 5 Canonization is a process of
- **a.** building cannons.
- **b.** recognizing saints.
- **c.** making Church laws.
- **d.** recognizing the holiness of particular people.

 6 Saints who served in America
- **a.** have not been canonized.
- **b.** include Elizabeth Seton and Isaac Jogues.
- **c.** include Andrew Kim and Charles Lwanga.
- **d.** none of the above

 7 Mary's principal privileges are:
- **a.** Mother of God and Virgin.
- **b.** the immaculate conception.
- **c.** the assumption.
- **d.** all of the above

 8 The immaculate conception means that
- **a.** Mary was free from sin from the time of her conception.
- **b.** Jesus was free from sin.
- **c.** the saints have no sin.
- **d.** Mary is a virgin.

 9 The Hail Mary
- **a.** was given to us by Jesus.
- **b.** includes the Magnificat of Mary.
- **c.** is called a solemnity.
- **d.** is the most common Catholic prayer to Our Lady.

10 Explain how we pray the rosary.

_____
_____
_____
_____
_____

Highlights for Home

Focus on Faith

Many tourists visit Mary, Queen of the Universe Shrine in Orlando, Florida. Here Mass is celebrated daily. Tourists are impressed by the beautiful rosary windows depicting saints of the North American Church.

Whether we can get to Orlando or not, the Church gives us the opportunity each year to honor Mary, Mother of Jesus and his first disciple. We celebrate her as Mother of God on January 1, as the Immaculate Conception on December 8, and in her Assumption on August 15. As families, we honor Mary by making her part of our home life (praying a Hail Mary or the rosary together, displaying an icon or statue, dedicating a garden to her, or perhaps pursuing a justice project for the "lowly").

Together with Mary, the entire communion of saints stands ready to befriend and intercede for us. Our prayers to them are ultimately prayers to God from whom all graces and blessings flow. To encourage your sons and daughters to get in touch with Mary and the saints is to share the treasures of your faith with them.

Conversation Starters

. . . . a few ideas to talk about together . . . .

◆ How does Mary's example challenge us to be more courageous disciples?

◆ How has Mary been a source of comfort or help to you?

◆ In what ways do you find the saints companions and examples of hope?

Feature Focus

The *Catholic ID* feature on page 167 reminds us that Catholics are encouraged to have patron saints as their special intercessors in heaven. The patron saint can also serve as a role model for the young person who has been given the saint's name at Baptism or Confirmation.

Reflection

In Mary's song of praise, the Magnificat, she proclaims thanksgiving for the privilege of her vocation as Mother of God and the first disciple of Jesus. Let us pray Mary's song with her to proclaim our thanks to God for all the great things that God has done for us. Reflect quietly on the following verses (Luke 1:46, 49–50).

My soul proclaims the greatness of the Lord;
my spirit rejoices in God my savior. . . .

The Mighty One has done great things for
me
and holy is his name.
His mercy is from age to age
to those who fear him.

PATHS OF PRAYER

Adult Focus

In the Gospel of Luke we read that Jesus told his disciples the parable of the persistent widow to teach them to "pray always without becoming weary" (Luke 18:1). Our days are taken up with much activity but we can always take a moment to turn our minds and hearts to God in prayer. Just as the young people practice math, vocabulary, or sports skills, they can develop the habit of praying daily—even when they are weary or "not in the mood." The Catholic tradition of prayer is rich and varied, rooted in daily praise, petition, intercession, and thanksgiving.

Chapter 15 provides the young people with an appealing variety of paths of prayer, from focusing on religious art in stained glass to scriptural and liturgical prayer. It clarifies for them the difference between contemplation, the act of attending thoughtfully to God without words or distractions, and meditation, the act of thinking about God, generally with the help of the Scriptures or other spiritual reading. Meditation can often lead to contemplation, as we move from thinking to "just being."

Although not all of these paths of prayer will appeal to every young person in the group, assure them that the chapter offers "something for everyone." Encourage them to share their own ideas about paths of prayer (through music, poetry, or nature).

Catechism Focus

The theme of Chapter 15 corresponds to paragraphs 2759–2776, 2700–2724, 1174–1178, 2697–2699, and 435 of the *Catechism*.

Enrichment Activities

Computer Connection
Have the young people design a screen saver that is a visual aid to them for one of the paths of prayer mentioned in the chapter. Have the young people exchange E-mail prayers with those with whom they communicate by computer.

Planning a Prayer Service
Involve the young people in choosing a theme of concern in their daily lives. Examples include: relationships with parents, loneliness, addictions, love and sexuality. Have them plan a prayer service integrating scriptural readings with popular music or video segments that speak to the theme. They might also compose a litany to Jesus, Companion of Youth.

Doing Dance Meditations
This activity may be done with the guidance of a liturgical dancer from your diocese, or with the video *Movement Meditations: To the Songs of Taize* featuring Carla De Sola, with Thomas Kane (Paulist Press). The video offers fourteen meditations involving simple movement patterns which the young people can follow. A booklet of instructions is included.

Teaching Resources

	Overview	Opening Prayer Ideas	Materials
SESSION 1	**Discovery:** To discover stained-glass windows as aids on the path of prayer.	Pray together Psalm 16:11. Write in your journals about joyful, faith-filled experiences.	These will be needed every session: texts, Bibles, highlighters or colored pencils, journals. • albums *Abba, Father* by Carey Landry (OCP) or *Songs of the New Creation* by the Dameans (GIA)
SESSION 2	**Exploring 1:** To explore ways of praying with Scripture.	Reflect on Jesus' words in Matthew 7:7–11. Write your reflections in your journal.	• posterboard, markers, rulers • group assignments on index cards • missalette or liturgical calendar • index cards or slips of paper • box or basket
SESSION 3	**Exploring 2:** To experience meditation and contemplation.	Do a breath meditation, praying the name of Jesus on each deep inhalation and exhalation.	• album *Instruments of Peace* by David Haas (GIA) or other reflective music of choice • CD or cassette player
SESSION 4	**Exploring 3:** To consider ways different prayers and sacraments can enrich our lives of prayer.	Pray together Psalm 17:6–9. Write three petitions for those who suffer from violence.	• four index cards with quotes and group assignments • display of sacramental objects • copies of handout *Perpetual Adoration*, page 174C • copies of handout *My Paths of Prayer*, page 185A
SESSION 5	**Putting It Together:** To give praise to God by praying Morning Praise of the Liturgy of the Hours.	Pray together Psalm 16:11. Give thanks for joys and abundant life.	• album *Most Requested Music for the Spirit from Joe Wise* (GIA) or other recordings • lectern, large Bible • two candles, bells (optional) • copies of *Highlights for Home*, page 185B

Supplemental Resources

Videos

My Peace I Give to You
Ignatius Press
P.O. Box 1339
Ft. Collins, CO 80522

St. Mark's Gospel
Palisades Home Video
P.O. Box 2794
Virginia Beach, VA 23450

Faith and Witness Journal:
Liturgy & Worship

For Chapter 15 see pages 60–63.

CHAPTER
fifteen

Perpetual Adoration

Do you know that twenty-four hours a day, 365 days a year, someone in the Church is praying for you?

Recently some parishes have answered Pope John Paul II's call for visits to the Blessed Sacrament by establishing the practice of perpetual adoration. Some parishes, with the permission of their bishops, have established special chapels which are open twenty-four hours a day, seven days a week. People come to spend an hour with Jesus as he asked his apostles to do on the night before he died (Matthew 26:40). The Blessed Sacrament is placed in a special container called a *monstrance* and placed on the altar for all to see.

Some parishioners sign up to spend one specific hour; others have invited family members or groups of friends to join them in quiet prayer. These people pray for others (especially the sick) and spend time praying with the words of Scripture or their own words to deepen their relationship with Christ and the Church.

Check to see if your parish or another parish nearby has established the practice of perpetual adoration. If not, you may still express your devotion and gratitude for Jesus' gift of himself in the Eucharist by making visits to the Blessed Sacrament in the tabernacle in your church. You may find the following prayer, written by Pope John XXIII, helpful to pray during one of your visits. Share the prayer with your family. Try to make a visit this week.

O living bread, that came down from heaven to give life to the world! O loving shepherd of our souls,. . . . you pour out your grace on families and peoples, we commend to you particularly the sick, the unhappy, the poor and all who beg for food and employment, imploring for all and every one the assistance of your providence; we commend to you the families, so that they may be fruitful centers of Christian life. May the abundance of your grace be poured out over all.

Paths of Prayer

You will show me the path to life, abounding joy in your presence.
Psalm 16:11

175

Objective: To discover stained-glass windows as aids on the path of prayer.

Introduction ___ min.

Opening Prayer: Distribute fine-line markers and invite the young people to inscribe the opening prayer from page 175 in their journals. Pray Psalm 16:11 aloud. Then encourage the group to recall times of joy and experiences of abundant life which they have experienced. Have them write brief descriptions of these times of joy and frame them in colorful symbols (balloons, bells, flowers, album covers).

While the young people are reflecting, play any thematic music. Suggestions include: "Oh, How Good" from the album *Abba, Father* by Carey Landry (OCP) or "All Our Joy" from *Songs of the New Creation* by The Dameans (GIA).

Have the young people share their experiences of joy on a voluntary basis. (These may include a great vari-ety of memories from an athletic or artistic performance to the deep enjoyment of a sunset or a mountain to a wonderful experience of liturgy.) Encourage the group to be open to all the everyday and extraordinary joys that Jesus wants them to experience. Pray Psalm 16:11 aloud together.

Chapter Warm-up: Point out that the cyclist in the photograph on pages 174 and 175 may be praying while pedaling. Have the young people brainstorm other activities that may be considered spiritual "exercise." Have volunteer recorders write the responses on the board. You may want to add the following suggestions: talking to God while dribbling a basketball or shooting hoops; thanking God for his great gifts while walking; praying or singing while doing pottery work on a wheel or with your hands; remembering God's presence while weaving, sewing, knitting, or crocheting.

Presentation ___ min.

◆ Have someone read aloud the definitions of prayer at the top of page 176. Call on others to complete the statement "Prayer is _____" in additional ways. (Examples: "Prayer is a relationship with God; a candle burning faithfully; a love song to the Lord; getting in touch with Jesus; an expression of praise; a cry from the heart; a joyful bike ride in God's presence; running at top speed with a grateful heart.")

◆ Ask volunteers to read pages 176 and 177. Have all underline in color or highlight the key concepts highlighted here.

◆ Invite responses to the window on page 176. Discuss why the young people think stained-glass windows can help someone to pray. Encourage the group to look more closely at the stained glass in their parish church (or other churches) to select those symbols or scenes that speak most effectively to them.

◆ Before beginning the window activity on page 177, you may wish to show the rose window and other stained glass shown on the video *Notre Dame Cathedral*. It is available from:

> Wellspring Media
> 65 Bleecker Street
> New York, NY 10012

◆ Distribute markers, colored pencils, or paint and brush kits. Invite the young people, working alone or with a partner, to complete the window activity described on pages 176 and 177. If you choose, put a list of Christian symbols on the board to help them get started.

- butterfly (Christ's resurrection)
- fish (Christ, baptism)
- lamb (Jesus, Good Shepherd)
- sparrow (least ones, dependence on God)
- wheat and grapes (Eucharist)
- olive branch (peace)
- palm branch (victory, triumph over death)
- thorns (suffering, sin)
- tree (abundant life)

Prayer is a path that leads to God; prayer is a window that reflects God's light; prayer is a heart open to God's love. What is prayer for you?

Windows of Prayer

In *prayer* we raise our hearts and minds to God. We ask God for the good things we need, we thank him for his gifts, we express our sorrow for sin, we pray for others, and we praise him for his goodness. With the help of the Holy Spirit and the tradition of the Church, we can pray in many ways. Here is one you might like to try.

We have seen them all of our lives: beautiful stained-glass windows, carefully crafted filters of light and color. We are drawn to them. Why? Because they help us to raise our hearts and minds to God.

The most famous and beautiful windows are called rose windows. They are circular. The circle is an ancient symbol of God and of eternity. Their interior panes fold out from the center like the petals of a rose. The rose window invites us to travel its paths and then to focus on the center.

Look at the empty stained-glass window here. How would you complete it? Here is a suggestion: Make this window into an expression of your relationship with God. Like a stained-glass window, this relationship has many dimensions. Think about the sacraments you have celebrated; you may want to symbolize each one in a section of your window. Think about your times of prayer both during the liturgy and alone. These could be symbolized in sections of your window. How do family and friends help you find God? Symbolize this in your window. Perhaps the Scriptures will find a place in your window as well.

176

Remind the young people to choose a title for their completed rose window. Allow about fifteen minutes for this activity. Then have volunteers act as tour guides and explain the significance of their rose windows.

e center of a stained-glass window is very
ortant. Everything else in the window revolves
und it. Sometimes the center of the window
ds a picture or icon of Jesus or
ry. Sometimes the center is a
le of color. Sometimes it holds a
ss, or a triangle to symbolize the
nity. What would you put in the
ter of your window? Perhaps you
ght insert a symbol of Jesus: the
ss as symbol of the paschal mystery
read and wine, the symbols of the
charist. What symbolizes the center
our relationship with God?

hough stained-glass windows are
rks of art, they are not usually given
es. However, you may want to title
rs. A title summarizes the meaning

ork. Choose a title to summarize the
aning of your stained-glass window.

agine that your window is one
the windows in a great
hedral. Act as a tour
de to explain the
aning of your
ndow, section
section, to
e group.

JOURNAL

Use your stained-glass window as a window
of prayer and reflection. Beginning with
the center, write a short prayer expressing
the meaning of each section of the window.
If one section symbolizes your Baptism, you
might write a prayer like this: "Thank you,
God our Father, for choosing me as one of
your children. Thank you, Jesus Christ our
Lord, for saving me and showing me the
way. Thank you, Holy Spirit, for guiding
my path. All praise to you! Amen."

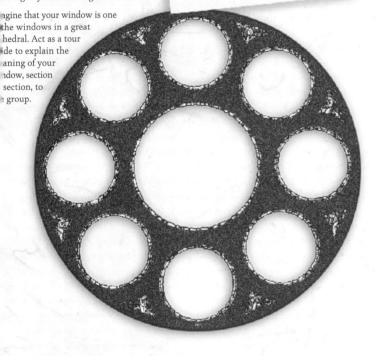

177

FORUM Assignment

✔ Read pages 178 and 179. Underline
in pencil the sentences that express
three main ideas.

✔ Briefly interview in person, on the
phone, or via E-mail one relative,
friend, priest, teacher or other person.
Ask, "How does the Bible help you to
pray?" Be prepared to share your
interview with the group.

Closing Prayer: Gather in a prayer
circle. Call on volunteers to share one
or more of their window prayers. After
each prayer, the group responds,
"Lord, you are the light of the world!"

Conclusion ___ min.

◆ Invite the group to do the journal exercise on page
177. The aim is to write one brief prayer for each section of their rose windows, beginning with the center.
If time is short, assure them that each prayer may be
brief, such as, "God, help me to trust you like the
sparrow does."

FOR SESSION 2

- posterboard, markers, rulers
- group assignments on index cards
- missalette or liturgical calendar
- index cards or slips of paper
- box or basket

SESSION 2

Objective: To explore ways of praying with Scripture.

Introduction ___ min.

Opening Prayer

Forum: Have the young people conduct the *Forum* as a TV talk show on a Catholic station. Invite two co-hosts to provide an introduction of the topic and call members of the audience forward to report on their interviews. After each report, a co-host may ask the "reporter" about any way in which he or she has used the Bible to pray. Other members of the audience may address questions or comments to the reporters. A co-host concludes the show by summarizing what has been shared.

Presentation ___ min.

◆ Have the young people form seven small prayer groups. Distribute Bibles, one sheet of posterboard per group, markers and rulers. Have group assignments printed on index cards as follows:

• *Group 1: Praying the Our Father*
  Look up both versions of the Our Father in the Gospels of Matthew and Luke. Make a poster of Luke's version of the Lord's Prayer. Be prepared to share how the two Gospel stories and the prayer differ.

• *Group 2: Praying Scripture Pictures*
  Do the prayer exercise on page 178. Write your responses in your journal. Make a poster encouraging others to pray with imagined Scripture pictures or scenes.

• *Group 3: Praying God's Word for the Day*
  Follow the directions in the text on page 179. Choose some verses from the Old Testament and others from the New Testament. Make a poster illustrating the verse your group likes best.

• *Group 4: Praying Today's Scripture*
  (Be sure this group has a list of the liturgical readings for today. These may be found in the missalette or on a liturgical calendar.) Follow the directions on page 179. Make a poster illustrating the verse or ideas your group finds most meaningful.

Praying with Scripture

The Sacred Scriptures can enrich our prayer immensely. They are the "faith record" of God's mysterious plan—what God has done in history and the revelation of God's plan for the world. A good way to pray is to take the Bible, read a passage, and then talk it over with God.

Praying with just one or two Scripture verses is a traditional and practical way to make prayer a part of our everyday lives. We can easily pray a short, easy-to-remember Scripture verse at work or play or during those "between times" we find ourselves in so often: between home and school, between lunch and recess, between the ending of one class and the beginning of another.

Here are several ways to pray with Scripture. Which appeal to you?

The Our Father

The whole gospel of Jesus Christ is summed up in the Our Father. It is the purest and most essential prayer of the Church. When we pray the Our Father, we pray with the attitude of Jesus and the Spirit of Jesus. We pray for what Jesus wants—that God's will be done on earth. As we pray the Our Father, we become one with Jesus and one with the Father in love and trust. The Our Father can be found in Matthew 6:9–13 and in Luke 11:2–4.

Scripture Pictures

When people asked Saint Ignatius Loyola for help in prayer, he advised them to picture a scene from Scripture and to put themselves into the scene. Tr it with Matthew 8:23–27. Imagine the people, the sounds, the smells; and especially, see Jesus as he speaks and acts. What is he saying to you? When you finish, write your thoughts in your journal.

• *Group 5: Praying with Scripture and Music*
  (If possible, have this group meet in a separate space where they can sing out loud. Provide them with a parish hymnal for ideas.) Follow the directions on page 179. Make a poster of your chosen verse or verses. Be prepared to sing your prayer.

• *Group 6: Praying a Scripture Exchange*
  (Provide this group with index cards or slips of paper, and a box or basket.) Follow the directions on page 179. Make as many verse cards as there are students in the class. Make a poster of the verse your group likes best.

• *Group 7: Praying the Name of Jesus*
  (If possible, provide this group with a separate space where they will not be distracted.) Practice the prayer as outlined on page 179. Make a poster encouraging others to pray the name of Jesus.

God's Word for the Day

...mpile a list of at least seven favorite Scripture ...sages. Choose one each day as your special ...se. Every time your mind is free or you are ...ween activities, recall your verse and say it to ...urself a few times. Here are two for your list:

..."Your word is a lamp for my feet,
   a light for my path" (Psalm 119:105).

..."I am the good shepherd, and I know mine ...and mine know me" (John 10:14).

Today's Scripture

...ing the Church's calendar of Scripture readings, ...d the readings for today. Read them and the psalm ...efully. If you find a verse or idea meaningful, stop ...d let it sink in. Stay with it as long as you like. Then ...on. Choose one of the verses, and recall it often ...ring the day.

Scripture and Music

...usic is a traditional and beautiful way to focus on ...e words and meaning of Scripture. Try setting a ...orite verse to a simple melody, perhaps in a ...antlike style. Create a harmony as well! You may ...nt to use a Scripture story or set of verses as the ...sis for an entire song. Saint John Chrysostom ...ote many Scripture hymns for the Church. Ask ... help!

Scripture Exchange

Spend some time looking through the New Testament. Write down, on an index card or a slip of paper, one or two verses you like. Collect them from the group in a box or basket. Then invite each group member to draw one. You may want to decorate or illustrate your verse on paper and display it.

The Prayer of the Name

"You shall name him Jesus" (Luke 1:31). The name of Jesus is a simple but powerful prayer, and using the holy name of Jesus in prayer is an ancient tradition in the Church. Begin by closing your eyes and becoming still. Breathe slowly and deeply. Then, as you breathe in, quietly say "Jesus." As you breathe out, you may want to say "Savior" or "peace" or another word that reminds you of Jesus. Continue this rhythm for as long as you wish.

An illuminated page of Gregorian chant, late fourteenth century

◆ Have volunteers share the statements they underlined on pages 178 and 179. Ask all to underline the key statements highlighted here.

FORUM Assignment

✔ Read pages 180 and 181. Underline in pencil the sentences that express five main ideas.

✔ Write at least five different ways you can help yourself become calm, peaceful, and undistracted. If one of your suggestions involves an audio or visual aid, bring it to share with your group.

Closing Prayer: Have prayer-group members display their posters and share their reflections on the seven ways of praying with Scripture.

Conclusion ___ min.

◆ If time allows, share with the young people the Church's tradition of *lectio divina* or reading of the holy Scriptures. Anyone who can read and sit still for ten to twenty minutes can pray through holy reading. The process is:

- Choose a scriptural passage.
- Read it through once. Then reread it more slowly or aloud.
- Ask the Holy Spirit to help you mull over and ponder the word of God you have just read.
- Write in your journal the message you have received in your own words.

FOR SESSION 3

- album *Instruments of Peace* by David Haas (GIA) (or other music of choice)
- CD or cassette player

SESSION 3

Objective: To experience meditation and contemplation.

Introduction ___ min.

Opening Prayer

Forum: Have the young people form small groups to share their ways of becoming calm, peaceful, and undistracted before prayer. Have the group members experiment with a few suggestions to see if these methods work for them.

Presentation ___ min.

◆ Have volunteers share the key concepts they underlined on pages 180 and 181. Then have them highlight or underline in color the statements highlighted here.

◆ Have the terms *vocal prayer*, *contemplation* and *meditation* printed on three large candles sketched on the board. Ask young people whose names begin with v, p, c, or m to come forward and "light the candles" by defining each term and drawing a flame above each in yellow or orange chalk. Take a survey to find out how many students feel most "at home with" each of these three ways of praying. Guide a brief dialogue on how our prayer choices may reflect our personalities and life experiences.

◆ Before sharing the Scripture meditation on page 181, invite the young people to occupy their own sacred space by separating from one another, sitting on cushions on the floor, or using any available prayer corners. (If possible, move outside or into a chapel.) Let the group know that we are about to experiment with a Scripture meditation. Their only task is to do their best to enter into the experience and focus their imaginations on the scene created by the narrator's voice. To introduce the meditation, play a song such as "We Walk By Faith" or "Healer of Our Every Ill" from the album *Instruments of Peace* by Marty Haugen (GIA).

With or Without Words

In our Catholic life of prayer, we often pray with words, aloud, and usually with others. This prayer with words is called *vocal prayer* because we pray not only with our minds and hearts but with our voices as well. The prayers we say during the liturgy are vocal prayers, as are traditional prayers such as the Our Father and the Hail Mary.

There are many paths to God in prayer. Vocal prayer is one of them. Once two sisters asked Saint Teresa of Avila how to find union with God. "Say the Our Father," responded Teresa. Sometimes when we say a familiar prayer carefully and thoughtfully, we gain insight into the meaning of the words. Then the words slowly fade away, and we find ourselves "just being" at peace in God. This is the prayer of contemplation.

Contemplation is the prayer of union with God. We might also call it the prayer of "just being with" God. If you look up the word *contemplation* in the dictionary, you will find: "the act of looking at attentively and thoughtfully." The prayer of contemplation is simply looking at God. As one saint described this kind of prayer, "I look at God and he looks at me."

Another path to union with God is praying with the words of Scripture, as we have seen. If we keep a special Scripture verse in mind during the day, we may find a new meaning in it. Or simply saying the words of Scripture quietly and peacefully can lead us to "just being with" God.

The path of meditation is another path to union with God. *Meditation* is simply "thinking about God," and it can easily flow into "being with" God. Most often we meditate on the Scriptures, but other spiritual books can be starting points as well, especially those that explain the Scriptures and inspire us to live the Christian life. For now let's choose a Scripture passage, Mark 10:46–52, for our meditation.

180

Then narrate the meditation on page 181, pausing after each question to allow for silent reflection. After the direction to "Take time to 'just be with Jesus,'" allow for a few minutes' silence. Then complete the meditation.

Scripture Meditation

[...b]efore meditating, it is a good idea to help yourself [bec]ome calm, peaceful, and undistracted. Sometimes [list]ening to soft background music can help. First sit [...] straight but comfortable position and close your [eye]s. Now let's try it.

[Ima]gine yourself sitting by the side of a dusty road. [You] look down the road. You are waiting for Jesus [to c]ome by. Already you see him in the distance, [sur]rounded by a large crowd.

[Sud]denly, across the road, you notice someone—[Bar]timaeus, a blind man. He, too, is waiting for [Jes]us. You hear him call out, "Jesus, Son of David, [hav]e pity on me." Jesus and the crowd are coming [clos]er. What do you hear? There is the calling of [Bar]timaeus, the buzz of the crowd, and someone [scol]ding Bartimaeus: "Quiet, blind man!" What do [you] see? There is Jesus, coming down the road. [The]re is Bartimaeus, alone and poor, the hot sun [beat]ting down on him.

Suddenly all is silent. Jesus is here—just a few feet away. "Call him," Jesus says. Someone runs to where Bartimaeus sits in the sun. "Take courage; get up, he is calling you."

Everything is happening right in front of you. You see Bartimaeus as he joyfully throws aside his cloak, springs to his feet, and comes to Jesus. You hear Jesus ask, "What do you want me to do for you?" Bartimaeus replies in a pleading voice, "Master, I want to see." Jesus tells him, "Go your way; your faith has saved you." Immediately Bartimaeus receives his sight and begins to follow Jesus.

But wait! Jesus is stopping again. He has seen you sitting there in your special place. Jesus calls to you, "Come here, my friend." You quickly stand up and go to meet him. Jesus looks at you with great love. "So—why were you waiting for me? What do you want me to do for you?"

Think a moment. What is your answer? What does Jesus say to you?

Take time to "just be with" Jesus a little while.

Now begin to say good-bye. Watch Jesus a moment as he turns to continue his journey of healing. Now begin your own journey back. Say good-bye to your special place. Then open your eyes slowly. Let us pray the Our Father together.

LOOKING BACK

Think for a moment about your experience. If there is anything about your meditation that you would like to remember, write it in your journal now.

Did your meditation (thinking about God) flow into contemplation ("just being with" God)? If not, there is no cause for concern. In prayer God always gives us exactly what we need. All prayer—vocal prayer, meditation, and contemplation—is a gift of God's life and grace. We need only take time to receive it.

181

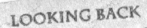

FORUMAssignment

✔ Read pages 182 and 183. Underline in pencil the sentences that express five main ideas.

✔ Find or compose one good "beginning" prayer and one good "ending" prayer. The beginning and ending may apply to a day, a meal, an assignment, an athletic or musical event, a gathering of family or friends, a youth retreat, or any other event.

Closing Prayer: Share the following advice on prayer from the anonymous author of the spiritual classic *The Cloud of Unknowing*:

> Lift up your heart to God with a
>   humble stirring of love;
> and mean God himself,
> and not what you can get from him.

Encourage the young people to remember this advice when they spend time with Jesus in wordless prayer.

Conclusion ___ min.

◆ Invite the young people to write a response to their meditation experience in their journals. Encourage them to write their responses to Jesus' question, "What do you want me to do for you?" They might also record what they believe Jesus' answer was or will be.

FOR SESSION 4

- four index cards with quotes and group assignments
- display of sacramental objects
- copies of handout *Perpetual Adoration*, page 174C
- copies of handout *My Paths of Prayer*, page 185A

Objective: To consider ways different prayers and using sacramentals can enrich our lives of prayer.

Introduction ___ min.

Opening Prayer

Forum: Have the young people sit in a circle with a prayer leader in the center. The leader, either at random or in order around the circle, calls on participants to share their "beginning" prayers. A recorder keeps a list of the kinds of beginnings chosen. If the group chooses, they may request copies of prayers they especially like and want to use. Or, all the prayers may be duplicated and collected in a booklet. The leader repeats the process for the "ending" prayers. The recorder reads his or her list of occasions chosen by the participants and seeks any additional suggestions for times when "beginning" and "ending" prayers might be offered by the young people.

Presentation ___ min.

◆ Call attention to the art on pages 182 and 183. Have the group compose captions that make a connection between the illustration and the theme, "Times for Prayer." Share several of these.

◆ Have volunteers share the key concepts they underlined on pages 182 and 183. Then have them highlight or underline in color the statements highlighted here.

◆ Have the young people form small groups. Group leaders draw an index card from a baseball cap or football helmet. On one side of the card is a prayer quote to be interpreted by the group. On the other side is an assignment for composing a prayer.

- Card 1
  Side A: "Do what you can do and pray for what you cannot yet do." (Saint Augustine)
  Side B: Write a prayer for the achievement of a seemingly impossible goal.
- Card 2
  Side A: "Lay before Him what is in us, not what ought to be in us." (C.S. Lewis)
  Side B: Write a prayer for guidance in knowing yourselves.

Times for Prayer

Jesus told the disciples that it is necessary to pray "always" (Luke 18:1). How is that possible? How would we ever get anything else done? One thing is certain: We will never be able to pray *at all times* unless we learn how to pray *at specific times*, times that we consciously pick out and set aside for prayer.

Certain times seem natural for prayer. All beginnings are good times for prayer, especially the beginning of each new day. As the light of the sun changes night into day, we are reminded of the light of Christ, which changes our night of doubt and uncertainty into a new day of hope and confidence in his victory. Each day is a gift. Each day is a day of Easter hope. Let us pray!

Other beginnings are also good times for prayer. It is good to pray at the beginning of a test, when you start your homework, at the beginning of a ball game, or each time you sit down to practice the piano. Some families pray together each time they begin a car trip.

The beginning of a meal is a traditional time for prayer. In a country where food is so plentiful, we sometimes forget that food is God's gift. Mealtimes are appropriate times to thank God for life and food, for family and friendship.

Grace before and after meals is an excellent time for spontaneous family prayer. As we gather at table, we remember one another's needs before God. "God, we thank you for this food. We ask you to bless Mom during these next days on her business trip. Help Tim as he studies for his history test tomorrow. Bless us all, keep us safe in this life, and welcome us in the next. Amen."

During Lent-Easter and Advent-Christmas time, the family meal can be an occasion for prayers that correspond to the liturgical season. During Advent the beginning of the evening meal is a good time to light the family Advent wreath.

Endings are also good times for prayer. As each day ends, we thank God for all that has happened during the day. The ending of the day also has an

182

- Card 3
  Side A: "Looking at art is one way of listening to God." (Sister Wendy Beckett)
  Side B: Write a prayer about enjoying God in the good things of life.
- Card 4
  Side A: "Everything one turns in the direction of God is prayer." (Saint Ignatius Loyola)
  Side B: Write a prayer about having a good time with your friends.

Allow about fifteen minutes for this activity. If time allows, share the prayers now. If not, collect them for sharing during Session 5.

◆ Distribute copies of the handout *Perpetual Adoration*. Discuss the richness of this faith practice. Encourage the young people to share what they have discussed with their families and friends.

FORUM*Assignment*

✔ Read pages 184 and 185. Underline in pencil the sentences on page 184 that express two main ideas.

✔ Complete the handout *My Paths of Prayer*. Use the Bible and any other appropriate resources.

Closing Prayer: Invite the young people to do the closing reflection on page 183 in their journals. If they choose, they might sketch the sacramental object they have received. Then their original blessing (for family, friends, home, activities or self) may be written inside the sketch or around the border. Share these as time allows.

...sociation with the ending of our lives. Thinking ...out death should not be grim or scary. The ...schal victory of Christ assures us that the death ...the body is the beginning of eternal life, and so ...en this aspect of evening is related to ...anksgiving.

...any Christians, as they go to bed, use the ...oments before falling asleep to think over the ...st day, to "examine their conscience," and to ...k pardon for any sins they have committed ...ring the day. Seeing each day in the perspective ...eternity puts the day's troubles in perspective.

...hatever times we pick to pray, it is important to ...tablish an *association*, to connect a time or activity ...ith praying, so that we get into a habit of prayer. ...ying a prayer each time you start your homework ...not a guarantee of great grades (though it ...uldn't hurt!), but it will help establish a habit. ...nless you get in the habit of praying regularly, at ...t times, you may end up not praying at all.

Sacramentals

Sacramentals are part of our daily lives. They are blessings, actions, and objects that the Church uses to prepare us for the graces of the sacraments. By objects, we mean things such as statues, medals, rosaries, candles, and crucifixes. By actions, we mean actions such as the sign of the cross, the laying on of hands, the sprinkling of blessed water. Blessings include the blessing of people, places, food, and objects. We bless ashes on Ash Wednesday and palms on Palm Sunday. Can you think of other times when we use blessings?

Unlike sacraments, which were instituted by Christ, sacramentals were instituted by the Church. The Church teaches us that sacramentals are never to be used in a magical or superstitious way or looked upon as good luck charms.

What sacramentals are part of your everyday life? You may want to write your own prayer, asking God's blessing on yourself, your family, your home, and your everyday activities.

183

Conclusion ___ min.

◆ From a display on the prayer table, pass around assorted sacramentals (words of blessings, rosaries, statues, medals, icons, candles, crucifixes). If possible, provide one for each young person. Invite responses to:

• How might these sacramentals help people to pray?
• Which of the examples we have here today are most helpful to you? Why?

Encourage the use of sacramental objects, actions, and blessings at home. Note that some families have small holy-water fonts in their home so that family members and guests can bless themselves before going to bed at night or whenever they choose. (Do not collect the sacramentals until after the *Closing Prayer*.)

FOR SESSION 5

• prayer symbols for group tables
• album *Most Requested Music for the Spirit from Joe Wise* (GIA) or other music
• lectern, large Bible
• two candles, bell (optional)

SESSION 5

Objective: To give praise to God by praying Morning Praise of the Liturgy of the Hours.

Introduction ___ min.

Opening Prayer

Forum: Have separate tables arranged for small group gatherings. If possible, array each table with a few symbols of two or more paths of prayer listed on the handout *My Paths of Prayer*. Have the young people form small groups for the sharing of responses. If available, play a recording on the theme of prayer. "Lord, Teach Us to Pray" from the album *Most Requested Music for the Spirit from Joe Wise* (GIA) or "Let the People Praise" from *Morning to Night* by The Dameans (GIA) are suggested.

Presentation ___ min.

◆ Have volunteers share the key concepts they underlined on page 184. Then have them highlight or underline in color the statements highlighted here.

◆ Involve the young people in preparing the prayer space and themselves for Morning Praise on page 185. Have a large Bible placed on a lectern and opened to Romans 8:14–16. Appoint a lector and a prayer leader. If possible, have two tall candles on either side of the lectern lit (or use battery-operated candles). Appoint a bell ringer who will sound the call to prayer. Practice bowing in unison for the Glory to the Father.

◆ Have the young people form two prayer groups and ask both to face the front of the room where the lectern is placed. Follow the directions at the bottom of page 184. Before praying Psalm 98, all sit in chairs, two sides facing each other. Follow the directions on page 185.

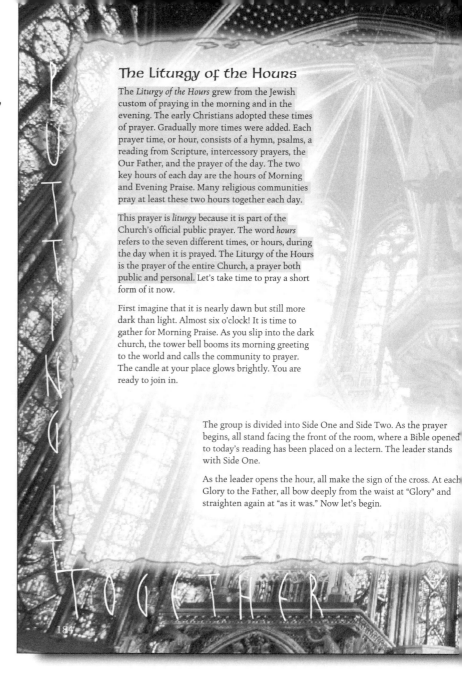

The Liturgy of the Hours

The *Liturgy of the Hours* grew from the Jewish custom of praying in the morning and in the evening. The early Christians adopted these times of prayer. Gradually more times were added. Each prayer time, or hour, consists of a hymn, psalms, a reading from Scripture, intercessory prayers, the Our Father, and the prayer of the day. The two key hours of each day are the hours of Morning and Evening Praise. Many religious communities pray at least these two hours together each day.

This prayer is *liturgy* because it is part of the Church's official public prayer. The word *hours* refers to the seven different times, or hours, during the day when it is prayed. The Liturgy of the Hours is the prayer of the entire Church, a prayer both public and personal. Let's take time to pray a short form of it now.

First imagine that it is nearly dawn but still more dark than light. Almost six o'clock! It is time to gather for Morning Praise. As you slip into the dark church, the tower bell booms its morning greeting to the world and calls the community to prayer. The candle at your place glows brightly. You are ready to join in.

The group is divided into Side One and Side Two. As the prayer begins, all stand facing the front of the room, where a Bible opened to today's reading has been placed on a lectern. The leader stands with Side One.

As the leader opens the hour, all make the sign of the cross. At each Glory to the Father, all bow deeply from the waist at "Glory" and straighten again at "as it was." Now let's begin.

184

Conclusion ___ min.

◆ Remind the young people to share *Highlights for Home*, page 185B, with their families.

Evaluation: Do the young people understand the paths of prayer that have been outlined? Are they prepared to experiment with various approaches to prayer in order to find the paths that will lead them closer to God?

Morning Praise

Leader: O God, come to my assistance.
All: Lord, make haste to help me.

One: Glory to the Father, and to the Son,
and to the Holy Spirit:

Two: as it was in the beginning, is now,
and will be for ever. Amen.

(*All sit in chairs facing each
other to pray Psalm 98.*)

Leader: Sing a new song to the LORD,
One: who has done marvelous deeds,

Two: Whose right hand and holy arm
have won the victory.

One: The LORD has made his victory known;
has revealed his triumph for the nations
to see,

Two: Has remembered faithful love
toward the house of Israel.

One: All the ends of the earth have seen
the victory of our God.

Two: Shout with joy to the LORD, all the earth;
break into song; sing praise.

One: Sing praise to the LORD with the harp,
with the harp and melodious song.

Two: With trumpets and the sound of the horn
shout with joy to the King, the LORD.

One: Let the sea and what fills it resound,
the world and those who dwell there.

Two: Let the rivers clap their hands, the
mountains shout with them for joy,

One: Before the LORD who comes,
who comes to govern the earth,

Two: To govern the world with justice
and the peoples with fairness.

(*All stand and bow.*)

One: Glory to the Father...

Two: as it was in the beginning....

(*All sit for the reading.*)

Reader: A reading from the letter
to the Romans (8:14–16).
(*Conclude with,*
"The word of the Lord.")

All: Thanks be to God.

(*All stand facing the lectern.*)

Leader: Let us pray as Jesus taught us:
Our Father

All: who art in heaven....
but deliver us from evil. Amen.

Leader: May the Lord bless us,
protect us from all evil
and bring us to everlasting life.

All: Amen.

(*All bow toward the word of God.*)

185

Videos

Available from:
Ignatius Press
P.O. Box 1339
Ft. Collins, CO 80522

- *To Everything There Is a Season:
  Meditations on the Four Seasons*
- *The Holy Rosary with the Pope*
- *The Juggler of Notre Dame*

Available from:
St. Anthony Messenger/Franciscan
Communications
http://www.americancatholic.org

- *Living from the Center: How to Pray*
- *Communion of Saints: A Litany of
  Saints Old and New*

Youth Update Pamphlets available from
St. Anthony Messenger Press:

- "Expanding Your Image of God"
- "Finding Your Own Way to Pray"
- "The Rosary's Mysteries Can Be Your
  Own"
- "Time Out for Peace: An Advent
  Retreat"
- "A Way of the Cross for Teens"

Additional Supplemental Resources

Book

William H. Sadlier's *Prayer Celebrations for the Liturgical Year*, written by Thomas H. Morris, is intended for young adolescents to use in preparing and celebrating communal prayer services during the liturgical seasons. Also included are celebrations for Reconciliation, Initiation, Pentecost, Thanksgiving, Mary, Mother of God, All Saints/All Souls, and "Beginnings and Endings."

CHAPTER *fifteen*

My Paths of Prayer

Take some quiet time to reflect and talk with Jesus about the paths of prayer that are best for you at this time of your life. Then complete the following statements.

Stained Glass or Religious Art

I (do/do not) feel drawn to this path because_____
_____.

One of my favorite themes in religious art is_____
_____.

Scripture

I (do/do not) feel drawn to this path because_____
_____.

One of my favorite ways of praying with Scripture is_____
_____.

A Journal

I (do/do not) feel drawn to this path because_____
_____.

One of my goals in using this path would be to_____
_____.

Contemplation or Meditation

I (do/do not) feel drawn to these paths because_____
_____.

I would like to experiment with one of these paths by_____
_____.

Sacramentals

I (do/do not) feel drawn to this path because_____
_____.

One sacramental that might really help me:_____
_____.

Highlights for Home

Focus on Faith

A modern spiritual writer has reminded us, "The truth is that we only learn to pray all the time everywhere after we have resolutely set about praying some of the time somewhere." No matter how many "sermons" we may give the young people about not neglecting daily prayer, they will tune us out unless they see that we ourselves make prayer a daily priority. If we begin and end the day with prayer, offer a blessing before and after meals, and seek God's guidance in times of decision-making, our young people will be more apt to value prayer.

Chapter 15 outlines various paths of prayer Catholics through the ages have used to come closer to God. A family dialogue on which prayer forms are most appealing to which individuals and why can be enlightening. It can also be an opportunity to support each other in a commitment to daily prayer, and to remember that even when our prayer feels dry as sawdust we should not give up. Even the driest prayer, as Julian of Norwich tells us, is of immense value. Jesus reminded her in a vision that "All believing prayer is precious to me."

Conversation Starters

. . . . a few ideas to talk about together . . . .

◆ What are the greatest obstacles to my daily prayer?

◆ How does one go about praying "always"?

◆ Which path of prayer do I find attractive? Can I pray this way all week?

Reflection

Most of us have trouble remembering that Jesus is always with us, whether we are lost in the crowd or alone in our rooms. Here is an excerpt from a traditional Celtic prayer. Pray it aloud. Try praying it to a drum or other musical accompaniment. Find a way to learn it by heart.

My Christ! my Christ! my shield, my encircler,
Each day, each night, each light, each dark:
  My Christ! my Christ! my shield, my encircler,
  Each day, each night, each light, each dark.

Chapters 1-7

Name _____

Circle the letter beside the **best** answer.

1 Catholic symbols and rituals are to be used
  a. carelessly.
  b. superstitiously.
  c. reverently in worship.
  d. sparingly.

2 The paschal mystery of Jesus is
  a. the story of Jesus' miracles.
  b. the passion, death, resurrection, and ascension of Jesus.
  c. the story of Jesus' birth.
  d. the story of the Last Supper.

3 *Liturgy* is
  a. the public prayer of the Church.
  b. the participation of the people in the work of God.
  c. the celebration of the paschal mystery.
  d. all of the above

4 The sacraments of initiation are
  a. Baptism and Confirmation.
  b. Baptism, Confirmation, and Holy Orders.
  c. Baptism and Eucharist.
  d. Baptism, Confirmation, and Eucharist.

5 The large open assembly area in a church is called the
  a. nave.
  b. narthex.
  c. apse.
  d. epiclesis.

Define the following terms.

6 symbol _____
_____
_____
_____

7 ritual _____
_____
_____
_____

8 sacrifice _____
_____
_____
_____

9 mystery _____
_____
_____
_____

10 conversion _____
_____
_____
_____

11 sacrament _____
_____
_____
_____

12 the sacrament of the Eucharist
_____
_____
_____
_____

Name the part or fixture of the church described.

13 The table of the Lord and the place where the sacrifice of the Mass is offered

_____

14 A lobby, porch, or vestibule

_____

15 The place in which the Eucharist is kept

_____

16 The reader's stand

_____

How would you reply if people asked you the following questions?

17 How can I become a member of the Catholic Church?

_____
_____
_____
_____
_____

18 Why do Catholics reserve the Eucharist in the tabernacle?

_____
_____
_____
_____
_____

19 What does it mean to celebrate the past, the present, and the future at the Eucharist?

_____
_____
_____
_____
_____
_____
_____
_____
_____

20 How does receiving the Body of Christ at the Eucharist connect us to the body of Christ, the Church?

_____
_____
_____
_____
_____
_____
_____
_____
_____

For extra credit

How does celebrating the paschal mystery of Jesus help you follow Jesus Christ in your everyday life?

ASSESSMENT

Name _____

Chapters 8-14

Circle the letter beside the **best** answer.

 1 Another name for the Lord's Day is
a. Sabbath.
b. Sunday.
c. Saturday.
d. Christmas.

2 The most important way Catholics praise God and honor the risen Christ is by
a. spending time in quiet prayer.
b. visiting the sick.
c. participating in the Eucharist.
d. spending quality time with family.

 3 *Mystagogy* is
a. the time spent in preparation for Easter.
b. the celebration of Pentecost.
c. a time for meditating on the mysteries of faith.
d. the three-day observance of Easter.

4 The sacrament of Reconciliation
a. celebrates our continuing conversion.
b. is a celebration of love and forgiveness.
c. strengthens us to grow in God's grace.
d. all of the above

 5 The laying on of hands is a sign of the sacrament of
a. Matrimony.
b. Eucharist.
c. Holy Orders.
d. Baptism.

Define the following terms.

6 Triduum _____
_____
_____
_____

7 neophyte _____
_____
_____
_____

8 absolution _____
_____
_____
_____
_____

9 viaticum _____
_____
_____
_____
_____

10 deacon _____
_____
_____
_____

11 indissoluble bond _____
_____
_____

Name the sacrament that is described.

12 The priest anoints each sick person with oil and makes the sign of the cross on the person's forehead and on the palm of each hand.

_____

_____

13 The free consent of the couple and the presence of a priest and two witnesses are the essential sign of this sacrament.

_____

_____

14 The candidate promises obedience to the bishop of the local church under whom he will serve.

_____

_____

15 Our relationship to God and to the community of the Church is restored.

_____

_____

How would you explain the following statements?

16 The communion of saints is both a tremendous responsibility and a source of hope.

_____

_____

_____

_____

18 As Catholics we honor the saints and express our devotion to them, but adoration is for God alone.

_____

_____

_____

_____

17 The liturgy enables us to pass from our past-present-future time into God's time of salvation.

_____

_____

_____

_____

19 Baptism is both a dying and a rising.

_____

_____

_____

_____

20 The gift of the Holy Spirit is a gift of mission.

_____

_____

_____

_____

For extra credit

What is your favorite liturgical season? Explain why.

Answer Sheet for Semester Tests

Midsemester Test

1. c **2.** b **3.** d **4.** d **5.** a

6. something that stands for or suggests something else

7. a symbolic action expressing our deepest beliefs

8. a ritual action that brings about and celebrates our joyful union with God

9. a truth that continually calls us to deeper understanding

10. the process of coming to believe that Jesus Christ is the Savior of the world. Literally it means, "turning around, going in the other direction."

11. a visible and effective sign, given to us by Christ, through which we share in God's grace

12. the sacrament of the Eucharist is the sacrament of the Body and Blood of Christ

13. altar

14. narthex

15. tabernacle

16. lectern or ambo

17. by joining the RCIA in your parish, becoming a catechumen, and receiving the sacraments of initiation (see page 70)

18. The consecrated Hosts can be taken to the sick and the dying; Catholics also have a long tradition of praying before the Blessed Sacrament reserved in the tabernacle.

19. At the Eucharist, we celebrate the past in the memorial of the Lord's Supper, the present in Christ's living presence today in his Body and Blood, and the future, because the Eucharist is a foretaste of the heavenly banquet.

20. When we receive the Body of Christ at the Eucharist, we also receive Christ living in each member of the body of Christ, the Church. We must treat each member of Christ's body as we would treat Christ himself.

(For extra credit) Accept reasonable responses.

Final Test

1. b **2.** c **3.** c **4.** d **5.** c

6. means "three days"—begins with the Lord's Supper on Holy Thursday and ends with evening prayer on Easter Sunday

7. newly initiated Christian

8. pardon, or being set free, from sin

9. means "on the way with you"—the Eucharist given to the dying

10. means "servant"—one of the ranks of Holy Orders

11. a bond that can never be broken

12. sacrament of the Anointing of the Sick

13. sacrament of Matrimony

14. sacrament of Holy Orders

15. sacrament of Reconciliation

16. It is a responsibility because everything we do, both good and bad, affects the rest of the body of Christ; it is a source of hope because we benefit by the holiness of the saints and the goodness of all the members of the body of Christ.

17. We adore and worship God alone because he is the creator of all. We honor the saints because they are friends of God, followers of Jesus, and can help us by their example and their prayers.

18. God's time of salvation is always now. In the liturgy, what happened in the past is made present now, and is a foretaste of the future (heaven). The liturgy does not divide up time, but makes God's salvation through Jesus Christ present now.

19. Baptism is a dying because it is a change from an old life to a new way of life, a Christian way of life. It is a rising because in Baptism we are given a new life in the risen Christ.

20. The gift of the Holy Spirit sends us out to others, just as the Holy Spirit sent the apostles out to tell others about Jesus on the first Pentecost. The Holy Spirit enables us to share in the mission of Jesus Christ, to help the kingdom to come in the world.

(For extra credit) Accept reasonable responses.

Computer Resources

For newspaper articles or prayers
Student Writing Center, a trademark of:
The Learning Company
6493 Kaiser Drive
Fremont, CA 94555
(1–800–852–2255)

For making crossword puzzles for review
WordCross, a registered trademark of:
Hi-Tech of Santa Cruz
202 Pelton Avenue
Santa Cruz, CA 95060
(1–800–425–5654)

For multimedia software program
Hyperstudio, a registered trademark of:
Roger Wagner Publishing
1050 Pioneer Road—Suite P
El Cajon, CA 92020
(1–800–421–6526)

For research
Prodigy, a trademark of:
Prodigy Services Company
445 Hamilton Avenue
White Plains, NY 10601
(1–800–776–3449)

THE LITURGICAL YEAR

"Christ's saving work is celebrated in sacred memory by the Church on fixed days throughout the year. Each week on the day called the Lord's Day the Church commemorates the Lord's resurrection. Once a year at Easter the Church honors this resurrection and passion with the utmost solemnity. In fact through the yearly cycle the Church unfolds the entire mystery of Christ and keeps the anniversaries of the saints" (General Norms for the Liturgical Year and the Calendar, 1).

The liturgy makes every day of our lives holy, especially when we celebrate the Eucharist and pray the divine office. We celebrate Sunday first of all, because Sunday is the day of the Lord's resurrection.

THE EASTER TRIDUUM

The three days of the Easter Triduum are the most important days of the entire liturgical year; during these days we celebrate the passion and resurrection of Jesus. The Easter Triduum begins with the evening Mass of the Lord's Supper on Holy Thursday. Its high point is the Easter Vigil. The Triduum ends with evening prayer on Easter Sunday.

The Easter Vigil celebrates the "blessed night" when Christ rose from the dead. The Church keeps watch as it awaits Christ's resurrection and welcomes new members of the body of Christ. The entire celebration of this vigil must take place at night.

THE EASTER SEASON

The fifty days from Easter Sunday to Pentecost are celebrated as one "great Sunday." These are the days we sing Alleluia and rejoice in our salvation.

THE SEASON OF LENT

During Lent we prepare to celebrate Easter. The liturgy of Lent reminds us of our Baptism. Catechumens prepare for the sacraments of initiation. All Catholics are urged to pray, fast, give alms, and do acts of penance.

THE SEASON OF ADVENT

The liturgical year begins with the first Sunday of Advent. Advent is a time of preparation for Christmas and for Christ's second coming at the end of time. We recall the long years of waiting by the people of Israel for the Messiah, and the faithfulness of Mary and Joseph to God's plan.

THE SEASON OF CHRISTMAS

Christmas is our celebration of Jesus' birth. It begins at the Vigil Mass on Christmas Eve and ends on the feast of the Baptism of the Lord. The season includes the events from Jesus' birth to the beginning of his public ministry.

ORDINARY TIME

Ordinary Time in the Church's year occurs between the Christmas and Lenten seasons, and after the Easter Season until the beginning of Advent. Ordinary Time is devoted to the mystery of Christ in all its aspects.

In this yearly cycle, we also venerate with a special love Mary, the Mother of God. We celebrate the memory of the martyrs and other saints. On Saturdays in Ordinary Time, if there is no obligatory memorial to a saint, a memorial of the Blessed Virgin Mary may be celebrated.

The liturgical year ends with the solemnity of Christ the King, the last Sunday in Ordinary Time.